CATHOLIC DEVOTION IN VICTORIAN ENGLAND

MARY HEIMANN

CLARENDON PRESS · OXFORD

1995

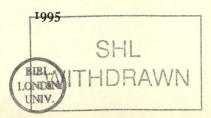

Oxford University Press, Walton Street, Oxford OX2 6DP
Oxford New York
Athens Auckland Bangkok Bombay
Calcutta Cape Town Dar es Salaam Delhi
Florence Hong Kong Istanbul Karachi
Kuala Lumpur Madras Madrid Melbourne
Mexico City Nairobi Paris Singapore
Taipei Tokyo Toronto
and associated companies in
Berlin Ibadan

Oxford is trade mark of Oxford University Press

Published in the United States
by Oxford University Press Inc., New York

British Library Cataloguing in Publication Data
Data available

Library of Congress Cataloging in Publication Data
Data applied for
ISBN 0-19-820597-X

1 3 5 7 9 10 8 6 4 2

Typeset by Graphicraft Typesetters Ltd., Hong Kong
Printed in Great Britain
on acid-free paper by
Bookcraft Ltd., Midsomer Norton, Avon

To the Goodalls: Morwenna, Elisabeth, Dominic, John, and especially David, for all their interest, encouragement, and love; for being a second family to me; and for being in part the reason for my admiration of the English Catholic community.

PREFACE

THE aim of this book is to incorporate devotion, that voluntary and explicitly religious aspect of the Faith, into a social and intellectual understanding of Catholicism in England in the second half of the nineteenth century and the early years of the twentieth. Although not of intrinsic devotional significance, the year 1850, which saw the formal reestablishment of the ecclesiastical hierarchy, has been taken as a convenient starting-point for this study and should enable it to complement several existing works which trace the history of the Catholic community up to that point. In many ways devotional *mores* which were established in the second half of the nineteenth century continued well beyond the outbreak of the First World War, arguably until the Second Vatican Council. Neither the *terminus ad quem* nor the *terminus a quo* will, therefore, be adhered to rigidly in the text.

This study has aimed to concentrate on the national scope of English Catholic developments from about 1850 to 1914. Inevitably, such an ambition has meant that the number of local sources used has had to be restricted for the sake of preserving the broad picture. However, through a deliberate concentration on sources which focus on the national dimension, this work may offer a useful introduction to those who, it is hoped, will be stimulated to pursue English Catholic devotional developments further at the local level.

Restrictions of space have meant that several related areas, including those of ecclesiastical architecture, hymnody, and the internal spirituality of religious orders, could not be accommodated in this work. Nor has it been possible to attempt a history of devotion in the whole of the British Isles in the period. Such subjects will nevertheless be alluded to from time to time.

I would like to thank the Principal and Fellows of Newnham College, Cambridge, for awarding me the Research Fellowship which enabled me to develop my doctoral thesis into this book. I am equally grateful to the staff and students of the college who helped to make Newnham such a pleasant place to spend three years.

Jane Garnett supervised the original version of this work with meticulous care and consistent encouragement. John Bossy was characteristically generous at every stage of research and writing: his scholarly example, careful criticisms, open hospitality, and many other kindnesses renewed my enthusiasm for the subject, and for research in general, at a number of critical points.

For intellectual stimulation and constructive criticism I am particularly grateful to Eric Wiley and David Goodall. My thanks also to Neil Gascoigne, John Cornwell, Frances Knight, and Sheridan Gilley. I owe a special debt of gratitude to Dinos Aristidou and Michaela Ross, whose love and friendship were, as ever, a fundamental source of strength and happiness.

The Catholic archivists of all the dioceses of England, and the religious of every community I approached, were both welcoming and generous. I am particularly grateful to the late Fr Columba Cary-Elwes of Ampleforth Abbey for his interest and kindly advice; to the headmaster of Downside, who showed me around the archives on one of the busiest days of the school year; to Robin Gard, archivist of Hexham and Newcastle, who took me scrambling on rocks by the sea after the archive closed; and to the community of St Dominic's, Stone, who welcomed me like a member of the family. My thanks also to Maurice Abbott, who lent me his own draft copy of a history of Our Lady's, Birkenhead; to Peter Waszak, who guided me through the parish archives of St Peter and All Souls, Peterborough, in his own time; and to Mgr Paul Hypher, Fr Jonathan Salt, and all the staff at All Souls, who gave me free rein with the archives and put me up at the Presbytery. Thanks also to Paul Burns of Burns & Oates, David Murphy of the Catholic Truth Society, Fr Dickie of the Westminster Archdiocesan archives, Fr Dennison of Oscott College, Fr Dolan of Nottingham Diocese, Fr Clifton of Southwark Archdiocese, Fr Lannon of Salford Diocese, Fr Marmion of Shrewsbury Diocese, Fr l'Estrange of Campion Hall, and Fr Bertram of the Oratory at St Aloysius in Oxford for help and advice. I am grateful to the staff of Oxford University Computing Service, and particularly David Rossiter, for patiently teaching me how to work the SAS software package which was used to construct the table and figures in the appendices; to Hilary Walford for scrupulous copy-editing; and to Paul Dempsey for help at the eleventh hour.

For permission to cite unpublished material my thanks to: Maurice Abbott; Pauline Adams; the Birmingham Oratory; Paul Burns; John Cashman; St Chad's, Birmingham; Gerard Connolly; Canon Seamus Cunningham; St Dominic's Convent, Stone; Dorset County Record Office; Downside Abbey; Durham Record Office; Fr Bernard Green; the Bishop of Hexham and Newcastle; Mrs Florence Julien; Desmond Keenan; Lancashire Record Office; the Bishop of Northampton; Elizabeth Roberts of the Centre for North-West Regional Studies; Captain G. M. Salvin; the English Province of the Society of Jesus; the Cardinal Archbishop of Southwark; Staffordshire County Council; Ralph Townsend; the Cardinal Archbishop of Westminster; the Metropolitan Borough of Wirral. In a few cases it was not possible to locate authors in order to obtain copyright permissions; but every reasonable effort was made to do so.

I am grateful to all of the above, and others whom there is not space to mention, for help of various kinds, direct and indirect. All faults or poor judgements in this work remain, however, very much my own.

MARY HEIMANN
Cambridge
January 1995

CONTENTS

1. Received Ideas   1

2. Devotions in Common   38

3. Familiar Prayers   70

4. A Community Apart   100

5. An English Piety   137

Appendices   174

Bibliography   201

Index   233

I
Received Ideas

CATHOLIC spirituality either fascinates or repels most outsiders. While pious images from the Middle Ages may seem sufficiently remote to be appreciated anthropologically or aesthetically, devotional objects characteristic of the nineteenth century continue to provoke a more naked response. English Catholics have more reason than most to be aware of the incomprehension or revulsion which certain manifestations of devotion, like plaster statues of the Virgin Mary, pictures of the Sacred Heart, or bottles of Lourdes water, can arouse in non-Catholics. These images, all of which were invented or popularized in the nineteenth century, are not only seen as strange or distasteful by many people; the piety they represent is often taken as a reflection of Catholic thraldom to papal authority. Bill McSweeney is not alone in believing that 'Catholic piety in the nineteenth century was a strategy carefully managed by Rome' and that 'the study of the daily rituals and practices of Catholics is important because it is through them that the Church exercises control'.[1] That some features of nineteenth-century devotion can still provoke such strong reactions would be reason enough to investigate their origins and context. But any consideration of the subject must start by examining devotion as it was understood by those who actually practised Catholicism in Victorian England.

A great deal of attention has already been devoted to the progress of the Catholic Church in England over the course of the nineteenth and twentieth centuries. Works abound which concentrate on its institutional development, political affiliations, and social significance. Scores of its bishops, clergy, religious, and laity have been the subject of biographies, both popular and scholarly: works which concentrate on the life and thought of a single Catholic of the period, John Henry Newman, could alone fill a small library. But no systematic account of the explicitly religious, or devotional, dimension of this self-proclaimed religious community has been written.

Given the widespread interest in English Catholicism which exists in

[1] B. McSweeney, *Roman Catholicism: The Search for Relevance* (Oxford, 1980), 38.

both specialist and non-specialist circles, and the strong reactions which Catholic spirituality can still provoke, it seems astonishing that no scholar should have attempted to trace the devotional history of the English Catholic community from 1850, the date at which its ecclesiastical hierarchy was formally re-established for the first time since the disruption of the Reformation. This absence is all the more striking since historians sympathetic to the community seem to be able to agree that devotion is central to understanding Catholicism. Donal Kerr has taken it as axiomatic that 'any proper assessment of a body whose stated purpose is spiritual should place first the devotional life of its faithful'[2] and John Bossy, in his study of English Catholicism in the period before 1850, acknowledges that devotion lies at 'the heart of the matter'.[3] Edward Norman, too, quite properly begins his general survey of *The English Catholic Church in the Nineteenth Century* by pointing out that 'beneath the official religious leadership of the Catholic Church in the nineteenth century—of the authorities and institutions whose activities are related in a study like the present one—there existed a sub-structure of rich spiritual enterprise'.[4] The lives of bishops and scholars, he goes on to explain, are 'rightly valued for shaping the course of events' but 'the substance, the largely unrecorded and forgotten labours and prayers of the local clergy and religious, provided the presence of Christianity visible to the sight of most ordinary people throughout the land'.

It is only relatively recently that this gap in the historiography of nineteenth-century English Catholicism has begun to be remarked upon, let alone filled. Sheridan Gilley, one of the very few who has begun to make inroads into the potentially vast field of popular devotion in the period, pointed out as long ago as 1972 that there was not 'yet any history of the devotional and theological impact of the ultramontane revival, though the materials are plentiful enough in readily accessible sources'.[5] More recently, in a review of Ann Taves's admirable work on Catholic

---

[2] Kerr goes on to explain that, since he has been asked to address the theme of the union, his paper will 'look more at the public and political face of the church' (D. A. Kerr, 'Under the Union Flag: The Catholic Church in Ireland, 1800–1870', in *Ireland after the Union: Proceedings of the Second Joint Meeting of the Royal Irish Academy and the British Academy, London, 1986* (Oxford, 1989), 23).

[3] J. Bossy, *The English Catholic Community 1570–1850* (London, 1975). The quotation is the title of his ch. 15, which discusses Catholic devotion up to the restoration of the hierarchy, pp. 364–90.

[4] E. Norman, *The English Catholic Church in the Nineteenth Century* (Oxford, 1984), 1.

[5] S. W. Gilley, 'Papists, Protestants and the Irish in London, 1835–70', in G. J. Cuming and D. Baker (eds.), *Popular Belief and Practice* (Studies in Church History 8; Cambridge, 1972), 266. (Originally published in *Recusant History* (1969–70).)

devotions in mid-nineteenth-century America, *The Household of Faith*, Bernard Aspinwall called her work a 'major contribution'. 'Would', he added, 'that we had comparable studies available of British Catholicism.'[6]

There are at least two reasons why Catholic devotion in England tends only to be alluded to in the occasional chapter or subsection in scholarly works, although it is often given a respectful nod before being passed over, as in the cases of Kerr and Norman. The first reason is that the subject concerns that most intimate and, to the historian, elusive phenomenon of man's spirituality. The nature of belief in the supernatural and the range of human religious feelings can never be identified with certainty, let alone categorized or quantified with any pretence at precision. Yet an attempt to incorporate the explicitly and self-consciously religious into social and political histories must be made if serious distortions in perceptions of Catholicism are not to result.

A second reason for the lack of attention paid to devotion as a subject in its own right is more idiosyncratic to the field of Catholic history in England. A tradition of long standing has perpetuated the notion that the divergent behaviour and views of English Catholics may best be understood through a dissection of its church membership into distinct, and often contrasting, sub-groups, whether ethnic, political, or, for want of a better term, social. Thus the 'old Catholics' have been contrasted with the 'converts' and especially the Oxford converts, the 'Irish' with the 'English', the 'English' with the 'Roman' or 'continental', and the 'liberal' with the 'ultramontane'. Such analytical devices can be useful and, up to a point, may be valid. Only a liberal–ultramontane divide over the issue of papal infallibility can make sense of Lord Acton's or Cardinal Manning's self-conscious party feeling at the time of the First Vatican Council, for example; and the distaste felt by some old Catholics for converts, of some English for the Irish, and the suspicion or impatience felt by some ultramontanes for the old Catholics are matters of record.

These categories have long been bracketed with their attendant 'ultramontane' or 'old Catholic', 'Roman' or 'English' devotions and devotional styles, which are alternatively treated as a reflection or a cause of such divisions. Thus Edward Norman, noting that 'from certain perspectives, the history of the English Catholic Church in the nineteenth century can appear as an accumulation of disputes', has stated that:

At the centre of most of the disputes lay the differences between the 'Roman' party within the Church, the Ultramontanes whose vision of the styles and claims

---

[6] B. Aspinwall, review article, *Heythrop Journal*, 31 (1990), 363.

of the triumphalist Rome which emerged from the humiliation of the French Revolutionary period was heightened (though not actually introduced to England) by the appointment of Wiseman as head of the new hierarchy in 1850, and the 'Old Catholics', conscious of their quiet English spirituality, their rootedness in the virtues of common English notions of liberty, and their antipathy to centralized authority.[7]

An analogous blending of devotional tastes with ethnic as well as political divisions can also be seen in Geoffrey Rowell's *Hell and the Victorians.* 'The nineteenth century', he writes,

was a time of unprecedented revival and change for Roman Catholicism in England. Already, at the beginning of the century, the feudal and restrained religion, centred on the old Catholic families, had begun to be challenged by the first Irish immigrants, and by new styles of devotion from the Continent.

These challenges, he continues,

became much greater in the course of the century, and the pattern of English Catholicism was further altered by the influx of converts from the Oxford Movement in the 1840s and 1850s. Tensions inevitably arose between Irish and English, converts and old Catholics, liberals and ultramontanes, and, whilst many of these were revealed in disputes over ecclesiastical organization and missionary strategy, they were also reflected in the contrast between the quiet devotion of the older English Catholicism, and the more exuberant worship and intense piety advocated by foreign missionaries, like Father Gentili, and supported by the Irish poor. The passing of Catholic Emancipation in 1829 finally opened the way for these new forms of piety to be put into practice, though the old Catholic community remained conservative and suspicious of change, and of their Protestant neighbours, for long afterwards.[8]

This passage succinctly sums up the arguments and assumptions of several generations of historians of nineteenth-century Catholicism. Since the devotional change which English Catholicism underwent in the latter half of the nineteenth century has generally been held to have been that of a triumph of ultramontanism over native or old-Catholic traditions, whether imposed directly from Rome or via the enthusiastic new converts on the one hand and the Irish immigrants on the other, the general perception seems to have been that, however interesting an examination of the *minutiae* of such a transfer of power might be, no new conclusions could be reached. Furthermore, the assumption that rigid distinctions existed between the supposed losers of this particular battle—the old or

---

[7] Norman, *English Catholic Church*, 3–4.
[8] G. Rowell, *Hell and the Victorians* (Oxford, 1974), 153.

native or English or liberal Catholics—and the winners—the ultramontanes or Romans or converts or Irish or continentals—has meant that changes in devotional practice in the period have been interpreted only in this context. Devotional practices and attitudes are used either to strengthen the argument for internal divisions through a contrasting of different styles and forms, or else to describe the defining characteristics of any one group implicitly placed within the same scheme of a sharply divided Catholic community. In short, the history of Catholic devotion in the nineteenth century has not been written because it has been assumed that, to the extent to which it could be uncovered, it would only confirm arguments already so well established in the historical tradition of English Catholicism as to make the exercise superfluous.

A rigid historiographical tradition has long hidden the subject of devotion as devotion. But to open the area to examination from a different perspective—one from which spirituality constitutes a subject of interest in its own right—can do more than simply redress the balance. It also calls in question a number of underlying historical orthodoxies. It is the aim of this book to put many of the assumptions of English Catholic historiography to the test, while at the same time uncovering the field of devotion as an independent area of interest. In so doing, it is hoped that the climate of religious feeling of the period *c.*1850–1914 will be successfully evoked and a fresh perspective offered on the religious behaviour of Catholics in England from the restoration of their ecclesiastical hierarchy in 1850 until the outbreak of the First World War.

The Second Spring and Catholic Revival

The most persistent of all historical orthodoxies about English Catholicism in the nineteenth century might, for convenience, be characterized as the 'second-spring' view. The term, which was first coined by John Henry, later Cardinal, Newman in a sermon which he preached at the first provincial synod of Westminster in 1852, was set in a text rich in poetic licence. 'I listen, and I hear the sound of voices, grave and musical renewing the old chant, with which Augustine greeted Ethelbert in the free air upon the Kentish strand,' Newman preached. 'Something very strange is passing over this land, by the very surprise, by the very commotion which it excites. It is the coming in of a Second Spring; it is a restoration in the moral world.'[9] The sentiment was apparently

---

[9] J. H. Newman, *Sermons Preached on Various Occasions* (London, 1857), 195–7 ('The Second Spring', 13 July 1852), as cited in Norman, *English Catholic Church*, 201–2.

beautiful enough to convince not only Cardinal Nicholas Wiseman, who, with many of the bishops and clergy, wept at its delivery,[10] but many subsequent generations of historians. In his introduction to *The English Catholic Revival in the Nineteenth Century* of 1899, Paul Thureau-Dangin uncritically cited Newman's sermon as evidence of what Catholicism was like before and after the revival;[11] Cuthbert Butler, in 1930, called the occasion of its reading 'a great event in the renewed life of the Catholic Church in England'[12] and explained that Wiseman's tears over the sermon were understandable, since the 'Synod may well have seemed to him as the re-birth of the Catholic Church in England, a re-birth the harbinger and earnest of a new life'.[13] Denis Gwynn, in 1942, still felt it valid to name his study of the Catholic revival in England after the famous phrase from Newman's sermon.[14]

Despite the accusation made by John Bossy in 1976 that the 'notion propagated by Newman, Wiseman and others around the mid-century, and thenceforth part of the folklore of English Catholicism, of a "Second Spring", a miraculous rebirth dating from somewhere around 1840' was no more than 'a piece of tendentious ecclesiastical propaganda',[15] a criticism which has been echoed by Gerard Connolly and Dermot Quinn in their doctoral theses of 1980 and 1986 respectively,[16] the notion survives largely unmodified in many more recent works—for example, Edward Norman's survey of 1984.[17] 'Throughout the country, Catholic chapels and churches were being built', Norman writes; 'a visible advance of the faith which, reinforced by the concession of Emancipation in 1829, elevated the expectations of the English Catholics and gave them that sense of what Newman . . . called "The Second Spring."'[18] Admitting that 'some

---

[10] As reported by Canon Crookall in G. Ramsay [K. O'Meara], *Thomas Grant: First Bishop of Southwark* (1874; 2nd edn., London, 1886), 78, and reproduced in C. Butler, *The Life and Times of Bishop Ullathorne* (2 vols.; London, 1926), i. 197.
[11] P. Thureau-Dangin, *The English Catholic Revival in the Nineteenth Century* (2 vols.; New York, 1899), i, pp. xxv–xxvii.   [12] Butler, *Life and Times of Ullathorne*, i. 196.
[13] Ibid. 198.
[14] D. R. Gwynn, *The Second Spring, 1818–1852: A Study of the Catholic Revival in England* (London, 1942).   [15] Bossy, *English Catholic Community*, 297.
[16] G. P. Connolly, 'Catholicism in Manchester and Salford, 1770–1850: The Quest for "le chrétien quelconque"' (Ph.D. thesis, 3 vols.; Manchester University, 1980), and D. A. Quinn, 'English Roman Catholics and Politics in the Second Half of the Nineteenth Century' (D.Phil. thesis, Oxford University, 1986).
[17] Though I have cited Norman here, other examples are not lacking. Josef Altholz, for example, called the 1840s 'years of intense creative excitement for the Catholics of England, marked by an intellectual revival, a wave of conversions, the reaction of a diocesan hierarchy, the enjoyment of emancipation and the promise of a "second spring"' (J. L. Altholz, *The Liberal Catholic Movement in England: The 'Rambler' and its Contributors 1848–1864* (London, 1962), 1–2).   [18] Norman, *English Catholic Church*, 8.

of . . . [Newman's] "Second Spring" was rhetorical embellishment', Norman rather undercuts the point with an embellishment of his own, arguing that it was none the less 'the justifiable exultation of those who had crossed to Rome and landed more safely upon her shores than they could have expected; it was the relief of ancient families whose recusancy was at last no longer the whispered tradition of the rural English catacombs'.[19]

The implications for devotion of the second-spring school of thought emerge clearly from the literature. Proponents of the second-spring view argue that Catholicism had been unable to express itself before the time of revival; they see the landmarks of the emancipation act of 1829, the restoration of the hierarchy in 1850, and the first provincial synod of 1852 as significant dates in paving the way for a free and full expression of the faith which had barely survived, and had been much dampened, by the hardship of the penal years. This expression of the faith took forms which have been held to be those championed by the ultramontanes, or advocates of 'Roman' and 'continental' devotions, and to have been imported by way of both Irish immigrants and the new orders and missionary priests from the Continent. These might be characterized as the more flowery aspects of Catholic worship, as well as, often, the more public: the recitation of the rosary, the following of the Stations of the Cross, attendance at Benediction of the Blessed Sacrament, participation in pilgrimages, and the use of devotions to the Sacred Heart, novenas, litanies, and May devotions. The use of devotional aids such as scapulars, medals, and rosaries, and more frequent communions and confessions, are also considered characteristic of the new age. The much-vaunted resistance of the native or old Catholics to what one might think, from this account, they would have embraced gratefully as the longed-for freedom to express a fully Catholic faith appears to pose no serious problem to the proponents of the second-spring view. Since none quite dares to suggest that the old Catholics suffered from a kind of Stockholm Syndrome (through which the victims of kidnapping come to love their oppressors), they are left to argue for an anachronistic, and hence slightly ridiculous, habit of 'timidity' born of the years of oppression, or else for an inherent coldness in temperament which can be excused neatly as being 'English'.

That such portrayals were first published in magazines renowned for their polemical views, and at times, such as the period surrounding the First Vatican Council, of particularly heated controversy between Catholics, ought to arouse our suspicions immediately. The *Month*, for example, a strongly pro-infallibilist journal at a time when views differed

[19] Ibid. 201.

sharply among Catholics as to the 'opportuneness' and appropriate scope of the impending definition of papal infallibility, lampooned what it referred to as the lingering 'Cisalpine' spirit among the old English Catholics. 'My friend is far from being a perfect representation of the old "Cisalpine" spirit,' an article of 1869 explained indulgently,

but he amuses me greatly by his timidity in matters of religious development . . . [he] has an old-fashioned way of fasting strictly on the eyes [?eves] of the Feasts of our Blessed Lady, but he can hardly make up his mind as to the statues of the Madonna . . . Nothing would induce him to miss one of the great 'Indulgences', but he thinks that converts go to Communion too frequently . . . He rejoices in the long prayers and litanies in the *Garden of the Soul*, and he knows the Penitential Psalms, and indeed, a great part of the Psalter, by heart . . . I suspect he has not yet acquiesced in the Hierarchy, and the prominent display of the Roman collar . . . He is in a constant state of protest against converts, and new Religious Orders, and foreign devotions . . . [I] need only add that of late he has been very nervous about the approaching Council . . .[20]

Since it is the winners who write history, we ought not to be surprised that the old Catholics have been portrayed in unflattering terms and the state of English Catholicism before the supposed adoption of the devotional forms of an 'ultramontane' spirituality painted in exaggeratedly dark hues. Yet such views have been uncritically adopted and perpetuated by many modern historians. Frederick Cwiekowski, for example, has claimed that the old Catholics 'resigned themselves to an attitude of inferiority that weakened their energy and sapped their ambition'. Some, he explains, 'gave the impression of being embarrassed or even ashamed of their faith: they attempted to conceal it from their neighbors and to minimize it, especially in regard to the papacy'.[21] Edward Norman, too, although more sensitive to the problems of bias of contemporary accounts of native English Catholicism,[22] has nevertheless felt it necessary to argue rather defensively, that 'in all truth, the traditional worship of the "Old Catholics", with its rejection of "continental" devotional practices . . . was,

---

[20] Anon., 'A Council on the Council', *Month*, 11 (1869), 477–8.

[21] F. J. Cwiekowski, *The English Bishops and the First Vatican Council* (Louvain, 1971), 7. Compare with Thureau-Dangin, for example, who argued in 1899 that 'Some of these Catholics became embarrassed, and almost ashamed, of their religion; they sought to dissimulate it with their neighbours, and to make them pardon it, by minimizing it as much as possible; notably, by displaying in their attitude towards the Pope an independence which approached rebellion' (Thureau-Dangin, *English Catholic Revival*, pp. xxvi–xxvii).

[22] See e.g. Norman, *English Catholic Church*, 10. He then undermines the point, however, as can be seen in the excerpt which follows in the text.

like Anglican worship at the start of the nineteenth century, extremely plain and subdued in tone'.[23]

John Bossy, Gerard Connolly, James Crichton, and other historians have refuted the now stale charges that native English Catholicism was particularly shallow or cold. Nor were they the first to find fault with this caricature. Fr Gosling, for example, in his introduction to Denis Gwynn's *Lord Shrewsbury, Pugin and the Catholic Revival* of 1946, regretted Newman's dismissal of the English Catholics in his second-spring sermon, and vindicated them, declaring that 'their religion was simple and undemonstrative, with a native tang to it that blended none too well with Wiseman's Roman practices, and even less happily with Faber's Italianate devotions; but in all essentials it was staunch and loyal'.[24] Horton Davies similarly protested in 1962 that the 'propagandists' of continental devotion who called the English school of spirituality 'insular, chill and restrained' brought charges which are 'difficult' to substantiate.[25] Of course, as Edward Norman aptly points out, 'the nineteenth-century Ultramontanes had an interest in representing [the English Catholic church's] devotional life as at a particularly low ebb', since the contrast 'threw their own achievements into a sharper light; it justified the decisiveness of the changes they sought to accomplish'.[26]

John Bossy in particular has sought, in his *The English Catholic Community*, to show that the spirituality of the old English Catholics, before its 'interior synthesis' was 'dissolved'[27] by the so-called revival of the 1840s, found perfect expression in the works of Bishop Richard Challoner and especially his extremely popular *The Garden of the Soul*, a work which 'achieved a comprehensive devotional structure which maintained the continuity of tradition while it renewed and adapted its data into forms appropriate to the situation'.[28] Bossy argues that by about 1750 *The Garden of the Soul* had come to replace the *Manual of Devout Prayers* as the most representative and formative spiritual work for the English Catholics, and 'was excellently calculated to provide the community with its devotional backbone during the following century',[29] that is to say, until about the time of the restoration of the hierarchy. Bossy's implicit admiration of the tolerant and charitable strain in Challoner's work, which

---

[23] Ibid. 9.
[24] S. J. Gosling, introduction to D. R. Gwynn, *Lord Shrewsbury, Pugin and the Catholic Revival* (London, 1946), p. xxiv.
[25] H. Davies, *Worship and Theology in England: From Newman to Martineau, 1850–1900* (4 vols.; London, 1962), iv. 23.   [26] Norman, *English Catholic Church*, 4.
[27] Bossy, *English Catholic Community*, 364.   [28] Ibid.   [29] Ibid. 365.

spoke of the faithful as 'Christians' rather than Catholics, and put its emphasis upon an 'individualistic and meditative, as opposed to collectivist and quasi-monastic'[30] piety (thus avoiding behaviour which would have seemed offensively sectarian to the Protestant majority of England), has been echoed in other quarters. Bernard and Margaret Pawley regret the loss of such an intrinsically ecumenical expression of Catholicism with the more strident and exclusive form which replaced it,[31] and James Crichton has spoken with profound admiration of the ' "Garden of the Soul Catholic" ' as being 'At least in England . . . one who was strong in the faith, somewhat reticent, solidly instructed and devout with a deep interior piety.'[32]

But, despite sporadic attempts to rehabilitate the old Catholics from descriptions which imply that they were devotionally deficient, the full ramifications of such criticisms have not been spelt out clearly, except, perhaps, in the works of John Bossy and Gerard Connolly; and these are concerned solely with the period before 1850. The ultramontane view that its own brand of Catholicism was Catholicism itself, and any deviation an inadequate rather than an alternative expression of the same essential faith, seems to have been broadly accepted by most historians. Since this acceptance rests largely on assumptions which have long been made about the nature of the faith of the Irish immigrants who flocked to England in the period, it is to the question of the impact of the Irish on English devotional life that we should now turn.

Irish Catholicism

The second-spring account sees the old-English Catholics as having been so cowed, through years of hardship and deprivation, that they lost their appetite for a vibrant and self-confident expression of the faith. It argues that several factors came to their (albeit partially resented) rescue. The first, which has already been mentioned, is the 'relief' which came in the shape of various legal reforms over the course of the late eighteenth

---

[30] Bossy, *English Catholic Community*, 364.

[31] Bernard and Margaret Pawley argue that 'As long as the "old Catholics" had an effective say in the government of the Roman Catholic Church in England there was a temper of moderation in what was said and done. But from the establishment of the hierarchy onwards the centralising ultramontane tendencies in Catholicism, beloved of converts and the new Irish immigrants, were bound to prevail' (B. Pawley and M. Pawley, *Rome and Canterbury through Four Centuries: A Study of the Relations between the Church of Rome and the Anglican Churches 1530–1981* (Oxford, 1981), 183).

[32] J. D. Crichton, 'Richard Challoner: Catechist and Spiritual Writer', *Clergy Review*, 66 (1981), 269.

century and throughout the nineteenth. Second-spring advocates assume that it was not until the passing of the Emancipation or Relief Acts of 1778, 1791, 1793, and 1829 that Catholics were able to profess their faith in England without fear of actual imprisonment. But this view, which presumes a direct correspondence between legislation as found on the statute books of the sixteenth, seventeenth, and eighteenth centuries[33] and real life over a period of two hundred years, makes better rhetoric than history.

As *The Oxford Dictionary of the Christian Church* points out, 'actual enforcement' of the Act of Uniformity of 1559, as of later and harsher statutes against recusants, priests, and Catholic landowners, 'waxed and waned under political pressures'. By the eighteenth century, 'judges and juries became increasingly unwilling to exact the full penalties'.[34] The amount of religious freedom which Catholics might exercise *de facto*, with due sensitivity to current judicial and popular opinion, needs to be considered as a corrective to the simple view of legislative reforms dictating practice. The Act of Toleration of 1689, for example, although it explicitly excluded Unitarians and Roman Catholics from its protection, was powerless to prevent Catholics from making use of its clauses. Bishop Burnet's claim that 'the Papists have enjoyed the real effects of Toleration, though they were not comprehended within the statute that enacted it', has recently been endorsed by the foremost historian of English Catholicism in the post-Reformation period.[35] According to John Bossy, the Toleration Act 'effectively abolished the offence of recusancy' and worked in practice 'as a charter for universal voluntarism', numbering Quakers, Unitarians, Jews, and Catholics among its unintended beneficiaries.[36] Although a much more severe 'Act for further preventing the growth of Popery' was passed in 1700, Bossy has been unable to find a 'single instance of a Catholic chapel actually being closed by any public authority between 1689 and the advent of legal status in 1791'.[37]

By the opening years of the eighteenth century, Catholic chapels attached to various foreign embassies in London had been functioning quite openly for over a century, and continued to draw English Catholics

---

[33] See M. D. R. Leys, *Catholics in England 1559–1829: A Social History* (London, 1961), for details of the penal laws themselves.

[34] F. L. Cross and E. A. Livingstone (eds.), 'Recusancy', in *The Oxford Dictionary of the Christian Church* (Oxford, 1957; repr. 1988), 1163–4.

[35] J. Bossy, 'English Catholics after 1688', in O. P. Grell, J. I. Israel, and N. Tyacke (eds.), *From Persecution to Toleration: The Glorious Revolution and Religion in England* (Oxford, 1991), 374.   [36] Ibid.

[37] Ibid. 375.

as well as foreigners to their Masses and Benedictions. Elsewhere through-out the country, as Bossy reminds us, 'custom and commonsense, not statute' had long decided what was acceptable: 'a low-profile building in the shape of a warehouse, something upstairs, something more chapel-like in a courtyard surrounded by other buildings—such precautions would meet the case.'[38] The sense of a second spring, that air of change in the middle of the nineteenth century which Newman and others found so exciting and which led the sanguine to cherish hopes of an imminent conversion of England to the True Faith, can hardly be attributed to parliamentary reform of the eighteenth and early nineteenth centuries.[39] Catholics in England had, after all, been managing to practise their reli-gion without too much difficulty from as early as the seventeenth century.

Second-spring optimism owed far more to the statistical boom of Catholicism in England from the 1840s than to the passing of so-called emancipatory statutes in 1829. This boom was evident to all in the spec-tacular growth of churches, the founding of religious orders, and other concrete expressions of a dramatically increasing number of adherents to the Faith within England. Although Tractarian secessions gave hope to some Catholics that a flood of Anglican converts might follow, the number of conversions from the Church of England remained relatively modest and was mainly of symbolic importance. It was the presence of the Irish immigrants, a steady stream from the previous century, but a torrent after the Great Famine, which occasioned excitement and gave rise to the second-spring account of the Irish appearing as holy reinforcements just at the critical moment. This version of the events assumes, of course, that the Irish who came to England were Catholic, and also that their brand of the faith was that 'true' Catholicism which expressed itself in those devotions which have been contrasted with the 'cold' and 'timid' forms favoured by the old Catholics of England. Recent scholarship would appear to call for a cautious approach to both assumptions.

'To put it rather crudely,' writes Gerard Connolly, 'the tradition of the

---

[38] J. Bossy, 'English Catholics after 1688', in O. P. Grell, J. I. Israel, and N. Tyacke (eds.), *From Persecution to Toleration: The Glorious Revolution and Religion in England* (Oxford, 1991), 375.

[39] As Bossy argues convincingly elsewhere, 'Anyone who tries to grasp the history of the English Catholic community as a community . . . must, I think, be struck by the relatively small part which external enactments, whether they emanated from the political or the spiritual sovereign, had in accounting for its existence, forming its characteristics, or alter-ing the course of its progress; the same, if we are considering the enactments of the English or British parliament, must I think be said for the beneficial legislation of this period [1791–1850] as for the repressive legislation of an earlier one' (Bossy, *English Catholic Community*, 296).

Second Spring sees a sudden miraculous reappearance of the old True Faith of England, emerging with strength and growth, once again, after years of wicked persecution.' On the strength of his impressively detailed study which tests the second-spring 'mythology' against the experience of the twin townships of Manchester and Salford, Connolly has argued persuasively that 'consideration of such becomes easier when seen not as the return of the True Faith, courtesy of the immigrant, but rather as the problems created by the conflict between the ratio of penetration and the ratio of practice'. Connolly argues that:

The conversion of a denomination into a church with what may be called, per-haps, sectarian habits or instincts towards practice, was in the end the only really relevant Catholic 'conversion' in England; moreover, for all the Tractarian admi-ration, it was in fact the only one ever likely to take place.[40]

In stressing that it is rather in terms of newly acquired 'sectarian habits or instincts towards practice' of the nominally Catholic than of literal conversion from Protestantism or atheism that any version of a second spring ought to be seen, Connolly has clearly made good use of recent studies both of contemporary Catholicism in Ireland and of Irish immi-grants in England. These suggest that, far from being in a position to give succour to a struggling English Catholic minority, a startlingly low pro-portion of Irish immigrants had any but the most nominal connection with the formal Catholic Church.[41]

The problem of establishing the degree to which many Irish, and particularly working-class Irish, were Catholic depends, of course, on one's understanding of the term 'Catholic'. That many Irish in London defined themselves as Catholic while not adhering to the formal practices of the Church, nor even appearing to believe in its most central tenets, as Booth and Mayhew found in their surveys of the poor of that city, only increases the difficulty. But even where the claim to Catholicism is clearly supported by evidence of religious behaviour and a firm adherence to the

[40] Connolly, 'Catholicism in Manchester and Salford', iii. 5–6.
[41] See Lynn Lees, who argues that 'Before 1850, the Catholic church in Ireland had succeeded only partially in imposing upon the Irish population acceptance of the religious practices decreed by the Council of Trent' (L. Lees, *Exiles of Erin: Irish Migrants in Victorian London* (Ithaca, NY, 1979), 165); and various articles in R. Swift and S. Gilley (eds.), *The Irish in the Victorian City* (Beckenham, 1985), especially Gerard Connolly's article 'Irish and Catholic: Myth or Reality? Another Sort of Irish and the Renewal of the Clerical Profession among Catholics in England, 1791–1918', pp. 225–53. Pauline Adams has argued that only approximately half of the Irish who emigrated to England were practising Catholics (P. A. Adams, 'Converts to the Roman Catholic Church in England, *circa* 1830–1870' (B. Litt. thesis, Oxford University, 1977), 22).

fundamental doctrines of the Catholic Church, the expression of faith,
mixed as it often was with 'superstitious' or at any rate nationally specific
customs such as the wake and pattern, may be viewed as either religious,
social, or nationalist in primary significance, depending on the view of the
commentator. Connolly argues that the real 'conversion' which occasioned second-spring enthusiasm entailed a move from 'what has been
vaguely called a "folk religion"' to a more orthodox Tridentine practice
of the Faith. 'For a significant sector of the population of Ireland in the
second half of the nineteenth century,' he maintains,

religious intuition involved attitudes qualitatively different from the discipline
of Tridentine Catholicism . . . not . . . better or worse: simply different. Numbers
of Catholics in Ireland may have remained, and assuredly did remain, personally
devout without frequent recourse to the Sacraments, and maybe even with only
minimal contact with the official Church.

Furthermore, 'to talk of neglect of practice in such circumstances is,
perhaps, to saddle one body of people with the value judgements of
another'.[42] Although a majority of incoming Irish may have retained, in
Connolly's words,

a loyalty to Catholicism *as they understood it*, for many their experience of habitual
practice was rudimentary and often non-existent. It would seem the English
missioner was, on the whole, forced to go out and *win* numerous immigrants to
the practice of Catholicism . . . He was about his first duty: to convert: not from
creed to creed, but from non-practice to practice.[43]

The difficulty in assessing what exactly constitutes adherence to the
Catholic Faith as opposed to superstitious beliefs or merely social habits
has been further complicated by a nationalist strain in much of the work
on Irish Catholicism. Several of those working on Irish spirituality have
stressed the loss of a native or Gaelic spirituality and its replacement with
European ultramontanism: this is Emmett Larkin's 'devotional revolution',[44] seen as the handiwork of Cardinal Paul Cullen, who allegedly
imposed an ultramontane brand of the Faith on a virtually (in the formal
sense) unpractising people. Michael Maher argues that, although the
ultramontanes may not have intended to undermine Irish spirituality, this

    [42] Connolly, 'Irish and Catholic', 233.
    [43] G. Connolly, '"*With more than Ordinary Devotion to God*": The Secular Missioner of
the North in the Evangelical Age of the English Mission', *North West Catholic History*, 10
(1983), 10.
    [44] E. Larkin, 'The Devotional Revolution in Ireland, 1850–75', *American Historical
Review*, 77 (1972), 625–52.

inevitably occurred as the new sensibility and practices filled the gap left by a native tradition which had been progressively undermined by a steady influx of English devotional texts.[45]

Other historians of Irish Catholicism have criticized the nationalist implications of these views. David Miller asserts that 'native Irish culture is not the source and strength of modern Irish piety', a conclusion which, as he points out, 'runs counter to long-standing popular and clerical opinion, which assumes that the rising tide of English language and ideas has been the principal threat to Irish piety'.[46] He posits instead the theory that change came about because of the perceived failure of traditional piety to prevent the Great Famine of 1845–7. 'When an element in a religious structure ceases to perform its role,' he reasons, 'the structural-functionalist expects the structure to change so as to perform the role in a different way. The devotional revolution was such a change.'[47] While such a functionalist approach as Miller's clearly has its limitations, it does at least take the debate out of the arena of competing nationalisms. His notion that an English–Irish polarity has been exaggerated would appear to be endorsed by other findings in the field. As Edward Steele has pointed out, the 'picture of Cardinal Cullen as a prelate whose brand of ultramontanism made him an inveterate opponent of Irish nationalism, both constitutional and revolutionary, ought not to have survived the work of Monsignor Corish, Fr MacSuibhne, and Dr John Whyte', since in many respects Cullen can be seen to have been sympathetic to Irish nationalism.[48]

For our purposes, these findings of the Irish historical community open up a range of questions and complications rather than providing any blueprint of a neat incorporation into England of a newly ultramontane Irish spirituality. If the Irish were not yet practising Catholics at the time of the more modest moves to the mainland which preceded the great exodus of the 1840s, and even as late as the time of the Great Famine (taken by many to have been the catalyst for change), then one should hardly cite them to support the contention that it was Irish immigrants

---

[45] M. Maher (ed.), *Irish Spirituality* (Dublin, 1981), 137.

[46] D. W. Miller, 'Irish Catholicism and the Great Famine', *Journal of Social History*, 9 (1975), 87. [47] Ibid. 91.

[48] E. D. Steele, 'Cardinal Cullen and Irish Nationality', *Irish Historical Studies*, 19 (1975), 239. See P. J. Corish, 'Cardinal Cullen and Archbishop McHale', *Irish Ecclesiastical Record*, 5th ser. 91 (1959), 393–408, and Corish, *The Irish Catholic Experience: A Historical Survey* (Wilmington, 1985), 226–58; P. MacSuibhne, *Paul Cullen and his Contemporaries* (5 vols.; Naas, 1961–77); J. H. Whyte, *Catholics in Western Democracies: A Study in Political Behaviour* (Dublin, 1981).

who 'strengthened' or 'laid the seeds' of the English Catholic revival. They would have been in no position to do either. Indeed, the much lamented 'leakage' of many Irish from the Faith once in England may have had nothing to do with their isolation in an unfriendly Protestant land, but rather attest to a continuation of their tradition of non-observance transplanted to the new country. On the other hand, they may well have brought with them 'superstitions' and folk traditions which they would have held to be expressions of their Catholicism; and one would expect that English ultramontanes would have seen both as every bit as much of a challenge as Paul Cullen did in Ireland.

Furthermore, if that strand of Irish historiography which sees the native Irish faith as having been undermined principally by English Catholic spirituality is correct, and if this happened before ultramontane reforms had been undertaken by Cullen, then the 'saintly reinforcements' from Ireland would, if anything, have brought with them a second-hand old-English Catholic, rather than an ultramontane, spirituality. There is some evidence to suggest that this may in fact have been the case. Donal Kerr mentions that in 1837, at any rate, the most popular devotional manuals in Ireland included *The Key of Heaven* and 'Challoner's works, especially *Think well on it* (in English and in Irish); meditations; and, above all, the *Garden of the Soul*'. Kerr argues that 'As more and more people learned to read English, the new prayer-books became the staple devotional diet of Irish homes. Indeed, the bundle that Paddy Leary took on his shoulder when he went off to Philadelphia almost certainly contained the *Garden of the Soul* or the *Key of Heaven*.'[49]

If Kerr is right, then we might expect the piety of the pre-Famine Irish, like that shared by their old Catholic counterparts in England, to have been brushed aside as a virtual irrelevance by ultramontanes, since it would not accord with their definitions of what Catholicism in its 'true' form should be. To the extent that Irish Catholics may have become, so to speak, old Catholic in devotion, one suspects that their religious expression would also have included traditions peculiar to Irish custom, which only adds a further complication. In order to assess which was the more decisive—the English impact on Irish spirituality or that of the Irish on the English (and again, one suspects that both processes were at work, probably simultaneously)—a much clearer picture of the development of Irish as well as of English spirituality will need to be drawn, and a more sophisticated explanation of the interaction between the two sought.

---

[49] D. Kerr, 'The Early Nineteenth Century: Patterns of Change', in Maher (ed.), *Irish Spirituality*, 139.

Since the various devotional influences of the old Catholic or English tradition, Cullen's domestic reforms, and those of the newly ultramontane English Catholics are likely to have reached different geographical areas of Ireland at different times, and to differing degrees, a careful examination of the places of origin of successive waves of Irish immigrants, and of the devotional imperatives specific to each time and place, will need to be made before much can be said of the significance of 'the Irish' for the development of English Catholic spirituality. It will not be possible to enter into these questions in as much depth as might be wished in this work, but caution will certainly be used in drawing on 'the Irish' to explain English spiritual developments.

Liberalism and Ultramontanism

Since the second-spring view of English Catholicism has come under attack from at least some quarters, another ostensibly comprehensive analysis has grown up in its place. This alternative perspective argues that the changes in English Catholicism in the period may best be understood as the outcome of a power struggle, both political and intellectual, between liberal and ultramontane factions within the English Church. Originally, the argument runs, these 'ultramontanes' were attractive, particularly through their advocacy of Roman devotions, even to some liberal Catholics and especially to the new converts. Thus Frederick Cwiekowski has made the point that 'Wiseman's program [to foster Roman devotions] was aided by some of the early English Catholic Liberals, many of whom were converts' and that 'part of their effort to emphasize lay activity consisted in promoting the "Roman devotions" about which many of the converts were so enthusiastic'.[50] Derek Holmes adds that these liberal sympathizers with ultramontanism were those Catholics 'who opposed the interference of the state in ecclesiastical affairs and who hoped that papal authority would enable the Church to meet the challenge of the age more effectively than rather conservative local hierarchies'.[51] In time, however, 'the more authoritarian and reactionary forces came to dominate the [ultramontane] movement and traditional as well as Liberal Catholics found themselves on the defensive'.[52] Cwiekowski agrees that, from what had been initially, if not quite a consensus, then at least a common ground

[50] Cwiekowski, *English Bishops*, 16–17.
[51] D. J. Holmes, *More Roman than Rome: English Catholicism in the Nineteenth Century* (London, 1978), 14.   [52] Ibid.

between the two factions, 'the Ultramontanists and the Liberals had a parting of ways'.[53]

According to this view, the division between liberals and ultramontanes grew increasingly marked through the late 1850s and early 1860s, and took its sharpest form from about 1860 until 1864, when the closure of the liberal magazine the *Rambler* and the publication of Pius IX's *Syllabus of Errors* showed which way the tide was turning. Thus Holmes has argued: 'By 1859 it was clear that the *Rambler* represented a distinct minority party within the English Catholic community and was opposed by the *Dublin Review* which was then in the hands of the ultramontanes.' With the battle lines so clearly drawn, it is easy to see why he has concluded that 'the end of . . . [the *Rambler*] effectively ended the English Liberal Catholic Movement. From now on, the Liberal Catholics in England were forced to act simply as individuals.'[54] According to Josef Altholz, Derek Holmes, and others, the defeat of the inopportunist lobby at the First Vatican Council came as the final death-knell[55] to any liberal hopes, and England was fated to become 'more Roman than Rome'. To the rhetorical question as to whether the Liberal Catholic 'movement' could 'survive and make its way in the new circumstances of English Catholicism', there could only be one answer: such liberals found themselves instead 'the rejected children of the Catholic revival'.[56]

This view of an ultramontane–liberal polarization is compelling in many respects. The condemnation by Pius IX of liberalism as one of the errors of the day in his *Syllabus of Errors* of 1864 remains notorious; and the adoption of anti-liberal rhetoric by ultramontanes in Victorian England can be amply testified by a perusal of contemporary issues of the *Month*, the *Dublin Review*, or the *Tablet*, or through an examination of the works and correspondence of certain outspoken figures like W. G. Ward and Henry Edward Manning. Lord Acton, Richard Simpson, Ignaz von Döllinger, and John Henry Newman all spoke in terms of 'party' at the First Vatican Council, identifying themselves with the liberal or inopportunist cause as Manning played the part of 'chief whip'[57] to the ultramontanes or pro-infallibilists. The *Rambler* did cease to operate under

---

[53] Cwiekowski, *English Bishops*, 17.

[54] Holmes, *More Roman than Rome*, 125. Altholz, *Liberal Catholic Movement*, 228.

[55] e.g. Altholz: 'The Munich Brief and the *Syllabus* had sounded the death-knell of Liberal Catholicism' but 'its agonies were prolonged until 1870 . . . as the Liberal Catholics struggled to salvage some fragments of accomplishment from the wreckage of their movement' (Altholz, *Liberal Catholic Movement*, 235).   [56] Ibid. 5–6.

[57] Shane Leslie first coined the term for Manning, and Butler called it 'happily chosen: he was the "chief whip" of the party; but Dechamps was the leader' (C. Butler, *The Vatican Council* (2 vols.; London, 1930), i. 130).

that title when first censured for its views by Rome, and although transmuted for a time into the *Home and Foreign Review*, voluntarily withdrew
from publishing altogether in 1864 to avoid the humiliation of being
expressly forbidden to continue.[58] But it is worth noticing that it
is where English matters touch international affairs that the 'party'
argument is at its most persuasive. It is in the context of the *Syllabus of
Errors* and of the First Vatican Council—in short, of primarily Roman
concerns and contemporary Roman policy—that a liberal Catholic
'movement' and ultramontane 'triumph' strike a chord which may sound
rather less in tune when applied to the case of England.

It is no accident that those who argue that English Catholicism may
best be viewed through the lens of a liberal–ultramontane struggle invariably invoke continental trends and examples to their aid. Thus Holmes
has placed England in a firmly European context in which 'an antithesis
between Liberalism and Ultramontanism replaced the earlier antithesis
between the freedom of Ultramontanism and the subjection to the secular
power which Gallicanism had too frequently involved'.[59] This was, of
course, very much how the contemporary Roman court—especially Pio
Nono himself and those closest to him, Prefect of Propaganda Cardinal
Barnabò[60] and Secretary of State Cardinal Antonelli[61]—viewed matters.
Those Englishmen who had lived and worked in Rome, and in close
collaboration with the Holy See, tended to see Catholic affairs in a similar
light, and to apply principles based on this Roman perspective even to
their own country. George Talbot, for example, as Papal Chamberlain
to Pius IX, wrote to Monsignor Searle[62] from Rome in January 1859: 'I
firmly believe that the animus of the whole movement against the Cardinal [Wiseman] is the Anglo-Gallican retrograde spirit which still reigns
in the old clergy of London.'[63] Similarly, Wiseman, whose formative
years (even before he became Rector of the English College) were spent
largely in Rome,[64] appointed the allegedly ultramontane Thomas Grant
to the diocese of Southwark in 1851 because he thought it 'a hot-bed of
"Anglo-Gallican" sentiment'.[65] Manning also echoed Roman concerns,

---

[58] See Norman, *English Catholic Church*, 306.

[59] Holmes, *More Roman than Rome*, 111.

[60] In May 1862, for example, Barnabò sent a circular letter to the English bishops
strongly criticizing the views of the *Rambler*. See e.g. Altholz, *Liberal Catholic Movement*,
186.   [61] It was Antonelli who first censured the *Rambler* from Rome. See ibid. 164.

[62] Searle was Wiseman's secretary at the time.

[63] As cited in Norman, *English Catholic Church*, 136.

[64] He grew up in Spain and Ireland. See ibid. 120–3 on Wiseman's early life and the
extent 'to which he stood, by background, outside the Old Catholic English world to which
he was later called' (p. 121).   [65] Cwiekowski, *English Bishops*, 33.

declaring that 'the Anglican Reformation has no perils for the Catholic Church; it is external to it, in open heresy and schism', but that:

Gallicanism is within its unity, and is neither schism nor heresy. It is a very seductive form of national Catholicism, which, without breaking unity, or positively violating faith, soothes the pride to which all great nations are tempted, and encourages the civil power to patronize the local Church by a tutelage fatal to its liberty. It is therefore certain that Gallicanism is more dangerous to Catholicism than Anglicanism. The latter is a plague of which we are not susceptible; the former is a disease which may easily be taken.[66]

Before we find ourselves swept along by the tide of such rhetoric, let us remind ourselves that the *Syllabus of Errors* and the moves, started in Rome, to define the infallibility of the pope were not, of course, made with England in mind. It was primarily the liberalism of native Italians, the consequences of whose movement had become ineluctably clear to him by the 1860s, which Pius IX meant to quash; and, if the Vatican's fears might have been well grounded when it came to the cases of Italy or France, the fact that the same principles were applied to England in no way suggests that they were appropriate to that particular case.

The silence of the vast majority of English Catholics on issues which, to judge by contemporary issues of the *Rambler* or *Dublin Review*, or from modern historians' accounts, amounted to a subversion of liberty by the ultramontanes must surely strike any student of English Catholicism. Why should only a few English Catholics—most notably Manning on the ultramontane side and Acton on the liberal—have spoken out about such issues as the imminent threat of Gallicanism to undermine the orthodoxy of Catholicism in England, or the sinister moves of the ultramontanes to subvert English freedoms through a sweeping definition of papal infallibility? Was this silence on the part of ordinarily outspoken, even querulous, English Catholics, as Holmes and Altholz imply, a symptom that the spirit of the liberal movement had been broken by the cessation of the *Rambler*?[67] To say so is to beg the question: one would expect more than one journal to have arisen in protest at such dark designs.

If we examine such debate as did exist on these and related matters, it emerges that virtually all who took a strong party line, whether liberal or ultramontane, were either foreign or in some other way outsiders, and saw the question primarily in a larger context than that of England, drawing parallels with the Continent which may not in fact have been

---

[66] As cited in ibid. 95.   [67] e.g. Altholz, *Liberal Catholic Movement*, 228.

applicable. Acton, fulminating against the ultramontane party, was largely the mouthpiece of Döllinger and was himself far more closely allied with the imperatives of German than of English Catholicism. Newman, baffled at not being able to muster more support in defence of an inopportunist position, had virtually no association with Catholics until his conversion and has long been recognized as having been peripheral in many respects to the core of English Catholicism.[68] He could imagine only that those who kept out of the fray, like Bishop William Ullathorne, lacked 'spirit' and he complained to Richard Simpson of the dearth of trustworthy allies to a liberal position.[69]

As for Manning, the lack of scruple which he exhibited in getting his favoured motion through the Council may well argue for his conscious adoption of a line which he knew would find favour with Rome as well as with that small circle of Englishmen who, like Talbot, had been in Rome so long that they had become genuinely Roman in outlook.[70] Certainly, Manning was not one to calm the fears of Roman authorities about the potential dangers of liberal Catholicism. When Talbot wrote to Manning to urge him to stand firm 'as the advocate of Roman views', Manning rather fanned the flames of mutual suspicions, declaring that Newman

has become the centre of those who hold low views about the Holy See, are anti-Roman, cold and silent, to say no more, about the Temporal Power, national, English, critical of Catholic devotions, and always on the lower side. . . . I see much danger of an English Catholicism of which Newman is the highest type. It is the old Anglican, patristic, literary, Oxford tone transplanted into the Church. It takes the line of deprecating exaggerations, foreign devotions, Ultramontanism,

[68] On Newman's position as an outsider see, for example, Norman, *English Catholic Church*, 327, and Gerald Parsons, 'Victorian Roman Catholicism: Emancipation, Expansion and Achievement', in G. Parsons (ed.), *Religion in Victorian Britain* (4 vols.; Manchester, 1988), i. 162.

[69] Newman to [William] Monsell, 3 Sept. 1869, in *The Letters and Diaries of John Henry Newman*, ed. C. S. Dessain *et al.* (31 vols.; Oxford, 1964–), xxiv. 326.

[70] David Newsome's recent appraisal of Manning offers a valuable corrective to the caricature which has been left to us by Edmund Purcell and Lytton Strachey. But, even in a highly sympathetic, not to say partisan, account of the Council's decrees such as E. E. Y. Hales's, Manning does not come out well. Defending the definition of infallibility, Hales grants: 'Yet it is still permissible to regret that even the semblance of pressure was brought to bear upon those at the Council who thought differently from the Pope on the main matters at issue. . . . if the opposition had not been irritated by Manning's tactics, and by the insertion of clauses at the last moment, it is likely that the majority would have been larger still, and fewer opportunities would have been given to hostile critics' (E. E. Y. Hales, *Pio Nono: A Study in European Politics and Religion in the Nineteenth Century* (New York, 1954), 312). See also D. Newsome, *The Convert Cardinals: John Henry Newman and Henry Edward Manning* (London, 1993), 7–12.

anti-national sympathies. In a word, it is worldly Catholicism, and it will have the worldly on its side, and will deceive many.[71]

For Manning, a man still capable at the end of his life of boasting of his captainship of the Harrow Eleven and his first from Balliol,[72] to have gone so far as to use the word 'English' pejoratively seems suspiciously as if he were feeding a known prejudice in his reader rather than offering an impartial view of the state of Catholicism in England. As Altholz aptly points out, Manning's 'sermons on the Temporal Power were regarded as extreme even by his own party and were delated to the Index; but he possessed a powerful friend at Rome in Monsignor Talbot, a Papal Chamberlain, and he was favourably regarded by the Pope himself'.[73]

It was the issue of the temporal power of the papacy and the future of the papal states which lay behind such unmeasured views from Rome and made any apparent hesitation or deviation on the part of Catholics the grounds for hostile suspicion.[74] In the climate of fear which justifiably surrounded that city, no exaggeration appeared too absurd if it seemed to show loyalty to the Holy See. The ultramontanes of England were correspondingly effusive. As Altholz has pointed out:

Manning was prepared to make the Temporal Power a dogma of faith . . . He had the enthusiastic support of Father Faber of the London Oratory, who emphasized the emotional side of Ultramontanism, personal devotion to the Pope and imitation of Roman practices. The intellectual leader of the Ultramontanes was W. G. Ward, who urged that all problems be solved by recourse to Rome and that every intimation of the will of the Pope was as binding on Catholics as dogma itself. Ward's too logical mind was delighted by the most absolute and extravagant statements.[75]

Altholz is undoubtedly right to stress that 'in the tense atmosphere of the 1860s there was little room for balanced views. The Church was regarded as being in a "state of siege", and the Ultramontanes sought to foster the mentality of inflexible resistance appropriate to a besieged army.'[76] But it is worth remembering that the self-styled 'liberal' opponents of such ultramontane extravagances were hardly more temperate in their

[71] As cited in Holmes, *More Roman than Rome*, 127.
[72] J. E. C. Bodley, *Cardinal Manning: The Decay of Idealism in France: The Institute of France. Three Essays* . . . (London, 1912), 14.
[73] Altholz, *Liberal Catholic Movement*, 131.
[74] Holmes argues that the Roman Question united the majority of 'Catholics who increasingly adopted an attitude of fundamental opposition to the "liberalism" of the age' (Holmes, *More Roman than Rome*, 116).
[75] Altholz, *Liberal Catholic Movement*, 131.   [76] Ibid.

rhetoric[77] as expressed in the *Rambler* and the *Home and Foreign Review*. They, too, through the influence of Döllinger and, through him, of Acton, were performing for a wider audience than that composed of English Catholics alone.

The badge of liberalism could evidently appeal to those whose familiarity with the Continent made the issues pertinent; it also had some relevance for those converts from Anglicanism who were acutely conscious of the effect which Roman recalcitrance over the 'new learning' in history and science, or the appearance of absolutist claims, would have on the Protestant world from which they came. As Newman once remarked with some bitterness: 'It is so ordered on high that in our day Holy Church should present just that aspect to my countrymen which is most consonant with their ingrained prejudices against her, most unpromising for their conversion.'[78] It was this effect of contemporary Roman policy appearing to feed the prejudices of English Protestants which the liberal converts fought so hard to avoid and which sometimes earned them accusations of dishonesty from native Catholics and ultramontanes alike.

But, despite the rather grandiose parallels which historians have drawn with the liberal and ultramontane movements of Germany, France, and Italy, the arguments of the extreme ultramontanes and liberals were, in England at any rate, restricted to a very small number of polemicists, mainly composed of outsiders whose arguments were furthermore exaggerated in the anxious desire to convince. Although such extreme views were certainly held, and by some influential Catholics, there is a danger in ascribing too much importance to what was, after all, the rhetoric of a few, albeit highly visible, figures. Dermot Quinn has aptly criticized the tendency of the English Catholic historical tradition to see its history as shaped by its bishops and cardinals and points out that Edward Norman has made Cardinal Vaughan, as Purcell made Manning before him, seem 'to reflect the era through which [he] lived'.[79] Such polemical exaggerations as those presented in Catholic journals at the time of the emotive issues of the *Syllabus of Errors*, the question of the temporal power, and

[77] While Manning urged the Catholics of England 'to separate themselves from the main stream of English society, which was heading towards "worldliness" and rationalism, and to show themselves "more Roman than Rome, and more ultramontane than the Pope himself "', an article in the liberal *Home and Foreign Review* 'shocked Monsell by implying there was a contrast between "Catholic" and "Christian" morality' (Altholz, *Liberal Catholic Movement*, 212 and 214 respectively).

[78] From W. P. Ward, *The Life of John Henry Cardinal Newman* (2 vols.; London, 1912), i. 14, and cited by Altholz, *Liberal Catholic Movement*, 231.

[79] Quinn, 'English Roman Catholics and Politics', 1. See E. S. Purcell, *Life of Cardinal Manning, Archbishop of Westminster* (2 vols.; London, 1896).

the definition of papal infallibility have left historians with a false impression of the strength and exclusivity of such divisions.

In fact, of course, there were other views and other Catholic journals to represent them: the *Chronicle* (1867–8), the *Weekly Register*, and Purcell's *Westminster Review* all managed to maintain more balanced views even at times when party feelings ran high. Indeed, as Bishop Chadwick pointed out, the *Westminster Review* rose in estimation precisely because of the moderate stance which it took at the time of the Council.[80] That a moderate like Ullathorne was believed, in 1865, to have 'the largest number of adherents among his countrymen' as a possible successor to Cardinal Archbishop Nicholas Wiseman, although he was viewed with suspicion at Rome, underlines the point.[81] The distaste which Ullathorne felt for such uncharitable, not to say distorting, pieces of propaganda as those we have seen, whether ultramontane or liberal, and which kept him quiet at the First Vatican Council, was no doubt the reason for the general silence among the English representatives there. Only in the face of a genuine threat would we expect to find defensive reactions: that so few were exhibited suggests the absence of a real threat more plausibly than a conspiracy of silence, whether due to crypto-Gallicanism, inherent recusant timidity, or triumphalist ultramontanism.

The Inadequacy of Devotional Categories

Although extreme liberal or ultramontane views were espoused by only a handful of Catholic polemicists in England, their characterizations of devotion have remained with us. The lampooning of devotional inadequacies or exaggerations may have been little more than rhetorical devices to serve an immediate purpose, but such name-calling has left its mark on the historiography of English Catholicism. Old slurs continue to shape perceptions of, and approaches to, devotion a hundred years after the debate which provoked them has been forgotten. As we have seen, second-spring and ultramontane-triumph schools of Catholic history continue to use devotional caricatures to strengthen arguments for internal divisions within the community. Depending upon which school is followed, it is either the Irish or the ultramontanes who are portrayed as loving pilgrimages, rosaries, and extravagant devotions (whether from 'true' devotion or mere slavishness), while the liberal Catholics and

[80] Cwiekowski, *English Bishops*, 163.
[81] Odo Russell to Earl Russell, 1 Mar. 1865, in N. Blakiston (ed.), *The Roman Question: Extracts from the Despatches of Odo Russell from Rome 1858–1870* (London, 1962), 308–9.

inopportunists are alternatively labelled quiet, timid, or rational in their old Catholic tendency to read Challoner's *The Garden of the Soul* for spiritual profit and to shy away from continental exuberance.

The most cursory examination of the devotional lives of even the most eminent and influential of English Catholics shows how misleading such stereotypes can be. Bishop Ullathorne, considered by Newman to have been sympathetic to the inopportunists at the First Vatican Council and long regarded as a bluff old English Catholic *par excellence*, has sometimes been claimed to have reintroduced the rosary into England, so notorious was his attachment to that devotion. He was also one of the first English promoters of the alleged apparitions of the Virgin Mary at La Salette. Newman, for all his misgivings about papal infallibility and his private difficulties with Rome, chose forms and objects of devotion for his fellow Oratorians in Birmingham which were anything but cold, English, or restrained. Manning, that quintessential ultramontane, was not particularly noted for a Roman flavour to his devotional life or for the warmth of his religious expression;[82] although he had a strong devotion to the Blessed Sacrament and to the Holy Spirit, it was rather Wiseman who cultivated the effusive devotional forms considered most characteristic of an 'ultramontane' spirituality. At the other extreme, Baron Friedrich von Hügel mystified some by the apparent anomaly of his attacking the Church through his modernist treatises, on the one hand, while showing fervent devotion, on the other. As Alec Vidler reports, Tyrrell wrote in 1908 to A. L. Lilley of their mutual friend:

The Baron has just gone. Wonderful man! Nothing is true; but the sum total of nothing is sublime! Christ was not merely ignorant but a tête brulé (*sic*); Mary was not merely not a virgin, but an unbeliever and a rather unnatural mother; the Eucharist was a Pauline invention—yet he makes his daily visit to the Blessed Sacrament and for all I know tells his beads devoutly. Bremond's French logic finds it all very perplexing.[83]

As will be seen in the next chapter, von Hügel did indeed 'tell his beads devoutly', and Cuthbert Butler also remembered how, after long walks together on Hampstead Heath,

[82] Manning's legendary asceticism seems to have extended to the avoidance of a clutter even of devotional objects. John Bodley was struck, when he visited the cardinal's home, that 'the only object of piety discernible in the dim lamp-light was a fine malachite crucifix on the mantlepiece' (Bodley, *Cardinal Manning*, 11).

[83] Tyrrell to Lilley, 14 Aug. 1908, as cited in A. R. Vidler, *A Variety of Catholic Modernists* (Cambridge, 1970), 117 n., and B. Reardon, 'Roman Catholic Modernism', in N. Smart, J. Clayton, S. Katz, and P. Sherry (eds.), *Nineteenth Century Religious Thought in the West* (3 vols.; Cambridge, 1985), ii. 158.

we always returned home by the little Catholic Church in Holly Place—it was his [von Hügel's] daily practice—and went in for a long visit to the Blessed Sacrament; and there I would watch him sitting, the great deep eyes on the Tabernacle, the whole being wrapt in an absorption of prayer, devotion, contemplation. Those who have not seen him so know only half the man.[84]

Differences over approaches to devotion certainly arose within the English Catholic community; but the familiar arguments that these reflected divisions between old Catholics and ultramontanes, converts and native Catholics, Irish and English, will not suffice as an explanation. Indeed, even the stereotype of strict opposition between Catholics who favoured Gothic and those who followed Roman styles of architecture does not seem very convincing. Although the subject of contemporary architecture falls outside the scope of this work, it seems worth mentioning that Augustus Welby Pugin's zealous promotion of the Gothic was considered highly eccentric by most English Catholics, and Cuthbert Butler was delighted to recall an occasion when W. G. Ward was 'paid in his own coin' by the equally intolerant Pugin.[85] In spite of some famous and extremely heated polemic on the subject, Catholics generally appear to have chosen the style of their parish churches for reasons of economy and personal taste, quite oblivious to 'party' significance. As Rory McDonnell has found in his study of church architecture, and an examination of any illustrated guide to English Catholic churches will readily confirm, the exterior of nineteenth-century Catholic churches was no sure guide to the sorts of devotions practised within.[86]

Theoretically at least, proponents of the new as of the old devotional spirit were largely in agreement as to the role which devotion should play within the Catholic community. 'In theology,' wrote F. W. Faber, the founder of the lavishly Italianate Brompton Oratory, and promoter of ultramontane devotion *par excellence*, 'devotion means a particular propension of the soul to God, whereby it devotes itself . . . to the worship and service of God'. It was not, he took pains to point out, 'to be confounded with fervour, no uncommon mistake . . .'.[87] Thus, Faber went on,

---

[84] J. P. Whelan, *The Spirituality of Friedrich von Hügel* (London, 1971), 16, extracted from *Baron von Hügel: Selected Letters, 1896–1924*, ed. B. Holland (London, 1927), 49.

[85] Butler, *Vatican Council*, ii. 42 n.

[86] Well-illustrated guides include E. M. Abbott, *History of the Diocese of Shrewsbury* (Bolton, 1987), and D. Evinson, *The Lord's House: A History of Sheffield's Roman Catholic Buildings 1570–1990* (Sheffield, 1991). See also R. McDonnell, 'Church Architecture as a Primary Document for Nineteenth Century Catholic History', paper read to the Catholic Record Society Conference, Plater College, Oxford, 1 Aug. 1990.

[87] F. W. Faber, *Growth in Holiness; or the Progress of the Spiritual Life* (London, 1854), 364.

it appears that devotion is a very grave, solid, hard-hearted, stout-willed, business-like affair, and not at all the sweet, fervid, heroic, graceful, tender thing it is often taken for. It is well when it has all the qualities these latter epithets imply. But when they are there, they add something to it, and do not express merely its own nature. If it did not sound like a play upon words, I would say that it is desirable we should have a more theological and a less devotional idea of devotion than we commonly have.[88]

As for devotions, those specific actions or prayers taken to be particular expressions of devotion, Faber explained that the Holy Ghost

also leads different souls, either by natural character or supernatural attraction, to different devotions, and gives them various lights upon them. Thus we have special devotions, and special saints to further them, to our Lord's Infancy, his Boyhood, His Active Life, His Passion, His Wounds, His Cross, His Risen Life, His Precious Blood, and His Sacred Heart, to His Mother, His Angels, His Apostles, and the various orders of His Saints.[89]

In stressing the acceptability of a variety of devotional approaches and emphases, Faber seems to have succeeded in his stated aim to 'harmonise the ancient and modern spirituality of the Church . . . and to put it before English Catholics in an English shape, translated into native thought and feeling, as well as language'.[90] The point would not have been lost on Newman, who wrote most earnestly to Mrs William Froude in 1855 that 'Catholics allow each other . . . the greatest licence, and are, if I may so speak, utter *liberals*, as regards devotions, whereas they are most sensitive about doctrine'. As he explained:

I shall not quarrel with any form of words *you* use about [Mary], or to her, so that it *does not state some untruth*, and I shall expect *you* not to quarrel with *me*, who refuse to use your forms and devotions. 'We praise thee, O Mary; we acknowledge thee, to be our Lady.' Is it the doctrine, or the taste of this, to which you object? I expect, the taste . . . Every nation and age has its own taste—and though there are invariable principles, we must allow a great latitude for such accidents. Think of the condescension of Almighty God comparing Himself to an eagle, with His Saints between His shoulders etc. etc.—There is no end of this, if you go on. Use your own taste, and let me use mine.[91]

He emphasized the same spirit of tolerance in a letter to Mrs Helbert of 28 September 1869: 'I don't see any doctrinal harm in St Buonaventura's Psalter—(I believe it certainly is *not* his)', he wrote, 'except that it is in very bad taste. Profaneness is often nothing more than bad taste and extravagance.'[92] The anti-opportunist and contributor to the *Rambler*

[88] Ibid. 364–5.   [89] Ibid. 371.   [90] Ibid., p. viii.
[91] Newman to Mrs William Froude, 2 Jan. 1855, in *Letters and Diaries*, xxvi. 342–3.
[92] Ibid. xxiv. 340.

Richard Simpson similarly stressed the latitude of the church, arguing that:

Catholicism is a fact, and not a theory. Whatever schools of thought have their existence within the Church, and are not cast out from her communion, are, *ipso facto*, shown to be consistent . . . with the generous spirit of historical Catholicism, which is tolerant of differences in doubtful matters, provided that unity is not broken in the necessary points of faith and morals.[93]

Even the Modernist George Tyrrell, for all his scepticism of some aspects of the Church's teaching, was adamant that

what has been revealed in Christianity is 'not merely a symbol or creed, but it is a concrete religion left by Christ to his Church'. The tenets of this religion were first expressed in the vivid, concrete, and totally unphilosophical language of fishermen and peasants. God 'has spoken their language, leaving it to others to translate it (at their own risk) into forms more acceptable to their taste'.[94]

Arguing, in an article entitled 'The Relation of Theology to Devotion', that 'Neither the metaphysical nor the vulgar idea is adequate, though taken together they correct one another', Tyrrell went on to explain that, 'taken apart, it may be said that the vulgar is the less unreal of the two'. As Nicholas Sagovsky has discovered, von Hügel read this article of Tyrrell's in draft and wrote to him that it was 'the finest thing you have yet done,—at least of those that I have read. It is really splendid. I thank God for it with all my heart.' It had, as he explained, given 'crystal-clear expression to [his] dearest certainties'.[95]

Even Frederick Faber, perhaps the most fervent exponent of ultramontane devotion in England, was prepared to admit that sobriety was perfectly compatible with devotion. The inopportunist and convert Newman and the intellects behind the modernist movement were equally convinced that the most effusive devotions could sometimes preserve a crucial element of the truth which mere intellectualizing might overlook. But, while Catholics could agree, at least in principle, on a definition of devotion, the unease which conflicting tastes and rival practices could arouse made it a perpetual struggle to maintain charity. 'Either we are lukewarm, or we are fervent,' Faber declared elsewhere. 'These are the ends of our whole voyage as proficients . . .'[96] He went still further in his conclusion to *The Growth of Holiness*, declaring that:

    [93] R. Simpson, 'Milner and his Times', *Home and Foreign Review*, 2 (1863), 557. Reproduced in Altholz, *Liberal Catholic Movement*, 213.
    [94] As narrated in N. Sagovsky, *'On God's Side': A Life of George Tyrrell* (Oxford, 1990), 72. See also G. Tyrrell, 'The Relation of Theology to Devotion', *Month*, NS 94 (1899), 473.
    [95] Sagovsky, *'On God's Side'*, 72–3.   [96] Faber, *Growth in Holiness*, 431–2.

fervour is the state of the saints on earth, and in one sense of the Blessed in heaven; and in its degree, it ought to be the normal state of all who are aiming at perfection. It is at once the growth of holiness, and the strength by which holiness grows. Every chapter hitherto has tended to this . . .[97]

It was this tendency towards hyperbole, which came dangerously close to implying that emotional intensity was the measure of religious commitment and the following of certain devotions the outward sign of such commitment, which made others within the fold uneasy. As an Anglican, Newman had shown caution with regard to an over-emphasis on religious feeling, writing that:

To be excited is not the *ordinary* state of the mind, but the extraordinary, the now-and-then state. Nay more than this, this *ought not* to be the common state of the mind; and if we are encouraging within us this excitement, this unceasing rush and alternation of feelings, and think that this, and this only, is being earnest in religion, we are harming our minds, and (in one sense), I may even say, grieving the peaceful spirit of God, who would silently and tranquilly work his divine work in our hearts.[98]

As a Catholic, he remained wary of the error of relying upon enthusiasm, as he saw it, which ultramontane Catholics like Faber seemed at times to imply was the sole sign of grace or the only path to a devout life. 'I suppose [Faber's *Growth in Holiness*] is a perfect magazine of valuable thoughts,' he wrote to Catherine Bathurst in 1855, 'but it must not make you scrupulous. What suits one person, does not another. To say that *every one* is joyful at first, is as untrue as the Evangelical notion, that everyone must pass through certain stages of conviction etc. etc.'[99] He had tried to bring out the point to Faber himself in 1851: 'The *end* of the Oratory Brothers is doubtless to *save the soul*,' he agreed, and therefore:

If any one or any Oratory, can arrive at this end by no means or by any means (allowable), let him do it. One can't prescribe one's own means to others. If you [at Brompton] can attain the end directly and immediately, by all means do it and use no means. I think I may say for certain that here [at Birmingham] we shall not be able.[100]

Newman's view evidently arose not only from a liberality of temperament but, perhaps more directly, from a candid recognition of his own

---

[97] Ibid. 441.

[98] J. H. Newman, *Parochial and Plain Sermons* (8 vols.; 1872–9), i, Sermon xx, p. 263, as cited in Davies, *Worship and Theology in England*, iv. 23 n.

[99] Newman to Catherine Anne Bathurst, 4 Apr. 1855, in *Letters and Diaries*, xvi. 436–7.

[100] Newman to F. W. Faber, 6 Apr. 1851, in ibid. xiv. 247.

limitations in this regard. These he had come to accept as a fact, whether or not a happy one: the light tone of regret mixed with resignation may, perhaps, be contrasted with the more strident tone of his Anglican writing on the same theme. 'All my life,' he wrote to John Gordon in 1853,

I have complained of [powerlessness], as I have called it. I mean a strange imprisonment, as if a chain were round my limbs and my faculties, hindering me doing more than a certain maximum—a sort of moral tether. People have said 'Why don't you *speak* louder? You speak, as far as you go, with such evident ease, you certainly can do more if you wish and try—' I can only answer, 'I can't.' I am kept in my circle by my moral tether, which pulls me up abruptly. So of my mind—I cannot feel more pain than a certain quantity, without fainting—it is my way at once. I cannot feel more devotion, unless something happened to my heart like St Philip's. I am an instrument which cannot be played on except in a certain way.[101]

Much of the argument which surrounded devotional change in England during the second half of the nineteenth century turned precisely on the point of how much importance ought to be attributed to feeling, and the degree to which specific devotions ought to be seen as the measure of, or the means of inculcating, a more fervent love of God. This debate affected the whole of the contemporary Catholic world, and it may therefore be useful to turn briefly to the experience of contemporary continental and American developments. Such an examination will also have the incidental advantage of enabling us to draw on historiographical traditions less constrained than those of Catholicism in England.

Ultramontanism and Revivalism

Leaving to one side for the moment the peculiarities of the English situation, it is striking that something like a Catholic revival appears, from historians' accounts, to have occurred at about the same time in most countries which boasted a Catholic population. The experience of a transformation of the Faith from one of non-practice (in the Tridentine sense) to one, not only of habitual practice, but of a showy and flowery expression of Catholicism, was certainly not peculiar to England. That such a transformation took place in Ireland at about the same time we have already seen. Analogous developments also appear to have occurred in France, the United States, and Germany, to name only a few instances.

Of the many possible causes which might account for such a coincidence of developments internationally, two immediately spring to mind.

---

[101] Newman to John Joseph Gordon, 4 Jan. 1853, in ibid. xv. 242.

The first is that such moves were directly encouraged by the papacy, at a time when its machinery had grown sophisticated enough to enable the Catholic Church to implement its will world-wide. Thus what had been merely an Italian variant of Catholicism, one national tradition among many which coexisted amicably within the same church, was now imposed on the entire Catholic world. This, in essence, is the argument of those who see the change in English Catholicism as reflecting the 'triumph of the holy see',[102] the victory of an ultramontane version of the faith over idiosyncratic variations which included that of the old-Catholic tradition of England.

A second possibility is that the shift in devotional tone might be explained as arising from a change in the intellectual and emotional climate of the times which, through a massive increase in publishing and the low cost of devotional texts, was able to spread far more widely than had been possible before. In a sense this explanation begs the question, since one would then wish to know why tastes should have changed. In part, of course, this might be accounted for by a widening of the market for devotional literature. That the tastes of working-class and lower-middle-class Catholics were being taken into account for the first time, since they could now afford to purchase works of spirituality, might go some way towards explaining the sudden popularity of devotional forms formerly disdained. The point has often been made that the new 'ultramontane' clergy tended to be drawn from the lower ranks of society, and so are presumed to have had a strong measure of sympathy with the tastes of those classes from which they had sprung. Yet Sheridan Gilley's findings that the 'vulgar' ultramontane tastes as expressed at the Brompton Oratory in London appealed to Catholics of all social classes would seem to suggest that caution ought to be used with such hard and fast assumptions about the relationship between taste and social class in devotional matters.[103]

Two possible explanations for the existence of an international change in the practice of Catholicism have been outlined, but it may well be that these represent two strands of an argument rather than mutually exclusive alternatives. Ann Taves has pointed out that most of the devotions which appeared in prayer-books in the United States at mid-century 'had been granted papal indulgences and thus had acquired an authorized

---

[102] See e.g. D. J. Holmes, *The Triumph of the Holy See: A Short History of the Papacy in the Nineteenth Century* (Shepherdstown, W. Va., 1978), *passim*.

[103] S. W. Gilley, 'Vulgar Piety and the Brompton Oratory, 1850–1860', *Durham University Journal*, NS 43 (1981), *passim*.

form . . . [which] meant that the devotions included in the prayer books were increasingly standardized'.[104] She has also pointed to papal indulgences attached to various confraternities, the approval which Pius IX gave to certain sites of pilgrimage and to the replication of the Lourdes shrine and sale of Lourdes water in the United States,[105] and prayers 'for the intention of the Sovereign Pontiff'[106] to support her central premiss of a 'centralization and standardization of practice' which was 'aggressively Roman'.[107]

As Taves herself recognizes, however, it is misleading to think of the devotions in question as Roman.[108] Devotions which came to be endorsed with papal approval in the form of indulgences did not necessarily originate in Italian spiritual manifestations. The French contribution to Catholic spirituality in the nineteenth century was particularly rich; but all countries with a Catholic population, including England, successfully petitioned that certain favoured devotions be granted this papal seal of approval. So there was nothing intrinsically Roman—in a spiritual sense—about the devotions which were approved by Rome. By choosing which devotions to accord indulgences, Rome did, of course, exert some leverage, but it is worth remembering that this relationship cut both ways. In practice, a devotion firmly established in the popular tradition, so long as it did not contradict doctrine, would tend to be granted approval retrospectively, as in the case of Lourdes. It would not necessarily, or even usually, be promoted from Rome. Since strong popular feeling towards a particular object or form of devotion always held the potential of emerging as a rival cult to those approved and brought into strict conformity with Catholic doctrine, this made perfect sense. Thus the mushrooming of indulgenced devotions during the pontificates of Pius IX and Leo XIII argues less for the substitution of spiritual for temporal power than for the need of the papacy to contain devotional developments while at the same time retaining the loyalty of a majority in the Catholic world. That the number of indulgenced devotions should have increased markedly at a period when the Church's future seemed most uncertain, first through the loss of the temporal power and then through the perceived problem of 'leakage' from the Faith, only reinforces the point.

In his study of French Catholicism in the period, Ralph Gibson has stressed the innate appeal of what he calls ultramontane piety, arguing that its attractiveness lay partly in its accommodation of older forms of

---

[104] A. Taves, *The Household of Faith: Roman Catholic Devotions in Mid-Nineteenth-Century America* (Notre Dame, Ind., 1986), 29.   [105] Ibid. 99.
[106] Ibid. 96.   [107] Ibid. 132.   [108] Ibid. 114–15.

popular devotion, which were transmuted skilfully into orthodox forms. Although the new clergy in France meant to stamp out what they considered to be abuses (much as Cullen's clergy were doing in Ireland), where possible they attempted to channel 'superstitious' practices into forms more intimately connected with the Tridentine church. Thus subtle changes to traditional prayers often 'involved trying to shift the emphasis away from the traditional attempt to manipulate the material world, towards more spiritual concerns'.[109]

Drawing on the work of Gérard Cholvy and Yves-Marie Hilaire, Gibson stresses the novelty of French 'ultramontanism' in accepting many aspects of popular traditions which would have been considered embarrassing, even contemptible, by most clergy in the eighteenth century. The willingness of 'Ultramontanes of the [Louis] Veuillot school' to prefer 'piety to intelligence and faith to reason', and to exhibit 'a credulous acceptance of the miraculous'[110] only endeared the Church to a people long attached to its 'superstitious' traditions. Gibson argues that this tolerance was symptomatic of a more 'fundamental change in religious sensibility that gradually got under way in France in the nineteenth century'. This all-important shift he sees as the move away from a religion of fear to a religion of love (both of God for man and of man for God). It can, Gibson argues:

be observed negatively in the decline of doctrines like the small number of the elect and the materiality of hell-fire, and positively in intensified Marian devotion, fervour for the Eucharist, a new attitude to the sacrament of penance typified by the rapid success of Liguorist moral theology—and much else.

It was this aspect of the new piety, Gibson concludes, which 'was working in favour of French catholicism in the second half of the nineteenth century, and which enabled it to withstand remarkably well—though with losses—the anticlerical offensive of the republic'.[111]

Given that hell-fire sermons remained a feature of Catholicism well into the twentieth century, and that the earlier tradition had its share of divine loving-kindness too, Gibson's thesis probably goes too far. His central argument that devotional change in the period may meaningfully be described as ultramontane also seems questionable, and will certainly be challenged with regard to the English case. But Gibson's fundamental

---

[109] R. Gibson, *A Social History of French Catholicism 1789–1914* (London, 1989), 144. See also G. Cholvy and Y.-M. Hilaire, *Histoire religieuse de la France contemporaine 1800–1930* (2 vols.; Toulouse, 1986). [110] Gibson, *Social History*, 240. [111] Ibid. 267.

point is an important one: it was surely because particular devotions came
to seem attractive, not because they were 'imposed', that devotional change
occurred. If we look again at the case of Ireland, it is hard to imagine how
a revolution in devotion such as that described by Larkin and other historians could have been forced upon an unwilling people; and the arguments that a gap left by an undermined Gaelic spirituality was filled by
the first alternative to come along seem highly implausible. If native Irish
spirituality was lost, then presumably this was because it had been abandoned for something which appeared more attractive to a new generation.

Another model worthy of consideration is that put forward by some
historians of contemporary Catholicism in the United States. Jay Dolan
has found that a Catholic revival, which began in the 1840s and aimed
primarily to convert the nominally Catholic, and especially the Irish
immigrant, to a devout life (i.e. to the practice of the Tridentine faith)
simultaneously ushered in the spread of 'ultramontane' devotional forms.
Dolan's concerns are quintessentially American in his attempt to place
the Catholic Church within the context of competing ethnic groups and
their associated sects, but arguably have a good deal of relevance to the
English situation as well. According to Dolan, the 'immigrant church'
was able to integrate into the mainstream of American religious life partly
because it adopted the evangelizing spirit of native Protestant sects.[112]
Dolan has found that Catholic revivalist techniques in the United States
included the use of parish missions and confraternities, both of which
encouraged participation in the sacraments and stressed the importance
of frequent communion and penance. These institutions were evidently
successful in rousing evangelical fervour until about the 1880s or 1890s,
by which time missions, although they had become a permanent feature
of Catholic life, no longer provoked the same enthusiasm as in the middle
decades of the century. While Dolan's argument is clearly specific to the
country of his study, it does draw attention to a central aspect of the
changes in Catholicism elsewhere. Gerald Parsons has also found that
the kind of evangelism promoted by Paul Cullen in Ireland, 'although
uncompromisingly and indelibly Roman Catholic in its specifics', nevertheless 'in overall tenor and appeal . . . shared much in common with
Protestant Revivalism and Anglican Ritualism'. It also 'shared with Revivalism the characteristic of tending to make more impact upon the
dormant or lax within the community than on those outside'.[113]

[112] J. P. Dolan, *Catholic Revivalism: The American Experience, 1830–1900* (Notre Dame,
Ind., 1978), *passim*.
[113] G. Parsons, 'Victorian Roman Catholicism. Emancipation, Expansion and Achievement', in Parsons (ed.), *Religion in Victorian Britain*, i. 172–3.

To point out that the devotional ethos which swept across the United States, Ireland, France, England, and elsewhere was 'evangelical' in tone or 'revivalist' in spirit is surely more useful and descriptive than to assert that it was ultramontane. In a masterly chapter which juggles the findings and criticisms of much recent work on English Catholicism, Parsons has cautiously concluded:

It has been said of Victorian Catholicism that, in its post-1850 turn to Ultramontanism, it became 'more Roman than Rome'. Certainly, even when far short of the most extreme versions of Ultramontanism, Catholic devotional life, both nationally and locally, was much more 'continental' and 'Roman' in 1900 than it was in 1829. 'More Roman than Rome' may be an exaggeration: more Roman than hitherto is not.[114]

Parsons's balanced appraisal is undoubtedly correct. One would find it difficult to dispute that Catholicism was in some sense more Roman by the end of the century than it had been at mid-century or before. But the statement is not of intrinsic significance: indeed, if we remove the subject of devotion from its usual methodological context, it becomes largely irrelevant.

Not one of the historians of non-English Catholicism whose work we have glanced at simply repeats the old chestnut that new devotional practices were forced upon native Catholics by an increasingly authoritarian Church of Rome. Neither do these scholars concur as to the cause of devotional change in the period. Naturally enough, each is concerned with the particular agents of change in his country of study, and each takes a different slant on the significance accorded to shifts in Catholic sensibility and practice. But all seem to have found that a new zeal entered the devotional life of Catholicism from about the late 1840s and certainly by 1850. Furthermore, all seem to be more or less agreed as to the outward manifestations of this change, whose analogous development in England has been termed 'ultramontane' by one English school of thought and 'truly Catholic' by another.

In England, as elsewhere, it seems that from about the middle of the nineteenth century more Catholics heard Mass, received communion, and went to confession, and did all of these things more often. Confraternities, sodalities, and other religious societies multiplied in number and grew in membership. What we might neutrally call the 'new piety' was also, we are told, characterized by participation in a range of newly popular devotions such as *Quarant'ore*, the Stations of the Cross, recitation of the

[114] Parsons, 'Victorian Roman Catholicism', 177.

rosary, and the making of novenas to such objects as the Infant Jesus, Mary Immaculate, St Joseph, and the Holy Family. 'Reparations' to the Sacred Heart, 'visits' to the Blessed Sacrament, participation in Corpus Christi processions, and attendance at Exposition, Benediction of the Blessed Sacrament, and pilgrimages to shrines all became a feature of nineteenth-century religiosity. Missions and retreats, those periodic re-newals or infusions of piety which became so characteristic an aspect of Catholic life in the nineteenth (and indeed the twentieth) century, also distinguish the new age of Catholicism. It is with such devotional mani-festations as these that this work will be primarily concerned.

It has been argued in this chapter that the devotional categories offered by the second-spring school of thought do not satisfactorily account for devotional change among the Catholics of England in the second half of the nineteenth century. It has also been stressed that to widen the mean-ing of the term ultramontane from a narrowly political definition to one describing a particular devotional outlook and a range of allegedly related views is to force the issue beyond an acceptable point. Even Holmes, arguing that the Catholics of England became 'more Roman than Rome' admits that 'not all English Catholics were Ultramontane', citing the more forceful observation of M. J. Whitty, editor of the *Liverpool Daily Post*, 'that the Ultramontanes did not represent the Roman Catholics of England and Ireland'.[115] It should, therefore, come as no surprise to find that recently published local studies of Catholic communities in England, like Gerard Connolly's earlier work on Manchester and Salford, appear to contradict assumptions long held by English historiographical conven-tion. Jennifer Supple, for example, has found that, although 'the second half of the nineteenth century is portrayed as the period during which the Ultramontane clergy took control of the Catholic Church from the hands of the old English clergy and laity', this did not happen in the allegedly ultramontane diocese of Beverley. If the standard account of a victory of ultramontanism and Romanization were 'true of England as a whole', she reasons, 'then it must surely be true of Yorkshire, where in 1861 the "thoroughly Roman" Robert Cornthwaite became Bishop of Beverley?'[116] While 'Ultramontanism, in all its guises, certainly had an influence on the Catholic Church in Yorkshire during this period,' Supple has evidently found it puzzling that 'there is also evidence of a continued attachment to old English attitudes and practices, even as late as the 1890s'. She concludes that, in Yorkshire at any rate,

[115] As cited in Holmes, *More Roman than Rome*, 120.
[116] J. Supple, 'Ultramontanism in Yorkshire', *Recusant History*, 17 (1985), 274.

What took place . . . was not the triumph of Ultramontanism but a gradual acceptance and assimilation of two different kinds of Catholicism, as the gentry who had formerly dominated the Yorkshire Church, and the old English clergy who served them, came to terms with the most Ultramontane of the English bishops and the younger priests who followed his example.[117]

Given the internal inconsistencies of both the second-spring and ultramontane-triumph schools of thought, it is not surprising that a close scrutiny of one English Catholic diocese should incidentally call into question the devotional assumptions of both historiographical traditions. Whether Supple's tentative hypothesis of the assimilation of 'two kinds of Catholicism' or a different explanation will prove the more accurate to describe the devotional behaviour of Catholics in England, however, will be considered in this work. An examination of English Catholicism which concentrates explicitly on devotion should give new insight into the religious dimension of the Catholic community, help to correct historiographical imbalances, and contribute to our understanding of the practice of the Faith in the late nineteenth and early twentieth centuries.

[117] Supple, 'Ultramontanism', 274.

2

Devotions in Common

CATHOLICS of all complexions and at all times would agree that devotion lies at the very centre of faith. Devotion in its broadest and most fundamental sense implies an earnest and deep love for God, and can hardly be measured. Although devotion is a private matter impossible for the contemporary, let alone the historian, to judge, manifestations which were generally thought by contemporaries to suggest a pious bent, or a serious religious commitment, are more open to scrutiny.

The historian's traditional measures of religious adherence—records of Mass and Easter attendances, baptisms, and the like—have generally been admitted to be inadequate, since the figures can only be taken as very loose approximations. Even if perfect, such statistics would not go to the heart of the matter, the motives and beliefs of the worshippers present, and the reasons for the absence of other self-styled Catholics. An examination of what are known in the Catholic Church as devotions and are, strictly speaking, extra-liturgical devotional actions, can compensate in part for the inadequacy of other indices. Since Catholic devotions are fully voluntary religious acts—the optional extras, so to speak, of religious adherence—they are less open to the charge of representing a lip service or merely social identification with a particular creed.

Apart from the general point that an analysis of devotions can help to uncover the religious dimension of the lives of many Catholics, there is an additional reason why such an approach is particularly appropriate for the study of Catholicism in the Victorian and Edwardian periods. One of the chief questions which divided nineteenth-century advocates of the new piety from those who favoured the old style was whether devotion to God was enhanced and encouraged, or to some extent cramped or inappropriately expressed, through such devotions as came to be increasingly rigid in form and universal in application. While Newman and others stressed that feeling could not be forced and that it was doctrine, rather than devotional expression or mere taste, which might legitimately be corrected, the kind of approach favoured by Faber could be taken to imply that true love for God would inevitably spill over into set devotional forms. A reluctance on the part of some Catholics to adopt devotions which were favoured by others could therefore be interpreted as revealing an inadequate or impoverished faith—in short, 'worldliness'. Newly enthusiastic or revivalist Catholics tended to emphasize that the tree of devotion would be known by its particular and distinctive fruit, while some conservatives objected that this was to interpret the love of God as consisting of mere feeling. Such traditionalists tended to remark that the bending of the will towards obedience was as legitimate an expression of the first commandment as any sensible emotion, however exotically or fervently expressed. An analysis of the spread, growth, and origin of devotions practised in the late nineteenth and early twentieth centuries offers more, therefore, than a mere narrative of devotional development. It also goes to the root of an important contemporary debate and can help us to assess how far the devotional approach favoured by enthusiasts such as the Brompton Oratorians was taken up by the mass of Catholics in nineteenth- and early twentieth-century England.

In order to avoid the *a priori* assumptions of both the second-spring and ultramontane-triumph schools of Catholic history, the less-loaded terms 'new piety', 'enthusiasm', and 'revivalism' have been used in lieu of 'ultramontane' or 'Roman' to describe the tone and forms of extra-liturgical Catholic worship which became characteristic of the period. Care will be taken not to follow the propagandists of the new devotions in assuming that an increase in devotions, or in certain kinds of devotions, may be equated with a more earnest faith, let alone the liberation of a somehow truer Catholicism from an ostensibly apologetic, weak, or timid old-Catholic tradition. For analogous reasons, the phrase 'popular devotions' will continue to be used sparingly. Just as the convention that the changes which overtook religious expression in the period be called 'ultramontane' implies an imposition from above, the notion of 'popular' devotions suggests a corresponding clamour from below. Both terms hint at an opposition or struggle which should not be assumed automatically. Although the term 'popular devotions' has sometimes been treated as an antonym for 'official' and in that sense formal church practices, it can also mean those devotions favoured by the many, those expressed in the vernacular, or those closest to the hearts of a particular social class or ethnic group. In order to refrain from prejudging the significance of devotions, all such terms, where possible, will be avoided, and an attempt will be made to establish and examine the facts of Catholic extra-liturgical devotional behaviour as impartially as possible. An analysis of change in the forms of religious expression should give an insight into the spirituality of several generations of English Catholics which has been largely hidden by polemical writings, both contemporary and modern.

Many devotions which originated in the nineteenth century, or have come to be associated with Catholicism of the Victorian and Edwardian periods, were church-based. This was *ipso facto* the case with all devotions which concentrated on the Eucharist, such as Benediction, *Quarant'ore* or the Forty Hours' Devotion, Exposition, and Visitation of the Blessed Sacrament. The Stations or Way of the Cross need not have been church-based but usually were, while images of the Sacred Heart, rosaries, and pictures or plaster statues of the Holy Family, St Joseph, the Blessed Virgin Mary, and the Infant Jesus could, of course, be contemplated either in church or at home, indoors or outdoors.

An analysis of the devotions which Catholic churches in England actually offered is the necessary prerequisite to any informed discussion of the popularity, extent, and significance of intrinsically church-linked devotions. Devotional services offered by churches have an additional significance for our subject, since they can be seen as an important meeting-point between the devotional imperatives prescribed by the Catholic hierarchy and those actually followed by a proportion of the Catholic laity. A further advantage in examining these devotions lies in the relative comprehensiveness of the information, which allows for regional and chronological comparisons to be made of devotional shifts across time and place.

A numerical table and fourteen figures are to be found in Appendices I and II at the end of this book. These are based on statistical information collected from the listings offered by all the churches, chapels, and stations in England and Wales in the *Catholic Directory* for the years 1850 to 1914. Information has been taken from the *Directory* for every fifth year,[1] each advertisement of a particular service, such as Benediction or *Quarant'ore* being counted once per church regardless of how many (or few) times the service was offered by that church in a given year. The statistics upon which the table and figures are based are only as reliable as the *Directory* itself. It will not be possible, in this work, to verify the statistics given in the *Directory* for so extensive a period and so large an area.[2] But they are likely to be more reliable than similar statistics given

[1] Except for the beginning and ending of the period, the gaps between 1851 and 1855 and 1910 and 1914 being, of course, four rather than five years.

[2] Spot checks comparing visitation returns (where they exist) and local directories seem to corroborate these figures, but it would be too time-consuming to undertake the task on a large scale, which would in any case still leave the numbers uncertain.

in visitation returns, since each church sent the editors of the *Directory* devotional information in the same spirit as it sent Mass and baptism times—to advertise its services to the public rather than to justify itself to ecclesiastical authority. Nevertheless, some churches may have chosen not to advertise their services at all, or may have neglected to advertise certain kinds of devotions; others may have forgotten to return their forms, and misprints may have occurred: for all these reasons it would be rash to take these statistics as corresponding exactly to the extra-liturgical offerings of Catholic churches in the period. They are intended to give an indication of broad devotional trends and do not pretend to an impossible scientific precision.

Since those devotions which took place outside church cannot hope to be measured as systematically as those routinely recorded in the *Catholic Directory*, there is also an inherent tendency to over-emphasize the importance of church-centred devotions at the expense of less well-documented, but equally significant, religious activity which took place outside church. Statistics of church-based devotions have the particular merit, however, of enabling us to assess the claims of the ultramontane-triumph school, whose arguments are concerned precisely with the role of the formal church machinery in influencing devotional behaviour. Devotions which were not tied to churches will be partially uncovered in the next chapter through an analysis of prayers. One final note of caution should be sounded before the table and figures in Appendices I and II are consulted: the *Catholic Directory* lists only services offered by, and confraternities, sodalities, and guilds attached to, churches, and not the numbers who participated in these. No estimate can be made from this information of the actual number of Catholics involved in church-based devotions at the national level. Nevertheless, it may be assumed that devotions would not continue to be offered by churches year after year if they did not attract at least some of the faithful; and the dramatic rise in the number of churches offering certain devotions would rather seem to indicate a difficulty in keeping pace with demand. Although a detailed examination of other sources, such as visitation returns and parish magazine articles and announcements, could not be undertaken for the whole of the country, spot checks have been made of selected parishes in the dioceses of Liverpool, Southwark, Northampton, Hexham and Newcastle, and Birmingham, and so should guard against any significant misinterpretations.

The devotional table and figures which are given at the end of this work[3] clearly show that only two church-based devotions were of overwhelming statistical importance to the English Catholic community. These two devotions were Benediction of the Blessed Sacrament and Public Rosary, each of which will therefore merit close scrutiny in this chapter. But before we go on to examine the two most popular of English Catholic devotions, it is worth noticing the startlingly low proportion of churches offering precisely those 'Italianate' devotions long assumed to have been so widespread as to have amounted to an ultramontane 'revolution' in Catholic devotion. These include such native Italian practices as Exposition of the Blessed Sacrament to prayer and adoration, and *Quarant'ore*, or Exposition of the Blessed Sacrament for forty hours' prayer and contemplation in memory of the forty hours Jesus spent in the tomb.

The Stations or Way of the Cross, which became a marked feature of English devotional life in the period, must rank next in order of importance after Benediction and Public Rosary. But although the Way of the Cross, perhaps because it is commonly known by its Italian name of *via crucis*, is frequently assumed to have been an ultramontane innovation, it is certainly misleading to think of it as Italian in any immediate sense: its medieval origins and promotion by Franciscans of all countries meant that it was certainly as widely available in nineteenth-century France as it was in contemporary Italy. The devotion, which symbolically followed the route leading up to the crucifixion (and was treated as equivalent to a pilgrimage to the actual sites of Christ's Passion in the Holy Land), had a much more limited appeal for the English, however. The Stations spread from London to Liverpool in the 1850s, becoming available in all dioceses by the 1860s. But even at a highpoint of 1875, when about a fifth of the churches in the archdiocese of Westminster catered for the *via crucis*, the figure seems relatively modest when compared with the 90 per cent and upwards of churches offering Benediction in dioceses such as Liverpool and Westminster, and the highpoint of about 80 per cent of these advertising Public Rosary. Furthermore, the proportion of churches offering the stations remained as low as 3 per cent or under in over half the dioceses throughout the period.

Nevertheless, those for whom the devotion held an appeal appear to

[3] See Table 1 in Appendix I, which gives the raw statistics of devotions offered by churches in England and Wales; and Figures 1–14 in Appendix II, which graphically represent the proportion of church-based devotions by diocese and year.

have felt its power strongly, and to have been attracted particularly by its penitential emphasis. This was certainly the case with Teresa Higginson of Bootle, whose long history of excessive self-mortification culminated in 'ecstasies' during which, to the mingled horror and wonder of onlookers, she violently re-enacted the scenes depicted in the Stations;[4] as for Lady Georgiana Fullerton, her biographer tells us that, when she performed her Stations, the 'very sound of her voice told how the passion had entered her soul'.[5] The statistical irregularity of the Stations, which can be seen in the devotional figures in Appendix II, indicates an unevenness in appeal which is also borne out at the diocesan level. Although the parish priest of St Mary's, Newcastle, was enthusiastic enough as early as 1854 to try to practise the devotion in spite of the fact that his church had no proper facilities for doing so,[6] the priest of a neighbouring church in the same diocese was still able, thirty years later, to reply to the relevant question in his visitation return that he had 'no knowledge nor certificate' applicable to the devotion.[7]

Devotions to the Sacred Heart, which were rarely advertised by English churches in the nineteenth century, had been both formalized and spread through French rather than Italian channels,[8] but held a respectable niche in English Catholic history. Although they only achieved widespread prominence after the famous visions of St Margaret Mary Alacoque in 1673–5, they had been known to Julian of Norwich in the fifteenth century and held a modest place in the recusant tradition from at least the time of Bishop Milner, who was particularly attached to this form of piety. The extent of the practice in England does not appear to have been markedly affected by the extension to the whole church of the Mass and Office of the feast by Pius IX in 1856, although Sacred Heart devotions

[4] This was in 1880. At about the same time she also developed stigmata, or the signs of Christ's wounds. See C. Kerr, *Teresa Helena Higginson: Servant of God 'The Spouse of the Crucified' 1844–1905* (London, 1927), 72, and A. M. O'Sullivan, *Teresa Higginson the Servant of God: School Teacher 1845–1905* (London, 1924), 130–1, for contemporary eyewitness accounts of this extraordinary performance.

[5] Anon., *The Inner Life of Lady Georgiana Fullerton* (London, 1899), 117.

[6] The priest announced that 'as the Stations have not yet [been] erected in the Ch.[urch] the Devotions will be said before the Rood Cross wh.[ich] has been indulgenced for the Devotion of the Stations' (Hexham and Newcastle Diocesan Archives, 'Notice Books 1854–1856', St Mary's, Newcastle, 26 Feb. 1854).

[7] Ibid., 'Visitation Papers', 1885, 'Esh Laude'.

[8] The popular seventeenth-century cult of the Sacred Heart, which was launched by Margaret Mary Alacoque's visions at Paray-le-Monial, took root in France and spread to Spain and Poland before being accepted with reluctance by Rome. For a concise account of the history of the devotion, see O. Chadwick, *The Popes and European Revolution* (Oxford, 1981), 64–6.

became a more pronounced feature in Catholic prayer-books from about 1875 for reasons which appear to have been quite unrelated to papal pressure.

It is perfectly true that devotions which can more legitimately be called Italian, such as some of those practised at the Brompton Oratory, became a part of the English Catholic devotional scene in the nineteenth century—but it was never a large part. The statistics of church-based devotions, far from corroborating the notion of a Roman or ultramontane triumph in devotional matters, indicate that native Italian practices met with a marked lack of enthusiasm from the mass of Catholics in England, although they always had a few admirers. Exposition of the Blessed Sacrament to prayer and adoration, although nearly half as widely available as the Stations of the Cross in London from about 1865, had still not reached even half of the dioceses of the country until the 1890s. Despite being associated by some historians with the Irish proletariat, this devotion never seems to have held much appeal for the Catholics of Liverpool, and appears to have left the dioceses of Beverley, Hexham and Newcastle, and Shrewsbury entirely untouched. As for *Quarant'ore*, or the Forty Hours' Devotion, the number of English Catholic churches offering the practice remained so low throughout the period that it accounted for less than 1 per cent of the churches of any diocese and consequently is not visible on the figures given in Appendix II.

Despite assumptions in histories of Catholicism that the existence in England of such devotions as Exposition and the Stations of the Cross indicates the success of an ultramontane revolution in the devotional habits of the English, the figures given in the *Directory* appear to indicate that these services catered for a distinct minority taste, which, although increasing from the 1860s to the 1880s, never came close to rivalling the appeal of either Public Rosary or of Benediction. Such devotions were, however, disproportionately high in London, as can be seen by examining the statistics for Southwark and Westminster dioceses in the figures of church-based devotions. This anomaly was probably due, at least in part, to the higher percentage of foreign Catholics in the capital, which included temporary residents such as diplomats and business representatives. As the seat of the hierarchy and principal archdiocese, it was in any case appropriate that London should aim to cater for all devotional requirements, however little in demand. Certainly, care must always be taken in generalizing from the case of a city as statistically eccentric as London. Since the only work specifically on Catholic devotions in England in the period, that of Sheridan Gilley, has concentrated exclusively on the capital,[9] assumptions made about the importance of so-called ultramontane devotions are understandable, if misleading, especially in their tendency to obscure the importance of the two most nationally important devotions, Public Rosary and Benediction of the Blessed Sacrament. No understanding of the devotional imperatives of English Catholicism can be grasped without a careful examination of these twin pillars of Victorian and Edwardian piety.

Historians who advocate the second-spring or ultramontane-triumph interpretations of English Catholicism have had little to say about Benediction. Usually, they restrict themselves to the single assertion that Benediction was one continental devotional import among the many which supposedly characterized the new Roman or ultramontane piety, devotions to the Sacred Heart, the rosary, *Quarant'ore*, and the Stations of the Cross being perhaps the better known of these. For those who are familiar with the historical literature, it may therefore come as something of a surprise to learn that in every single diocese of England from 1850 to 1914 it was not Sacred Heart devotions or *Quarant'ore*, but Benediction of the Blessed Sacrament which was the most commonly offered of all extra-liturgical practices. Furthermore, the proportion as well as the absolute number of churches which catered for the devotion continued to rise, and dramatically, throughout the period.

By the beginning of the twentieth century, Herbert Thurston, the Jesuit historian, could reproduce the observation that 'The modern English Catholic . . . knows only two church services—Mass in the morning, and Benediction in the evening; and he is fast coming to regard the two as of equal importance', with only a mild qualification that 'however exaggerated this statement may be, there is undoubtedly an element of truth underlying its extravagance'.[10] His view is endorsed by the *Catholic Dictionary*, which, by 1917, judged Benediction to be 'a rite which has now become very common in the Catholic Church'.[11] In an investigation of 1905 into

[9] Sheridan Gilley has argued that 'Catholic London enjoyed a kind of informal pre-eminence in the English Church' since the London diocese 'alone could cast a shadow of the Counter Reformation's continental glories' through the agency of the French, Sardinian, Neapolitan, Spanish, Portuguese, and Bavarian embassy chapels, but he readily admits that Catholics were more numerous in southern Lancashire and the West Riding. The importance which he attributes to such 'continental' influence in any case begs the question. See S. W. Gilley, 'The Roman Catholic Mission to the Irish in London, 1840–1860', *Recusant History*, 10 (1969), 125.

[10] H. Thurston, 'Our English Benediction Service', *Month*, 106 (1905), 394.

[11] W. E. Addis and T. Arnold (eds.), *A Catholic Dictionary* (9th edn., London, 1917), 77–8.

'Our English Benediction Service', Thurston went so far as to declare that

its occurrence at least weekly is now assumed as a matter of course; so much so that a priest who neglected to provide Sunday Benediction for his people would be regarded by many as more seriously wanting in his duty than if he gave up preaching, or omitted to distribute ashes on Ash Wednesday.[12]

So what was this most popular, albeit least described, of all English Catholic extra-liturgical activities? The devotion itself was simple enough, consisting of a short service which the *Catholic Dictionary* describes as follows:

The priest takes the Host from the tabernacle, places it in the monstrance, and then puts the monstrance containing the Host on a throne above the tabernacle. The priest then incenses the Blessed Sacrament, while the choir (at least in England) usually sing the 'O Salutaris Hostia'. Next the Te Deum, the Litany of the Blessed Virgin, or some other canticle or antiphon, is sung, followed by the 'Tantum Ergo', during which the Blessed Sacrament is again incensed, and the prayer 'Deus, qui nobis', &c., is recited. Finally, the priest, mantled with the veil, makes the sign of the cross with the monstrance over the people.[13]

If the ultramontane-triumph school were correct in viewing the drive for devotional change in England as coming directly from Rome, then we should expect to find that Benediction was either a continental import favoured by and promoted from Rome, or else an Italian custom which was spontaneously imitated by English Catholics. In fact, neither appears to have been the case. Despite its deep-rooted appeal for English Catholics, the rite was quite a novel one in the development of Catholic devotion and ritual. 'Few of our fellow-Papists realize how relatively modern Benediction of the Blessed Sacrament is', Thurston pointed out in 1905,[14] adding that 'few understand that the existence of such a rite is still almost ignored by the Church's official ceremonial'.[15] As Thurston explained,

whatever we possess in the way of a formal ritual for Benediction is only of recent and local development. No official mandate has been issued to the Church at large prescribing what is to be done. Hence rubricists have to guide themselves by what

---

[12] Thurston, 'Our English Benediction Service', 394.

[13] Addis and Arnold (eds.), *Catholic Dictionary*, 77–8. The dictionary adds that 'The Congregation of rites orders this Benediction to be given in silence; probably to show that it is not the earthly, but the Eternal Priest who in this rite blesses and sanctifies his people. If a bishop gives Benediction of the Blessed Sacrament, he makes the sign of the cross over the people three times' (p. 78).

[14] Thurston, 'Our English Benediction Service', 394. The *Catholic Dictionary* also points out that 'the rite is comparatively modern' (Addis and Arnold (eds.), *Catholic Dictionary*, 78).   [15] Thurston, 'Our English Benediction Service', 394.

is enjoined for the feast of Corpus Christi or by the Papal Instruction for the *Quarant'ore*.[16]

Rome gave no sign which might be mistaken for approval during the Victorian and Edwardian periods; it was not until 1958 that the Sacred Congregation of Rites explicitly affirmed that Benediction served a 'true liturgical function'.[17]

Nor was the devotion Italian, Italianate, or even continental in the form in which it was practised in England. Thurston traces the development of the service from 'the original *Salut*, or *Salve*, or *Lof*, or *Laudi*, as it was variously called in different countries' and which 'might be directed to our Lady, or to the angels, or to any of the saints, or to the Holy Ghost, or the Passion of our Lord' and could 'consist of the Rosary, or the *Salve Regina*, or the *De profundis*, or almost any recognized form of prayer',[18] pointing out that in these medieval precursors to Benediction 'the *Salut* itself was the substantial element, the exposition and final blessing were only accessories'.[19] The distinguishing features of the modern and English service of Benediction of the Blessed Sacrament, Thurston argues, are 'first its relative brevity, and secondly the inclusion of the *O Salutaris* as its introductory and invariable element'.[20] Both of these distinctive features appear to have come about through

an imitation of this practice [of opening with the 'O Salutaris'] prevalent both at Douai and St Omers [*sic*] where so large a proportion of the English clergy during the seventeenth and eighteenth centuries will first have become familiar with that short service of exposition of the Blessed Sacrament which we now call Benediction.[21]

As for the more immediate origins of the rite, Thurston found that 'it is in the first or one of the early editions of the *Garden of the Soul*, that venerable English prayer-book compiled about 1740 by Bishop Challoner, that a recognition of anything like our modern Benediction service first finds a place'.[22] He then reproduces Challoner's version of the service, remarking that

It will be noticed that prayers for the Church and the King are intimately bound up with the service [as found in Challoner], but that, with this exception and

---

[16] Ibid. 402.
[17] J. G. Davies (ed.), *A New Dictionary of Liturgy and Worship* (London, 1986; 1991), 89. Until then official views went only so far as to admit that 'The general law of the Church permits Benediction, both morning and evening, on the feast of Corpus Christi and during its octave. For a good reason the bishop may grant permission for this devotion on other occasions' (C. Pallen and J. Wynne (eds.), *The New Catholic Dictionary* (London, 1929), 109). [18] Thurston, 'Our English Benediction Service', 395.
[19] Ibid. [20] Ibid. 400. [21] Ibid. 402. [22] Ibid. 398.

saving for the omission of any explicit reference to the Litany of Loreto, the form is substantially identical with that to which we are accustomed.[23]

That the service of Benediction was actively practised in England, and not merely recommended, during the recusant period can be confirmed by an examination of pre-1850 advertisements in the *Laity's Directory* which certainly go back as far as 1823 and presumably beyond, although earlier editions of the *Directory* unfortunately omit to give details of any church services or extra-liturgical devotions. Its placement in early editions of *The Garden of the Soul* suggests that it was most commonly subsumed in the service of Compline in Challoner's day, but was certainly taking place independently as well from at least as early as 1823, when churches in places as diverse as London, Bridgewater, Whitby, and Coventry advertised Benediction as a separate service.[24]

In tracing the origins of the rite, Thurston considered the possibility of an indirect influence from the sixteenth-century Italian practice of *Oratio sine intermissione* alluded to by St Charles Borromeo which 'seems to have been a type of devotion intermediate between the Forty Hours and our modern Benediction'.[25] As he points out elsewhere, 'there can be little doubt, I think, that the service which is now so simple and so familiar, is of composite growth'.[26] While Thurston's association with the liturgical movement of the turn of the century and his interest in tracing a peculiarly English Catholic tradition should keep us on our guard, it is only after a painstaking and scholarly consideration of a myriad of possible origins that he appears to find the Douai–St Omer–Challoner route the most persuasive. There seems to be no reason to doubt his conclusion.

By 1850, then, thanks to the influence of Challoner's *The Garden of the Soul*, the practice of Benediction of the Blessed Sacrament already boasted

[23] Thurston, 'Our English Benediction Service', 400.

[24] See the *Laity's Directory* for that year. The devotion evidently appealed to the poor, like the two thousand or so members of Romney-terrace, Marsham St, in Westminster, whose congregation was made up 'almost exclusively of poor labouring people' and whose church offered up 'Mass at 11 o'clock, with benediction of the B. Sacrament . . . for the *benefactors of the chapel*, both living and dead'. At Clarendon Square in Somerstown Benediction was offered at 6 o'clock in summer or 5 o'clock in winter. But the service was also available at more exclusive addresses like Chelsea New Chapel, where 'Vespers with benediction' was offered at 3.30. At Court House, Cannington, near Bridgewater, Benediction followed Vespers at 5 o'clock. At St Mary's, Coventry, it was offered only on the first Sunday of the month, and at Whitby only on holidays (*The Laity's Directory for the Year 1823* (London, 1823)).

[25] H. Thurston, 'Benediction of the Blessed Sacrament. III. The Benediction', *Month*, 98 (1901), 187.

[26] H. Thurston, 'Benediction of the Blessed Sacrament. I. Seeing the Body of the Lord', *Month*, 97 (1901), 587.

over a century of history as a distinctively English rite. It needed neither promotion from Rome nor the influence of Irish immigrants and zealous converts to assure it of an enduring popularity; on the contrary, it was established firmly enough in the English Catholic tradition for its origins to have been obscured and for its faint whiff of unorthodoxy to have been forgotten by all but a few liturgical scholars. Indeed, by Thurston's day the

O Salutaris, Litany of Loreto, *Tantum ergo*—these in the popular mind constitute[d] 'Benediction', and the English traveller on the continent look[ed] with a certain suspicion on the variations which he [found] there, as though they were something new-fangled and not altogether quite orthodox.[27]

Thurston attributes the overwhelming popularity of Benediction among English Catholics partly to the uniformity of the service, by which he presumably means its geographical as well as historical coherence, arguing that 'It is this last tendency towards uniformity which has, I think, contributed more than anything else to the hold which the service has taken upon the hearts of the people in modern times'.[28] Elsewhere he stresses the 'brightness, brevity, and uniformity of the rite, the last two points being much more conspicuous in England, or in countries influenced by England, than elsewhere'.[29]

That the service was a compact one, and generally offered at the convenient time of 7 or 8 o'clock on a Sunday evening, as well as on additional days in some parishes, filling the gap which the Anglican church met with Evensong, might seem a sufficient explanation to account for its popularity. Certainly, these factors must have added to the attraction of the service; but they would only account for such remarkably high levels of popularity as we have seen if Benediction had been a formal requirement of the church. Benediction, however, was a purely optional affair, and not in any way a substitute for attendance at Mass, or for the meeting of other religious obligations, since neither the requirements of confessing nor of communicating could be fulfilled there. Nor was it granted indulgences in its specifically English form, hardly a surprising fact given Thurston's point that it was tolerated rather than approved by Rome, although some of its components, such as the (albeit optional) Litany of the Blessed Virgin, met with warmer approbation. Thurston does allude once, in passing, to 'the quite modern development of the practice of "visiting" the Blessed Sacrament, which undoubtedly has

---

[27] Thurston, 'Our English Benediction Service', 394.   [28] Ibid.
[29] Ibid. 396.

much to say in the matter'[30] of the increased popularity of the devotion, but seems to feel on firmest ground with his argument for the intrinsic neatness of Benediction and of its uniformity, which also, of course, implies familiarity.[31]

Although it was enshrined in its full form in that prayer-book which is frequently used as a synonym for old English Catholicism, *The Garden of the Soul*, and which has been criticized by some advocates of ultramontanism as apologetic and timid, the rite of Benediction, however idiosyncratic in the international context of the Catholic world, was about as distinctively Catholic as a service in a Protestant country could be. Concentrating almost exclusively on the mystery of transubstantiation, with a brief reference to the prominence of the Virgin Mary in the recitation of her Litany of Loreto; heightening the priestly functions and particularly emphasizing the priest's role as 'eternal' rather than natural, the service would have had a natural appeal for champions of the priest-hood like Henry Edward Manning or W. G. Ward. Its use of the expo-sition of the sacrament and the blessing of the people with the 'captive victim' in the monstrance would also complement, as Thurston's remark suggests, the new strain in devotional imperatives which was responsible for the promotion of such 'ultramontane' practices as *Quarant'ore*, visits to the Blessed Sacrament, and Exposition of the Blessed Sacrament. As F. W. Faber put it, in characteristically effusive language, 'Better far to flutter like a moth round the candles of a gay Benediction, than to live without love in the proprieties of sensual ease and worldly comfort.'[32] It is no doubt because it had elements which corresponded with the new piety that several historians have spoken of the service of Benediction in the same breath as these other devotions, and easily bracket all together as Roman or ultramontane, implying that Benediction was yet another foreign import among a host of devotional innovations.[33]

But the service of Benediction was likely to have as much innate appeal for the old-English Catholic as for his ultramontane counterpart. As we have seen, Benediction was English in its formation as a distinctive rite,

---

[30] Thurston, 'Our English Benediction Service', 396.   [31] Ibid. 402.

[32] As cited in C. Jones, G. Wainwright, and E. Yarnold (eds.), *The Study of Spirituality* (London, 1986), 429.

[33] Thus Norman seems to speak of 'new devotions' in the same vein as this old Catholic favourite in his discussion of Fr Luigi Gentili's importance in bringing a new religious sensibility to England. See E. Norman, *The English Catholic Church in the Nineteenth Century* (Oxford, 1984), 227. Ann Taves does not seem to distinguish very clearly between novel and traditional devotional elements, either (A. Taves, *The Household of Faith: Roman Catholic Devotions in Mid-Nineteenth Century America* (Notre Dame, Ill., 1986), 11).

its roots lay deep in the recusant tradition, and it remained virtually unaltered from the time of Challoner. It would, in fact, be difficult to find a more quintessentially old–Catholic devotion, if one considers its distinguished pedigree from Douai to Challoner. In his discussion of the transformation of the inessential elements of the continental *salut* to those central and fixed in the English version of Benediction, Thurston, as an English Catholic, can hardly contain a note of confidence bordering on the smugly proprietorial. 'Now it hardly needs saying', he declares,

that our point of view at the present day, and especially here in England, is quite different from [that of viewing the devotion's elements as inessential]. The service which we call 'Benediction' is looked upon as something complete in itself. The exposition of the Blessed Sacrament and the blessing imparted at the end are no longer mere accessories, but they constitute the main appeal to the piety of the faithful, and it is to honour the Blessed Sacrament in this way that the congregation assemble. They may perhaps be puzzled, if ever they advert to it, by the incongruity of singing the Litany of our Lady at a service which is seemingly consecrated to the veneration of the Holy Eucharist, but the familiarity with all its elements gives a certain sense of oneness to the whole; and the name 'Benediction' no longer in our minds connotes the mere act of blessing with the monstrance, but it includes all that takes place there from the *O Salutaris*, sung as the tabernacle door is opened, to the final *Adoremus* with which the service usually concludes.[34]

The appeal of the service of Benediction was certainly as strong for a Garden-of-the-Soul Catholic as for his newer Catholic counterpart. That it held an equally strong attraction for working- as for middle- and upper-class Catholics is borne out by the sheer number of churches offering the devotion. Benediction was no separate devotion exclusively for those of a quiet or genteelly English bent; nor was it solely of interest to enthusiasts of the Brompton Oratory or spiritual dogmatists like Manning and Ward. The son of a patternmaker and a machinist from Preston recalled in later years how 'we were all connected with St Ignatius Parish and in St Ignatius service there would be what they called in those days, Benediction, a major service in the evening in the church'.[35] Herbert, later Cardinal, Vaughan was equally attached to the devotion: as he wrote to Lady Herbert of Lea in 1867, he could not 'possibly see Tiz.

---

[34] Thurston, 'Our English Benediction Service', 395–6.
[35] From Elizabeth Roberts's interview with Mr S. 4. P. (b. 1915, of Preston, son of a patternmaker father and a machinist, afterwards teacher, mother), unpublished manuscript from the Centre for North-West Regional Studies, University of Lancaster. I am grateful to Elizabeth Roberts for this reference.

Confessions here to-night. Mass and Benediction to-morrow',[36] and again: 'Tizzy said something about your driving her over here. To-morrow and Saturday Benediction is at 5. On Sunday service at 4 and Procession of the Blessed Sacrament round the grounds, weather permitting, in case you come.'[37]

Cardinal Wiseman knew at which services to reach the greatest number of his flock when, in 1852, he urged the Catholic community to give thanks for the restoration of the hierarchy through 'an act of thanksgiving, either at the close of Mass, or at Benediction in the evening' at which the '*Te Deum* . . . will be sung (or recited where no music is ordinarily performed); and the Prayer for thanksgiving will be inserted in every Mass'.[38] The habit of using Benediction both to attract congregations and to mark any church festivity with special solemnity was as common at the parochial as at the national level. The Eucharistic Congress of 1908, unsurprisingly, opened and closed with Benediction;[39] but Canon Moser, parish priest of All Souls church in Peterborough, in the smallest English diocese of Northampton, could think of no more fitting mark of respect when, in 1895, his congregation was to move from its modest chapel in Queen Street to its modern premises, than to hold a final Benediction service there. As its assistant curate, Dudley Cary-Elwes, later recalled with nostalgia: 'We can imagine the final scenes on that memorable day, and the thoughts that filled the hearts of all of the last Benediction in the old Queen Street Chapel, the scene of so many divine gifts to the rapidly growing congregation . . .'.[40]

Benediction was the second great service in the church which an English Catholic, of whatever social class or ethnic group, was likely to feel a

[36] Vaughan to Lady Herbert, 13 Aug. 1867, in *Letters of Herbert, Cardinal Vaughan, to Lady Herbert of Lea 1867 to 1903*, ed. S. Leslie (London, 1942), 16.

[37] Vaughan to Lady Herbert, 11 June 1868, in ibid. 97.

[38] [N. Wiseman], Synodal Letter to the First Synod of Westminster, 17 July 1852, in *The Synods in English: Being the Text of the Four Synods of Westminster, translated into English . . .*, ed. R. E. Guy (Stratford, 1886), 267.

[39] Benediction brought the congress to an end on 13 September 1908, when, as a kind of *tour de force*: 'public Benediction of the Most Blessed Sacrament was to be given by the Cardinal Legate from the balcony . . . The Catholic Boys' Brigade mounted a guard of honour on the opposite side of Ashley Place, and between them and [Westminster] Cathedral stood line upon line of altar-servers, members of confraternities, British and foreign clergy and laity. Every window and gallery was occupied; it was a sight not easily forgotten. There was a stir in the balcony above, and the crowd beneath, notified of what was passing, sang with fervour and emotion the Benediction hymns . . . (H. Thurston (ed.), *Report of the Nineteenth Eucharistic Congress, held at Westminster from 9th to 13th September 1908* (London, 1909), 18, 601–2).

[40] D. Cary-Elwes, 'Catholic Peterborough, Past and Present', *St Francis' Magazine*, NS 48 (1921), 111.

desire to attend. It may be—although there is no more than the faintest
hint of this—that this appeal was enhanced, for some, by superstitious
beliefs which could be attached to the service. In late medieval France a
common prayer to be said at the elevation of the host during Mass
included the petition 'deliver us by this your most Holy Body which is
held on your altar from all impurities of mind and body and from all evil
and danger, now and for ever'.[41] John Bossy has argued persuasively that,
even after the elevation had been combined with the hymn 'O Salutaris
Hostia' and evolved into the separate service of Benediction, 'the salvation in question [was] still the salvation of soul and body, and the enemies
[were] still real enemies'.[42] That visits to the Blessed Sacrament and
blessing with the Blessed Sacrament should have continued to be thought
by some to be good for the health of the body as well as the soul seems
a strong possibility, and one not likely to have been altogether discouraged by some advocates of the new piety.

   Although Herbert Thurston was troubled to find that St Augustine
believed a plaster made of the Blessed Sacrament to have cured a man
from blindness,[43] and explicitly distanced the nineteenth and twentieth
centuries from 'a more primitive age [when] the line which separated
religious ritual and therapeutics was by no means clearly defined',[44] he
probably protested too much. After all, a celebrated account of just such
a miraculous cure had been translated into English and published by
Lady Georgiana Fullerton in 1866,[45] and folk tradition claims that the
first English Catholic to be cured at Lourdes was a Liverpool Catholic
called Jack Traynor who had been paralysed from war wounds at Gallipoli. It seems significant that it was not at the grotto but 'as he was
blessed by the blessed sacrament [that] he suddenly felt that he wanted to
get up, to move and get away' and was found to have been miraculously
healed.[46]

   While there is no evidence to suggest that most English Catholics
would have gone so far as to expect a miracle cure while attending

   [41] J. Bossy, 'Christian Life in the Later Middle Ages: Prayers', *Transactions of the Royal
Historical Society*, 6th ser., 1 (1991), 147.   [42] Ibid.
   [43] Repeating Augustine's account, he remarks: 'Now whether the story be true or
false . . . the striking feature is that the great doctor of the western Church should record
it without any hint that he disapproved the action of Acatius's "religious mother"'
(H. Thurston, 'Reservation in its Historical Aspects', *Month*, 130 (1917), 240).
   [44] Ibid. 238.
   [45] J. P. Verdenal, *The Miracle at Metz Wrought by the Blessed Sacrament, June 14, 1865*,
trans. G. Fullerton, from *Relation de la guérison d'une malade* (London, 1866).
   [46] B. Green, 'Adieu Mass', *Ampleforth Hospitalité de Lourdes Newsletter*, 16 (1992), 7. See
also R. Cranston, *The Miracle of Lourdes* (New York, 1955; 1988).

Benediction, the central mystery of transubstantiation, itself improbable enough in natural terms, was hardly likely to create a climate of instinctive scepticism. Bruce Marshall's fictional Father Smith, who

always loved the service of Benediction, because it was so beautiful with our Lord there all White in the centre of the monstrance, and he sometimes wondered why lay-people wanted to go to concerts and theatres at all, when they could have so much more pleasure praising and adoring God this way[47]

may have been rather sanguine; but an element of theatre no doubt played its part in contributing to the appeal of this most popular devotion. Benediction was in every way calculated to appeal to the mass of English Catholics: in its Englishness and its familiarity, in its blending of native tradition with the devotional imperatives of those most influenced by recent continental developments, in its conciseness and convenience, and, finally, in its theatre and sense of the mysterious.

That Benediction contained all those elements necessary to ensure it widespread Catholic support also made it a natural target for exploitation by those who wished to nudge Catholic devotion into more extreme, or at any rate more exclusive, directions. But even such a superficial modification of the rite as a change in the English translations which accompanied the Latin hymns does not appear to have been favoured by nineteenth-century readers of *The Garden of the Soul*. Up-to-date translations, which were included in the 1877 version of Challoner's prayer-book, were dropped in the next edition (1883), which returned to the older, familiar translations.[48] Occasional attempts by the hierarchy to redirect the rite were not much more successful. The *Manual of Prayers for Congregational Use* of 1886, the first post-1850 prayer-book to be 'prescribed by the Cardinal Archbishop and Bishops of England', reminded readers that, since 'it is the desire of the Cardinal Archbishop and Bishops of the province of Westminster, that public as well as private prayers and intercessions be

[47] B. Marshall, *All Glorious Within* (London, 1944), 43–4. This view may have been coloured by nostalgia as well, since Marshall's novel, although set in the inter-war years, was not published until the Second World War. It was set in Scotland rather than in England, but it was the English service of Benediction which was being referred to, and Catholics of both countries appear (not altogether surprisingly, given their proximity, common language, and similar circumstances) to have been kindred in matters of devotion.

[48] See [R. Challoner], *The Garden of the Soul: A Manual of Spiritual Exercises and Instructions for Christians Who, Living in the World, Aspire to Devotion* (London, 1856), in the Miniature Golden Manual series; a new edition prescribed 'by lawful authority' (London and Derby, 1877); a further edition 'approved by the Cardinal Archbishop of Westminster' (London, 1883); and a London edition of 1899. The objectionable new translation slightly pre-dates the period under consideration, and appears to have been published first in Birmingham in 1844 in 'a new and amended edition' boasting 'permissu superiorum'.

constantly offered up to God for the conversion of England', the bishops
had resolved, on 2 May 1869, 'that the Exposition and Benediction of the
Blessed Sacrament on the second Sunday of every month shall be for this
intention'.[49] It added that 'the following prayers, composed by His
Eminence Cardinal Wiseman, may be said on this and other occasions,
even during Exposition of the Blessed Sacrament'.[50] These prayers included effusive petitions, like the one which begged that Jesus should:

look graciously upon our beloved country . . . that, acknowledging once more the
dignity of this holy Virgin, they may honour and venerate her with all affection
of devotion, and own her as Queen and Mother. May her sweet name be lisped
by little ones, and linger on the lips of the aged and the dying . . . that this Star
of the Sea being their protection and their guide, all may come to the harbour of
eternal salvation . . .[51]

The 1886 *Manual* also included the direction that 'after the Benediction,
and before the *Divine Praises*, the following may always be recited or sung
by Priest and Congregation "For the conversion of England. Spare, O
Lord, spare Thy people, and be not angry with us for ever. *Thrice*."'[52]
That such prayers and intentions were left optional, despite constant
reminders of their existence as forms which might be followed,[53] may
indicate conflicting tastes among the bishops over the matter, an 'enthusiastic' contingent desiring the rubric to be included along with Wiseman's
effusive prayers, the defenders of the traditional simplicity of Benediction insisting that any such tinkering with Challoner's handiwork be left
explicitly optional.

The novelty was not taken up with much zeal in the country at large,
it would seem, since in 1890, at the bishops' meeting held at Whitsuntide,
it was felt necessary to raise the point a third time, 'it [being] resolved to
direct that, at Benediction on the Second Sunday of the month, there be

---

[49] *Manual of Prayers for Congregational Use* (London and Derby, 1886), 274.
[50] Ibid. 274. In 1867 the bishops had agreed '1. To consider, and mention in the *Directory*, the Benediction usually given in all Churches and Chapels on the second Sunday of
each month, as offered for the Conversion of England; 2. to petition for the extension to all
England of the Indulgence granted by His Holiness to the Faithful who pray for the same
intention; and 3. To request the Archbishop to prepare a set of prayers for the use of the
Faithful containing this Indulgence' (Westminster Archdiocesan Archives, 'Manning 1867–
1891', Acta, Low Week Meeting of the Bishops, 2 May 1867, xxi).
[51] *Manual of Prayers*, 276.   [52] Ibid. 277.
[53] The *Manual of Prayers for Congregational Use* further emphasized the point with a
second reference to the 'Supplication of the Conversion of England' to be held after
Benediction, in a note on p. 342 under the rubric for 'The Rite of Exposition and Benediction of the Blessed Sacrament', p. 331. Music for the same was brought to the attention of
readers in an appendix on p. 188, and in the preface to the manual on p. vii.

sung or recited either the *Litany of Intercession for England*, as in the "Manual of Prayers", or the prayers which precede it; with one *Hail Mary*.[54] The same resolution also called for an instruction to be sent to the clergy 'recommending the revival of the practice instituted by Father Ignatius Spencer, of saying one *Hail Mary* daily for the Conversion of England'.[55] A perusal of the *Catholic Directory* would appear to confirm this picture of reluctance on the part of Catholics in England to accept novelties in their cherished rite, since only one church, in the diocese of Salford, advertised Benediction for the Conversion of England from 1893,[56] and this in spite of the fact that the bishop of the diocese had been explicitly urging the adoption of the practice from at least as early as 1870.[57] At about the same time, an unsuccessful attempt was made to graft the Roman conception of Benediction on to the English observance. At the bishops' meeting of 1889, 'leave was given for Messrs. Burns and Oates to publish a new edition of the *Ritus Servandus*, for Benediction, etc., together with certain additions, and with corrections to bring it into conformity with the text of the *Rituale*, as approved in Rome'.[58] Yet another attempt was made to tamper with the rite on the occasion of the sacerdotal jubilee of the pope in 1908, when the bishops recommended that 'In England, on the day when the Jubilee is to be kept, there should be, in all Missions where it may be possible, Exposition of the Most Blessed Sacrament, with special prayers for the intentions of the Holy Father, and if possible, a Solemn *Te Deum* during Benediction.'[59]

The inherent popularity of the service of Benediction may have left it open to attempts at manipulation by some members of the hierarchy; but this innate appeal made the devotion equally open to pressure from below. Members of the hierarchy were certainly worried by the possibility that the Blessed Sacrament might not be accorded proper respect, as when Bishop Goss of Liverpool considered it 'for the present . . . better not to have procession of the B.[lessed] S.[acrament]' at St Michael's in 1866, since 'it is the most solemn of all rites & requires more than your

---

[54] Westminster Archdiocesan Archives, 'Bishops' Meetings 1858–1909', Acta, Meeting of the Bishops at Whitsuntide, 1890, xi. 231.   [55] Ibid.

[56] This was St Gertrude's Convent in Manchester. See annual issues of the *Catholic Directory* from 1893.

[57] See Lancashire Record Office, The Parish Priest, St Augustine's Church, Preston, RCPa 1/16, 'St Augustine's Parochial Notice Book, 29 May 1870–27 December 1874', e.g. 9 Oct. 1870.

[58] Westminster Archdiocesan Archives, 'Bishops' Meetings 1858–1909', Acta, 1889, vi. 221.

[59] Westminster Archdiocesan Archives, 'Bishops' Meetings 1858–1909', Acta, Meeting of the Bishops in Low Week, 1908, vii. 387.

Church as yet possesses to be carried out rubrically'.[60] He was similarly nervous at the thought of the Blessed Sacrament being housed in a church near Wigan which he thought 'in its present ruinous condition . . . not fit to be the home of the Blessed Sacrament'.[61]

As well as wishing to protect church practices from disrespect, the records of the bishops' meetings also hint at a certain anxiety to contain such devotional enthusiasm as might threaten the centrality of approved worship. The balance between encouraging a warm love of God and restraining spontaneous outbursts of religious feeling which departed from the teaching of the church, or appeared to obscure its own liturgy, was always a delicate one. From at least as early as 1871 the bishops attempted to restrain the number of 'different translations of various psalms, lately appeared in certain prayer-books', resolving unanimously that 'all Scripture quotations should be made from the authorized Douay version'.[62] The preface to the *Manual of Prayers for Congregational Use* of 1886 clearly pointed out that

the popular use of devotions in the vernacular has always been universal in the Church, and in this country our congregations are to be encouraged in the regular and frequent use of them, especially on account of the doctrinal and moral truths with which they continually inform the mind, while at the same time they nourish and strengthen the soul.[63]

The preface went on to warn, however, that

while the use of popular devotions is warmly recommended, the difference between liturgical and extra-liturgical services must be borne in mind. The former are always in the language of the Church; they are prescribed and regulated by the Holy See, and are not open to modification by any local authority. The latter are open to the revision, direction, and approval of the Bishop of the diocese, and may be used privately and popularly, but never as forming part of the solemn liturgy of the Church.[64]

It was for this reason that the bishops' *Manual* attempted to ensure that the two kinds of religious service be strictly and clearly differentiated, and the integrity of the Church's preferred forms given precedence over the uncontrolled variety and innovation to which spontaneous

---

[60] Lancashire Record Office, The Archbishop of Liverpool, RCLv 5/2 Box 14, 'Bishop Goss's Letter Book 1855–1872', Alexander Goss to Mr Tobin, priest of St Michael's, West Derby Road, Liverpool, 6 May 1866, fo. 105.

[61] Ibid., Alexander Goss to Fr Bury, 1 July 1867, fo. 152.

[62] Westminster Archdiocesan Archives, 'Bishops' Meetings 1858–1909', Acta, Meeting of the Bishops in Low Week, 1871, x. 45.

[63] Preface to the *Manual of Prayers*, p. vii.   [64] Ibid., p. viii.

religious expression was always liable. Thus the *Manual of Prayers for Congregational Use* insisted that 'the popular devotions that are used before and after Mass are to be recited by the Priest without chasuble and maniple; and at Exposition of the Blessed Sacrament the novenas, or other special prayers in the vernacular, must be said before the *Tantum ergo*'.[65] In 1890 it was again stressed that 'in approving the "Manual of Prayers", there was no intention to prohibit the public use of prayers not therein contained, but only to forbid "variety of version", and verbal and textual alterations of the forms printed in the "Manual" '.[66] It would seem that, while the hierarchy believed Benediction to be of spiritual profit to the laity, it was anxious to ensure that the Mass and other requirements of practice not be overshadowed by so cherished a devotion, and that the Blessed Sacrament be approached with the right kind and degree of reverence.

The most popular of English Catholic devotions was hardly 'ultramontane', although it did appeal, among others, to those whose piety has been called ultramontane. It was not imposed upon the English people by Rome, which simply tolerated it; or by the English Catholic hierarchy, whose occasional attempts to reinterpret or steer it were generally unsuccessful. Its popularity was unrivalled, perhaps in part precisely because pressure neither from above nor from below ever managed to damage its integrity. It remained, old-English Catholic devotion though it was, the primary extra-liturgical service of the nineteenth- and early twentieth-century Church, now swelled with Irish immigrants and converts as well as native Catholics.

After Benediction, the most popular Catholic devotion in England from 1850 until well beyond 1914 was the rosary. The devotion, which was popularly believed to have been revealed to St Dominic in the thirteenth century by Mary herself, is, of course, that familiar 'form of prayer in which fifteen decades of Aves, each decade being preceded by a Pater and followed by a Gloria, are recited on beads',[67] while a separate mystery is contemplated during the recital of each. The rosary is divided into three sets of five decades, each known as a corona or chaplet, which gives the broader theme, so to speak, of each set of mysteries to be considered. As the *Catholic Dictionary* explains:

[65] Preface to the *Manual of Prayers*, p. viii.
[66] Westminster Archdiocesan Archives, 'Bishops' Meetings 1858–1909', Acta, Meeting of the Bishops at Whitsuntide, 1890, xvii. 235.
[67] Addis and Arnold (eds.), *Catholic Dictionary*, 732.

In the first chaplet the five joyful mysteries are the subjects of contemplation— viz. the Annunciation, Visitation, the Birth of our Lord, His Presentation in the Temple, His being found after the three days' loss. The sorrowful mysteries contemplated in the second chaplet are the Agony in the Garden, the Scourging, the Crowning with Thorns, the Carrying of the Cross, the Crucifixion. The glorious mysteries, which are allotted to the third chaplet, are the Resurrection of Christ, His Ascension, the Descent of the Holy Ghost, the Assumption and Coronation of the Blessed Virgin.[68]

This rosary, most familiar as a string of beads used to keep track of the number of prayers recited, could be shaped more discreetly as a 'rosary ring' of ten beads or a decade, worn on the finger and used for counting; or it could consist of a group of fifteen people, known as the 'living rosary', who united every month to recite the whole of the rosary together. When advertised by churches, the 'Rosary' meant the public recitation of this Dominican rosary of fifteen decades (referred to hereafter as 'Public Rosary'),[69] which was usually led by a priest and followed, with or without beads, by the congregation.

The already marked, but rapidly increasing popularity of Public Rosary among English Catholics in the latter half of the nineteenth century might, at first glance, seem to challenge the notion put forward in this work that changes in devotional practice did not arise from Roman imperatives, whether directly or indirectly. Considered an ultramontane and Irish devotion *par excellence*, its mushrooming popularity might be taken to reinforce arguments for an ultramontane revival. Alternatively, it might seem to support Jennifer Supple's notion of the accommodation in England of two distinct forms of Catholicism—in which case those on their way to Benediction presumably would have passed others on their way to recite the rosary in a church which catered for their separate taste. If the latter were true, we might expect to see an inverse correlation between churches which offered Benediction and those which offered Public Rosary. But the figures which illustrate the proportion of churches offering various devotions in each diocese clearly show that dioceses with

---

[68] Ibid.

[69] Apart from this most common rosary, there existed several variations. As the *Catholic Dictionary* points out, 'A popular manual by Labis, translated by an English Passionist, enumerates the following rosaries besides the Dominican—viz. that of St Bridget, 7 Paters and 63 Aves, in honour of the joys and sorrows of the Blessed Virgin and the 63 years of her life; that of the Seven Dolours, a Servite devotion; that of the Immaculate Conception, approved by Pius IX in 1855; the Crown of our Saviour, attributed to Michael of Florence, a Camaldolese monk, in 1516, and consisting of 33 Paters, 5 Aves, and a Credo; the Rosary of the Five Wounds, approved by Leo XII in 1823 at the prayer of the Passionists' (ibid. 733).

a high proportion of churches advertising Benediction had a correspondingly high proportion of churches which catered for Public Rosary.
Furthermore, the two devotions tended to grow at about the same rate,
although the absolute numbers for Public Rosary remained smaller than
those for Benediction.

That this statistical relationship between the growth of Public Rosary
and Benediction was complementary rather than competitive within dioceses can be ascertained from a closer examination of the *Catholic Directory*. This shows that churches which offered Public Rosary invariably
offered Benediction as well, the usual procedure advertised being 'Benediction of the Blessed Sacrament followed by the Rosary' or 'Benediction
and the Rosary', which indicates that the two services were being offered
to the same congregation. An (albeit cursory) examination of visitation
returns does not suggest that it was normal practice to leave at the inter-
mission, so to speak, between the two services. Furthermore, although
the rosary is often assumed to have been a particularly Irish devotion,
a traditionally English Catholic parish like St Peter's, Lytham, was enthusiastic enough to set up more than thirty parish-based rosary 'circles'
in 1856; and these were continuing to draw Catholics of English as well
as Irish origin for at least the next nineteen years.[70] There is no evidence
to suggest that the rosary was a devotion which appealed to a different
sort of Catholic from one who would attend Benediction.

The rosary hardly divided Catholics from one another. But the common assertion that its practice had gradually been lost after the Reformation and needed to be restored to the English people in the nineteenth
century remains to be answered. If true, this alleged fact would strengthen
the case for the appearance of an ultramontane devotional revolution
which went against the grain of the old-English or recusant tradition. A
pious legend has been circulating for about a hundred years, and can still
be heard in some Dominican circles, which claims that it was Bishop
Ullathorne, under the influence of Margaret Mary Hallahan, who reintroduced the rosary into England after generations of neglect. This
rumour may have contributed to the significance attributed to the rosary
even by serious historians. Frederick Cwiekowski claims, for example,
that

[70] Members of the first 'circle', for example, included the names Marshall, Pendlebury,
Haythornthwaite, Walmsley Smith, Stanhope, Fox, and Hargreaves as well as Malley,
Reilly, Gillett, Davis, etc. Members generally seem to have been enrolled by family, and
although there was a high proportion of women, men were also represented. Lancashire
Record Office, The Bishop of Lancaster, 'Circle Lists of the Confraternity of the Living
Rosary, 6 June 1875', RCLy 7/13.

At Coventry . . . [Ullathorne] had as a fellow worker Mother Mary Hallahan, a Dominican secular tertiary with whom he later founded an institute of Dominican tertiary nuns. It was owing to her initiative that Ullathorne introduced such practices as May devotions, processions, public rosary and benediction. This was the first place in England where some of these practices were introduced.[71]

Edward Norman has also asserted that

it was Wiseman's highest task, as he saw it, to revivify English devotional life, and that he did . . . The Forty Hours' Devotion was introduced, and the Rosary—'the devotion so little understood, nay, often so much slighted, even by good people in our country'—was encouraged . . .[72]

We have already seen the danger in ascribing much significance to the mere existence in England of any particular devotion, as with the case of *Quarant'ore*. But if Wiseman thought it shocking that the rosary was not practised more widely, and was even disdained by some, his upbringing and formation in Italy probably meant that he was making an unfair comparison, and certainly a contentious one, in implying that it was undervalued by the Catholics of England and therefore needed an infusion of ultramontane piety to bring it to the forefront of the English devotional scene.

However central the rosary may have been to Italian devotional life, it was far from slighted in the English recusant tradition. As Ann Taves has acknowledged, although in a rather dismissive tone, 'Like de Sales's *Introduction* [*to a Devout Life*], *The Garden of the Soul* acknowledged the importance of Mary and the saints, but did not give them much prominence; it included only two devotions, Benediction of the Blessed Sacrament and the rosary.'[73] The rosary was not only included in every reissue of Challoner's spiritual classic; it also held an honoured place in the old English Catholics' 'penny catechism', and rosary beads can still be seen in the homes of many recusant Catholic families. The devotion was certainly in regular use among the English Catholics at Douai in 1712, when Challoner complained of the inquisitiveness of spies at the English College who,

If any one should chance to tell something favouring us . . . [for example the] two pair of beads to be said every week by one of [th]e Philosophers . . . theyd [*sic*] be

[71] F. J. Cwiekowski, *The English Bishops and the First Vatican Council* (Louvain, 1971), 30. Butler also claims that 'in Coventry [Ullathorne] was instrumental in introducing for the first time in England such devotions as the public Rosary, processions with the image of the Blessed Virgin, more frequent Benedictions' (C. Butler, *The Life and Times of Bishop Ullathorne* (2 vols.; London, 1926, i. 153).

[72] Norman, *English Catholic Church*, 142.   [73] Taves, *Household of Faith*, 72.

very inquisitive into [th]e affair till they understood it and [the]n penned it all down.[74]

Yet it is true that there was a certain ambiguity surrounding this least intellectual of devotions.

When Herbert Thurston investigated the origins of the rosary with characteristic thoroughness, and published his discovery[75] that the devotion was not in fact started by St Dominic, he met with some strong reactions. His chief antagonist, a Dominican scholar and contributor to the *Rosary* magazine named Fr Wilfrid Lescher, published contradictory accounts of the history of the rosary, pestered the editors of the *Catholic Encyclopedia* about the matter,[76] and wrote rather grimly to Thurston that 'we are not engaged in a controversy. I did not begin it, but I shall go on to the end and others also are ready to defend our cherished inheritance.'[77] But if one Dominican, whose association with the devotional magazine the *Rosary* betrays a clear bias, was determined to protect the supernatural sanction alleged to be attached to the devotion, less partial members within the Catholic community were also far from pleased at the prospect of any tampering with pious tradition.

Aidan Gasquet (former prior of Downside Abbey, future cardinal, and historian in his own right), while freely admitting that the revelatory vision to St Dominic was a 'pious belief' or 'legend',[78] felt obliged to write a rather testy letter to Thurston, stating that, while he did not think Thurston 'had gone on a wrong historical principle of the Rosary', he was not enamoured of 'the *general* principle of knocking traditions on the head because there was no absolute documentary evidence for them. If there be documents to disprove a mere tradition it is quite another matter'. 'Are you,' he wondered,

going to deal with other 'pious legends' in their turn. St Maurus & St Placid for example & the 'Nine Fridays'. As far as I am concerned you are most welcome

[74] M. Trappes-Lomax, *Bishop Challoner: A Biographical Study Derived from Dr Edwin Burton's 'The Life and Times of Bishop Challoner'* (1936; London, 1947), 9.
[75] See H. Thurston, 'The Rosary', published in instalments in *Month*, 96–7 (1900–1). This series of articles included an investigation into the Dominican legend of the origins of the devotion to which he returned in 1916 with 'Genuflexions and Aves: A Study in Rosary Origins', *Month*, 127 (1916), 441–52.
[76] See Society of Jesus (British Province) Archives, Thurston papers, 'Rosary' folder, letter from *The Catholic Encyclopedia* to Thurston, 6 Dec. 1912, *passim*.
[77] Ibid., Lescher to Thurston, 7 Dec. [?1912].
[78] 'I have always believed, since I went into the subject years ago, that the vision of S. Dominic was probably and almost certainly a pious legend . . . If the Dominicans like to cling to their "pious belief", they I believe fully admit that it is merely a pious belief' (ibid., A. Gasquet to Thurston, 15 Mar. 1901).

but you must not complain if people cry out when you tread on their 'favourite corns'. . . . I shall read your article with pleasure but I feel that you are belabouring a very dead horse.[79]

Small wonder that a few years later, in 1906, the story began to circulate that Thurston had been summoned to the death-bed of a prominent Jesuit father only to be told: 'Bertie, spare the Blessed Trinity.'[80] A conjunction of thoughts as ambivalent as Gasquet's also came from the pen of Bertrand Wilberforce, OP. Congratulating Thurston on exposing myths, Wilberforce wrote that he had 'never been able to believe that our H.[oly] F.[ather] S.[aint] Dominic began or in fact had anything to do with the Rosary, since I read the "vita Fratrum" and the early lives', but added, as an afterthought, 'Of course do not quote me.'[81] His letter concludes, rather touchingly, with the sentence, *à propos* of nothing in particular, 'I love the R.[osary] because the Church tells me it is a devotion pleasing to God.'[82]

Something of the emotional investment involved can be glimpsed in a letter sent to Thurston by a nun of the Convent of the Holy Sepulchre in which she declared that 'this is spilt milk—that our Holy F[athe]r. S.[aint] Dominic was not the instigator of the Rosary I suspected as a girl at home. I remember my *terror* when, later, I read your first articles. The secret locked up in my heart would be divulged through the world!' But again there is a surprising afterthought: 'However no others teach you to love the Rosary as the poor Dominicans do, & saying it has been one of the greatest joys in my life', she concludes.[83] Even the sceptical Thurston rounded off his contributions to the *Month* with the confession that:

What I most regret in this rather abrupt conclusion of the series of articles on the second of our popular devotions, is my inability to speak, as I intended, in deprecation of the charge brought against the Rosary, that it is an exercise of vain and mechanical repetitions. Whatever may be the history of its origin and first development, the Rosary, for the learned and unlearned alike, is not only one of the simplest prayers, but also, as I sincerely believe, one of the most helpful means by which the soul may learn to live continually in the thought and presence of the son of God made Man.[84]

[79] Ibid.

[80] This plea was said to have been uttered by Fr Gallwey, but the anecdote is almost certainly apocryphal. See J. H. Crehan, *Father Thurston: A Memoir with a Bibliography of his Writings* (London, 1952), 66.

[81] Society of Jesus (British Province) Archives, Thurston papers, 'Rosary' folder, Bertrand Wilberforce OP to Thurston, 12 Nov. 1900.   [82] Ibid.

[83] 'Rosary' folder, S. Mary Catherine to Thurston, 6 Jan. 1913.

[84] H. Thurston, 'The Rosary', *Month*, 97 (1901), 404.

The rosary, perhaps because of its inherent repetitions, simplicity, and accessibility to the illiterate, seems to have provoked a mixture of feelings, not so much within the Catholic community, dividing Irish from English and ultramontanes from old Catholics, but within Catholic individuals themselves. A certain embarrassment, mingled with the feeling that the recitation of the rosary had special devotional qualities not easily articulated by the intellect, seems implicit in the warm attachment shown even by critics of the mythology which surrounded the devotion. This can be felt in the odd conjunction of Sister Mary Catherine's and Wilberforce's thoughts on the matter and the irritated tone of Gasquet's ostensible approval of the application of historical rigour to the investigation of its origins. More recently, a Benedictine has pointed out that:

As a prayer the Rosary has great depth and flexibility for all its apparent simplicity, resembling in its purpose the Jesus Prayer of the Orthodox Church. Thus its heart is not so much the reciting of regular prayers as the contemplation of the underlying mysteries, or basic incidents in the life and work of Jesus.[85]

Is it fanciful to detect a slight note of defensiveness in this passage, a salutary reminder that the rosary may be of devotional use even to the learned, since the question just might arise? The very fact that the point might only be hinted at, and never stated too baldly, reveals something of the tension between head and heart, doctrine and devotion, which accompanied much of the intensification of English Catholic devotion in the late nineteenth and early twentieth centuries.

There is another reason why a certain ambiguity and even embarrassment should have surrounded the use of the rosary in England which, although it should not be overstressed, undoubtedly affected some. A range of evidence suggests that a folk tradition connecting rosaries with the revelations of St Bridget and characterized by a concentration on numbers which lent itself to the superstitious or semi-magical lingered on in some quarters despite an ostensible concentration on the fully orthodox Dominican rosary. The 'revelations' of St Bridget of Sweden (not to be confused with the second patron saint of Ireland who is variously known as St Bride, Brigid, or Bridget) had long been associated with a special 'rosary of St Bridget' consisting of seven Paters and sixty-three Aves, 'in honour of the joys and sorrows of the Blessed Virgin and the 63 years of her life'.[86] This rosary or 'Chaplet . . . said in honour of

---

[85] C. Cary-Elwes, *Experiences with God: A Dictionary of Spirituality and Prayer* (London, 1986), 185–6.   [86] Addis and Arnold (eds.), *Catholic Dictionary*, 733.

the sixty-three years which, it is said, the most holy Mary lived on earth'[87] was presumably formulated and spread through the order which the saint is thought to have founded in the fourteenth century, the Brigittines,[88] and was indulgenced by a series of popes: Leo X in 1515, Clement XI in 1714, Benedict XIV in 1743, and twice by Leo XIII, in 1886 and 1897.[89]

This series of indulgences reflects both the grass-roots appeal of the devotion and the perceived need to distinguish it from the rosary proper; but it seems that attempts to differentiate the two clearly were only partially successful. In the second half of the nineteenth century, a whisper of the supposed 'revelations' of St Bridget could be heard in some meditations recommended for use in connection with the Dominican rosary. An 1854 edition of *The Garden of the Soul* which was published in Dublin gives the instruction, for the second sorrowful mystery, 'Let us contemplate in this mystery, how our Lord Jesus Christ was most cruelly scourged in Pilate's house: the number of stripes they gave him being about five thousand, as it was revealed to St Bridget.'[90] In a London edition of 1856, too, the popular legend is preserved, although its source is not named: 'our Lord Jesus Christ was most cruelly scourged in Pilate's house: the number of stripes they gave him being about five thousand.'[91] An Edinburgh edition of 1874 leaves Pilate's house and the number of stripes revealed to St Bridget firmly alone, suggesting instead that 'how our Lord . . . was delivered by Pilate to the fury of the Jews, fastened to a pillar, and there most cruelly scourged'[92] should be the matter to be contemplated in the mystery. This was in turn softened in the London edition of 1883, which concentrates on 'how our Lord . . . was delivered by Pilate to the fury of his enemies, and being fastened to a pillar, was most cruelly scourged'.[93] It would seem that the hierarchy was concerned

[87] Ibid.   [88] Ibid. 95.

[89] According to the *Raccolta*, 'It is requisite, in order to gain these Indulgences, that the Chaplet, being made either of six or of five decades, should be blessed by the superiors of the monastic houses or other priests of the Order of St Saviour, otherwise the Order of St Bridget, or by one with the necessary faculties' (*The Raccolta; or Collection of Indulgenced Prayers*, ed. T. Galli (London, 1909), 151–3).

[90] [R. Challoner], *The Garden of the Soul: A Manual of Spiritual Exercises and Instructions for Christians . . . Enlarged Edition* (Dublin, 1854), 305.

[91] [R. Challoner], *The Garden of the Soul: A Manual of Spiritual Exercises and Instructions for Christians . . . New Edition. Miniature Golden Manual* (London, 1856), 294.

[92] [R. Challoner], *The Garden of the Soul: A Manual of Devotion. A New Edition . . .* (Edinburgh, 1874), 359.

[93] [R. Challoner], *The Garden of the Soul: A Manual of Spiritual Exercises and Instructions . . . A New Edition. Approved by the Cardinal Archbishop of Westminster* (London, 1883), 262.

to weed St Bridget out of the recitation of the rosary through successive approved versions of popular prayer-books.

If so, the bishops were not entirely successful in removing the legend, with its perceived dangers to orthodox belief, from the popular mind. As late as 1919 Thurston found in circulation two distinct copies of an extraordinary document calling itself 'The Revelations of St Bridget'. This gave an account of a supposed 'Revelation . . . made by the mouth of Our Blessed Saviour to St Bridget, who desired to know somewhat of the Passion he endured', which consisted of an itemization of the precise number of blows, stripes, sighs, beard-pullings, and spittings which Jesus endured, given in fifteen separate instances. The document assured readers that 'all persons who say devoutly Seven Paters and Seven Aves with the Creed every day for 15 Years, in honour of my Passion, shall enjoy the blessings herein mentioned'. These included a curious blend of the spiritual and temporal:

They shall receive a plenary indulgence from all their sins. They shall not suffer the pains of Purgatory. If they die before the 15 years are ended, they shall enjoy the same happiness as if they had suffered martyrdom. I [Jesus] will come myself to receive their souls and bring them to everlasting bliss. Whosoever will carry this Revelation about them shall be preserved from crimes, neither shall they die suddenly. If a woman with child will carry this Revelation and perform this devotion, she shall have a safe delivery. In whatever part of the house this Revelation is kept that place shall not be infected with any contagious distemper. Whosoever will carry this Revelation, and perform the devotion, the most glorious and Blessed Virgin will appear to them three days before their death.— Amen.[94]

Thurston was not one to dismiss such a document lightly: in his manuscript collection at Farm Street is carefully preserved a comparable item in the form of a chain letter which required a certain prayer to be said and passed on to nine others. This prayer promised that its users would be immune from poison, a sudden death, and would fear neither thunder nor lightning; it also claimed to cure fits, to see a woman through a safe delivery, and to give three days' warning of death, while those who laughed at it would suffer. This 'Red Cross Chain', allegedly found 'on the grave of our Lord Jesus Christ' in the year 303, 803, or 1003, according to different editions, was apparently circulating in at least two forms in Ireland in 1897, and caused a certain amount of scandal when it was

---

[94] As reprinted in H. Thurston, 'Uses that are Really Superstitious', *Month*, 133 (1919), 57–8. See Appendix III for the full text of this 'revelation'.

found to be in use by soldiers at the front in the First World War, by which time 'those who passed it by would meet with misfortune, and those who sent it on would be free from casualty'.[95]

Thurston evidently saw a worrying connection between such superstitious 'devotions' as 'The Revelations of St Bridget' and other folk beliefs concerned with the saint, such as those which found their way into editions of approved prayer-books. He thought it worth stating explicitly that 'We believe that there is no serious foundation in the authentic works of St Bridget of Sweden for any of the computations which are sometimes attributed to her in books of devotion.' As he pointed out:

even the clause often introduced at the public recitation of the Rosary 'The number of stripes they gave Him being above 5,000, as was revealed to St Bridget,' was declared, as long ago as the seventeenth century, by Gonsalvo Durantus, the editor of her Revelations, to be altogether without authority.[96]

Although most Catholics would have been scandalized by the kind of nonsense 'revelations' which were incorporated into the 'Red Cross Chain' and 'Revelations of St Bridget', these undoubtedly evolved in part because the line between piety and superstition was not always drawn sharply, either in theory or in practice. When Mother Digby lay dying at the Sacred Heart in Ixelles, Janet Stuart kneeled

motionless at the foot of Reverend Mother Digby's bed. But whenever children and others came in with rosaries with which to touch the hands, she would rise, take them and reverently lay them for a moment on the bed, then return them to their owners . . .[97]

Sheridan Gilley has found that in London, too, during the

lying-in-state that preceded the funerals of Irish girls of special piety . . . [t]he poor would bring rosaries and medals to be sanctified by contact with the hands and throat of the corpse, which was placed 'amidst lights and flowers, with a wreath of roses on her brow, and a crucifix on her breast'.[98]

[95] See T. O'Doherty, 'A Scandalous Imposture', *Irish Ecclesiastical Record*, 5th ser., 12 (Nov. 1918), 421–2, and Society of Jesus (British Province) Archives, Thurston papers, 'Red Cross Chain' folder, *passim*.

[96] Thurston, 'Uses that are Really Superstitious', 58.

[97] M. Monahan, *Life and Letters of Janet Erskine Stuart: Superior General of the Society of the Sacred Heart 1857 to 1914* (London, 1922), 293.

[98] The quotation is from G. Fullerton, *Faithful and True: The Life of Elizabeth Twiddy* (London, 1900), originally published as *Apostleship in Humble Life* (London, 1860), 9, cited in S. W. Gilley, 'Vulgar Piety and the Brompton Oratory, 1850–1860', *Durham University Journal*, 43 (1981), 20.

Catholics brought up on romantic verses of piety, such as those composed for student recitations at the Society of the Holy Child Jesus schools in about 1870, would have been unlikely to scoff at such behaviour. Set texts for pupils at St Leonards-on-Sea included 'A Legend of the Rosary' in which a pious orphan who once forgot to say her rosary was visited by the Virgin Mary herself and sorrowfully reprimanded. Though the child died that very same day, the poem assured its readers that 'Pilgrims to Our Lady's shrine / Would often go to see / Her grave, whom Mary's self had taught / To say the rosary'.[99] Even some authorized devotional manuals seemed to invite, rather than to discourage, credulous responses to the rosary through the wording of their advertisements. The simple or poorly educated might be forgiven for imagining the rosary capable of securing temporal benefits of the kind suggested in the spurious 'revelations' we have seen, when they bought penny editions of works such as *The Fifteen Saturdays of the Rosary. A Most Efficacious Devotion to Obtain Any Special Favour. Published by a Dominican Father*, which the *Irish Rosary* in Dublin and the Catholic Truth Society in London brought out in 1900, and which advertised the albeit carefully chosen words of Pope Urban IV that 'the Rosary daily procures many advantages to Christian people', of Pope Leo X that 'the Rosary was instituted against the dangers which threaten the world' and Pope Adrian VI that 'the Rosary is a means of overcoming the devil'. The instrumentalist interpretations which such statements might evoke undoubtedly also played a part in giving the rosary its deep and widespread appeal.

It has been shown that neither of the two most popular devotions in England, Benediction of the Blessed Sacrament or the rosary, was in fact new to the English Catholic scene. Each had an honourable and well-documented pedigree enshrined in that foremost manual of recusant piety *The Garden of the Soul*; no plausible case can be made for the imposition of either devotion by an authoritarian Rome without, or of infiltration via converts or immigrants within, the English community. Yet both became far more important to the ordinary devotional life of the Victorian English Catholic. Not only did the absolute number of churches offering Benediction of the Blessed Sacrament and Public Rosary rise at an exhilarating rate, but the *proportion* of churches which catered for both services rose dramatically and inexorably throughout the period. The point to be made, then, is not that the nature of English Catholicism was

---

[99] Anon., *Legends of Our Lady and the Saints; or, Our Children's Book of Stories, In Verse, Written for the Recitations of the Pupils of the Schools of the Holy Child Jesus, St Leonards-on-Sea* (London, 1870), 122.

transformed from without, nor even that it was permitted to express its full nature at long last, but rather that elements which had always been within its own tradition accelerated at a newly dramatic rate.

The wider causes for this momentum will be examined in the chapters which follow. But it may be pointed out now that the rosary, just like Benediction, offered a point of unity between Catholics of different social and ethnic backgrounds, and of various intellectual and devotional temperaments. As Baron von Hügel wrote, in gratitude for his own spiritual education:

the new Helper sent me by God [Huvelin] advised me that my prayer should now be mainly informal—more prayer of quiet type; but that there should always remain short vocal prayers morning and night, Mass and Holy Communion twice a week, with Confession once a week or once a fortnight; and . . . one decade of the rosary every day—this especially to help prevent my interior life from losing touch with the devotion of the people. After over thirty years of this mixed *régime*, I am profoundly convinced of the penetrating sagacity of this advice.[100]

It appears to have become something of a pious *cliché* in the nineteenth century to say that the rosary, which was initially resisted by some as childish,[101] was a good devotional exercise for those to whom it appealed and also for those to whom it did not, since it was better than nothing for those who were incapable of a more sophisticated piety and was humbling for those who might otherwise suffer from spiritual pride. This perspective may be seen as a bridge between Catholics of differing emotional and intellectual tempers, and as calculated to justify the position of each while at the same time humbling both. It is here that Catholicism may be seen at its most charitable and inclusive, in a word its most catholic. Certainly, Catholics as different from one another as Newman and Faber, Ullathorne and Wiseman, Thurston, von Hügel, Acton, Manning, and any number of illiterate Irish or English, could all say their rosary together, and meet together at 8 o'clock for Benediction.

---

[100] As cited in *Spiritual Counsels and Letters of Baron Friedrich von Hügel*, ed. D. V. Steere (London, 1964), 116.

[101] See Augusta Drane, for example, who reports that 'the Rosary was quite in disuse at this time among the Catholics of Coventry, and even Sister Margaret [Hallahan]'s immediate companions thought it a childish sort of devotion, in which they joined chiefly to please her' (A. T. Drane, *Life of Mother Margaret Mary Hallahan* (London, 1929), 73). It may also have been thought effeminate by some: it was perhaps to reassure those who might think the rosary an unmanly sort of devotion that the legend of Cardinal Vaughan's attachment to it was put about. As Edward Norman reports, 'As a boy he had been keen on sports, and used, apparently, to say his rosary beneath hedgerows on summer evenings, with his gun in his other hand, waiting for the rabbits to come out' (Norman, *English Catholic Church*, 351). Vaughan was born in 1832, so presumably this tale, if reliable, would refer to piety of the 1840s and 1850s.

3
Familiar Prayers

HOWEVER religion may be defined by outsiders, whether as a purely sociological or even a psychological phenomenon, to the believer the essence of Christian faith lies in the personal relationship believed to exist between the creator and the creature. Prayer, whether petitionary, adulatory, or intercessory, is therefore central as the chief means of communication between God and man. So it is no accident that those Catholic devotions which have already been examined have consisted of prayers, as those said with the aid of a rosary; or of services incorporating prayer, as with Benediction of the Blessed Sacrament; or of objects or representations meant as a focus for particular prayers, as with the Way of the Cross, Exposition of the Blessed Sacrament, *Quarant'ore*, and devotions to the Sacred Heart.

There was nothing unique to Catholics in this central concern with prayer as an expression and measure of piety or devoutness. 'Faith', Luther claimed, 'is prayer and nothing but prayer', and the nineteenth-century evangelical Schleiermacher declared that 'To be religious and to pray—that is really one and the same thing.'[1] But, although all Christians would agree on the fundamental importance of prayer, the objects, subject, and forms of Catholic prayers could differ from those of other denominations. The rise and fall in popularity of particular prayers within the Catholic community therefore gives the best insight that can be glimpsed, not only of denominational difference, but also of internal shifts in spiritual emphases over time.

This most central aspect of devotion, also the most private, is correspondingly difficult for the historian to recapture. An attempt will be made in this chapter first to identify the most popular, which will be defined as the best-selling, prayer-books in circulation among English Catholics in the period. The next object will be to pinpoint and analyse those individual prayers which appear most distinctive of the piety of the community. Finally, changes both in prayer-books and in favourite prayers

---

[1] Cited in F. Heiler, *Prayer: A Study in the History and Psychology of Religion*, trans. and ed. S. McComb (New York, 1932), p. xiii.

will be examined in order to try to understand the devotional imperatives of the mass of English Catholics when at prayer.

Unfortunately, none of the relevant records of the great Catholic publishing houses of the period, those associated with the names of Ward, Sheed, Lambert, Burns, Oates, Washbourne, and Richardson, seem to have been kept for the period 1850–1914.[2] This means that no authoritative figures can be given for the frequency of publication of any Catholic manuals of devotion or collections of prayers produced in England. But the contents of the three copyright libraries of England—the British Library, Cambridge University Library, and the Bodleian—do give a fairly good indication of the relative rates of publication of different prayer-books between 1850 and 1914.

Those Catholic prayer-books which appear most frequently in the British, Cambridge University, and Bodleian libraries and may therefore be surmised to have been the best-selling in England during the period are, in approximate order of importance: *The Garden of the Soul*, the *Raccolta*, *The Key of Heaven*, the *Manual of Prayers*, and the *Jesus Psalter*. Although a host of other collections of prayers were brought out simultaneously, including reissues of well-established works such as the *Crown of Jesus* prayer-book, *The Golden Manual: A Guide to Catholic Devotion*, and *The Path of Holiness* or *Vade Mecum*, as well as more specialized works of piety which concentrated on particular devotions such as the *bona mors* or Sacred Heart, none of these devotional rivals appears to have sold particularly well in the post-1850 period.

Missals printed in English during the period seem to have been limited to *The Roman Missal for the Use of the Laity* (London, 1852 and 1890) and *The Roman Missal Adapted to the Use of the Laity* (London, 1887), which began to be reissued in the 1890s along with *A Popular Missal for the Use of the Laity* (London, 1893; 2nd edn., 1898) and *The Missal for the Use of the Laity, arranged by Provost Husenbeth* (London, 1897). These English translations of the Latin liturgy did not, of course, stray into the field of 'devotions' or 'instructions' for hearing Mass, and so were not competitors with traditional accompaniments to the service like that provided by Challoner. Although the influence of the continental liturgical movement can be detected from the fact that missals began to be published in greater numbers in the 1890s, the notion of greater lay involvement in the liturgy

---

[2] Burns & Oates, for example, although still very much in existence, lost most of its records in the Blitz. But according to Mr Paul Burns, the present editor, it is doubtful that comprehensive publication lists were ever kept (letter to the author, Feb. 1992).

proper does not seem to have begun to take root until about 1910 in England and seems unlikely to have filtered down to the majority of Catholics until after the First World War.[3]

It is the pervasive and persistent influence of that work which has been so closely associated with the recusant or old Catholic period, *The Garden of the Soul*, which emerges most strikingly from the dry listings of prayer-book publications. As Michael Trappes-Lomax pointed out in the 1930s, albeit from a resolutely second-spring perspective:

The popularity of this book may be gauged from the fact that Challoner himself brought out seven editions in seventeen years; its influence, from the fact that a hundred years later a large part of the Catholics of England was known by its name, the expression 'Garden-of-the-Soul Catholics' being used to distinguish the hereditary Catholics, with their undemonstrative piety, from later converts with a tendency towards imported flamboyance in devotion.[4]

Challoner's devotional classic continued to be easily the most frequently reprinted Catholic prayer-book in England throughout the period 1850–1914. Following its many pre-1850 editions came the 'miniature golden manual' of 1856, a new Burns & Oates edition of *c*.1870 and another, by R. Washbourne, in 1872, as well as an abridged or 'little' edition in 1873. A new Edinburgh edition was published in 1874 and two more were brought out by T. Richardson & Sons in 1877, one published under the usual title and another called 'Parochial'. *Instructions and Devotions for Hearing Mass . . . (from the Garden of the Soul)* was published separately, also in 1877, in which year another *Parochial Garden of the Soul* and a new edition by T. Richardson & Sons also came out. Another Washbourne *Little Garden of the Soul* appeared in 1878, as did an edition of 1883, and two of 1884. These were followed by an edition combined with the *Manual of Prayers* of 1892; an edition of 1896; and another of 1899. A further edition, which also advertised Sacred Heart and Way of the Cross devotions, was published in 1900, as was *Sunday Evening Devotions . . . [Extracted from The Garden of the Soul]*. Yet another version, printed in shorthand, appeared in 1902.

No other prayer-book was reissued with anything like the frequency of *The Garden of the Soul*. Even the official Roman prayer-book known as

---

[3] See e.g. F. L. Cross and E. A. Livingstone (eds.), *The Oxford Dictionary of the Christian Church* (Oxford, 1957; repr. 1982), 829–30.

[4] M. Trappes-Lomax, *Bishop Challoner: A Biographical Study Derived from Dr. Edwin Burton's 'The Life and Times of Bishop Challoner'* (1936; London, 1947), 37.

The Raccolta: or Collection of Indulgenced Prayers, first published in 1807 and granted a special decree of approbation from the Sacred Congregation of Indulgences in 1849, did not appear in English until Ambrose St John published his translation of the work in 1857.[5] Although it found a modest market in England, selling enough copies to merit a fifth edition by 1880 and a sixth (edited by R. G. Bellasis) by 1909, this does not compare very favourably with the twenty editions of *The Garden of the Soul* which the Bodleian and British libraries alone can boast. The *Raccolta* seems to have been treated, even by the English bishops, rather as a reference work of Roman imperatives than a treasured volume of spiritual nourishment. That it was unsuited to meet the day-to-day devotional needs of English Catholics seems clear from the fact that an alternative prayer manual was soon proposed by the bishops themselves, who felt, at least as early as 1871, that it was 'desirable to have some acknowledged standard version [of the different versions of prayers in the prayer-books now printed]' and requested the Bishop of Shrewsbury to collect the best versions for the next meeting.[6]

When he reported back at the following Low Week meeting, Bishop James Brown considered versions of prayers as found in *The Garden of the Soul*, *The Crown of Jesus Prayer-Book*, *The Path of Heaven*, and *The Ursuline Manual*, but chose the time-honoured versions of *The Garden of the Soul* as the standard from which to measure any deviant forms to be included in a new and exclusively recommended manual of prayers for the Catholics of England. Justifying his choice, Brown stated, in a revealing tautology, 'that the "*Garden of the Soul*" appeared to be the radix of all the others: that in its new editions there were but few changes; but that in other prayer-books many changes had been made in prayers taken from the "*Garden of the Soul*"'.[7] He then suggested that 'the words of the "*Garden of the Soul*" should be retained for the "*Te Deum*", "*Veni Creator*", "*Jesus, the only thought of Thee*," &c.; and that a common standard should be followed in all public services' and 'undertook to report on the editions of the "*Garden of the Soul*"'.[8]

---

[5] The original title was *Raccolta di Orazioni e pie Opere per le quali sono state concedute dai Sommi Pontefici le S. Indulgenze.* Thurston tells us that it was first published in 1807, and that 'Besides editions and translations appearing elsewhere, new Roman editions were published in 1810, 1812, 1814, 1818, 1825, 1831, 1834, 1837 and 1841. The edition of 1849 was accompanied by a special Decree of approbation from the Sacred Congregation of Indulgences' (H. Thurston, 'The Memorare', *Month*, 132 (1918), 269 n.).

[6] Westminster Archdiocesan Archives, 'Bishops' Meetings 1858–1909', Acta, Meeting of the Bishops in Low Week, 1871, x. 45.   [7] Ibid., 19 Apr. 1872, xiv. 51.

[8] Ibid.

This project took a while to get going: it was two years before 'it was resolved to authorise the Cardinal Archbishop [Manning] and the Bishop of Southwark [James Danell] to treat on the subject of printing the collection of authorised English prayers, to be sent round on slips to the Bishops',[9] and a further five years before 'the Bishops resolved to request the Cardinal Archbishop and the Bishop of Southwark to undertake the revision of the authorised version of prayers for public use'.[10] In 1883 it was finally 'agreed that the first Derby edition[11] of the Garden of the Soul be the basis of the Manual' and the 'proposed *Contents*, as printed by the Bishop of Nottingham [Edward Bagshawe], were considered, and, after sundry omissions and additions, approved'.[12] The task of preparing the *Manual of Prayers* for publication and of sending proof-copies for the bishops' approval was then delegated to the bishops of Salford [Herbert Vaughan] and Nottingham [Edward Bagshawe]. In 1884 'Specimen sheets were laid upon the table'.[13] The bishops' approved prayer-book was eventually published in 1886 as the *Manual of Prayers for Congregational Use* (London and Derby).

Bishop Brown was not alone in feeling strongly that versions of prayers as found in *The Garden of the Soul* ought to be preserved. Although some purists in the hierarchy considered altering traditional versions of the *Te Deum* and Doxology on the grounds that translations in current use among English Catholics had been borrowed from the Protestants, even Herbert Vaughan found their argument historically dubious as well as uncharitable and impractical.[14] As he asked rhetorically of the Bishop of Shrewsbury in 1884:

were the English Bishops to publish a new translation of the Doxology, would they succeed in getting it adopted—even by their own flocks? Is there not a very

[9] Westminster Archdiocesan Archives, 'Bishops' Meetings 1858–1909', Acta, Meeting of the Bishops in Low Week, 1874, xi. 83.   [10] Ibid., Low Week 1879, xii. 140.
[11] This edition could not be found in any of the major English Catholic or British copyright libraries and may no longer exist. We can probably assume that the 1877 Derby edition, which has been consulted, preserved original translations and only added extra material; but we will not know for certain, until a first Derby edition comes to light, which 'additions and omissions' were approved. Attempts to find Brown's report on editions of *The Garden of the Soul*, and Bagshawe and Vaughan's proof copies, which Manning and Danell also worked on, have not been any more successful.
[12] Westminster Archdiocesan Archives, 'Manning 1867–1891', Acta, Meeting of the Bishops in Low Week, 5 Apr. 1883, xx. 173.   [13] Ibid., 1884, xix. 180.
[14] Shrewsbury Diocesan Archives, 'Gloria Patri', Vaughan to Knight, 23 Dec. 1884, fo. 2. This letter from Herbert Vaughan, Bishop of Salford, to Edmund Knight, Bishop of Shrewsbury, gives a rare glimpse into the concerns surrounding the bishops' prayer-book revisions. It has therefore been reproduced in full in Appendix IV to this work.

strong feeling among Catholics to hold to their traditions & customs? Would not a large number of the clergy feel an equal repugnance with the laity to make this change?[15]

The decision of the majority of the bishops to keep to the time-honoured and familiar versions of prayers as found in *The Garden of the Soul* expressed a feeling which appears to have been shared by the majority of the book-buying Catholics in England. Of the other volumes of spirituality which Brown mentioned as possible sources of prayers for a new recommended text, only one edition of *The Crown of Jesus: A Complete Catholic Manual of Devotion, Doctrine, and Instruction* has been found in an English copyright library, that printed at London and Derby in 1862; no English post-1850 edition of *The Ursuline Manual* (also known as *The New Manual of Catholic Devotion* or *The Spirit of Prayer*) is to be found in the British or Bodleian libraries until 1923,[16] and the Catholic *Path of Heaven* does not appear in the British, Cambridge University, or Bodleian library catalogues at all.

If we turn from these prayer-books, whose contents Brown found to have been drawn from *The Garden of the Soul* in any case, the picture does not alter substantially. *The Key of Heaven: A Manual of Catholic Devotion*, which could boast thirty-three Dublin editions by 1839, was reissued a further five times in Ireland between 1850 and 1914 but only three English editions of the same period can be found in the combined stores of the English copyright libraries.[17] Another devotional manual, the *Catholics [sic] Vade Mecum: A select Manual of Prayers for Daily Use*, appears to have been published only once during the period, in 1851. A variety of other devotional manuals evidently catered for an even smaller share of the devout Catholic market.[18] Since Challoner's devotional

---

[15] See Appendix IV for the full text of this letter.

[16] The Cambridge University Library does have one post-1850 version, *The Ursuline Manual, or a Collection of Prayers, Spiritual Exercises . . . Arranged for the Young Ladies Educated at the Ursuline Convent, Cork* (Dublin, 1875), but this is clearly Irish both in origin and intended use.

[17] *The Key to Heaven: A Manual of Prayers. With Epistles and Gospels* (1884), another edition of 1884, and a *Child's Key of Heaven. A Prayer Book for Catholic Children, Compiled from Approved Sources* of 1904. The original title of what came to be known as *The Key of Heaven* was *The Poor Man's Manual; or, Devout Christian's Daily Companion*, but the title had evidently been changed by about 1820.

[18] e.g. *Private Devotions, for Every Day in the Week*, abridged from the *New Manual* [of Devotions] in 1852; *A Catholic's Manual of Instructions and Devotions* (Liverpool, 1867); a tenth edition of *Catholic Hours, or, The Family Prayer-Book* (1868); *Practical Meditations for Every Day in the Year on the Life of . . . Jesus Christ, by a Father of the Society of Jesus* (1868); *The Catholic Prayer Book. A Short Manual of Private Devotions* (1888), etc.

classic unquestionably remained the favourite prayer-book of the English
Catholic community until at least the First World War, we would do well
to begin our examination of prayers in the post-1850 period with a closer
look at *The Garden of the Soul.*

The assumption that the spirit of Catholic piety of the recusant period
may be divided sharply from that of the post-1850 period underlies
virtually all writings on the subject of English Catholicism in the post-
Reformation period. As we saw in Chapter 1, a contrast between the two
ages is often expressed, by a convention which seems to date from about
the time of the First Vatican Council, in the polemical terms 'Garden-of-
the-Soul' as opposed to 'ultramontane' or, properly speaking, 'Roman'
Catholicism. For a recent expression of this entrenched account, one may
look, for example, to Richard Luckett, who asserts that 'Challoner the
author defined a period', and supports this with Canon Burton's observation of 1909 that:

So successful was [*The Garden of the Soul*] in training up a large class of Catholics
whose devotion was marked by a definite character, that in later days the expression
'Garden-of-the-Soul Catholics' came to be employed as distinguishing the old
hereditary members of the faith from those who entered the Church at the time
of the Oxford Movement, and whose devotions under more directly Roman
influence, such as that exercised by the Oratorians, were more fervid and expansive
in expression.[19]

The fact that *The Garden of the Soul*, far from being abandoned in the
post-1850 period, continued to be the staple devotional text for the vast
majority of Catholics living in England is, therefore, a point worth making explicitly, if only to insist that the distinction between the ostensibly
old-fashioned Garden-of-the-Soul Catholic and his later, allegedly
ultramontane, counterpart is at the very least a misnomer. Not only did
The Garden of the Soul remain the most popular manual of prayer in England throughout the nineteenth century and well into the twentieth, but,
as we saw in the last chapter, the two devotions which held an important
place in the prayer-book from its earliest days remained the overwhelm-
ingly, indeed the increasingly, popular expressions of religious feeling in
the period which followed the restoration of the ecclesiastical hierarchy.
    No second-spring enthusiast or ultramontane-triumph propagandist,

---

[19] R. Luckett, 'Bishop Challoner: The Devotionary Writer', citing E. Burton, *The Life
and Times of Bishop Challoner* (2 vols.; London, 1909), i. 130, in E. Duffy (ed.), *Challoner
and his Church: A Catholic Bishop in Georgian England* (London, 1981), 71–2.

certainly no educated Catholic or historian of Catholicism, could deny the magnitude of debt which the English Catholic community owed to the prodigious output of its most celebrated bishop of the recusant period. Nor would any deny that the influence which Challoner's writings had upon the English Catholics' religious life was profound. As that ultramontane *par excellence* Nicholas Wiseman marvelled, in an article for the *Dublin Review* of 1842, it was Challoner who had

alone furnished us with a library of religious works, the privation of which would create a void, not easily to be filled up by many other men's writings. The catechism from which we learnt the first rudiments of our faith, that by which we early became acquainted with sacred history, or versed in controversial discussion, the prayer-book with which we have been most familiar, the meditations which have afforded daily instructions to us in families and communities, many of our most solid and most clear works of controversy, the charming records of our fathers in the faith, the missionary priests, the martyrology of our ancient Church and many other works, we owe to this really great and good man; and we know not what we should have done, or what we should have been without them. He supplied, in fact, almost the entire range of necessary or useful religious literature for his Catholic fellow-countrymen, and that at a time when such a supply must have been truly as a boon from heaven.[20]

There is no question that Challoner's influence during the penal years, that formative period of post-Reformation English Catholicism, was of paramount importance to the community. But the extent to which the distinctive piety of the recusant period was able to survive the changed circumstances of the latter half of the nineteenth century is open to debate. Modern historians generally agree that the Challonerian vision as expressed in *The Garden of the Soul* did not linger on beyond 1850. This view is implicit in Eamon Duffy's *Challoner and his Church*, in John Aveling's introduction to *The Handle and the Axe*, and in many works which rely upon their arguments; but it has been most forcefully put forward by John Bossy in his *The English Catholic Community*. In this highly influential work, Bossy argues that *The Garden of the Soul* perfectly represented the devotional outlook of the English community from about 1750 until about 1850, but that from about the time of the restoration of the hierarchy the new enthusiasm of second-spring advocates altered the essentials of this tradition beyond recognition. Drawing on Bossy's work, Gerard Connolly stresses that successive nineteenth-century revisions of *The Garden of the Soul* might better be called

---

[20] As cited in ibid. 71.

'deformations', since they cumulatively amounted to a despoilation of the recusants' 'refreshing willingness to ignore uncharitable references to Protestants and non Catholics generally'. Connolly argues that, for Challoner, unlike his second-spring and ultramontane successors, 'the threat to the Catholic christian came from the vanities of the world, and he [Challoner] sought the conversion of "poor sinners", a phrase not meant to be a pseudonym for the majority of his fellow Englishmen'.[21]

In order to determine whether there was in fact an essential point of devotional difference between English Catholics of the two ages traditionally associated with the sobriquets 'Garden of the Soul' and 'second spring' or 'ultramontane', it will be of importance to establish whether *The Garden of the Soul* can be said to have remained the same essential work throughout the period 1750 to 1914 or whether, as John Hilton has put it, 'though the title remained popular, the contents suffered'.[22] If, as Bossy, Connolly, and Hilton suggest, it was only nominally the same book from as early as 1850, the detail of that transformation and its implications will need to be examined with a good deal more care than has hitherto been taken or been recognized to be necessary. Was the essential character of the original *Garden of the Soul* changed through successive editions? And, if so, how best might that change be described, and what can it tell us about the devotional outlook of the English Catholic community in the nineteenth and early twentieth centuries?

A cursory comparison of successive nineteenth-century editions of *The Garden of the Soul* with Challoner's 1755 version[23] might, at first, lead one to suppose them to be different works. Nineteenth-century editions are much longer, arranged differently, and include a number of devotions alien to Challoner's original, such as prayers for the conversion of England, *Quarant'ore*, prayers to St Joseph, and devotions to the Sacred Heart. The unadulterated work's alternative title 'A Manual of Spiritual Exercises and Instructions for Christians who (living in the world) aspire to Devotion', as Bossy has pointed out, gives a good deal of important information which is worth briefly recapitulating here.

    [21] G. P. Connolly, 'Catholicism in Manchester and Salford, 1770–1850: The Quest for "le chrétien quelconque"' (Ph.D. thesis, 3 vols.; Manchester University, 1980), i. 492.
    [22] J. A. Hilton, '"The Science of the Saints": The Spirituality of Butler's Lives of the Saints', *Recusant History*, 15 (1980), 189.
    [23] *The Garden of the Soul* was first issued in about 1740, but continued to be republished under Challoner's auspices until his death in 1781. Since Bossy and others agree that *The Garden of the Soul* had not formed the 'backbone' of the community's spirituality until the 1750s, the 1755 edition will be used as the stereotype version throughout this discussion.

Challoner's work addresses itself explicitly to Christians, rather than to Catholics, setting the inclusive and non-confrontational tone so admired by Connolly, Bossy, Duffy, and others, and which is contrasted with the sectarian flavour which was to replace it in the nineteenth century. The work also deliberately allows the notions of living in the world and of aspiring to devotion to coexist, with implications, often pointed to, for the spiritual importance of the layman. As Connolly argues, 'The ideal [in Challoner] . . . is that of the sanctification of the christians [*sic*] daily life not a swoon for life everlasting . . . [a] contrast [which] will assume greater importance later on, when the Nineteenth century is considered . . .'.[24] Finally, Challoner's use of the expression 'spiritual exercises' is no accident, since his *Garden of the Soul* is heavily reliant upon St Francis de Sales's *Introduction to the Devout Life*. Challoner aims to provide a practical guide for the incorporation of the unworldly aims of devotion into ordinary life, and follows de Sales in suggesting exercises, instructions, and meditations to that end.

Before we go on to examine the development of *The Garden of the Soul* in the nineteenth century, let us look first at the contents of the stereotype or 1755 edition in a little more detail. The work opens with a summary of Christian doctrine, followed by 'a morning exercise' which includes the Lord's Prayer, Hail Mary, Apostles' Creed, and *Confiteor*, as well as 'acts' of faith, hope, and charity. Ten meditations of St Francis de Sales and instructions and devotions for hearing Mass are followed by various psalms; more acts of faith, hope, love, and contrition are given, along with 'an universal prayer for all things necessary to salvation'. The Lord's Prayer is explicated and the Athanasian Creed given. Rubrics and prayers for 'Vespers, or Even-song' are included, as are those for 'Complin' and 'Benediction of the Blessed Sacrament'. Evening prayers, complementing the 'morning exercise', incorporate an examination of conscience and are followed by a reminder of the virtues to be exercised each day. The rest of the book is taken up with further devotional 'flowers' to be 'plucked' as desired from the eponymous devotional garden. These include the rosary, St Bernard's hymn 'Jesus, the only thought of thee . . .', *Ave Maria Stella*, various aspirations and ejaculations, 'affections', resolutions and meditations, instructions and devotions for confession, mental exercises to prepare for death, prayers for the dead, and litanies of Jesus and of Our Lady of Loreto. The manual ends with a prayer 'for the whole state of Christ's church upon earth and all the intentions of the Indulgence' and closes with the Jesus Psalter.

---

[24] Connolly, 'Catholicism in Manchester and Salford', i. 484.

The first nineteenth-century edition of *The Garden of the Soul* which was published after the restoration of the hierarchy, that of 1854, did not in fact depart very far from the stereotype edition. Rather, it took particular care '[to retain] all that is in general use in the original editions, and nearly in the same order', but also added devotions 'which now form a necessary part of every Catholic prayer-book, such as the "Stations of the Cross", "Visits to the Blessed Sacrament", "Devotions to the Sacred Heart, &c."' as well as daily prayers and other devotional material taken from *The Key of Heaven*, 'thus combining in one volume the advantages of both'.[25]

Although this edition, published nearly a hundred years after the stereotype version, certainly added to the selection of devotional 'flowers', it is hard to see how such changes can justly be characterized as a 'deformation' of the original. Newman, for one, thought the tone of *The Key of Heaven* so obviously in keeping with 'English style' that he was willing to doubt publicly, in his famous *Letter to Pusey*, whether the Anglican divine would 'find anything to displease' him in either *The Garden of the Soul* or *The Key of Heaven*, since he did 'not observe anything in them which goes beyond the teaching of the Fathers, except so far as devotion goes beyond doctrine'.[26] By 1877, not only was material from *The Key of Heaven* included as a matter of course, but so were the '*Quarant'ore*, or forty hours devotion', the *Angelus*, St Bernard's Prayer (also known as the *Memorare*), prayers and a hymn to St Joseph. Prayers for the conversion of England, the *bona mors* or 'exercises for a happy death', and acts of reparation and consecration to the Sacred Heart were still later additions, but had come to seem a necessary part of the English Catholic repertoire by the time of that version of 1892 which amalgamated *The Garden of the Soul* with the bishops' own *Manual of Prayers for Congregational Use*.

Despite the obvious differences in size and content of later editions of *The Garden of the Soul*, it is worth noticing that the basic elements of Challoner's original text were carefully preserved rather than discarded, however overshadowed by extraneous material they had become. Furthermore, if we were to confine ourselves to a comparison of directions given for the devotions which the English most cherished, not only Benediction and the rosary, but also those designed for what the catechism assured Catholics was the 'most devotional' of acts, that of 'assisting' at

---

[25] Preface to [R. Challoner], *The Garden of the Soul: A Manual of Spiritual Exercises and Instructions for Christians . . . New Edition. Miniature Golden Manual* (London: Burns & Lambert, 1856), p. iii.

[26] As reproduced in C. Butler, *The Life and Times of Bishop Ullathorne* (2 vols.; London, 1926), i. 358.

Mass, we would be hard pressed to find evidence in successive versions of *The Garden of the Soul* of anything approximating to a 'despoliation' of the original. Of the many post-1850 revisions in existence, none of those editions which were both new and hierarchically approved[27] departs substantially from Challoner's stereotype edition in this most important respect. On the contrary, each post-1850 reissue retains Challoner's 'Devotions for Mass' virtually intact, keeping not only to his close shadowing of the formal Latin liturgy, but also, in all but a few minor points, to his own language and characteristic tone of earnestness blended with instruction. Thus the 1856, 1877, 1883, 1892, and 1899 editions begin, just like the 1755 version, with a prayer 'O almighty Lord of heaven and earth, behold I, a wretched sinner, presume to appear before thee this day', which quickly turns to a reminder of five purposes for which the Mass should be offered before recapitulating the more emotive strain of the opening prayer with 'Oh! be thou pleased to assist me in such manner by thy grace, that I may behave myself this day as I ought to do in thy divine presence . . .'.

So few and so insubstantial were the changes to Challoner's own text in what is arguably the most central of his devotions that they may easily be dispensed with. Some minor changes involved bringing Challoner's language up to date, as when 'salutary' was evidently thought better than his choice of 'wholesome' in a prayer at the preface; or, in the same part of the Mass, when 'eternal' was substituted for 'everlasting'. Challoner's *Garden of the Soul* was also brought into line with Victorian conventions of punctuation, so that 'O' became 'Oh!' and 'catholic church' went into upper case. Less trivial textual changes were rare and do not seem to have reflected any substantial change: from the 1877 version onwards a short prayer, which was explicitly set apart as optional, and which in no way departed from the spirit of Challoner, was added to the Offertory;[28] in 1883 another prayer was added at the Elevation to include a pious thought

[27] In other words that 'New Edition, Containing: Devotions to the Blessed Sacrament, to the Sacred Heart, to St Joseph, and a Collection of Indulgenced Prayers' which was published by Thomas Richardson & Sons in 1877 'By Lawful Authority'; the version brought out by R. Washbourne in the same year; the 'New Edition. Approved by the Cardinal Archbishop of Westminster' which Burns & Oates brought out in 1883; the 1892 edition which combined *The Garden of the Soul* with the *Manual of Prayers for Congregational Use* and which, although published by James Duffy & Co. in Dublin, advertised itself as the 'Version prescribed by the Cardinal Archbishop of Westminster and the Bishops of England'; and a version, bearing an *imprimatur*, which was brought out by R. & T. Washbourne in 1899.

[28] See e.g. [R. Challoner], *The Garden of the Soul: A Manual of Spiritual Exercises, in Which Are Included Many Devotions of Recent Practice, and Approved of by the Church* (London, 1877), 45–7.

for the faithful departed,[29] and this was moved elsewhere, but preserved intact, in the 1899 version.[30] Only one nineteenth-century version of *The Garden of the Soul* actually seems to have changed Challoner's tone and emphasis in this sacrosanct rubric of what was itself a treasured prayer-book; and since this single example of 1874 was Scottish rather than English, it need not concern us overmuch.[31]

Although many of Challoner's devotions, and particularly those for Mass and Benediction, were carefully preserved over the course of the following century, there is no denying that, throughout the rest of the manual, the choice and order of material changed enough over time that arguments for its 'despoliation' do have some force. The steadily increasing bulk of *The Garden of the Soul* shows that more and more new material was thought suitable for inclusion in the text, and a good deal, although by no means all, of this new material was explicitly Catholic rather than universally Christian. Furthermore, while the 1856 and 1877 versions (which used Challoner's text as the basic material or skeleton for a work to which a number of devotions were added) managed to preserve Challoner's own emphasis on the Ten Commandments and the Meditations of St Francis de Sales, such clarity of focus became blurred through the sheer bulk of material in later editions. *The Garden of the Soul*, as it became increasingly inclusive, incorporated some devotions—chaplets to the Sacred Heart, litanies to Mary, and prayers for the conversion of England—of precisely the exclusively Catholic kind which a contemporary Protestant would have been likely to find offensive, and which tend to undercut the apparent compatibility with Protestantism of the original work. But even these changes do not constitute such a radical departure from the spirit of Challoner as one might at first imagine.

Those who argue that Challoner's *Garden of the Soul* was essentially different from Victorian and Edwardian reissues tend to stress that Challoner was more ecumenically minded, and also less other-worldly in his aims than the later ultramontanes. Both points have some validity, but rest upon exaggerated characterizations of the devotional lives of both the

---

[29] '*At the Memento of the Dead*. I offer thee again, O Lord, this holy sacrifice of the Body and Blood of thy only Son, in behalf of the faithful departed, and in particular for the souls of [*here name those you wish to pray for*]. To these, O Lord, and to all that rest in Christ, grant, we beseech thee, a place of refreshment, light and peace. Through the same Christ our Lord. Amen.'

[30] [R. Challoner], *The Garden of the Soul. A Manual of Devotion Containing Devotions to the Sacred Heart, Way of the Cross, Ordinary of the Mass* . . . (1899), 50–1.

[31] This was [R. Challoner], *The Garden of the Soul. A Manual of Devotion. A New Edition, Containing Devotions to the Sacred Heart* . . . (Edinburgh, 1874).

recusants and of the legally recognized Catholics who succeeded them. Although Challoner's stately Georgian prose, combined with the relatively small number of exclusively Catholic practices which he included, may give an impression of accommodation, his *Garden of the Soul* could certainly never be mistaken for a Protestant work. We have already seen how Benediction, the rosary, and intercessionary prayers to the saints formed an important part of English Catholic devotion from the start; and these would also have struck a contemporary Protestant as strange and to that extent offensive.

Nor should these facts surprise us: it was Challoner, after all, already the author of *The Unerring Authority of the Catholick Church, in Matters of Faith . . . In Which the Infallibility of the Church of Christ is Demonstrated . . .*, who was appointed 'controversial writer' to the English Chapter from 1736 until 1757 and who published, in 1745, *Britannia Sancta: or the Lives of the Most Celebrated British, English, Scottish and Irish Saints: Who Have Flourished in these Islands, from the Earliest Times of Christianity, Down to the Change of Religion in the Sixteenth Century.*[32] It was also Challoner who carefully compiled the *Memoirs of Missionary Priests*, and who cherished what Alban Butler assured Lawrence Mayes in 1747 was a 'very earnest and pressing [wish] to have the affair of the offices of the English Saints mentioned by him, finished soon and granted'.[33] The fact, as Sheridan Gilley reminds us, that 'polemics figure largely in Challoner's literary output' to an extent that 'no study of the man can ignore them'[34] is a useful reminder that Challoner, and the recusant Catholics he represented, also felt themselves to be different from their Protestant neighbours, however more universally Christian the expression of their sentiments may seem in comparison with what was to follow.

Michael Trappes-Lomax has stressed that behind Challoner's *The Memoirs of Missionary Priests*, as behind his later efforts for the restoration of English saints to the liturgy, there lies a quiet national piety: 'these men were English; they had died nobly; it was right that they should be commemorated.'[35] But he might just as easily have pointed out that 'these men were Catholic', acknowledging the implicit reminder to the Protestant majority that the English recusants were as conscious of their idiosyncratic history as Catholics as of their identity as Englishmen. Not only did Challoner's interest in preserving—and, to some extent, creating—

---

[32] Trappes-Lomax, *Bishop Challoner*, 71.
[33] Alban Butler to Lawrence Mayes, 16 Nov. 1747, as cited in ibid. 72.
[34] S. W. Gilley, 'Challoner as Controversialist', in Duffy (ed.), *Challoner and his Church*, 90.   [35] Trappes-Lomax, *Bishop Challoner*, 46.

the sense of a distinctive English Catholic history pave the way for the nineteenth-century Catholic 'ghetto' mentality, but so did his uncompromisingly Catholic, if now seldom remembered, works of controversy.

The arguments that Challoner's piety was in some sense practical and this-worldly, in contrast with the 'swoon'[36] for life everlasting which was to follow, and that he presented an 'individualistic and meditative, as opposed to collectivist and quasi-monastic'[37] piety also seem to call for some circumspection. We have already seen how several of Challoner's most treasured devotions, like Benediction and the rosary, included elements which have tended to be associated with the 'enthusiasm' of the latter half of the nineteenth century. His own devotional practice only reinforces the sense of common ground between recusant and post-1850 English Catholic spirituality. 'In the very midst of business,' Barnard tells us, Challoner

frequently raised both his heart and eyes to God by short ejaculations, which could frequently be perceived by those who happened to be in his presence . . . And he made it his constant and invariable practice (which all his acquaintance observed) to renew the love of God in his heart whenever he heard the clock strike, by signing himself with the sign of the Cross, and saying, *O my God, teach me to love Thee in Time and Eternity*: which practice he also recommended to all the faithful, and for that reason inserted it in the Catechism which he published for the instruction of children.[38]

Although Challoner's distinctive voice in *The Garden of the Soul* grew fainter over the course of the nineteenth and early twentieth centuries amid a plethora of devotions to the *bona mors*, the Stations of the Cross, and *Quarant'ore*, in devotional terms the difference between his original prayer-book and its subsequent reissues was one of degree rather than of kind.

Sheridan Gilley has remarked that, in his capacity as compiler and writer, Challoner 'avoided rather than strove for originality'.[39] The aim of his works, whether devotional, historical, or controversial, was to popularize and above all to 'transmit the mainstream Douai tradition which he had received'.[40] Michael Trappes-Lomax has also stressed that 'Challoner neither was trying to supersede the old (incidentally, he published a

[36] Connolly, 'Catholicism in Manchester and Salford', i. 484.

[37] J. Bossy, *The English Catholic Community 1570–1850* (London, 1975), 364.

[38] Trappes-Lomax, *Bishop Challoner*, 67. His catechism also included emotive bits of piety like 'Come, my dear Jesus, and take full possession of my soul'. See e.g. *An Abridgment of Christian Doctrine: or, the First Catechism. Published for the Use of the London District* (London, *c.*1820), 57.   [39] Gilley, 'Challoner as Controversialist', 90.

[40] Ibid.

revision of the *Manual* in 1758) nor was the originator of that form of piety later to be described as "Garden-of-the-Soul"'. Challoner's intention, argues Trappes-Lomax, was rather

to produce a useful supplement to the books already in existence, and in doing so he drew on earlier sources wherever they suited that purpose—they included *Ten Meditations out of the first part of St Francis de Sales's Introduction to a Devout Life*, and *A Prayer taken out of Mr Gother's Works, for obtaining Contrition*. And 'Garden-of-the-Soul' piety itself was no new thing. He had learned its elements from Mr Gother, and it had upheld Catholicism in England for years before he was born.[41]

Nineteenth- and twentieth-century 'improvements' to *The Garden of the Soul* seem to have been taken in very much the same filial spirit as Challoner's own. Revisions aimed rather to intensify devotional elements already present within the recusant tradition than wilfully to subvert the 'faith once delivered' as mediated through the community's most cherished bishop, Challoner. Devotional continuity was tacitly recognized even by advocates of the new style. Although the 'ultramontane' Wiseman found much of the spiritual legacy of the eighteenth century cold and overly restrained, he explicitly distanced Challoner from such criticism. Of the 'truly venerable, learned and saintly Dr Challoner', he declared in 1842, 'it would be both unjust and ungrateful were any English Catholic to speak in terms other than of profound admiration and sincere respect'.[42] Manning similarly observed, in a letter to the fourth synod of Westminster in 1873, that 'We have now a literature growing up, partly original, partly translated from other languages, which for variety and excellence promises gradually to supply much of our need.' But he took care to add that:

In commending our modern works, we do not mean to give them precedence in solidity and truth of expression over our older books. In devotion indeed we should rather commend the writings of our Catholic forefathers, to whom the realities of persecution taught a deep and simple piety, such as men learn in suffering, and would desire to rest upon in the hour of death.[43]

Challoner's quintessentially old-Catholic or traditional English devotion was hardly disparaged even by a self-styled ultramontane like Manning or a lover of Italian spirituality like Wiseman.

[41] Trappes-Lomax, *Bishop Challoner*, 37.
[42] N. Wiseman, 'Prayer and Prayer-books', *Dublin Review*, 13 (1842), 482.
[43] [H. E. Manning], Synodal Letter to the Fourth Synod of Westminster, 12 Aug. 1873, in *The Synods in English: Being the Text of the Four Synods of Westminster, translated into English . . .*, ed. R. E. Guy (Stratford, 1886), 296.

Nevertheless, conceptions of how warmth and earnestness in religion ought properly to be expressed had shifted, and many Victorian Catholics found eighteenth-century devotional style dry and unfeeling. As Wiseman put it, 'while we are grateful for all that we have received, we may be forgiven if we ask for more. Holy desires may grow . . . And we believe sincerely that the longings of our people after a higher spirit of devotion is, and has for some time been, on the increase.'[44] To a post-nineteenth-century but pre-Vatican II English Catholic like Trappes-Lomax, 'believing, it may be, and possibly with justice, that increase in external devotions tends to development in spirituality', it is not altogether surprising to read that the impression given to him by the exercises in *The Garden of the Soul* should have been 'one of excessive length and aridity—they include, for instance, Communion at eight stated times a year, and preparatory meditations suited to the seven preceding days'.[45] Nor is it astonishing, given the increased currency of the second-spring perspective from the mid-nineteenth century, that it should have become a truism by Trappes-Lomax's day to believe that Catholicism had 'got beyond that stage'. As he explained, in apology for what had come to seem a restrained devotion among the recusants, 'the eighteenth century Catholics were in that stage . . . they could only cultivate a secret garden'.[46]

Nineteenth- and early twentieth-century changes to *The Garden of the Soul* are best understood, not as an ultramontane subversion of the recusant tradition, but as attempts to reappropriate a cherished manual of piety by recasting it into the idiom of the day. Just as Challoner had attempted to transmit a distinctively English Catholic tradition of piety through a medium which aimed to renew fervour and to promote methods for 'daily sanctification', so did Victorian and Edwardian editors of his prayer-book. Each wrote in the language of his time, and each meant to present the essentials of the Faith in terms which would move the hearts of his contemporaries. But just as Bowdlerizations of Shakespeare seem, from a late twentieth-century perspective, to have lost something essential to the genius of the original, so nineteenth-century alterations to *The Garden of the Soul* may seem to us to have damaged the integrity of Challoner's message. As Trappes-Lomax has perceptively pointed out: 'The difference between the *Garden of the Soul* and its predecessors was that it gave as it were the theory as well as the practice: it was a treatise on the spiritual life, as well as a collection of exercises therein.'[47] This

[44] Wiseman, 'Prayer and Prayer-books', 482.
[45] Trappes-Lomax, *Bishop Challoner*, 38.   [46] Ibid.   [47] Ibid.

particularly appealing feature of Challoner's *Garden of the Soul* was gradually undermined by a Victorian *penchant* for eclecticism. The increasing sense of clutter of the 1856 and 1877 versions finally reached its logical conclusion in 1892. It was at this point, when the material from *The Garden of the Soul* was interlaced with that of the *Manual of Prayers for Congregational Use*, that what was published under the traditional title became rather a reference manual of devotional options for every conceivable occasion than the single volume of instruction and devotional guidance which had been Challoner's original contribution. This change in the function of *The Garden of the Soul* was tacitly and widely recognized from about the 1880s, at which time Challoner's subtitle 'a manual . . . for Christians who, living in the world, aspire to devotion' was dropped in favour of merely informative titles like *The Garden of the Soul. A Manual of Spiritual Exercises and Instructions.*[48]

But the analogy with Bowdler's Shakespeare is not perfect. Changes to *The Garden of the Soul* were not undertaken solely for reasons of taste, but also reflected changed circumstances in publishing which saw increased competition among prayer-books, themselves the product of a widened market for such literature. In a climate of increasingly sophisticated religious publishing and marketing techniques, special interest groups such as the young, schoolchildren, families, or scouts were targeted;[49] particular devotional needs, such as the art of dying happily, the Stations of the Cross, and the Sacred Heart were also catered for,[50] while still

---

[48] In England, Challoner's original title seems to have been dropped first by R. Washbourne in its edition of 1872. In Scotland it had been dropped by 1874, but it was preserved by Thomas Richardson & Sons of London and Derby until at least 1877. Burns & Oates preserved the subtitle as late as 1883 but finally dropped it in 1884. No post-1884 edition seems to have preserved Challoner's ecumenically worded and expressive subtitle.

[49] e.g. *The Catholic Penny Prayer Book: Designed for the Use of Schools* (London, 1873); *The Children's Prayer Book of Catholic Devotions*, ed. H. Hill (1900); *The Catholic Scout's Prayer Book* (Catholic Truth Society, 1912); *Manual of Prayers for the Use of Catholic Youth . . .* (1892).

[50] Manuals which catered for particular devotions included, by subject: *Mourning for the Dead. Pious Exercises for November and Times of Bereavement* (London, 1900); *A Devotional Exercise to Prepare the Soul for Death* (London, 1902); *The English Catholic's Manual of Devotions for the Stations . . . for Use During Lent . . . by the Editor of the English Catholic's Book of Family Prayers* (Oxford, 1871); *A Manual of Affective and Practical Devotion to the Sacred Heart of Jesus*, trans. and ed. by the Pious Society of Missions (2nd edn., 1873); *The Litany of the Holy Face* (London, 1884); *A Simple Explanation of the Litanies of the Holy Name of Jesus, of the Blessed Virgin Mary, and of the Saints* (London, c.1850). Collections by religions included extracts from the *Book of Devotions used at the Jesuits' Church of the Immaculate Conception in Farm Street* (1856) and *Bands of Love. Intercessions Based on Mental Prayer on Subjects Connected with the Life of Our Lord and the Mysteries of the Catholic Faith*, by H. M. Kyle, a Carmelite tertiary (1903).

more publications were meant for use during particular seasons of the liturgical year.[51] This was not, of course, a peculiarly Catholic phenomenon: Anglicans, too, produced devotional works intended for distinctive markets, and the increased overall output of devotional manuals by many denominations was designed to meet the demand of an increasingly diverse and often discriminating pool of consumers.

Faced with a much larger potential market, both through a massively increased demand for Catholic books in England, and dramatically reduced publication costs which in turn meant low book prices for the consumer, a prime worry of the English hierarchy was to retain what control it could over the publication of manuals which set themselves up as rivals to officially sanctioned texts. Not only did official representatives of the Church fear unorthodoxy in prayers and devotional practices which might, in all innocence, become popular; but the existence of separate translations from Latin, Italian, French, Polish, or German prayers could lead to the absurd situation, which was only exacerbated by the increased mobility of members, of congregations being unable to recite prayers together. One has only to note how few prayer manuals carried official ecclesiastical sanction in the shape of an *imprimatur*, and to read reiterated complaints in the minutes of bishops' meetings, to see that this anxiety was perfectly well founded.

Since the English bishops' own recommended *Manual of Prayers for Congregational Use* did not have the natural advantage of being widely known by name and sanctioned by generations of use, it is not surprising that the hierarchy should have exercised control where it could, by turning Challoner's *The Garden of the Soul* into what became in effect an anthology of authorized prayers for English Catholic congregations. Although this hid, perhaps even undermined, the idiosyncratic flavour of Challoner's original, it is worth remembering that it also preserved a good deal more of the native English Catholic tradition than would have been the case had the *Raccolta*, or indeed the bishops' own *Manual of Prayers*, been so favoured. That the Catholics of England, who voted with their pocket-books, stayed loyal, on the whole, to *The Garden of the Soul* rather than to any Roman, French, Irish, or even newfangled English

---

[51] e.g. for Advent: *The Holy Child: The Life and Work of . . . Jesus* (1857); *The Holy Child Jesus, Thoughts and Prayers* (1859); *The Twelve Mysteries of the Holy Childhood* (Birmingham, 1857); and *Pictures of the Childhood of Jesus* (1889). Lenten meditations and prayers included: *The Holy Week of the Passion and Death of . . . Jesus Christ* (1867); *The Hours of the Passion [in verse]* (1898); and *Meditations on the Passion of Our Most Holy Redeemer* by A. G. Mortimer (1903).

compilations which, from about the 1870s, contained a fair number of the same prayers, suggests that they believed, however historians may have assessed the change in their devotional habits, that they were remaining true to their own tradition, and that in becoming more outwardly devotional they were only responding to Challoner's exhortation to earnestness or true devotion in the practice and apprehension of their faith.

Successive revisions to *The Garden of the Soul* gradually turned it from a formative work of piety, capable of defining the approach and influencing the spirituality of generations of English Catholics, to a mere anthology with as little inherent guidance as might be found in any other collection of prayers. Since the very function of the prayer-book appears to have changed beyond recognition during the period under scrutiny, a detailed analysis of the contents of its later versions will not be able to tell us much about the devotional habits of its readers.

In an extremely interesting and painstaking analysis of Catholic devotions in the United States in the mid-nineteenth century, Ann Taves has based her arguments for an increasingly Romanized conception of extra-liturgical worship almost exclusively on the evidence of the devotional content of the most widely selling prayer-books in the United States during the period. Thus she demonstrates that, while 64 per cent of prayer-books included the rite of Benediction of the Blessed Sacrament between 1790 and 1840, 75 per cent of those issued between 1840 and 1880 did so; that while 21 per cent included prayers to St Joseph before 1840, 88 per cent did so after 1840; that 7 per cent included the Way of the Cross before 1840 but 88 per cent afterwards, and so forth. While her research is clearly of importance in pointing to broad trends and in giving some empirical basis to a discussion of changes in devotional practice, there are at least two dangers in treating such findings in isolation, one methodological and one interpretative.

The fact that a given percentage of prayer-books included a particular devotion does not leave us any the wiser as to how many individual Catholics used the prayer in question. This problem is similar to the one which was discussed earlier in relation to statistics of the number of churches in England and Wales which offered extra-liturgical devotions. Just as statistical information taken from the *Catholic Directories* can only be used safely when taken together with impressionistic evidence gleaned from biographies, correspondences, and the close scrutiny of particular parishes, so the sort of evidence presented by Taves is of limited value in itself.

A second *caveat* in relying upon such information as Taves uses has to do with the changing role of prayer-books which we have just seen. The fact that many devotions came to be included in a single text such as *The Garden of the Soul* does not mean that all should be accorded equal weight. That Benediction was included in only 11 per cent more prayer-books in the United States after 1840 than before undoubtedly suggests that it had become more popular, but does not mean that it was 11 per cent more widely practised: if American developments mirrored English ones, Benediction will have become far more popular than that. Nor does the fact that 88 per cent of prayer-books after 1840 included an indulgenced form of the devotion of the Stations of the Cross, while only 7 per cent had done so formerly, mean that these figures represent a change in practice of that magnitude. Naturally, one would expect there to be some correlation between the availability of a devotion—by means of both the number of churches willing to cater for it, and the existence of prayer-books to make its form widely available—and its practice. But the mere fact that a prayer was included in a text does not indicate how often, by whom, or even if, it was actually used. The inclusion of indulgenced devotions as a matter of courtesy to the Holy See; the devotional bent of a particular author or of the bishop to whom he might submit his work for approbation; a desire on the part of an editor to be exhaustive; all these motives, which have little to do with the views or tastes of the reading public, may have played a role is deciding which versions went to press, and cannot be assumed to indicate their real popularity. If we are to guard against some of the dangers of an exclusively Tavesian analysis of English prayer-books, we will do well not to take analyses of the contents of prayer-books too seriously, and to be sure to use such information only in conjunction with other, albeit more impressionistic, evidence for the popularity of specific prayers.

When, in a series of articles published in the *Month* between 1914 and 1918 on the theme of 'Familiar Prayers', Herbert Thurston selected eleven prayers for special scrutiny, the prayers which he believed to be representative of English Catholic worship suggest a different devotional picture. Those prayers which he considered to be the most common among English Catholics at the time of writing, an opinion which none of his readers disputed in the press, were: the Sign of the Cross, the Our Father (in English), the *Anima Christi*, the *Veni, Sancte Spiritus*, the *Confiteor*, the Hail Mary, the *Salve Regina*, the *Regina Caeli*, the *Memorare*, the *De Profundis*, and the *Gloria Patri*.

The most striking fact about this selection is the antiquity and universality of most of the prayers. Not one was distinctively Victorian, let alone the direct result of an ultramontane revolution of the 1850s; most pre-dated even the Counter-Reformation period. Making the sign of the cross on the forehead certainly goes back to Augustine in the fourth century, and arguably as far back as the end of the second century, since Tertullian mentions the 'sign' but without describing it.[52] The Our Father is, of course, scriptural; the *Gloria Patri* or 'little doxology' has ancient Jewish roots but existed in its modern Christian form from about the fifth century;[53] and the *Veni, Sancte Spiritus*, which has been variously attrib-uted to Robert, king of France (d. 1031), Pope Innocent III, and Cardinal Stephen Langton, was certainly both composed and popularized no later than the eleventh or twelfth century.

That several of these prayers—the Sign of the Cross, the Our Father, and the *Confiteor*, were used liturgically in the most common of all Catholic acts of worship, the Mass, undoubtedly accounts for their familiarity and corresponding popularity. The Hail Mary would have become most fa-miliar from the rosary, the catechism, and the service of Compline, but also from its recitation before each canonical hour, and from the *Angelus*. The antiphon *Salve Regina*, which closes the services of Compline[54] and Lauds,[55] and was, as Thurston demonstrates, closely related to the service of Benediction of the Blessed Sacrament (as well as to the *Memorare* or Prayer of St Bernard), also had ample reason to be well known. Likewise the *Regina Coeli*, which signalled the end of the offices of the breviary during Easter.[56] The *De Profundis* was, of course, remembered from the Office of the Dead, and Thurston argues that it was through the old practice of 'the "Bidding Prayers", the English equivalent of the French *prône*, recited after the Offertory on Sundays in every parish church at the principal Mass' that the laity were made most familiar with it. He also notes that, in the Ireland of his day, the prayer was normally recited after

[52] J. G. Davies (ed.), *A New Dictionary of Liturgy and Worship* (London, 1986; 1991), 247.

[53] H. Thurston, 'The Gloria Patri', *Month*, 131 (1918), 406. This was the prayer which came dramatically to Janet Erskine Stuart's mind when she wrote of the end of her novitiate in 1889: 'My seven years are ended! What grave lessons have I learned! . . . The wild songs have died out of my memory . . . instead of them, I hear great psalm tones rushing through the pine trees, echoing from the rocks in glorious music; "Glory be to the Father, and to the Son, and to the Holy Ghost." This is the song that the voice of the torrents shouts forth to heaven, and the stars give it back to me on earth . . .' M. Monahan, *Life and Letters of Janet Erskine Stuart: Superior General of the Society of the Sacred Heart 1857 to 1914* (London, 1922), 72.   [54] H. Thurston, 'The Salve Regina', *Month*, 128 (1916), 258.

[55] W. E. Addis and T. Arnold (eds.), *A Catholic Dictionary* (9th edn., London, 1917), 752.   [56] Ibid. 718.

Mass.[57] The *Veni, Sancte Spiritus*, one of only four sequences[58] which
were retained in the Roman missal after its revision in the sixteenth
century, was pentecostal in subject and in use. This prayer, known
colloquially from the Middle Ages as 'the golden sequence', appears to
have appealed to Christians of other denominations as well: according to
Thurston, it deservedly 'occupie[d] an almost unrivalled position in the
hymnody of the church' and 'its aptness of phrase and intense devotional
feeling [had] aroused the enthusiasm of writers of every creed'.[59]

It is worth stressing that a widespread familiarity with the prayers just
mentioned would tend to emphasize the continuity rather than the dis-
junction of Catholic devotional practice in England, both historically and
geographically. Certainly, those devotions deemed characteristic of nineteenth-century ultramontanes, such as reparations to the Sacred Heart,
prayers to St Joseph, the Holy Family, or to Our Lady of Lourdes, are
conspicuous by their absence. But while the majority of Thurston's
'familiar prayers' would have been well known to Catholics, and indeed to
most Christians, across national boundaries and over time, the popularity
of two of his choices, the *Anima Christi* and the *Memorare*, is not so
readily explained. It is to these prayers that we will now turn.

Of all the prayers which Thurston chooses as 'familiar' to the ordinary
English Catholic (by which he seems to mean known by heart, rather
than simply recognized), only the *Memorare* and the *Anima Christi* appear
to have reached widespread popularity without the benefit of long association with the liturgy. The second, as Thurston himself admits, was
not, perhaps, quite so popular in England after all. 'Although the *Anima
Christi* is found in most modern prayer-books,' he writes, 'and although
it has of late years received quasi-liturgical recognition by being included

---

[57] H. Thurston, 'The "De Profundis" ', *Month*, 132 (1918), 368.

[58] A sequence is defined by the *Catholic Dictionary* as 'A rhythm sometimes sung between the Epistle and Gospel; also called a "prose", because not in any regular metre . . .'.
The others were the ' "Victimae Paschali", at Easter (attributed to Wipso, chaplain to
Conrad II, eleventh century) . . . "Lauda, Sion", at Corpus Christi (by St Thomas of
Aquin); the "Dies Irae" in Masses of the Dead (by Thomas of Celano, d. *circa*. 1250). A
fifth prose, "Stabat Mater", by Jacopone da Todi, on the two feasts of the Seven Dolours,
must have been added very recently, since neither Le Brun nor Benedict XIV recognizes it.
Other sequences are found in the Missals of religious orders . . . etc.' (Addis and Arnold
(eds.), *Catholic Dictionary*, 774).

[59] He also notes that it was sung with gusto at the Eucharistic Congress of 1908. In an
article which is permeated with his own delight in the sequence, Thurston appears to find
most satisfactory 'the fact that, with all its intense devotional feeling, it is so adequate and
dignified' (H. Thurston, *Familiar Prayers* (London, 1953), 54–6 (from his original article in
the *Month* of June 1915).

in the supplementary matter of the Roman Breviary, it would probably be rash to assume that all Catholic readers know it by heart . . .'[60] The text, that granted indulgences by Pius IX in 1854, and which was, by 1915, 'alone in current use',[61] was perhaps included through pressure from a less representative Catholic lobby. At any rate, and despite the popularity in the period of the English hymn 'Soul of my Saviour' which expressed the same sentiments, the only English work concerned with the specifically Roman devotion seems to have been the semi-official *Prayers on the Anima Christi*, brought out by the Catholic Truth Society of London in 1900. That the indulgenced version of the prayer was confined to this collection may suggest that, however highly thought of in Rome, it did not strike much of a chord with most English.

Precisely the opposite seems to have been the case with the other extraliturgical prayer to be considered, the *Memorare*, or Prayer of St Bernard. Thurston notes that the prayer 'never met with the official and liturgical recognition accorded to, let us say, the *Te Deum* or the *Salve Regina*'. Yet, in spite of this, 'it is nevertheless a prayer which many people know by heart and which is now almost invariably included in our manuals of devotion'.[62] That it was genuinely and spontaneously popular in England seems clear from the fact that a multitude of different versions of the prayer appeared in a range of nineteenth- and early twentieth-century English prayer-books. As Thurston pointed out, one cannot help but be struck by

such diversities as the following [which] force themselves upon one's notice. The translation . . . from the Appendix to the Catechism [Burns & Oates] begins 'Remember, O most loving Virgin Mary, that never was it known', &c. The translation in the *Manual of Prayers for Congregational Use*, 'Version prescribed by the Cardinal-Archbishop and Bishops of England' and issued in 1886, opens thus: 'Remember, O most loving Virgin Mary, that it is a thing unheard of that any one ever had recourse to thy protection', &c. The English translation of the *Raccolta*, made originally by Father Ambrose St John, and officially approved in 1857, but published in many editions subsequently, runs 'Remember, O most gracious Virgin Mary, that never was it known', &c. This version has apparently been adopted in the American *Raccolta* . . . Other translations begin: 'Remember O most holy Virgin Mary', or again 'Remember, O most pious Virgin Mary'. In these last two cases the rendering can hardly be called accurate, but for the most part there is no ground for complaint except the lack of uniformity.[63]

---

[60] H. Thurston, 'The Anima Christi', *Month*, 125 (1915), 493.   [61] Ibid.
[62] H. Thurston, 'The Memorare', *Month*, 132 (1918), 269.   [63] Ibid. 270–1.

That at least as many as five distinct versions of the prayer were still circulating in 1918, and this in spite of the fact that Pius IX had granted indulgences to only one version of the prayer as early as 1846, that version which was in turn incorporated into the twelfth and 'thoroughly revised' edition of the *Raccolta* of 1849, would seem to indicate that the prayer held a broad-based appeal in England which was quite unrelated to pronouncements from the Vatican.

Since the prayer was not introduced from Rome, one might imagine that it stemmed from the recusant tradition. But in fact the prayer is not to be found in early editions of popular English prayer-books. Thurston 'sought for it in vain in the early editions of the *Primer*, the *Manual of Prayers*, and the *Garden of the Soul*' and surmised that it probably came to England by way of France, since it 'was . . . for France alone that Pope Pius IX. On 25th July, 1846, first enriched this prayer with a 300 days' indulgence *toties quoties* and a plenary indulgence once a month'.[64] It seems first to have found a place in the newly revised Birmingham edition of *The Garden of the Soul* of 1844, a full two years before Pius IX saw fit to grant the prayer any indulgences, and from which date it was included in virtually every reissue of the favourite English Catholic prayer-book.[65] It was also included in devotional appendices to the English Catholics' penny catechism from about 1880. So the *Memorare* evidently became an English Catholic favourite in the post-1850 period for reasons which had no direct connection either with papal directives or with native tradition. How then are we to account for its widespread appeal, and what can it tell us about the devotional understandings of those who used it?

The variations of the prayer to which Thurston drew attention, and which he dismissed as at worst a nuisance of inconsistency, do give hints as to how the prayer may have been used which in turn shed light on reasons for its appeal. In the 1844 Birmingham edition of *The Garden of the Soul*, the prayer, which is given as 'The Prayer of St Bernard' and in English only, takes the following form:

Prayer of St Bernard

Remember, O most holy Virgin Mary, that no one ever had recourse to your protection, implored your help, or sought your mediation, without obtaining

[64] H. Thurston, 'The Memorare', *Month*, 132 (1918), 269. On 11 Dec. 1846 the indulgence was extended to the rest of the Catholic world and the prayer incorporated in the twelfth edition of the *Raccolta di Orazioni e pie Opere per le quali sono state concedute dai Sommi Pontefici le S. Indulgenze* (Rome, 1807; 12th edn., 1849).

[65] Of the versions of *The Garden of the Soul* we have been considering, it was included in those published in 1854, 1856, 1872, 1874, 1877, 1883, and 1892, and omitted in those of 1884 and 1899.

relief. Confiding therefore in your goodness, behold me a penitent sinner sighing out my sins before you, beseeching you to adopt me for your child, and to take upon you the care of my eternal salvation.

Despise not, O Mother of Jesus, the petition of your humble client, but hear and grant my prayer.

A different translation, included alongside the Latin text, and given as the '*Memorare* or Prayer of St Bernard' in the 1856 edition of *The Garden of the Soul* gives this alternative:

Memorare or Prayer of St Bernard

Remember, O most gracious Virgin Mary, that never was it known, that any one who fled to thy protection, implored thy help, and sought thy intercession was left unaided.

Inspired with this confidence, I fly unto thee, O Virgin of Virgins, my mother. To thee I come; before thee I stand, sinful and sorrowful.* O Mother of the Word Incarnate, despise not my petitions, but in thy mercy hear and answer me. Amen.

* Here you may make your request.

It will have been noticed that this second version omits the explicitly spiritual request to 'take upon you the care of my eternal salvation', intended perhaps as a cautious corrective to any rash use which might be prompted by the assurance of 'relief'. Rather, it leaves the meaning of the prayer ambiguous enough to support either a spiritual or a more instrumental interpretation. But, although the new version allowed greater room for less spiritual motives and even encouraged the making of specific requests in an explanatory footnote, it was at the same time more cautious about appearing to promise results, replacing the demand to 'grant' my prayer with that to 'answer' my prayer.

That the *Memorare* might, in some ecclesiastical circles, seem to invite unorthodox uses was presumably the reason why one prayer-book of 1874 chose to apply the prayer to the Sacred Heart, and still more innovatively, to 'Our Lady of the Sacred Heart', in what seems a fairly clear attempt to capitalize on the native appeal of the prayer in order to direct enthusiasm to other devotional ends. This prayer-book gives the following:

Memorare to the Sacred Heart

Remember, O most sweet Jesu, that it has never been heard of in any age, that those who had recourse to thy Sacred Heart implored its assistance or claimed its mercy in vain. Filled and animated with the most lively confidence, O Heart, King of Hearts, I come, I fly to thee, and sighing beneath the weight of my sins, I prostrate myself before thee. O Sacred Heart, despise not my feeble prayers, but graciously hear and grant my petitions, thou, thyself, the heart of the best fathers; and may he who gave thee to us, by thee also receive our prayers. Amen.[66]

and also:

Memorare to Our Lady of the Sacred Heart

Remember, [Our] Lady of the Sacred Heart, the boundless power which thou possessest over the heart of thy Divine Son. Confiding entirely in thy merits, I now implore thy protection, O glorious Queen of the heart of Jesus, of that heart which is the inexhaustible source of all graces, and which thou canst open at thy will, in order to pour down upon mankind all the treasures of love and mercy, of light and salvation which it contains; grant me, I implore thee, the favour which I ask for. . . . No! I cannot meet with a refusal; and since thou art my mother, I beseech thee to hear and grant my prayer.[67]

Another variant of the prayer, Ambrose St John's translation, was included in the 1857 English edition of the *Raccolta* but was presumably meant only as an informative supplement to the Latin version, which was given first. Certainly, it is hard to imagine the following stilted translation being readily committed to memory:

Remember, Mary, tenderest-hearted Virgin, how from of old the ear hath never heard that he who ran to thee for refuge, implored thy help, and sought thy prayers, was forsaken of God. Virgin of virgins, Mother, emboldened by this confidence I fly to thee, to thee I come, and in thy presence I a weeping sinner stand. Mother of the Word Incarnate, O cast not away my prayer; but in thy pity hear and answer. Amen.[68]

It was none of these versions, however, but a third variant of the *Memorare* proper which, despite its being 'one of the only too numerous English translations', Thurston chose to print in his article on the origins of the prayer, not 'as the best, but as likely to be the most widely familiar, since it is now included in the Appendix to what in remote pre-War days was still correctly described as the "Penny" Catechism'.[69] This version, as can be seen below, took neither the precaution of directing requests to

---

[66] [R. Challoner], *The Garden of the Soul. A Manual of Devotion. A New Edition, Containing Devotions to the Sacred Heart, Visits to the Blessed Sacraments [Sic], Way of the Cross, Bona Mors, Indulgenced Prayers, Administration of the Sacraments* . . . (Edinburgh, 1874), 328–9. [67] *Ibid.* 364.

[68] *The Raccolta; or Collection of Indulgenced Prayers*, ed. T. Galli, trans. A. St John (London, 1857), 196. The Latin ran as follows: 'Memorare, O piissima Virgo Maria, non esse auditum a saeculo quemquam ad tua currentem praesidia, tua implorantem auxilia, tua petentem suffragia, esse derelictum. Ego tali animatus confidentia, ad te, Virgo virginum, Mater, curro, ad te venio, coram te gemens peccator assisto; noli, Mater Verbi, verba mea despicere, sed audi propitia, et exaudi. Amen' (ibid. 195–6).

[69] Thurston, 'The Memorare', 269.

explicitly spiritual ends, nor that of minimizing the implicit promise of direct results:

Prayer of St Bernard

Remember, O most loving Virgin Mary, that never was it known that any one who fled to thy protection, implored thy help, and sought thy intercession, was left forsaken. Filled, therefore, with confidence in thy goodness, I fly to thee, O Mother, Virgin of Virgins; to thee I come, before thee I stand a sorrowing sinner. Despise not my words, O Mother of the Word, but graciously hear and grant my prayer.[70]

Small wonder that Janet Erskine Stuart, who was later to become superior-general of the Society of the Sacred Heart, converted in 1879 on the strength of the prayer. 'Did I ever tell you how Our Lady first came into my life?', she wrote to a friend in 1909:

It was by the Memorare . . . it took me off my feet at once, for it was so daring a statement that I thought it could not have lived if it had been a lie, and I said it constantly and clung to it as the first definite something that seemed to come authentically after my seven years of groping in the dark.[71]

It seems clear that the whole thrust of the prayer was of reassurance and the all but certainty of being helped, while at the same time quite specific requests, whether for temporal or spiritual favours, were apparently being invited from the faithful. Attempting to generalize about so personal and private a matter as responses to particular prayers is a delicate matter for the historian, and will necessarily involve what is perhaps a dangerous degree of speculation. But it would seem that intrinsic to the *Memorare* were several elements common to those which we have already seen in the English Catholic approach to its most widespread devotions, the rosary and Benediction. Above all a prayer of reassurance which stressed the direct accessibility of the supernatural, the immediacy of the *Memorare* was likely to be reassuring in a comparable sense to that of being blessed by Christ himself in the Blessed Sacrament, or of pleasing Mary through a close attention to the devotion through which she was particularly honoured and associated.

Just as a whiff of the superstitious blended with the miraculous in the service of Benediction, which was appealing not only in its concentration on the central mystery of transubstantiation, but also in its vague association with curing and protecting from harm, so the quasi-miraculous stories which surrounded the rosary seem to be of a piece with some understandings of the bold claim central to the *Memorare*. Those who went to Benediction more to be protected than to worship, or who did not draw such a distinction, may similarly have said the *Memorare* for direct intervention in the shape of a cure, or a safe journey, with confidence in results beyond simply those of being heard. Open to the most spiritual of interpretations, it was above all the prayer's immediacy, its concrete offer of tangible results, which no doubt accounted for the breadth of its popularity.

In the prayer-book produced by the monks of Ampleforth Abbey for the boys of Ampleforth College, a tacit distinction is drawn between the two sorts of uses, as if individual boys might vary in their requirements, or different moods and circumstances might dictate which version would be needed on any given occasion.[72] The more high-flown St Bernard's Prayer, given in an appendix of 'Prayers and Hymns for Special Occasions', was taken from Dante's *Paradiso*, canto 33. The only stanza, the third, which seems to bear any relation to the *Memorare* was given in the following awkward translation, which was hardly calculated to arouse a sense of the immediate accessibility of the Blessed Virgin:

Lady, so great art thou and such thy might, that he who would have grace and has not recourse to thee would have his desire fly up without wings. Thy bounty not only succours all that ask, but often freely foreruns the asking.[73]

But the same prayer-book also included, as an untitled morning prayer which follows immediately after the rubric 'Let us turn to our blessed Lady, and beg her most earnestly to help us in all necessities this day':

Remember, O most loving Virgin Mary, that it is a thing unheard of, that any one ever had recourse to thy protection, implored thy help and sought thy mediation, and was left forsaken. Filled, therefore, with confidence in thy goodness, I fly to thee, O Mother, Virgin of virgins; to thee I come, before thee I stand, a sorrowful sinner. Despise not my words, O Mother of the Word, but graciously hear and grant my prayer. Amen.[74]

---

[72] A pupil of Ampleforth in the 1940s and 1950s recalled 'the habit, inculcated at school, of saying the *Memorare* at the outset of a journey' (D. Goodall, 'How I Pray: 6. Habit of a Lifetime', *Tablet*, 246 (1992), 467).

[73] *Devotions and Prayers: A Book for the Use of the Boys of Ampleforth College at the Benedictine Abbey of Saint Lawrence the Martyr* (Ampleforth, 1933), 161.

[74] Ibid. 4.

That at least two distinct uses of the prayer had come to be incorporated in this Benedictine prayer-book of 1933 reinforces the impression of an increasing tolerance towards naïve as well as sophisticated approaches to devotion within the Catholic community. Catholics as highbrow as Tyrrell and Newman were careful to defend what they saw as genuine expressions of piety, however simple or vulgar these might appear to refined tastes. Others, like Faber and John Brande Morris, went even further, positively encouraging childlike expressions of affection for and trust in God and the saints, which they themselves adopted with equal enthusiasm. While some English Catholics thought the latter approach smacked of affectation (and many found Faber's addressing of the Virgin Mary as 'mamma' particularly irritating[75]), the sentiments which such expressions embodied were theologically irreproachable and, as Newman and Tyrrell would have been the first to admit, probably closer to the spirit of Jesus's teaching than any number of lofty intellectualizations. However much embarrassment naïve views of prayer, like naïve views of the rosary or of Benediction, might privately have caused some English Catholics, such approaches were increasingly central to others within the community, and had come to be tacitly tolerated, whether in charity or in diffidence, by all.

[75] See R. Chapman, *Father Faber* (London, 1961), 148.

4

A Community Apart

OVER the latter half of the nineteenth century, English Catholic conceptions of devotion widened in a way which was calculated to encourage active participation from as many members within the community as possible. Not only did manuals of prayer offer an increasingly wide choice of prayers, even the hallowed *Garden of the Soul* being significantly expanded, but the greatest possible latitude, in that tolerant spirit which was advocated by Catholics as diverse as Faber, Newman, Tyrrell, and von Hügel, was allowed in approaches to individual prayers such as the *Memorare* and to a range of understandings of traditional devotions like Benediction and the rosary. Hand in hand with this trend towards devotional inclusiveness within the community, there developed an equally strong tendency for Catholics to wish to separate from those outside the fold. These shifts in attitude, which were of social as well as devotional importance, can be traced in successive editions of the catechism and also in the growth and nature of exclusively Catholic societies.

Too little attention has been paid to catechisms in assessing the development of English Catholicism in the period, despite the fact that this summary of the Faith was, for most Catholics, the single most authoritative source of church doctrine, whose phrases, memorized in childhood, would readily spring to mind in the face of any religious question. The importance of the catechism from this point of view was one of which the English bishops seem to have been particularly conscious. When, on 8 February 1869, the bishops who were gathered in Rome for the First Vatican Council began discussion on the proposal that a standard elementary catechism[1] be adopted for the whole church,

great divergence of opinion was manifested, especially on the proposal that Bellarmine's catechism, in use at Rome, should be the norm; the German bishops were very adverse to the supplanting of Canisius' catechism by any other, it being in universal use throughout the German lands, and most excellent in itself.[2]

Representing the other side of the debate, a Spanish bishop declared, with no little rhetorical flourish, that:

[1] This was the fourth *schema* of Discipline and Canon Law.
[2] C. Butler, *The Vatican Council* (2 vols.; London, 1930), i. 228.

as the Pope said: 'I lay before you a universal catechism for the Church of God, all we bishops should say "So be it, so be it," and nothing more. He who sitteth on the throne, surrounded by the four and twenty elders, is the Roman Pontiff surrounded by the bishops, who, as often as and along with him they decree something in faith or discipline, cast their crowns before the throne, saying, "Benediction and glory and wisdom and thanksgiving and honour to our God for ever and ever." And so when the supreme Pontiff says a catechism is necessary, let us cast down our crowns, and say . . .'[3]

Not altogether surprisingly, given such a high-handed tone, it was not only the Germans who took exception to the papal initiative. English bishops William Clifford of Clifton diocese and William Vaughan of Plymouth both objected strongly that such a catechism, if it were to be enforced at all, ought to be the work of the Council and not simply a papal directive.

As Cuthbert Butler's account of Vatican I suggests, underlying the discussion of a universal catechism lay a question of principle related to the issue uppermost in everyone's mind—the manner of defining and the extent of the proposed dogma of papal infallibility. Frederick Cwiekowski has shown that concern over the catechism was shared by many bishops of the minority group who believed the anticipated definition of papal infallibility to be 'inopportune':

Only if the catechism were drawn up by bishops elected by the council or if the text were examined and approved by the council fathers would it truly be a catechism of the council. The impression that the bishops had relinquished their responsibilities, the minority argued, would thus be avoided.[4]

The bishop of Lausanne and Geneva, acting as head of the deputation on the *juxta modum* votes of 4 May, declared testily that such objections

fell into three classes: those who wanted the catechism recommended, not imposed; those who wanted the council, not the Holy See, to draw up the catechism; and those who saw difficulties of application. [Bishop William] Vaughan's *modum* was among those cited as examples of the second group. Did the objections of this group, the *relator* asked, evidence a lack of devotion to the supreme pontiff, the vicar of Christ and supreme head of the Church? Was this council to seem lacking in devotion, love and obedience to the pope?[5]

There is no doubt that veiled protests at the proposed dogmatic definition, which concentrated on a point of principle concerning the relations

[3] Ibid.
[4] F. Cwiekowski, *The English Bishops and the First Vatican Council* (Louvain, 1971), 151–2.
[5] Ibid. 153.

between pope and council, account for much of the heat generated by the catechism debate, even among the English. This issue was surely in Clifford's mind when he proposed an amendment to the text of the decree requiring the new catechism to be based on Bellarmine's,[6] the effect of which would have been to avoid any impression that the new catechism had to stick slavishly to Bellarmine's text and to permit greater use of other catechisms.[7] There was also the point that Bellarmine's close association with theological justifications for the doctrine of papal infallibility made him a particularly contentious name to bandy about in the context of a universal catechism. There were resonances to the very name Bellarmine since, although 'the doctrine [infallibility] had been implicit in the Church through the centuries, representing the centralization of the infallibility of those protected in all truth by the promise of Christ himself', it had 'been expressed in a systematic theological form by Bellarmine'.[8] Edward Norman argues that, 'As a symbol of the "Roman" influence of the nineteenth-century Ultramontanes', the

issue of Infallibility only too easily came to appear as a weapon of neo-triumphalism in a Papacy anxious to exercise a spiritual autocracy over a world which had stood aside while the temporal patrimony of the Church was stripped away.[9]

But while the German and Spanish positions at the Council may have been fixed entirely by the debate over papal jurisdiction, as Butler's excerpt from the proceedings and Norman's commentary imply, there are hints that the issue at stake was not solely one of authority as far as the English bishops were concerned.

English protests at the threatened replacement of their own time-honoured catechism may have been straightforward enough. On their rare visits to Rome, most of the English bishops—Manning is a notable exception—give the impression of innocents abroad rather than of hard-nosed politicians at the centre of ecclesiastical power. The majority had too little Latin to be able to follow much of the debate at the First Vatican Council, where they spent enjoyable breakfasts chuckling over reports of themselves in *The Times*; at the Canonization of the Japanese Martyrs in

---

[6] Clifford thought the text should be amended to read 'ob oculos habitis imprimis praedicto venerabilis cardinalis Bellarmini Catechismo, tum etiam aliis in christiano populo magis pervulgatis catechismis'. The sense of this seems to be: 'having before our eyes in the first place the aforementioned catechism of the venerable Cardinal Bellarmine, then those catechisms better known among the Christian people [should also be considered].'

[7] See Cwiekowski, *English Bishops*, 150.

[8] E. Norman, *The English Catholic Church in the Nineteenth Century* (Oxford, 1984), 306.

[9] Ibid.

1862 they appear to have thoroughly enjoyed, though with a touch of disbelief, the pomp and grandeur of their surroundings. As Ullathorne gaily wrote home:

I confess to have sinfully pocketed a white dove reposing on sugar, and a singular old gentleman in blue wings and yellow hat, and a muffler for toothache; intending to carry them to a certain St Dominic's, at Stone; in punishment for which theft they broke and melted in my pocket . . . Some of the vases of sweets had little Cardinal's hats on top of them; and it was quite pleasant to offer them to one's neighbour, and assure the fortunate prelate that his new honour came from the Pope.[10]

Small wonder that Dermot Quinn, summarizing his doctoral thesis on English Catholics and politics in the period, has despaired of the bishops' lack of political acumen, calling them 'naïve beyond the ordinary in their political endeavours'.[11]

Given the apparent lack of guile of the majority of the English bishops, they probably meant precisely what they said. Although Clifford did object to the principle that the English should have to follow central directives, what is less often noticed is that he also thought that 'the work of Bellarmine was more apt for particular use, than for the needs of the universal Church. He himself thought it impossible to get a catechism as extensively used and approved as that of Canisius.'[12] William Vaughan, addressing the only topic which moved him sufficiently to make him speak out publicly at the Council, went further:

He thought Bellarmine's work least adaptable to the needs of the times. The questions and responses were much too long, and too involved for the abilities of children; for the children of the poor in England and her colonies, he judged, they were impossible. It was the needs of such poor that ought to be the concern of the council.[13]

It has generally been assumed that the catechism debate at the Vatican Council was nothing more than an oblique dispute over the authority of the papacy. Cwiekowski implies this in the thrust of his chapter which

---

[10] C. Butler, *The Life and Times of Bishop Ullathorne* (2 vols.; London, 1926), i. 245–6.

[11] D. A. Quinn, 'English Roman Catholics and Politics in the Second Half of the Nineteenth Century' (D.Phil. thesis, Oxford University, 1985), short abstract.

[12] Cwiekowski, *English Bishops*, 149. Canisius was not only a contemporary of Bellarmine's, but a fellow Jesuit; both expounded equally well the orthodoxy of the Counter-Reformation. To judge by the number of editions of Canisius' several catechisms, and especially his *Summa Doctrinae Christianae* (or *Catechismus Major*) of 1554, Clifford seems to have been speaking no more than the truth when he argued that it would be impractical to attempt to impose Bellarmine's longer and less well-known catechism upon Catholics already well used to that of Canisius.   [13] *Ibid.* 150.

examines the catechism question and which he has subtitled 'the taking of sides'. Butler, in his own account of the Council, puts it slightly less forcefully, explaining that 'the great debate on Church and Papacy had begun and was engrossing the entire attention of all, so that catechism and discipline had faded out of view'.[14] Manning's account of Vatican I— despite, or perhaps because of, the defeat[15] for the ultramontane party over the catechism question—leaves the debate unmentioned.[16]

But, although a genuinely ultramontane contingent, which one might have expected to close ranks at the prospect of a Holy See on the brink of invasion, saw the issue in such terms, it does not follow that the minority view was actually intended to be disloyal. There may have been reasons intrinsic to the proposed catechisms themselves, rather than merely their symbolic importance, which caused Vaughan and Clifford to wish to preserve their own English catechism, and therefore to oppose Bellarmine's so vehemently. James Hennessey, at any rate, has found the ultramontane interpretation, that the issue turned solely on the question of authority, difficult to justify. 'The entire second debate on the elementary catechism is a strange one,' he muses:

The catechism *schema* itself was peculiar. In effect, the fathers were asked to give the Roman authorities *carte blanche*, and both spokesmen for the deputation persisted in treating objections as professions of disloyalty to the Holy See. In his final summation for the deputation, Bishop Etienne Marilley of Lausanne and Geneva put the charge very baldly. He declared that those who demanded that the catechism be the work of the council were saying equivalently that they did not trust the pope, and that they were affording journals hostile to the Church the opportunity of claiming that there was a division between the pontiff and the

---

[14] Butler, *The Vatican Council*, i. 231.

[15] Despite mollifying arguments that 'Toutefois, les évêques pourront publier à part des leçons catéchétiques pour donner à leur diocésains une instruction plus ample ou pour réfuter les erreurs courantes dans leurs milieux' and that such reforms need not be made 'tout d'un coup, mais par des modifications successives que les évêques prépareraient dans les conciles provinciaux, en travaillant par exemple sur le texte de Canisius', the English desire for episcopal discretion in the choice of catechism was heeded: 'Quant aux détails, on prendra modèle, non seulement sur le catéchisme de Bellarmin, mais encore sur ceux qui sont les plus répandus. Conformément au désir de quelques Pères, on a dit que la version devrait être fidèle plutôt que littérale et que les leçons ajoutées par les évêques pourraient êtres insérées dans le texte mais en les distinguant très exactement' (E. Mangenot, 'Catéchisme', in *Dictionnaire de théologie catholique*, eds. A. Vacant and E. Mangenot (17 vols.; Paris, 1899–1950), ii (1903), cols. 1960–1).

[16] 'As to the labours of the other sections,' he wrote, 'on Discipline, on Religious Orders, on Missions and the Oriental Churches and on Rites, no comment need be made. The world has little interest in them, and takes no notice of them. The one object of its hostility is the Definition which has affirmed the divine authority of the head of the Church' (H. E. Manning, *The True Story of the Vatican Council* (London, 1877), 84).

bishops. It is very difficult, to say the least, to find substantiation for these accusations.[17]

Although the issue of infallibility undoubtedly was, as Butler put it, 'engrossing' the attention of the bishops at the expense of full concentration on the catechism question, this does not mean that there was no intrinsic significance to the less publicized debate. That Newman was suspicious of Clifford's or Ullathorne's commitment to the inopportunist cause, lamenting with Acton and Simpson the dearth of reliable 'party' men, should remind us to be cautious in attributing to English Catholic bishops the labels 'liberal' or 'ultramontane' and to interpreting their every opinion in the context of a struggle between these two poles. As has already been seen, party rhetoric at the Council, however much it may reveal about the state of alarm in Roman circles, can be highly misleading when applied to English Catholic concerns. The matter of English catechisms will therefore be examined as a subject of interest in itself.

The history and use of Catholic catechisms in England might be imagined to be a fairly straightforward matter to establish. Indeed, in successive editions of *The Oxford Dictionary of the Christian Church*, F. L. Cross and E. A. Livingstone sum up post-Tridentine Catholic catechisms in a few sentences:

During the following centuries a flood of R[oman] C[atholic] catechisms appeared; in many countries, e.g. in France, there was a different one approved for each diocese; in England one superseded all others: *A Catechism of Christian Doctrine*, first issued in 1898, popularly called the 'Penny Catechism'. This was based on R.[ichard] Challoner's *Abridgement of Christian Doctrine*, first published in 1759.[18]

This account is confirmed in its various components by other reference works: E. Mangenot, for example, declares in the *Dictionnaire de théologie catholique* that 'les évêques d'Angleterre et du Pays de Galles ont approuvé un seul et unique catéchisme pour l'usage de leurs diocèses: *A Catechism of Christian Doctrine, London, 1898*'.[19] The *New Catholic Encyclopedia* agrees that '*An Abridgement of Christian Doctrine*, is attributed to B[isho]p Richard Challoner (1691–1781). This book, which has the

[17] J. Hennessey, *The First Council of the Vatican: The American Experience* (New York, 1963), 169–70.

[18] F. L. Cross and E. A. Livingstone (eds.), *The Oxford Dictionary of the Christian Church* (Oxford, 1957; repr. 1988), 249.   [19] Mangenot, 'Catéchisme', col. 1957.

merit of simple, direct language, formed the basis of the later English "penny catechism".[20]

The first anomaly occurs in successive editions of Herbert McCabe's introduction to the Catholic Truth Society's *The Teaching of the Catholic Church. A New Catechism of Christian Doctrine*, in which he refers to 'the older *Catechism of Christian Doctrine* (Catholic Truth Society, London, 1889) which is still in use in this country'.[21] The discrepancy in the year of publication might easily be explained as a misprint, inadvertently perpetuated, which meant to refer to the same Challoner-based catechism of 1898. But this explanation would not account for an anecdote related in Kathleen O'Meara's biography of Thomas Grant, of a near-sighted student who enraged the bishop by not appearing to show proper reverence at the elevation of the host, leading him to exclaim: 'What sort of faith is this? Why, a child that knew its penny catechism wouldn't behave so!'[22] Even if the story is apocryphal, the biography was published well before either 1889 or 1898, and so the term 'penny catechism' must pre-date any landmark abridgement of doctrine of the 1880s or 1890s. Furthermore, catechisms which appear to be editions of the penny catechism go back at least as far as 1859, and arguably as far as 1820 or even to the eighteenth century if earlier editions of what is clearly the same abridgement of doctrine may be considered the same essential work. And this does not take account of the other, rival catechisms which existed in England throughout the period. To complicate matters further, no catechism exists in the three English copyright libraries (the Bodleian, Cambridge University, and British libraries) which bears the significant dates of either 1889 or 1898.

In order to begin to make sense of such anomalies, it seems worth attempting to piece together the history of catechisms in England in a more general way. According to Dom Stephen Marron, oral catechizing was a church practice from ancient times which continued in this loose form until Luther's booklet of doctrine for children prompted Peter Canisius to retaliate with a written catechism to 'counteract this evil'.[23] This catechism was soon followed by others, notably, among those in use in England, Laurence Vaux's *Catechism, or Christian Doctrine necessary for*

[20] W. J. McDonald, *et al.* (eds.), *New Catholic Encyclopedia* (17 vols.; New York etc., 1967–79), iii. 214.

[21] Catholic Truth Society, *The Teaching of the Catholic Church. A New Catechism of Christian Doctrine* (London, 1985), 3.

[22] G. Ramsay [K. O'Meara], *Thomas Grant: First Bishop of Southwark* (1874; 2nd edn., London, 1886), 473.

[23] S. Marron, 'Bishop Challoner and our Catechism', *Douai Magazine*, ns 9 (1936), 116.

Children and Ignorant People (1562), translations of Bellarmine's and Canisius' catechisms, and Henry Turberville's *Abridgment of Christian Doctrine* (*c*.1649), which came to be known as the *Doway Catechism*. Marron argues that 'Bellarmine's catechism retained its popularity in England as a catechism for children . . . right up to the middle of the eighteenth century'[24] and was an influence upon Turberville's 'original one in the sense that it was not a mere adaptation of any preceding catechism'.[25] It is this Bellarmine-influenced *Doway Catechism* of Turberville's which Marron takes to be the real parent of the penny catechism, by way of the *Doway Abstract* (possibly by Fr John Gother), which was in turn abridged and simplified to *A Short Abridgment of Christian Doctrine for the Instruction of Beginners* (1745).[26] This *Short Abridgment*, the first catechism to start with the direct question 'Who made you?', was 'in all probability'[27] the text which Challoner 'revised and enlarged' into the catechism for which he is known and which Marron describes as a 'sort of compromise between the *Short Abridgment* and the *Doway Abstract*'.[28]

Herbert Thurston argues that the earliest English catechism entitled to claim parentage of what was later to become the penny catechism is that of 1728, of which 'there have been since . . . at least three notable revisions, in 1836, 1858, and 1888, each of which involved verbal changes of moment and the addition of some new matter, but which need not be more particularly described here'.[29] The earliest catechism found which resembles this proto-penny catechism is *An Abridgment of Christian Doctrine: or, the First Catechism. Published for the Use of the London District* (London: Keating, Brown, & Co., Printers to R. R. the Vicars Apostolic, *c*.1820), which makes no claim to be approved or exclusively prescribed, however; indeed it is bound together with an apparently alternative *Second Catechism*, or *Abstract* of the Douai catechism. Also, at a cover price of $2\frac{1}{2}d$., it cannot strictly speaking be called a 'penny' catechism. The next stage towards the development of an exclusive and national penny catechism appears to have come in the shape of that *Abridgment* of 1836 which Thurston mentions,[30] this time 'Revised, Improved, and Recommended by Authority, for the Use of the Faithful in all the

---

[24] Ibid. 117.   [25] Ibid.
[26] This also seems to be the view of the *Catholic Encyclopedia*. See C. G. Herbermann *et al.* (eds.), *The Catholic Encyclopedia* (17 vols.; London, 1907-), v. 87.
[27] Marron, 'Bishop Challoner', 120.   [28] Ibid.
[29] H. Thurston, 'The "Douay Abstract" and the "Short Abridgement"', *Tablet*, ns 117 (1911), 10. I am not sure that Thurston is right about this, as will emerge in what follows.
[30] *An Abridgment of Christian Doctrine . . .* (London, 1836).

Districts of England' and also carrying with it an approbation by the vicars apostolic and coadjutors of England that the catechism be used by the 'Faithful in our respective Districts'. No mention is made, however, of any recommendation for its exclusive use.

The first version in the Bodleian, Cambridge University, or British libraries which dates from after the restoration of the hierarchy would appear to corroborate Stephen Marron's view that 'uniformity seems to have been first secured after the establishment of the hierarchy by [an 1859 edition]',[31] a fact which was also known to James Crichton, and strangely appeared to him to have been well enough established by 1981 to be alluded to without comment.[32] This is the *Large Type Edition. Catechism of Christian Doctrine, Approved for the Use of the Faithful, in all the Dioceses of England and Wales* which was granted an *imprimatur* in 1876, and so was presumably printed after that year, but still bore an approbation from Nicholas Wiseman of 1859 which 'approve[d] of this Edition of the Catechism, in our own name and that of the other Bishops, and prescribe[d] its exclusive use'. It was also copyrighted by the publishers Thomas Richardson & Sons of Derby and London, although Rockliff Brothers in Liverpool published the same text as the *Catechism of Christian Doctrine, with the Questions Numbered. Approved for the Use of the Faithful, In all the Dioceses of England and Wales* in *c.*1876. This publication bore the *imprimatur* of the bishop of Liverpool.

That this 1859 version was still being reprinted in 1876 suggests that the 1859 version remained the only 'approved' post-1850 version of the catechism in existence until about 1880, when a new revision (which will be discussed in more detail later) was published. Indeed, this hypothesis would seem to be supported by the existence of other 1859 versions of the catechism, also published in the 1870s, whose titles would seem to imply that this 1859 version had become 'the' catechism: Henry Gibson published his elaborated version of the 1859 text as *Catechism Made Easy* (Liverpool, 1865–77); the Revd John B. Bagshawe's *The Catechism Illustrated by Passages from the Holy Scriptures* . . . came out in London in 1870, and the *Ten Thousand. The Explanatory Catechism of Christian Doctrine* . . . appeared, again from a London press, in 1877. 'The catechism' was enough, apparently, for the faithful to know which version

[31] Marron, 'Bishop Challoner', 120.

[32] 'All through the nineteenth century and indeed until recently,' he writes, 'he [Challoner] was spoken of as the author of the "Penny Catechism" which for about a hundred years (from 1859 onwards) was imposed on children of all ages' (J. D. Crichton, 'Richard Challoner: Catechist and Spiritual Writer', *Clergy Review*, 66 (1981), 271).

was meant, there no longer being the need, as there had been in 1820, to specify *An Abridgment . . . or, the First Catechism* as opposed to *The Second . . . Being an Abstract of the Douay Catechism.*

It would seem that no revisions to the text of the catechism took place throughout the next two decades, despite a substantially larger demand for catechisms from the 1870s as evidenced by a proliferation of versions of the 1859 text and the spread of the Confraternity of Christian Doctrine, which had been recommended by the first provincial synod of Westminster in 1852, and whose aim was to catechize as widely as possible. According to advertisements published by churches in the *Catholic Directory*, only London responded immediately to the synod's suggestion, setting up confraternities in Southwark and Westminster. Salford and Shrewsbury dioceses followed suit in 1855, while Beverley and Liverpool waited until 1858 and 1859 respectively. By the 1870s, however, the confraternity was well represented in the dioceses of Salford, Shrewsbury, Hexham, and Liverpool, which suggests that an ever-increasing number of Catholics were learning the same text. Although in 1883 the bishops still found cause for complaint that although the 'Catechism is usually given publicly in the Churches on Sunday' the 'Confraternity of Christian Doctrine, though recommended by the First Provincial Synod of Westminster, is not generally established; and that in many Missions Catechetical instruction is given by voluntary teachers', such quibbling was the mark of inflated hopes in the wake of an already substantial success.[33] The catechism was of particular importance, since it remained the only source of official instruction in the Faith which, because it was learned by heart, was as accessible to illiterate as to educated Catholics.

It was thus at a point when the catechism was widely disseminated among Catholics of all classes that, in 1877, 'the Bishop of Salford [Herbert Vaughan] proposed that a Revision of the [1859] Catechism should be made' to which 'the Bishops assented . . . and the Bishops of Shrewsbury [James Brown] and Salford were requested to undertake it'.[34] In the following year 'the proofs of the new Catechism were revised and approved . . . [and] the Bishops of Birmingham [William Ullathorne] and Salford [Herbert Vaughan] were requested to bring out the Catechism as soon as it could be got ready'. They 'were also requested to compile a first, or preparatory Catechism, extracted from the new Catechism; and to send proofs of it to the Bishops'.[35] In 1879 it was reported that 'the text

---

[33] Westminster Archdiocesan Archives, 'Bishops' Meetings 1858–1909', Acta, Meeting of the Bishops in Low Week, 1883 (3 Apr.), iv. 170.   [34] Ibid. 1877, xiv. 118.

[35] Ibid. 1878, xxii. 135.

of the new Catechism was finally revised and approved'.[36] This revision was probably published in 1880,[37] and certainly at some point between 1878 (1877 is the year of publication of the last two 1859 versions found in the copyright libraries)[38] and 1883, when a version of the catechism appeared which helpfully carries on its front cover the notice 'NB—This revised Edition of 1883 may at once be known by its containing two questions on Character in Chapter vi, page 40'.[39]

To enter into the intricacies of nineteenth-century revisions to the penny catechism may seem a mere exercise in pedantry. But the changes from the 1859 version of the catechism, in use by the faithful for the next twenty years, to that edition current in the first few years of the 1880s, the version which continued to be reprinted throughout the remainder of the century[40] and to be read by an increasing number of Catholics, although dismissed by Stephen Marron as 'slight',[41] were by no means insignificant. None of the 1859 versions, for example—and despite the

[36] Westminster Archdiocesan Archives, 'Bishops' Meetings 1858–1909', Acta, Meeting of the Bishops in Low Week, 1879, xxi. 142.

[37] Two copies of a catechism have been traced which, although undated, contains all the changes from the 1859 to the 1883 version except for the omission of the two questions on character. This version is likely, then, to pre-date 1883—an impression reinforced by the fact that it is unnumbered (as was the 1859 text, except in one edition which took the trouble to advertise this feature in its title), whereas from 1883 versions of the catechism were numbered as a matter of course. Finally, the Bodleian Library catalogue, for reasons of its own, gives it the tentative date of *c.*1880. See *A Catechism of Christian Doctrine, no. II. Approved by the Cardinal Archbishop and the Bishops of England and Wales, and Directed to be Used in All their Dioceses* (London and Derby, *c.*1880).

[38] See *Tenth Thousand. The Explanatory Catechism of Christian Doctrine* . . . (London, 1877), and H. Gibson, *Catechism Made Easy, being a Familiar Explanation of the Catechism of Christian Doctrine* . . . (3 vols.; Liverpool, 1865–77).

[39] See *A Catechism of Christian Doctrine, no. II* . . . (London, 1883). In 1882 'the Very Rev. Canons Dunderdale, Scott, and Wenham, the Rev. Walter Richards, D.D., and the Rev. T. A. Burge, O.S.B., were appointed as a committee to revise the Catechism [presumably the current, i.e. *c.*1880 version] and to present their joint report at the next Bishops' Meeting' (Westminster Archdiocesan Archives, 'Bishops' Meetings 1858–1909', Acta, Meeting of the Bishops in Low Week, 1882, xv. 163). At the following meeting 'the report of the Committee of Revision was read. It was decided by the Bishops—1. That the repetition of the words of the question should be retained in the answer; 2. That the Bishops of Leeds and Salford should confer together and collate the two Catechisms, and report to the Meeting later on' (ibid. 1883, iii. 170).

[40] See e.g. *A Catechism of Christian Doctrine, no. II. Approved by the Cardinal Archbishop* . . . (London and Derby, 1883); *190th Thousand. The Explanatory Catechism of Christian Doctrine, Chiefly Intended for the Use of Children in Catholic Schools* . . . (London, 1884); *A Catechism of Christian Doctrine, no. II. Approved by the Cardinal Archbishop* . . . (Manchester, 1887); *A Catechism of Christian Doctrine, no. II. Approved by the Cardinal Archbishop* . . . (London, 1883); G. E. Howe, *The Catechist: or, Headings and Suggestions for the Explanation of the Catechism of Christian Doctrine (No. 2)* . . . (2 vols.; Newcastle-on-Tyne, 1895); *A Catechism of Christian Doctrine, Approved by the Cardinal Archbishop* . . . (London, 1903), etc.   [41] Marron, 'Bishop Challoner', 120.

fact that they continued to be reprinted after the First Vatican Council had declared papal infallibility to be a dogma of the church—contained any reference to this declaration, although they did not go as far as Keenan's Irish catechism, an adoption of the catechism of the Diocese of Montpellier, which until 1870 contained the question and answer: 'Q. Must not Catholics believe the Pope in himself to be infallible? A. This is a Protestant invention.'[42] For a number of years after 1870 the *Controversial Catechism* dropped the question altogether rather than amend its answer: it was not until about 1896 that it inserted: 'Q. What do Catholics believe concerning the Infallibility of the Pope? A. That the visible Head of the Church on earth received from Christ the same prerogative of Infallibility which . . . [belongs] to the Church by divine institution.'[43]

The relevant section of the English catechism, which treats of the ninth article of the Apostles' Creed, ran as follows in the 1859 version:

Q. Has not the Church a visible Head on earth?
A. Yes; the Bishop of Rome, who is vicar of Christ.
Q. Why is the Bishop of Rome the head of the Church?
A. Because he is the successor of St Peter, whom Christ appointed to be head of the Church.
Q. How do you prove that Christ appointed St Peter to be head of the Church?
A. Because he said to him: 'Thou art Peter, and upon this rock I will build my Church, and the gates of hell shall not prevail against it. And to thee I will give the keys of the kingdom of heaven.'
Q. What is the bishop of Rome called?
A. He is called the Pope, which word signifies Father.
Q. Is the Pope our spiritual Father?
A. Yes; he is the spiritual father of all the faithful.[44]

---

[42] S. Keenan, *Controversial Catechism: or, Protestantism Refuted, and Catholicism Established, by an Appeal to Holy Scriptures, the Testimony of the Holy Fathers, and the Dictates of Reason; in which Such Portions of Scheffmacher's Catechism as Suit Modern Controversy are Embodied* (London, Manchester, and Edinburgh, 1854), 112.

[43] S. Keenan and G. Cormack, *Controversial Catechism . . .* (London, New York, etc., 1896), 111.

[44] Where 1859, 1880, and other 'versions' are referred to, the particular revision of the catechism under discussion may be identified by its date of publication. But since it is confusing to refer to variants of the catechism which are not distinguished by separate titles, page references will be given in each case to a single catechism whose distinctive title will make clear which particular 'version' is meant, even if this appeared after its original publication as a *Catechism* or *Abridgement of Christian Doctrine*. In this case, for the text of the 1859 version of the catechism, see *Large Type Edition. Catechism of Christian Doctrine, Approved for the Use of the Faithful, in all the Dioceses of England and Wales* (London and Derby, 1876), 13–14. This edition will be referred to hereafter as the *Large Type Edition*.

So far the 1859 version of the catechism and the later catechisms of *c*.1880 and after were virtually identical. But sandwiched between the last answer and 'Q. Has the Church of Christ any marks by which we may know her?' (question 94 in the later catechisms) came three additional questions (nos. 91–3 in these later catechisms):

91. Is the Pope the Shepherd and Teacher of all Christians?
    The Pope is the Shepherd and Teacher of all Christians, because Christ made St Peter the Shepherd of the whole flock when He said, 'Feed my lambs, feed my sheep.' He also prayed that his 'faith' might never fail, and commanded him to 'confirm' his brethren. *John* xxi. 15, 16, 17; *Luke* xxii. 32.
92. Is the Pope infallible?
    The Pope is infallible.
93. What do you mean when you say that the Pope is infallible?
    When I say that the Pope is infallible, I mean that the Pope can not err when, as Shepherd and Teacher of all Christians, he defines a doctrine concerning faith or morals to be held by the whole Church.[45]

This delay between the definition of infallibility at the First Vatican Council and its incorporation into 'approved' catechisms, a delay of not less than ten years, would appear to indicate a reluctance to adopt the Vatican decrees which goes well beyond that recalcitrance of a few years on the part of a mere handful of the English faithful which has generally been assumed. It was perhaps because of tactful avoidance of the issue in the catechism that England never reached a crisis point like that which led to the breakaway movement of the German, Swiss, and Austrian Old Catholic Churches. Of the English Catholics, even Lord Acton, despite his celebrated reluctance to submit to the newly defined dogma in 1870, never actually became estranged from the Church.[46]

An earlier definition, that of the Immaculate Conception, was accommodated much more quickly in England. Dogmatically defined in 1854, the following questions pertaining to the doctrine appeared in the English penny catechism from 1859 and were kept in later revisions:

Q. Are all mankind conceived in sin?
A. Yes; all mankind, except the Blessed Virgin, who by a special privilege and

---

[45] See e.g. *190th Thousand. The Explanatory Catechism of Christian Doctrine, Chiefly Intended for the Use of Children in Catholic Schools* ... (London, 1884), p. 18. This catechism, which gives the version 1880 and after, will be referred to hereafter as *190th Thousand*.

[46] David Mathew has suggested that Acton's 'faith, perhaps all the more profound for being rather unardent in its temper, passed through these vicissitudes' (D. Mathew, *Catholicism in England* (1936; London, 1948), p. 224).

grace of God, through the merits of her Son, was conceived without the stain of original sin.[47]

But the later versions made this doctrine more explicit with an additional question:

118. What is this privilege of the Blessed Virgin called?
This privilege of the Blessed Virgin is called the Immaculate Conception.[48]

On another point of Marian devotion, a question in the later revision which came under the section concerning the Lord's Prayer subtly strengthened the emphasis on the Hail Mary. The original ran:

Q. Why do we say the Hail Mary so often?
A. To put us in mind of the Incarnation of God the Son, and to honour His blessed Mother.
Q. Why does the Catholic Church show such devotion to the Blessed Virgin?
A. Because she is the Immaculate Mother of God.[49]

By the 1880s the first question had become more specific:

160. What is the chief prayer to the Blessed Virgin which the Church uses?[50]

and question 164 '*Why should* we frequently say the Hail Mary?'[51] replaced '*Why do we*'.[52] A further question was also inserted:

165. Have we another reason for often saying the Hail Mary?
We have another reason for often saying the Hail Mary,—to ask our Blessed Lady to pray for us sinners at all times, but especially at the hour of our death.[53]

Two further questions clarified, but also implicitly increased in importance, Mary's role:

167. How is the Blessed Virgin Mother of God?
The Blessed Virgin is Mother of God because Jesus Christ her Son, who was born of her as man, is not only man but is also truly God.
168. Is the Blessed Virgin our Mother also?
The Blessed Virgin is our Mother also, because being the brethren of Jesus, we are the children of Mary.[54]

It seems significant that, at however long an interval, changes were made to the catechism to incorporate the two most notable, and controversial,

[47] *Large Type Edition*, 18.   [48] *190th Thousand*, 20.
[49] *Large Type Edition*, 24.   [50] *190th Thousand*, 26.   [51] Ibid. 27.
[52] *Large Type Edition*, 24. Here and elsewhere in textual comparisons of different versions of the catechism, the italics are mine.   [53] *190th Thousand*, 27.
[54] Ibid. 28.

decrees of Pius IX's pontificate, the two which would have struck the Protestant majority of England as the most offensive: papal infallibility, and the intercessory role and Immaculate Conception of Mary. The newer catechism of the 1880s also stressed the separateness of the Catholic faith in other ways. An entirely new question under the section concerning the Ten Commandments read:

178. How do we expose ourselves to the danger of losing our Faith?

> We expose ourselves to the danger of losing our Faith by neglecting our spiritual duties, reading bad books, going to non-Catholic schools, and taking part in services or prayers of a false religion.[55]

Similarly, where the 1859 catechism had asked:

Q. And what is the duty of parents and of other superiors?

A. To take proper care of all under their charge, and to bring up their children in the fear of God.[56]

the revised version answered its question 201 with: 'The duty of parents towards their children is to provide for them, to instruct and correct them, and to give them a good Catholic education.'[57] Again, where the 1859 catechism was content to define matrimony as 'a sacrament by which the contract of marriage is blessed and sanctified', with a brief discussion of its special grace when received worthily,[58] the later version emphasized its Catholic exclusiveness with additional questions:

309. What is a 'mixed marriage'?

> A 'mixed marriage' is the marriage between a Catholic and one who, though baptised, does not profess the Catholic faith.

310. Has the Church always forbidden mixed marriages?

> The Church has always forbidden mixed marriages, and considers them unlawful and pernicious.

311. Does the Church sometimes permit mixed marriages?

> The Church sometimes permits mixed marriages, by granting a dispensation, for very grave reasons and under special conditions.[59]

As well as emphasizing the distinct and exclusive character of membership in the Catholic Church, revisions to the catechism also tended to

---

[55] *190th Thousand*, 30.   [56] *Large Type Edition*, 31.   [57] *190th Thousand*, 35.
[58] *Large Type Edition*, 47.
[59] *190th Thousand*, 57. Although the change was not incorporated into the catechism until *c*.1880, the bishops had 'agreed that it would be expedient to insert in the revised edition of the Catechism, after the commandments of the Church, the unlawfulness of mixed marriages, or some explanation of the evils which so frequently result from them' four years earlier. Westminster Archdiocesan Archives, 'Bishops' Meetings 1858–1909', Acta, Meeting of the Bishops in Low Week, 1876, xvi. 100.

tighten what might formerly have been interpreted as the 'optional extras' of devotion into virtual requirements. We have already seen the shift in the treatment of the Hail Mary. Analogous changes of a word here or there changed the tone of the revised catechism to one which was far more prescriptive. Thus '*May* we ask the Saints and Angels to pray for us?'[60] became '*Should* we ask the Saints . . .? We should . . .',[61] and '*Is it allowable* to give [the saints and angels] any kind of honour?'[62] shifted to '*What kind* of honour or worship should we pay to the Angels and Saints?'[63] Similarly, 'And *is it allowable* to honour relics, crucifixes and holy pictures?'[64] became '*What honour* should we give to relics, crucifixes and holy pictures?'[65] The difference in tone between the almost cajoling note of the 1859 catechism and the more bullying one of the later revision may also be seen in the question concerning the sacraments. Thus, in 1859:

Q. Is it a great happiness to receive the sacraments worthily?
A. Yes, it is the greatest happiness in the world.[66]

became, as question 252 in the revised catechism:

Ought we to have a great desire to receive the Sacraments?
We ought . . . because they are the chief means of our Salvation.[67]

Other revisions to the 1859 catechism stressed, or made more explicit, the role of the Church in providing services which were simultaneously becoming more insistently demanded of the faithful. Whereas 'indulgence' had previously been defined as 'a remission of the temporal punishment which often remains due to sin, after its guilt has been forgiven',[68] it now became 'a remission, *granted by the Church*, of the temporal punishment . . .',[69] etc. A new Commandment of the Church made it an obligation 'to contribute to the support of our pastors'.[70] The Church itself, previously revered as the maintainer of all truths,[71] became the 'Ark of Salvation', the emphasis shifting from the treasures housed to the house itself.[72] While these conceits were not novelties in the history of the Church, their cumulative effect, when explicitly chosen to be included in a short text, and one, moreover, which was being learned by rote by an increasingly large proportion of the faithful, was to present the emphasis

[60] *Large Type Edition*, 23.
[61] *190th Thousand*, 26.
[62] *Large Type Edition*, 28.
[63] *190th Thousand*, 31.
[64] *Large Type Edition*, 28.
[65] *190th Thousand*, 32.
[66] *Large Type Edition*, 39.
[67] *190th Thousand*, 45.
[68] *Large Type Edition*, 45.
[69] *190th Thousand*, 54.
[70] Ibid. 35.
[71] *Large Type Edition*, 15.
[72] *190th Thousand*, 17.

of an English Catholic's self-definition in a manner which was far more assertively Catholic.

The most striking effect of the 1880s revisions to the English Catholic reference work of Christian doctrine was to highlight the denominational exclusiveness of membership in the Catholic Church as distinct from the broader Christian fold. In general, more emphasis was placed, in the shape of additional questions, on the sacraments and especially on the Mass. Again, not only was greater importance implied by a more thorough grounding in distinctive features of Catholic faith, such as the doctrine of transubstantiation; but the importance of attending Mass was made still more serious. Although the obligation of hearing Mass had, of course, been included among the Commandments of the Church in earlier versions, the revised catechism of *c*.1880 reiterated this command with an additional question to drive the point home: 'Is it a mortal sin to neglect to hear Mass . . .? It is a mortal sin . . .'.[73]

The distinction drawn between the explicitly Catholic and the more broadly Christian was not always overt, as in discussion of 'mixed' marriages or Catholic schooling, but was also implicit in recommended devotions. As well as emphasizing the sacraments, and especially the Mass, as the most devotional of acts, the catechism included, as part of the Christian's Daily Exercise, 'little indulgenced prayers' which 'you would do well to say often to yourself during the day'.[74] The earlier version had also recommended the recitation of 'little prayers', but without insisting that these be indulgenced.[75] The prayers were different, too. In 1859 the prayers which were recommended might just as easily have been recited by a devout Anglican or Methodist:

O Lord, teach us to do Thy holy will in all things. Lord, keep me from sin. May the Name of our Lord be for ever blessed. Come, my dear Jesus, and take full possession of my soul. Glory be to the Father, and to the Son, and to the Holy Ghost. As it was in the beginning, is now and ever shall be, world without end. Amen.[76]

But the later indulgenced prayers included, along with 'Glory be to the Father . . .' the following recommended prayers:

In all things may the most holy, the most just, and the most lovable will of God be done, praised, and exalted above all for ever.

O Sacrament most holy, O sacrament divine, all praise and all thanksgiving be every moment thine.

[73] *190th Thousand*, 41.   [74] Ibid. 66.   [75] *Large Type Edition*, 58.
[76] Ibid.

Praised be Jesus Christ, praised for evermore.

My Jesus, Mercy; Mary, Help.[77]

These new prayers clearly stressed the importance of the sacrament dispensed by the Church, while at the same time giving Mary nearly as much prominence as her son, the whole expressed in the vivid, simple, and fervent tone of the new Catholic style. That such memorable and direct language was partly devised with working-class readers in mind may be surmised from the introduction of a new question under the eighth commandment in the revised catechism of the 1880s:

218. Is it dishonest in servants to waste their master's time or property?
    It is dishonest in servants to waste their master's time or property because it is wasting what is not their own.[78]

The changes to the 1859 version of the catechism which we have seen would not necessarily strike one immediately. Indeed, they do not seem to have been noticed by historians. If one were to scan the pages of a revised catechism, one might easily overlook reworkings which characteristically took the form of an added clause here or a changed word there, and tended not to intrude on the beginning of sentences. Yet the cumulative effect of such apparently minor revisions was enough to alter significantly the tone and slant of this official presentation of the fundamentals of the Catholic faith as practised and understood in England. Even in the later revisions, after the practice of numbering the questions had been adopted, alterations were carefully introduced so as not to disrupt the numbering. It would appear that those who revised the catechism took care that changes should not be particularly striking. This might reflect a certain self-consciousness at the notion of introducing change in what, as a summary of Christian doctrine, might be imagined to be unchanging and unchangeable. Or it might suggest a sensitivity to the way in which the appearance of change would affect the task—or even the faith in authority—of parents testing their children on the contents of 'the' catechism from their own memory. But it may also indicate a certain canniness on the part of the hierarchy in introducing changes which, if detected, were thought to be unlikely to find favour with at least some Catholics in England.

How can change in the presentation of doctrine over the course of the nineteenth century be accounted for, and why should it have occurred in

---

[77] *190th Thousand*, 66.   [78] Ibid. 38.

so marked a form in about 1880? One might be tempted to explain the phenomenon as an ultramontane subversion of traditional English Catholic teaching. But, if this were so, one would expect revisions, or at least debate on the subject, to have occurred a good ten, and arguably thirty, years earlier than it in fact did. Furthermore, as we have seen, most English bishops at the First Vatican Council were adamant that the English catechism be preserved rather than replaced. In view of the fact that the Roman party at Vatican I was defeated when it tried to impose Bellarmine's catechism on all Catholics, we might wonder whether an ultramontane faction within the English episcopate, thwarted in 1870, later tried to redress the balance by bringing the English catechism into closer conformity with Roman models through the back door. The possible existence of such a faction requires some careful consideration, since disputes and animosities among the English bishops, which have been painstakingly documented in many accounts of the community and in the biographies of individual bishops, were certainly never lacking.

As Edward Norman has pointed out, 'the history of the English Catholic Church in the nineteenth century can appear as an accumulation of disputes'.[79] The division of funds of the old diocese of London into Southwark and Westminster soon after the restoration of the hierarchy soured relations between bishops Thomas Grant and Nicholas Wiseman for the rest of the decade. Ill feeling also remained between Henry Manning and George Errington after the former's institution of the Oblates of St Charles and attempts to 'reform' St Edmund's College. This reform was allegedly proposed over the head of its president, Weathers, through 'a Vice-President with all the untamed enthusiasms of Herbert Vaughan in his youth, and with him two or three other Oblates'.[80] According to tradition, it was this disagreement which culminated in the defeat of Wiseman's *schema* for the government of the ecclesiastical colleges at the third provincial synod held at Oscott in July 1859 and further divided cardinal and bishops from one another. Fresh resentments accumulated during the build-up to, duration, and aftermath of the First Vatican Council. Manning was particularly singled out for blame, and his easy accusations of 'Gallicanism' and 'worldliness' hardly helped to calm tempers or to allay mutual suspicions. The resentments provoked by such rows certainly coloured relations among members of the episcopate throughout the period under discussion. What is not clear, however, is that such disputes, however keenly felt, were ever successful in dividing

[79] Norman, *English Catholic Church*, 2.
[80] Butler, *Life and Times of Ullathorne*, i. 209.

the majority of bishops into clear-cut political camps when it came to deciding matters of devotion and doctrine as opposed to those of jurisdiction or authority.

If anything, it would seem that a good deal of care was taken by the episcopate to ensure that revisions to its devotional and doctrinal texts, *The Garden of the Soul*, the *Manual of Prayers for Congregational Use*, and the penny catechism, should not be the sole work of any single party. After all, the two bishops who were appointed by general consent to undertake the *c.*1880 revision of the catechism were James Brown and Herbert Vaughan. Between them, this pair might be expected to have guaranteed a compromise position since, if one were to assign them party appellations, they would have found themselves at opposite poles. Herbert Vaughan, one of Manning's Oblates, was capable of the kind of invective so characteristic of Manning, as when he wrote to Wiseman in 1857 that Ullathorne, whom he called 'Monsignor *Ego Solus*' behind his back, had revealed his 'true colours' as 'Anglican and Gallican in the strongest way'.[81] Bishop Brown, on the other hand, had a strong aversion to being pushed around by ecclesiastical authority; as he wrote to Ullathorne at the time of the Council: 'I have taken occasion to object to one of the conclusions in his [Manning's] Pastoral. I don't see why the whole Episcopate is to be made a mere empty speaking-trumpet of.'[82] During the Errington case, which Edmund Purcell has summed up as that '. . . prolonged struggle—in which Manning in reality was the prime mover—to deprive Dr Errington of his right of succession to Westminster . . . [and which] symbolised and summed up all the other pending disputes between Cardinal Wiseman, the Chapter, and his suffragan bishops'[83] his allegiances were made clear. When Ullathorne, 'on behalf of the other bishops, visited Rome in support of Dr Errington's cause, and was favourably listened to by Cardinal Barnabò and the Cardinals of Propaganda', he was joined by William Clifford and ' "the two Dr Browns" [Thomas of Newport and James of Shrewsbury, who], as Manning reported to Talbot, took sides with the coadjutor'.[84]

Nor was James Brown an enthusiast for uncritically adopting Roman practices: we have already heard his *cri de cœur*, during episcopal discussions about the *Manual of Prayers for Congregational Use*, that the prayers of *The Garden of the Soul* be retained as the standard for any new and

---

[81] Ibid. i. 236–7.

[82] As cited in S. Leslie, *Henry Edward Manning: His Life and Labours* (London, 1921), 216.

[83] E. S. Purcell, *Life of Cardinal Manning, Archbishop of Westminster* (2 vols.; 1896), ii. 81.

[84] Ibid. 93.

approved collection of prayers. Although Brown was moved from the committee for revising the catechism once the proofs were ready, his place was filled by another moderate, Ullathorne, who was no more likely to find favour with self-styled 'anti-Gallicans' like Manning or Talbot. Even Herbert Vaughan, as we have seen in connection with prayer-book revisions, was reluctant lightly to accept newfangled translations, tending to favour (and not only for pragmatic reasons) the preservation of what 'has been for 300 years',[85] even if thought by some to be tainted with Protestantism.

That the English bishops managed to agree on changes to the catechism despite mutual mistrust over other issues suggests that 'improvements' to the catechism were not seen by most as a party matter. Neither must the changes we have seen necessarily be interpreted as primarily political in significance. After all, for all that many English bishops thought the declaration of papal infallibility to have been inopportune in 1870, most, including Ullathorne and Newman, believed the doctrine to be true. The issue had become so explosive around 1870, through exaggerated interpretations of the doctrine and a mounting polemic which twisted the question into one concerning loyalty towards or betrayal of the papacy, that the English bishops evidently thought it best left alone until tempers and uncharitable suspicions had had time to subside. The speed with which the bishops were willing to incorporate the dogma of the Immaculate Conception, on the other hand, in a climate far less heated than that of *c.*1870, suggests that this doctrine was seen simply as acknowledging reverence to the Virgin Mary. Despite later ultramontane rhetoric, it is hard to see how it could have been meant to express 'obedience' to the Holy See: English bishops were concerned first and foremost with the state of Catholic faith and devotion in England, not with international views of the papacy.

Although the English bishops evidently believed by about 1880 that the catechism should be made more explicitly Catholic and church-centred, it does not follow that they were motivated by ultramontane concerns, let alone attempting to 'obey' Rome. A new question in the revised English catechism of *c.*1880 which condemned secret societies, for example, although apparently in harmony with papal objections to the Freemasons, that *bête noir* of the *Syllabus of Errors* of 1864, was far more likely to have

---

[85] 'Is it desirable to draw a fresh & additional distinction between Catholics & the English people, by declaring, after 300 years, that we can no longer use the same version of the Doxology?' he wondered (Shrewsbury Diocesan Archives, 'Gloria Patri', Vaughan to Knight, 23 December 1884, fo. 2; See Appendix IV for the full text of this letter).

been adopted in England with the Fenians in mind.[86] Rome's tendency to mistrust all rival societies to the Church was treated with greater circumspection by the English bishops, who seem to have considered each case on its individual merits, weighing the dangers to faith in a firmly English context. Edward Bagshawe's determination to exclude Odd Fellows from Catholic membership, for example, was not welcomed by a majority in the English hierarchy, who evidently found the society harmless and stated that, 'as a fact, the exclusion of Members of this Society from the Sacraments has never been enforced'.[87] Similarly, 'As to Catholics becoming members of the "Primrose League", no decision was come to' at the bishops' Low Week meeting in 1884, 'each Bishop being left to his own judgment. But it was held that a Catholic could not make the declaration, as laid before the Meeting, without an explicit and express reservation.'[88]

Changing perceptions of the place of the Catholic community within England do not seem to have turned on party disputes, which could nevertheless be responsible for much unpleasant invective. Nor do they appear to have reflected a straightforward ultramontanism. How then are we to account for their increasingly sectarian emphasis? There seem to be two points worth bearing in mind here. The first is that we might expect a text of purely hierarchical imperatives, composed without input from the laity, to take a more church-centred line than a prayer-book would. The second is that it would be astonishing if that increased stridency which was characteristic of all English denominations from the early nineteenth century should not also have affected official presentations of Catholicism in England. Both points would seem to be borne out by the fact that changes to the catechism which took place well before the restoration of the hierarchy already showed a tendency towards the increasingly church-centred and denominationally specific.

In 1820, a question concerning the humanity of Jesus found '*Q. Was he always man? A. No: but only from his incarnation*'[89] sufficient. The

---

[86] 'Is it sinful to belong to any Secret Society? It is sinful to belong to any Secret Society that plots against Church or State, or to any Society that by reason of its secrecy is condemned by the Church . . .'. This was question no. 204. See e.g. *190th Thousand*, 35.

[87] Westminster Archdiocesan Archives, 'Bishops' Meetings 1858–1909', Acta, Meeting of the Bishops in Low Week, 1883, xxiv. 174.

[88] Ibid. 1884, xxiv. 180. Neither of these societies was, as far as I know, actually secret; nor was either in the business of plotting against Church or State. But their use of ritual and oath-taking would certainly have been held in suspicion in Rome as uncomfortably reminiscent of the Freemasons.

[89] *An Abridgment of Christian Doctrine: or, the First Catechism. Published for the Use of the London District* (London, *c*.1820), p. 7.

revised catechism of 1836, however, added a further question: 'What do
you mean by his incarnation?', in answer to which Mary was now explicitly included: 'A. I mean his assuming human nature when he was conceived and made man, in the womb of the blessed Virgin Mary.'[90] This
1836 revision also gave the pope fuller prominence. In 1820, following on
from the point that the pope is the visible head of the church on earth,
came the question: '*Q. Why is he called the Pope?* A. Because the word
Pope signifies *Father*; and the Bishop of Rome, as the head of the Church
under Jesus Christ, is the common father of all the faithful.'[91] In 1836 the
same matter was broken into three separate questions and answers, as if
to drive the point home:

Q. Why is the Bishop of Rome the head of the Church?
A. Because he is the successor of St Peter, whom Christ appointed to be the head
   of his Church.
Q. What is the Bishop of Rome called?
A. He is called the Pope, which word signifies Father.
Q. Is then the Bishop of Rome our Spiritual Father?
A. Yes: he is the Spiritual Father of all the faithful.[92]

While this 1836 *Abridgment of Christian Doctrine, Revised, Improved, and
Recommended by Authority for the Use of the Faithful in All the Districts of
England* was in turn content with 'Q. Can the Church err in what she
teaches? A. No; she cannot err in matters of faith',[93] the 1859 version
added 'for she is our infallible guide in both'.[94] Similarly, where the 1836
version found 'Q. What is forbidden by [the third commandment]? A.
The third commandment forbids all unnecessary, servile work and sinful
profanation of the Lord's day' sufficient,[95] the next revision added 'Q.
Why are we commanded to rest from work? A. That we may have time
and opportunity for prayer, going to the Sacraments, hearing instructions, and reading good books.'[96] The priest's role in baptism was also
made explicit. The question of 1836 had asked: 'Q. How is baptism
given? A. By pouring water on the child, while we pronounce the words
ordained by Christ.'[97] In 1859 the following was inserted before the question: 'Q. Can no one but a Priest baptize? A. In case of necessity, when

---

[90] *An Abridgment of Christian Doctrine, Revised, Improved, and Recommended by Authority
for the Use of the Faithful in All the Districts of England* (London, 1836), 8–9.
[91] *An Abridgment . . . or, the First Catechism (c.1820)*, 14.
[92] *An Abridgment* (1836), 15–16.   [93] Ibid. 17.
[94] e.g. *Large Type Edition*, 15.   [95] *An Abridgment* (1836), 30.
[96] *Large Type Edition*, 30.   [97] *An Abridgment* (1836), 38.

a Priest cannot be had, any one may baptize.'[98] Finally, the denominationally neutral opening of the 'Christian's Rule of Life' 'Q. Of what religion
are you? A. By the grace of God, I am a Christian'[99] was omitted from
1859 onwards.

Although the shift towards greater denominational distinctiveness was
most marked from about 1880, it was already evident in revisions to the
catechism which took place as early as the 1830s. Plainly, neither the restoration of the hierarchy in 1850 (which post-dated this trend) nor the
declaration of papal infallibility in 1870 (whose dogma it did not seem
opportune to include for ten years) had much to do with the change. A
more plausible explanation may be sought in that general trend towards
denominational assertiveness in England which began in the aftermath of
the French Revolution, and which accelerated sharply from about 1880
because of heightened perceptions of 'leakage' and dechristianization.[100]

The trend towards Catholic exclusiveness which was reflected in subsequent revisions to the penny catechism was not welcomed by all English Catholics. Some evidently felt that the later changes went further
than simply to press doctrinal and devotional differences with other Christians. What seemed to some laymen to be going too far was the tendency
of bishops to restrict the social freedom of Catholics, advocating their
literal separation from the rest of society through independent schooling,
reading matter, and family life. 'Our law did not say—do not look on a
woman, because it leads to danger of adultery; but to look with lust is
adultery,' scribbled Richard Simpson in the back of a notebook, probably
in the 1870s: 'It was a new definition of the extent of the law, not a
margin added to it to guard against the danger of the breach.' But, he
went on to complain,

this power . . . saying, not only 'all occasions of sin are to be avoided', but 'this &
that are occasions of sin, so often & so generally that they are forbidden to all' is
now claimed by the ecclesiastical authorities. Don't go to Oxford, or you will lose
your faith; don't be educated in mixed schools, it is an occasion of losing your
religion; don't intermarry with people of other religions, it is an occasion of
dishonouring God—They do not push on the law, extend it, but they add other
laws to it, as margins to prevent it [?straying] out & hedges to protect it. They do
not (they cannot define) to go to Oxford is to lose faith, whoso[ever] goes to a
mixed school is irreligious, whoso[ever] marries a Protestant dishonours God—
But they say, whoso[ever] does these things runs into such danger of committing
the sins, that these things may & must be generally forbidden. And thus new laws

---

[98] *Large Type Edition*, 39.   [99] *An Abridgment* (1836), 50.
[100] This shift will be examined in more detail in the next chapter.

are made, which themselves will in time require their own hedges & fences—We shall be forbidden to go within five miles of Oxford, or to pass through a street where there is a mixed school, or to dance or dine with a young person of the other sex.[101]

Other educated laymen echoed Simpson's frustration; and Newman was particularly noted for railing against what seemed an absurd episcopal over-sensitivity to the 'contaminating' influences of the Protestants, particularly in the matter of education. But, despite the occasional complaints, it seems likely that many humble Catholics were persuaded of the episcopal point of view, while others waited patiently for the tide to turn. As Cuthbert Butler wrote with feeling,

in no part of the world could there be found a more staunchly Catholic, loyal, devoted and devout, and long-suffering body of educated Catholic laymen than the English Catholics of the 'sixties, old Catholics and converts alike; and they had to suffer long in this matter of university education for the ideas of their ecclesiastical leaders.[102]

Although some laypeople evidently found the new stress on Catholic exclusiveness a troubling departure from tradition, the English bishops at least appear to have agreed upon its importance. In their struggle to maintain control over the transmission of the Faith in the face of fierce denominational competition and the perceived threat of widespread religious ignorance and indifference, it is not surprising that the hierarchy should have insisted upon the authority and distinctiveness of the Church with new zeal. But cumulative textual changes to the catechism, for all that they projected an increasingly sectarian image, were not ultramontane in the sense of slavishly following Roman imperatives. Nor were they the work of an ultramontane contingent within the English hierarchy, since the bishops were careful to protect this delicate area of the transmission of doctrine from overtly party prejudices. Rather, the majority of bishops, and with particular vehemence from about 1880, evidently felt that the protection of Catholics from unedifying outside influences was the necessary prerequisite to their salvation. How social and devotional conceptions of Catholicism came thus to be increasingly linked, and how far the goal of Catholic separation from 'the world' was attained, may best be seen, perhaps, through an examination of those societies deliberately intended to promote the development of a Catholic world within England: guilds, sodalities, and confraternities. It is to these societies that we will now turn.

---

[101] Downside Abbey Archives, Richard Simpson MSS, undated jottings in Notebook 8 entitled 'Shakespeare', fos. 9–10.   [102] Butler, *Life and Times of Ullathorne*, ii. 39.

Remarkably little is known about Catholic societies in the nineteenth and early twentieth centuries. Despite some scholarly advances in the shape of work on the Society of St Vincent de Paul,[103] and Hugh McLeod's stimulating comparative study of the role of nineteenth-century Catholic organizations in places as diverse as the Netherlands, Germany, the United States, Switzerland, Belgium, Austria, France, and Great Britain,[104] relatively little progress has been made since Sheridan Gilley pointed out in 1977 that the history of the 'the significant range of . . . Catholic institutions with a social purpose' has yet to be written.[105] Adequate justice cannot be done in a few pages to a subject which deserves the attention of a book to itself; this brief discussion will nevertheless attempt to explore the social and devotional implications of the increased prominence of exclusively Catholic sodalities, guilds, and confraternities within England.

That Catholic societies of one kind or another were established in most of the dioceses of England and Wales by about 1865, and throughout the country by 1880, may be confirmed by an examination of Table 1 in Appendix I to this work. A more detailed examination of the *Catholic Directory* reveals that, by the same date, virtually every Catholic church in England had some sort of society attached to it, and often several. Patterns of church advertisements[106] would seem to indicate that Catholic societies were formed partly in response to changing church needs as identified by the hierarchy. Thus from roughly 1850 to 1860 societies which aimed to provide basic services like catechizing for newly founded churches were widely established,[107] while over the next two decades

[103] B. Aspinwall, 'The Welfare State within the State: The Saint Vincent de Paul Society in Glasgow, 1848–1920', in W. J. Sheils and D. Wood (eds.), *Voluntary Religion* (Studies in Church History 23; London, 1986), 445–59. See also J. Davies, 'Parish Charity: The Work of the Society of St Vincent de Paul, St Mary's, Highfield St, Liverpool, 1867–1868', *North West Catholic History*, 17 (1990), 37–46.

[104] H. McLeod, 'Building the "Catholic Ghetto": Catholic Organisations 1870–1914', in Sheils and Wood (eds.), *Voluntary Religion*, 411–44.

[105] S. W. Gilley, 'Papists, Protestants and the Irish in London, 1835–70', in G. J. Cuming and D. Baker (eds.), *Popular Belief and Practice* (Studies in Church History 8; Cambridge, 1972), 266.

[106] See also Appendix V to this work, which gives a chronological list of all guilds, confraternities, and sodalities attached to churches in England and Wales for the same sample of years as those taken for the statistics of devotions which are given in Appendices I and II, i.e. every fifth year from 1850 to 1914.

[107] This service was provided by the Confraternity of Christian Doctrine, which was first established in 1852. By 1855 the confraternity was well represented in Salford, Westminster, and Shrewsbury dioceses; by 1860 it had spread to Southwark and Beverley as well; and by 1865 had also reached Hexham and Newcastle and Liverpool. See Table 1, Devotional statistics of the churches, chapels, and stations in England and Wales, 1850–1914, in Appendix I to this work.

there was a marked increase in devotional societies proper, of groups such as the Sodality of the Children of Mary and the Apostleship of Prayer. From the 1870s and 1880s societies which were designed to provide Catholics with denominationally specific clubs or services, like various young men's guilds and young women's societies, became a marked feature of diocesan development.

But while broad hierarchical concerns and emphases may be detected in the functions of some of the confraternities adopted by or created in England, the presence of most cannot be accounted for so simply. Neither does the mere fact that Catholic societies became widespread in England give much insight into their actual importance. As Ralph Gibson has pointed out, in contemporary France nineteenth-century confraternities such as those of the Rosary, Scapular, Blessed Sacrament, and Sacred Heart, although 'set up by the clergy in most parishes . . . do not . . . tell us very much about a possible nucleus of fervent Christians'. These societies, Gibson has found, 'Despite the fact that the obligations of membership were scarcely onerous . . . often existed on paper only, and had to be periodically revived by clerical initiative.'[108] Furthermore, 'Where membership lists survive and bear witness to their activity, they suggest that young people were enrolled *en masse* by the *curé* after their first communion, or pushed and prodded into signing up at a later date.' According to Gibson, 'where they did function, they seem to have been not so much organizations of religious fervour as centres of female sociability'.[109]

Such a dismissive approach might, at first sight, seem to be warranted in the English case as well. Hugh McLeod has found that 'membership of confraternities tended to be low', at least among the London-based societies for boys and young men which he examined.[110] Caution should be exercised before presuming a direct parallel with the French situation, however. The Confraternity of the Living Rosary at St Peter's, Lytham, which was launched by the parish priest in 1856, for example, was still managing to attract thirty-seven rosary circles of about thirty members each in 1875,[111] and the Confraternity of the Sacred Heart was similarly able to appeal to 364 members in the same year.[112] Since Sacred Heart devotions, which came to be included in most English prayer-books, were evidently practised by a significant minority of Catholics, the fact that

[108] R. Gibson, *A Social History of French Catholicism 1789–1914* (London, 1989), 168.
[109] Ibid. [110] McLeod, 'Building the "Catholic Ghetto"', 420.
[111] Lancashire Record Office, The Bishop of Lancaster, RCLy 7/13, 'Circle Lists of the Confraternity of the Living Rosary, 6 June 1875'.
[112] Ibid. RCLy 7/14, 'Roll of Members of the Confraternity of the Sacred Heart of Jesus, 6 June 1875'.

devotions 'for a happy death' (which it was the business of the Bona Mors Confraternity to promote) were similarly included, and often advertised in the *Catholic Directory* by individual churches as well,[113] would seem to indicate a grass-roots appeal for at least some devotional confraternities.

The deep and complex question of possible differences between 'male' and 'female' piety lies beyond the scope of this work. But, in England at least, while women appear to have participated in confraternities in higher proportions than men did, societies which were open to both sexes and which have left membership lists, like those of the Rosary and of the Sacred Heart at St Peter's, Lytham,[114] were not exclusively feminine in membership. Women, who were generally responsible for transmitting the Faith to children, whether as mothers, nuns, or lay teachers, seem to have been disproportionately prominent in every aspect of Catholic practice, from attendance at church services to participation in extra-liturgical devotions and enrolment in devotional societies. Since men, albeit in smaller numbers, were also involved in all of these activities, it seems to me that one can justifiably speak of Catholic rather than of gender-linked piety.

Although some Catholic societies varied in popularity from parish to parish, others were evidently important to Catholics throughout the country. The French-inspired laymen's society of St Vincent de Paul (SVP), first brought to England in 1844, and which had come to be well represented in every diocese in the country by 1880,[115] merited specific mention in at least one edition of *The Garden of the Soul*. This included familiar prayers like the Our Father, Hail Mary, creed, and doxology as opening 'Prayers for the Conference of St Vincent de Paul' to be 'used at the weekly meetings'.[116] Closing prayers were specifically tailored for the SVP:

---

[113] In 1870, for example, churches in Liverpool, Northampton, Nottingham, and Westminster explicitly advertised the devotion.

[114] Lancashire Record Office, The Bishop of Lancaster, RCLy 7/13, 'Circle Lists of the Confraternity of the Living Rosary' and 'Roll of Members of the Confraternity of the Sacred Heart of Jesus', RCLy 7/14, 6 June 1875.

[115] The SVP was already well represented in Salford, Hexham and Newcastle, and Westminster dioceses by the 1860s, but expanded markedly over the next twenty years. By 1880 Westminster archdiocese could boast thirty-three branches of the society, Birmingham diocese eight, Clifton four, Hexham and Newcastle seven, Leeds two, Liverpool twenty-four, Middlesbrough two, Northampton one, Nottingham three, Plymouth two, Salford four, Shrewsbury one, and Southwark seven. See *The Catholic Directory* (London, 1880), 98–237.

[116] [R. Challoner], *The Garden of the Soul: A Manual of Spiritual Exercises, in Which are Included Many Devotions of Recent Practice, and Approved of by the Church* (London: R. Washbourne, 1877), 397.

Most Gracious Jesus, who didst raise up blessed Vincent for an apostle of the most ardent charity in thy Church, pour forth upon thy servants that same fervour of charity, that for the love of thee they may with a most ready heart bestow their good upon the poor, and spend themselves for their souls.[117]

At St Chad's cathedral in Birmingham, where the society had been established in 1865 by Bishop Ullathorne, members were continuing to meet once a week at least as late as 1904.[118]

Membership in the Sodality of the Children of Mary came to be an equally common experience for Catholic girls as membership of the SVP was for adults of both sexes. The confraternity was already well represented in Lancashire by 1875, where at least four parishes in the diocese could boast branches.[119] While Catholic circles in Lancashire may have been especially 'devout',[120] the fact that the Children of Mary were invariably represented at Catholic processions and on grand occasions throughout the country suggests that they had a much wider national appeal. At St Chad's in Birmingham by 1904 the Children of Mary processed in honour of the Blessed Virgin once a month,[121] and St Peter and All Souls church in Peterborough thought the confraternity important enough to add a special chapel for its members in 1909.[122] Recalling the Catholic processions of her girlhood in Southwark which were 'really lovely because no matter how hard up people were, they would really dress their kids up for that', even a non-Catholic like Alice Ivison knew that 'some used to have blue dresses and white, and they were called Children of Mary'.[123]

While no doubt providing a place for Catholic girls to meet and talk,

[117] An additional prayer 'for benefactors' begged: 'Vouchsafe, we beseech thee, most tender Jesus, thy grace to the benefactors of the poor who hast promised a hundredfold and a heavenly kingdom to them that do works of mercy in thy name. R. Amen' (ibid. 398).

[118] Anon., *A History of St Chad's Cathedral Birmingham 1841–1904: Compiled by the Cathedral Clergy* (Birmingham, 1904), 131.

[119] See *The Catholic Directory* (London, 1875), 191–9.

[120] See W. J. Lowe, 'The Lancashire Irish and the Catholic Church, 1846–1871: The Social Dimension', *Irish Historical Studies*, 20 (1976), 129–55. Mrs Julien, born in Cheshire in 1920, thought that 'English Catholic devotion in the North—especially Lancs—was intense from all I ever heard in my childhood' and remembered that 'There was still deep devotion when I lived there in 1928–1933', at which time the headmistress of her school 'encouraged all her pupils to receive Holy Communion daily if possible; weekly if not' (letter from Mrs F. Julien to the present writer, 12 Mar. 1990).

[121] Anon., *History of St Chad's*, 133.

[122] D. Cary-Elwes, 'Catholic Peterborough, Past and Present', *St Francis' Magazine*, NS 49 (1921), 141.

[123] P. Schweitzer and C. Wegner (eds.), *On the River: Memories of a Working River* (London, 1989), 40.

there is no reason to suppose that the society's aims 'to fly from evil, to advance in Christian piety, in probity of life, and in the practice of the duties of their state'[124] were not taken seriously. Aspiring members could not join until they had at least made their First Communion, had been in the Sodality as aspirants for a minimum of three months, and had 'given proof of true piety and devotion'.[125] Once enrolled, they were expected to say morning and evening prayers, recite their rosary and go to Mass (every day if possible), to confess their sins, to take communion weekly,[126] and to go on a retreat of at least four days every year.[127] Again, among that select minority of Catholics who became famed as stigmatics or visionaries, and whose lives have consequently been documented in pious biographies, several seem to have belonged to the Tertiaries of St Francis.[128] While this fact may simply indicate that Catholics of a particularly pious bent tended both to be attracted by this quasi-monastic institution and to be susceptible to visions, it is just as likely to reflect a more general membership which happens not to have been documented in the case of less-celebrated lay Catholics.

Since at least some confraternities appear to have held a genuine appeal for many Catholics, their range of function and, above all, their common spirit seem worth exploring in more depth. What may at first seem a bewildering variety of objects and function among Catholic confraternities, sodalities, and guilds of the period might for convenience be classified into three groups. A first kind competed directly with non-Catholic or secular social clubs, like the Boys' and the Girls' guilds, created from around 1870 as rivals to Protestant boys' and girls' clubs, or the Confraternity of Christian Mothers, which similarly targeted a particular sub-group within the community for social interaction and solidarity. A number of men's societies and confraternities also aimed to promote social intercourse among Catholic men. Groups for working men, young men, young women, unmarried women, Catholic married women, and

---

[124] *The Child of Mary's Little Handbook: A Manual of the Rule, Ritual and Devotion for the Use of Sodalities of Children of Mary affiliated to the Primaria, or Arch-Sodality, of the Immaculate Virgin and of St Agnes* (London, 1901), 25.   [125] Ibid. 29.

[126] 'If not once a week, then once a fortnight; but never less than once a month' (ibid. 39).

[127] Ibid. 40.

[128] As well as being the case with various continental visionaries and ecstatics, this was also true of Lancashire Catholic and stigmatic Teresa Higginson (see A. M. O'Sullivan, *Teresa Higginson the Servant of God: School Teacher 1845–1905* (London, 1924), 189) and American visionary Adele Brice (A. Taves, *The Household of Faith: Roman Catholic Devotions in Mid-Nineteenth-Century America* (Notre Dame, Ind., 1986), 101). Ralph Gibson has found that tertiaries were 'a standard feature of the more religious parts of rural France' (Gibson, *Social History*, 107).

children covered every conceivable state of a Catholic's life and enabled
him or her easily to find a social niche amongst like-minded Catholics.[129]

Other confraternities targeted specific good causes within the Catholic
community, such as the Converts' Aid Society, set up 'for erstwhile
Tractarian parsons',[130] the League of English Martyrs of the 1890s which
aimed 'to assist convert clergyman and others', and which met with the
warm approbation of the English bishops in 1894;[131] or the Immaculate
Conception Charity 'for the protection of poor children whose faith or
morals are in danger'.[132] Night Refuges set up for 'Men, Women, and
Children of Good Character', started in the 1860s as the 'Night Refuge
for Women of Good Character', and numerous temperance societies,
such as the Temperance Guild of Our Lady and St John the Baptist or
the Temperance Guild of St Patrick, also fall into this category.

The particularly widespread society of St Vincent de Paul, which
aimed to relieve the sick poor, feed the hungry, and bury the destitute
dead, but had substantial latitude to undertake other charitable works,[133]
also brought together Catholics who might not otherwise have met. As
Lady Georgiana Fullerton wrote warmly to Lady Herbert of Lea upon
the latter's conversion to Catholicism in 1866: 'It gave me great pleasure
to hear that you were affiliated to the Sisters of St Vincent of Paul. So
have I been for the last three years, and I am happy to think we shall have
a common object of interest.'[134] Other societies were created to supply

---

[129] e.g. The 'Young Men's Society', started at Our Lady's, Birkenhead in 1859 (E. M.
Abbott, 'The Foundation of Our Lady's, Birkenhead', *North West Catholic History*, 18
(1991), 14); 'The Men's Sodality' at St Chad's, founded in 1901 (anon., *History of St
Chad's*, 132–3); the 'Catholic Boys' Brigade', 'Catholic Women's League', 'Catholic Young
Men's Society', etc., among the societies listed at Newcastle in 1911 (anon., *The Second
National Congress, Newcastle Upon Tyne, 4th–8th August, 1911. Handbook and Souvenir*
(Newcastle, 1911), 89). That such societies had been started at Newcastle long before is
evident from references to the 'Young Men's Society', etc., in Notice Books from as early
as 1854 (Hexham and Newcastle Diocesan Archives, 'Notice Books 1854–1856', Wednesday, ? Sept. 1854). See Appendix V to this work for the full range of such societies.

[130] R. K. Donovan, 'The Denominational Character of English Catholic Charitable
Effort, 1800–1865', *Catholic Historical Review*, 62 (1976), 211.

[131] Westminster Archdiocesan Archives, 'Bishops' Meetings 1858–1909', Acta, Meeting
of the Bishops in Low Week, 1894, xix. 267.

[132] Southwark Archdiocesan Archives, file J89, pamphlet entitled 'Immaculate Conception Charity' (n.d.; pre-1900), 1.

[133] See e.g. Birmingham Archdiocesan Archives, 'St Chad's Cathedral Records', 13 (29
Sept.–31 Dec. 1880) 'Regulations of the Confraternity of St Vincent de Paul, as it is
Established in Birmingham' (1843), insert between fos. 10–11, which reminded members
that 'as the object of the Confraternity is to do as much good as possible . . . however
carefully rules for such an institution may be drawn up, they will necessarily want modify-
ing and changing with the irresistible change of circumstances'.

[134] As cited in anon., *The Inner Life of Lady Georgiana Fullerton* (London, 1899), 56–7.

poor Catholics with a library of 'good books'[135] or of sound clothing, like the 'Catholic Clothing Club' at Newcastle which was undertaken by 'several ladies' in 1867, and which proposed that aspiring 'members may deposit any sum from 1*d.* to 2*d.* per week. This will help parents, ['servants' crossed out] &c. to lay by during the year in small sums [a] sum that will procure for them & their children warm & useful clothing.'[136] Such groups also included societies whose purpose was to raise money for church provisions or functions, such as various altar societies, church choir guilds, and embroidery and needlework guilds.

A last broad category of Catholic societies is composed of those which were devotional societies strictly speaking, and which included, although they were not restricted to, many French and Italian, as well as German and international models. These societies had as their object the promotion of certain kinds of prayer or devotional action, or of a particular way of life, and were often associated with a pre-existing religious order. The Third Order of St Francis enabled laypeople to participate as nearly in the Franciscan monastic tradition as was compatible with life in the world. Members of the Order, also known as Tertiaries, took solemn vows of chastity and poverty, but these were not strictly binding and were renewable at intervals of a year. In his preface of 1893 to a manual and rule-book of the sodality, Herbert Vaughan assured aspiring Franciscan tertiaries that, however, undemanding the rules of membership might seem, 'If they are faithfully and fervently observed, simple as they are, they will certainly lead the soul to a high perfection.' As an illustrative example, Vaughan pointed to

the third Rule, which prescribes grace before and after meals. To say grace devoutly seems a little thing. It is treated by many as insignificant and below their notice. Look at Catholics in all conditions of society. How few regularly make the sign of the cross and say their grace before and after meals! Some neglect doing so from human respect; they are afraid of being noticed by non-Catholics; others from want of recollection, others from being in a sad state of indifference. Yet here is a simple little practice by which Catholics may make open profession of faith and give good example without offence. Who knows but that they might incline Protestants towards the true religion by this practice?[137]

---

[135] See e.g. a parish notice like that at St Mary's, Newcastle, which advertised in 1867 that 'The library will be open for the circulation of books this evening after vespers' (Hexham and Newcastle Diocesan Archives, 'Notice Books 1867–1871', 8 Dec. 1867, 6).

[136] Hexham and Newcastle Diocesan Archives, 'Notice Books 1867–1871', 8 Dec. 1867, 5.

[137] H. Vaughan, Preface (1893) to *Franciscan Tertiary Manual* . . . (Pantasaph, 1904), pp. xii–xiii.

Tertiaries, who were entitled to wear the scapular, or symbolic yoke, of the Order, chose a way of life intermediate in its religious intensity between that of the full Franciscan and that of an ordinary Catholic layman. Lady Georgiana Fullerton, who joined the Third Order of St Francis in 1857, certainly took her vows seriously: 'Behold now is the accepted time, behold now is the day of salvation,' she wrote, on the eve of her joining:

To-morrow morning, the anniversary of my beloved child's last Communion, I am to be admitted into the Third Order of St Francis, and I firmly purpose and intend, by God's grace, that it be the beginning of a new life, strictly dedicated to God and to His service.[138]

Similar lay organizations were also catered for by the Carmelites and the Dominicans, and by religious confraternities such as the Apostleship of Prayer, for whose *Almanac of the Apostleship* Lady Georgiana Fullerton composed a poem in 1890,[139] but which disappointed a parish priest in the diocese of Hexham and Newcastle by leaving his own congregation cold.[140]

Although the three loose classifications outlined account for the aims and activities of Victorian Catholic confraternities, sodalities, and guilds, divisions were not so sharp in practice. Rather, a broader perception of devotion which was increasingly held in common tended to undercut ostensible differences of function. Gibson has implied that those few confraternities in France which managed to be successful were those which served an almost purely social function, however sanguine priests may have been that they would increase devotion. Not only do many confraternities in England seem to have been more popular than Gibson has found their French counterparts to have been, but the distinction which he draws between the 'social' and the 'devotional' seems a misleadingly anachronistic one. As Robert Donovan has pointed out, 'philanthropy, defense, and proselytizing were not separated'[141] in the minds of the promoters of Catholic charities in England, and the same might be said of advocates of ostensibly other-worldly devotional societies.

By far the largest number of English Catholic societies of the period mixed the three functions which have been outlined, blending the explicitly

---

[138] This was on 4 May 1857. Anon., *The Inner Life*, 43.   [139] Ibid. 103.

[140] The parish priest of the Church of the Sacred Heart and English Martyrs at Thornley filled out his visitation return of 1911 as follows: '6. Confraternities. *a.* name of each? Apostleship Prayer. *b.* Is it canonically established? yes. *c.* does it flourish? no' (Hexham and Newcastle Diocesan Archives, 'Visitation Papers', 'Thornley', 28 May 1911).

[141] Donovan, 'Denominational Character', 208.

devotional with either the socially useful or the pleasantly sociable. The Young Men's Society at Our Lady's, Birkenhead, which had been established in the diocese in 1859, set aside specially reserved times for confession,[142] and notices like that of October 1859 that 'Members of the Y.M.S. will attend at the funeral of their brother . . . [and] will wear crosses, but with black ribbons'[143] or of February 1863 that members 'must all be in the school room at 2 for the funeral of Michael Riley'[144] became a feature of parish life. In 1866 members of the society were taken on an excursion to Holywell, where it was hoped that they would 'conduct themselves in a becoming manner to repair in some way the scandal given there on former occasions'.[145]

A similar blend may be seen in the temperance society known as the Association of the Cross, which held the social aim of encouraging Catholic men to take a pledge of moderate drinking, but did so in vividly religious terms which had devotional implications. Aspiring members presented themselves at a special monthly Mass where they took an oath by God's help 'never to misuse intoxicating drinks; but on the contrary, to use them very sparingly, and even to endeavour, if I can do so without injury to my health, to abstain from them altogether'.[146] Praying to Mary 'to present this my resolution to the Father of Mercies and God of all consolation, and to obtain for me the grace to be ever faithful to it',[147] they knelt to receive a two-and-a-half foot wooden cross from the hands of the priest. This cross, which the new member vowed to 'embrace . . . as the Standard, the Emblem, and the Christian principle of the privation which I impose upon myself, and upon all those who are dependent upon me', was taken home after the service, to be presented to the man's wife and children in the same way. It was then to be placed 'in a conspicuous part of the chief room of the house, where, according to the rule of the Association, it should remain 'to remind the family . . . of the resolution it has taken to make a special practice of the virtue of Temperance . . . [and] to practise the Christian virtues of which the Cross is the fruitful source'. Obligations of membership included the daily recitation, by a member of the family at the foot of the wooden cross, of five Our Fathers and five Hail Marys for the intention of the Five Wounds of Our Lord and for the

---

[142] This was on some Saturdays from 2 to 9 o'clock (E. M. Abbott, 'History of Our Lady's—Birkenhead', unpublished manuscript kindly lent by the author, 1991, fo. 8).

[143] Ibid., fos. 8–9. See also Abbott, 'The Foundation of Our Lady's', 14.

[144] Abbott, 'History of Our Lady's', fo. 9; 'The Foundation of Our Lady's', 14.

[145] Abbott, 'History of Our Lady's', fo. 11.

[146] Southwark Archdiocesan Archives, file J89, 'Constitution of The Temperance Society of the Cross' (n.d.; pre-1900), 2.　　　　[147] Ibid.

spiritual benefit of all the members of the society.[148] Thus a society specifically created to combat a particular social evil—that of alcoholism—was also the means of spreading the unrelated practice of saying particular prayers, contemplating the five wounds of Jesus, and of having a tangible sign of denominational allegiance prominently displayed in the home.[149]

Even a society as apparently restricted in function as the altar society at St Chad's, Birmingham, whose primary purpose was to make linen cloths, albs, and other articles for liturgical use, dedicated itself to the Blessed Sacrament and decided also to undertake a charitable work by providing clothing for the poor of the parish.[150] This mixing of the practical and other-worldly, which made such a strong appeal to English conceptions of piety, may be seen most vividly perhaps in the enthusiastic reception which was given to the Society of St Vincent de Paul and of the philosophy which underpinned it. Indeed, this society, whose founder saw the alleviation of the poor as a means to a devotional end, that of Catholic charity in the giver and Catholic holiness in the recipient,[151] was brought to England by former Quaker and editor of the *Tablet* Frederick Lucas as a sort of Catholic antidote to 'the "Protestant" Poor Laws' which he 'contrasted . . . to medieval charity where men "made themselves familiar with wretchedness, and by personal sympathy, no less than pecuniary aid, strove to mitigate the sufferings under which the afflicted were bowed down"'.[152]

Other confraternities which made an appeal to the English shared this conception of *caritas*: Franciscan tertiaries, for example, were similarly expected to practise poverty themselves, and to empathize with Catholics of all states of life through the common pursuit of an ideal of spiritual perfection. Renewing the more *ad hoc* vow which she had made nineteen

[148] Southwark Archdiocesan Archives, file J89, 'Constitution of The Temperance Society of the Cross' (n.d.; pre-1900), 2.

[149] The president of the Catholic Total Abstinence League of the Cross at Our Lady's, Birkenhead insisted that the pledge be given only on Wednesday evenings at 7.30 p.m. so that members could also benefit from Public Rosary, Instruction, and Benediction, which were offered beforehand. See E. M. Abbott, 'Our Lady's, Birkenhead: Growth, Destruction, Resurgence and Renewal', *North West Catholic History*, 19 (1992), 48.

[150] Birmingham Archdiocesan Archives, St Chad's Cathedral Archives, 'St Chad's Confraternity of the Blessed Sacrament', Altar Society Minute Book, 14 Nov. 1867–11 Nov. 1895, 18 May 1868.

[151] As Donovan reports, the founder of the Society, Frédéric Ozanam, made explicit that, for all its works of relief, 'Notre but principal . . . ne fut pas de venir en aide au pauvre, non; ce ne fut là pour nous qu'un moyen. Notre but fut de nous maintenir fermes dans la foi catholique et de la propager chez les autres par le moyen de la charité' (Donovan, 'Denominational Character', 205).   [152] Ibid. 206.

months before with the consent of F. W. Faber, who acted as her spiritual director, Lady Georgiana Fullerton made a further and 'firm resolution' in 1857 to

practise poverty in every way in my power . . . To try not to allow in myself anything that I am not obliged to, that would be unbecoming in a religious . . . I will try, as the rule directs, to keep to two meals a day. If I take anything else, to let it be only a bit of dry bread . . . To make a careful and attentive study of my rule, observing every point of it keeping to the spirit, if I cannot to the letter, examining myself upon it, and noting down my transgressions. I will make my meditation to-morrow on the Five Wounds of Our Lord, with ardent prayers to St Francis to obtain for me the five virtues of humility, obedience, mortification, love of poverty, and patience.[153]

That there should have been a good deal of overlap and similarity between societies ostensibly this-worldly and other-worldly should not surprise us in view of the widespread attempts to bring religious earnestness or devotion into the lives of ordinary Catholics. We have already seen how a mixture of the worldly and unworldly was tolerated, and even encouraged, in approaches to Benediction, the rosary, and the *Memorare*. Even what have been called 'strictly devotional' societies were the spiritual equivalents of temporal mutual assistance societies, and operated along analogous lines. Just as burial guilds functioned as friendly societies, the weekly contributions of each member going to create an insurance fund which could be tapped by members in the event of a death in the family, so devotional societies took as contributions the prayers of their members, supernatural credit which could be stored for the moment of death and judgement. Similarly, indulgences, which reduced the amount of temporal punishment due to sin by an agreed number of days, could sometimes be spread among members who performed set devotions. Thus the members of the Living Rosary acquired both the spiritual benefits due to their individual performance in the recitation, and those indulgences due to the group as a whole, each member taking the credit, so to speak, for the combined actions of the full confraternity. Such attractive rates of spiritual interest could only be acquired through a collaboration with other Catholics.

The more devout an individual Catholic aspired to be, the more he was thrown back into the company of other Catholics. To join a purely this-worldly organization, such as a mutual benefit society or a boys' club, a Catholic was usually given some Catholic prayers to recite, and was, at

[153] Anon., *The Inner Life*, 43–4.

the very least, nominally under the patronage of a particular saint, or of a divine or Marian attribute. Were he to aspire to a more spiritually ambitious role, choosing to share the yoke of the Franciscans or to join in the Apostleship of Prayer, he was restricted by the rules of his chosen devotional society. Thus the spiritual life of the nineteenth-century Catholic was increasingly bound up with his social role within the wider Catholic community, not only through his church, school, hospital, and at times of socially recognized importance such as his birth, marriage, and death, but also in his leisure hours, his insurance policies, and in the direction of his spiritual growth.

5
An English Piety

ASSUMPTIONS about the nature of the English Catholic community have hidden the subject of devotion from direct scholarly attention and prejudged the significance of devotional change in the nineteenth century. The preceding chapters have shown how devotion, far from exacerbating differences between Irish and English, old Catholics and converts, ultramontanes and liberals, effectively provided a common language to articulate that specifically religious dimension of life which was shared by Catholics as Catholics. In its accommodation of the piety of the humble and illiterate, its sentimentality and simplicity of expression, and above all its revivalist tendencies, this new English spirituality had a good deal in common with contemporary Catholic developments abroad. But Catholic devotion in nineteenth- and twentieth-century England was not primarily characterized by an importation of popular Italian manifestations or the straightforward implementation of Roman imperatives. Just as Marian apparitions were almost entirely confined to France in the period, and cults surrounding bleeding statues were restricted to southern Italy, so English Catholic piety manifested itself in ways which may have been influenced by, but were distinct from, those of neighbouring Catholic countries.

The Catholic revival in nineteenth-century England was just that: the attempted renewal and vigorous reappropriation of a distinctive religious outlook among Catholics, both nominal and practising, living in England. But, despite second-spring propaganda, which held that the faith had been virtually lost during the penal years, and the ultramontane charge that the recusants' faith was tainted or incomplete, it was an invigorated English recusant tradition, not a Roman one, which was most successful in capturing the imagination of Catholics living in England from the middle of the nineteenth century to the early years of the twentieth. This tradition was not reproduced exactly, but was filtered through contemporary idiom and made both more attractive and more accessible to what had come to be a majority of uneducated and poor members within the community. Thus the longer litanies and prayers from the eighteenth-century *Garden of the Soul* were replaced with shorter, more sentimental ones which were in better keeping with Victorian taste; and simple approaches to devotions and prayers were not only tolerated from Irish proletarians but positively encouraged among English aristocrats as well.

For all the romantic longing for a feudal England which Augustus Welby Pugin or Ambrose Phillipps de Lisle might express, for all Wiseman's love of Roman forms, or the dogmatic insistence of W. G. Ward or Henry Edward Manning that orthodoxy lay only in the exact imitation of Rome, English Catholicism did not in fact become 'more Roman than Rome' after the restoration of the hierarchy in 1850. It was Challoner's rather than Bellarmine's catechism which was reissued throughout the nineteenth and early twentieth centuries, to be memorized by increasing numbers of the faithful; and it was *The Garden of the Soul* rather than the Roman *Raccolta* which continued to be used by Catholics living in England, whether for private prayer or in assisting at Mass or Benediction. Furthermore, those extra-liturgical forms which came to be practised with increasing regularity were devotions which had also been favourites in the recusant tradition: Benediction and the rosary. Alarmed Roman pronouncements in the aftermath of crises such as the godless revolutions of France, the stripping of the temporal power of the papacy, and the development of rival ideologies to Christianity may have helped to urge Catholics, in England as elsewhere, to feel that devotion ought to be increased, earnest religion reappropriated, and confessionalism made manifest. But Catholics were culturally idiosyncratic in their precise understanding of the details of what such earnest devotion consisted in.

The devotional life of English Catholics may have changed in tone and emphasis during the period, but it is difficult to justify the common assertion that it became 'Roman', for all that it became more distinctively Catholic. The devotional tastes of nineteenth- and twentieth-century English Catholics continued to be influenced, although not dictated, by continental, and especially French, habits, practices, and perceptions, as they had been during the eighteenth century. Foreign Catholic practices, which were routinely recorded in the Catholic press and accessible in a range of newly translated devotional works, were also made known through confraternities, retreats, schools, and missions as sponsored by a variety of international religious orders. These were an obvious source of spiritual choice and inspiration, and it was partly through the prominence given to certain devotions by these communities that a number of specifically Roman, as well as continental, devotional practices were made known to, and consequently adopted by, some English Catholics.

But religious orders could not dictate approaches to a laity exposed to so many rival influences any better than the hierarchy could: while a convent school might emphasize one devotion, the local priest, passing missioner, retreat father, confraternity, family, neighbours, and library all offered alternative approaches. Although some particularly celebrated English Catholics, like Faber, were especially drawn to Italian practices, others felt equally at liberty to choose spiritual forms to suit their idiosyn-cratic devotional palates: Canon William Moser of Peterborough, for example, preferred German Catholic ones.[1] And, while many expressed loyalty to Rome and the pope, especially during the troubled 1860s, even 'devotion to the pope' was not normally an expression of party affiliation but rather one of broad denominational allegiance or personal religious inclination. Jennifer Supple has found that Yorkshire Catholics, although happy to sing Faber's hymn 'God Bless Our Pope', hesitated to contrib-ute to Peter's Pence collections. Her cautious conclusion that 'reluctance to send money to Rome was probably no more than a typical Yorkshire reluctance to part with hard-earned "brass"'[2] does not seem entirely convincing in view of the fact that Yorkshire churches, like English Catholic churches elsewhere, were largely paid for by the 'pennies of the poor'. In practice, 'devotion' to the pope as a symbol of holiness and as denominational figurehead was perfectly compatible with a reluctance to wish to have much to do with the bureaucracy and machinery of Rome, still less with the real man who filled the office. As Desmond Keenan has argued persuasively, even in contemporary Ireland,

On the evidence available one cannot speak of a swing from a non-papal, or anti-papal feeling to a strongly pro-papal feeling, still less from virtual Gallicanism to outright Ultramontanism . . . it would seem that pro-papal feeling increased in line with the emphasis on other specifically Catholic doctrines. One could possi-bly regard it as a 'devotion' to the Pope similar to the other 'devotions'.[3]

Nor did the mere fact that a devotion was Roman mean that it was required of the faithful: its place of origin certainly did not guarantee its general acceptance among that increasing number of Catholics in England

---

[1] Moser's concern for the souls in purgatory, which amounted to a one-man crusade in their cause, was deeply influenced by the work of a priest of Munich, Louis Gemminger, which Moser translated as *All Souls' 'Forget-Me-Not': A Prayer and Meditation Book for the Solace of the Poor Souls in Purgatory* . . . in 1890. All his efforts for parish fund-raising centred around this theme. He also chose a German artist to design the Stations of the Cross for his church, evidently finding German style more to his taste than Roman.

[2] J. F. Supple, 'Ultramontanism in Yorkshire, 1850–1900', *Recusant History*, 17 (1985), 277.

[3] D. J. Keenan, 'The Catholic Church in Ireland 1800–1860: A Social and Sociological Study' (Ph.D. thesis, Queen's University, Belfast, 1979), 282.

who responded to Challoner's frequently republished challenge to 'aspire to devotion'. We have already seen how a common reverence for the Blessed Sacrament led English Catholics to treasure their own Benediction service where continentals had alternative versions of the same rite, or might prefer to show devotion to the same object through *Quarant'ore* or Exposition of the Blessed Sacrament.

Nor were other continental spiritual fashions necessarily adopted wholesale. Although Lourdes had its own railway station as early as 1866 and was therefore easily accessible, at least to the wealthy, the first official English Catholic pilgrimage there did not take place until 1883; and none of these English visitors was cured or witnessed miracles.[4] Yet a modest native tradition of miraculous cures pre-dated this most celebrated French shrine by at least fifty years. Holywell in northern Wales, which had been vigorously championed by the vicar apostolic of the Midland District John Milner in 1805,[5] continued to attract some faithful throughout the century.[6] The many celebrated accounts of miracles at Lourdes undoubtedly heightened the expectations of pilgrims to Holywell, and probably contributed to the popularity of the Welsh shrine, which seems to have been particularly intense in 1894;[7] but here as elsewhere continental developments did not initiate British ones.

Catholics in England were certainly aware of and, to varying degrees, influenced by the models and range of spiritual choice offered by Catholic countries across the channel and which were made easily accessible to the

[4] See anon., *The English Pilgrimage to Lourdes May 1883: By One of the Pilgrims* (London, 1883), 16, 6.

[5] Milner publicized Winefrid White's cure at the well, which, in his view, demonstrated that 'even in this age of domineering vice and incredulity, *God hath not left himself without testimony . . .* or to speak in plain terms that an EVIDENT MIRACLE has been wrought among us' (see J. Milner, *Authentic Documents relative to the Miraculous Cure of Winefrid White* (London, 1805), 25, as cited in J. F. Champ, 'Bishop Milner, Holywell, and the Cure Tradition', in S. Mews (ed.), *Religion and National Identity* (Studies in Church History 18; Oxford, 1982), 153–64).

[6] Mary Bowness of Gainsborough, for example, made a pilgrimage to St Winefred's well in 1844, perhaps for a safe delivery rather than a cure, since her child was born there. C. Kerr, *Teresa Helena Higginson: School Teacher and Mystic 1844–1905* (Edinburgh, 1928), 11.

[7] Herbert Thurston recalled in 1916 that there had been an 'unusual profusion' of miraculous cures in 1894 (H. Thurston, 'Holywell in Recent Years', *Month*, 128 (1916), 38–51). This fact also drew comment at the time: see e.g. M. Maher, 'Holywell in 1894', *Month*, 83 (1895), 153–82. But Gerard Manley Hopkins was contemplating the mystery of the well in his 'Maidens' Song from St Winefred's Well' at least as early as 1882. See G. M. Hopkins, 'The Leaden Echo and the Golden Echo', in *The New Oxford Book of Victorian Verse*, ed. C. Ricks (Oxford, 1987), 423–4. Hopkins composed the poem in 1882 and it was published in 1918.

English through a surfeit of cheap devotional literature as well as through international Catholic organizations. But the problems which confronted the English Catholic hierarchy were first and foremost English problems, and the religious instincts of the community came more directly from English than from foreign sources. It was not the paradox which a long-standing historiographical tradition would make it appear that the Catholic Church in England should have remained distinctively English while at the same time heightening the importance and encouraging the frequent use of exclusively Catholic practices.

English Catholicism in the nineteenth and early twentieth centuries has tended to be treated in isolation from developments which affected other English Christians. In part this is the legacy of contemporary anti-Catholic feeling which took it as axiomatic that Catholicism, being 'Roman', was essentially un-English. This historiographical tendency has been further exacerbated by the fact that a great number of Catholics living in England during the period were Irish, and still more were perceived to be so, the distinction between first and subsequent generations not being drawn very carefully, and definitions of ethnicity being in any case highly subjective. But English Catholicism was not only for the English-born. Whatever the place of origin or cultural allegiance of a Catholic living in England in the nineteenth century, and despite the many social and economic factors which might divide him or her from others within the denomination, 'English' and 'Irish' Catholics managed to find a common spiritual ground which was acceptable to the sensibility of each. This English (or, if one prefers, English–Irish) Catholic devotion, which gave Catholics at the very least a common language, but often a sense of supernatural kinship as well, had been prepared by a long history of mutual spiritual influence between England and Ireland prior to 1800. But this inclusive spirit came to be explicitly and widely held as a principle of mutual toleration from about the middle of the nineteenth century.

We might easily characterize Christianity in England in the nineteenth century as having been marked successively by assertiveness in the aftermath of the French Revolution, a revivalist spirit from the 1840s, heightened worries about dechristianization from about 1880, and, for some, a fashionably frivolous reaction to Victorian earnestness from the beginning of the Edwardian period until the sobering effects of the First World War. However generalized and simplistic such a summary may be, what is striking is the extent to which it describes English Catholic developments as well as it does those of other English denominations.

Just as Protestant denominations in England concentrated much of their attention on the perceived need to revive a pre-lapsarian enthusiasm and moral earnestness into what was perceived to be the religious indifference of the day, so did the Catholic community. The movement of renewal within English Catholicism which gathered momentum in the 1840s, in parallel with the Oxford Movement in the Church of England, seems to have come about partly through a romantic desire to recreate the medieval ages of faith. This desire was not, of course, exclusively Catholic or even proto-Catholic. While an intense romanticism led Pugin to convert, not only Tractarians and Camdenians but also many ordinary readers of Sir Walter Scott were affected to a lesser degree. This revivalism of the English Catholic Church, although rooted in common English perceptions and related to analogous Anglican developments, was sustained in its sense of mission by the challenge to accommodate vastly increased numbers of both practising and nominally Catholic immigrants over the next few decades. But for all that the problem of large-scale immigration was peculiar to Catholicism, concerns for lapsed Irish were also mirrored in the Anglican and dissenting churches' efforts to reclaim the many nominal but 'indifferent' adherents among the poor of the great industrial cities.

From about 1880 the English Catholic hierarchy, like the leaders of other Christian groups, perceived widespread secularization in England to be a real and immediate threat, and felt itself to be in increasing competition with rival denominations for unclaimed souls. Such a view may in fact have been an over-reaction, since membership in the Catholic Church continued to rise at a faster rate than that of other English churches, and even membership in the Church of England did not begin actually to decline until 1910.[8] Nevertheless, the rate of church growth did slacken; and, as Owen Chadwick has pointed out, churchmen's worries about the future of Christianity were at their most acute during this decade which saw an atheist elected to Parliament, in which the effects of biblical criticism and the *Origin of Species* were held to have left

---

[8] R. Currie, A. Gilbert, and L. Horsley have summarized a range of statistics of denominational allegiance as revealing that Catholic membership was characterized by 'high growth between 1800 and 1840; very rapid growth between 1840 and the 1860s, and still high, but rather slower growth between the 1860s and 1970'. Signs of Protestant decline came sooner: the same indices show 'high growth between 1800 and 1840; lower growth between 1840 and 1910; and a decrease between 1910 and 1970' (R. Currie, A. Gilbert, and L. Horsley, *Churches and Churchgoers: Patterns of Church Growth in the British Isles since 1700* (Oxford, 1977), 24).

their mark on popular belief, and atheism was being espoused even by respectable people.

An Anglican bishop summed up the mood of the 1880s when he declared that

you found unbelief everywhere, in your club or your drawing-room. You might hear it from the lady next to whom you sat at dinner. You found it lurking in the newspaper, or the novel. You found parents who watched their children saying their prayers at their knee, and wondered what would happen when the child went away to school or university, or asked themselves 'What will my innocent daughters think when they imbibe the poison of infidelity from the first novel they borrow from the circulating library?'[9]

It was in this alarmist atmosphere that Catholics encouraged the growth and spread of exclusively Catholic social, charitable, and devotional societies to protect the faithful from the insidious influences of 'the world'. At about the same time, the English Catholic hierarchy attempted to separate its members from rival Christian influences through a strong discouragement of 'mixed' marriages and non-denominational education. Increased stress on the devotional as well as the doctrinal peculiarities of the Catholic creed was mirrored in the self-protective responses of other communities of belief. As Hugh McLeod has pointed out, 'This was the age of the self-built ideological ghettos—Catholic, Protestant, liberal, socialist.'[10]

David Mathew once remarked that 'a phrase such as Edwardian has no meaning for those below a certain income-level'.[11] But after Victoria's reign, too, English Catholic developments had a broad similarity to Protestant ones. An earnestness continued to mark the religious sense of many humble Catholics, as it did the faith of their Protestant neighbours; but the newly light-hearted, even irreverent, tone of a G. K. Chesterton found a middle-class audience which was glad to be diverted from at least some aspects of Victorian heaviness. The point should not be overstressed: such apparent frivolity did not disturb a deeper seriousness where the Faith was concerned, and which can be detected in the deliberately surprising other-worldliness of Chesterton's Father Brown, the apologetic writings of his contemporary Hilaire Belloc, and the popular acclaim which was given to Edward Elgar's rendition of Newman's *Dream of*

[9] O. Chadwick, *The Victorian Church* (2 vols.; London, 1966–70; 1987), ii. 112.
[10] H. McLeod, *Religion and the People of Western Europe 1789–1970* (Oxford, 1981), 36.
[11] D. Mathew, *Catholicism in England* (1936; London, 1948), 241.

Gerontius.[12] Nevertheless, Chesterton, like others of his generation, evidently felt increasingly uncomfortable with prescription and generally preferred to amuse or gently to suggest than too blatantly to instruct.[13]

In each phase of the development of the Christian churches in England which has been outlined, the Catholic case finds an obvious parallel in those of other denominations. Since English Christians faced similar problems and imbibed a common atmosphere, it should come as no surprise to learn that English Catholic devotion in the period had a great deal in common with contemporary Protestant spirituality. Indeed, some aspects of English piety in the period, Catholic and Protestant, were so alike as to seem virtually indistinguishable. Other devotional tendencies, although evidently prompted by similar feelings, nevertheless seem to have been focused rather differently in the two traditions. In this final chapter the broad spectrum of a Victorian and Edwardian Catholic sensibility will be sketched, beginning with those aspects of devotion which Catholics and Protestants held most closely in common.

Earnestness and Anxiety

Although deliberately and self-consciously distinct devotional forms became a pronounced feature of Catholic piety in the nineteenth century, the earnestness and religious intensity which underlay English Catholic practices seems particularly characteristic of Victorians of all denominations. In an extreme form, this could amount to a 'conversion', which, although one thinks of the term as primarily an evangelical one, was also familiar to Catholics, who used it to distinguish mere membership, as evidenced in outward manifestations of denominational adherence like baptism, from a vivid and personal apprehension of the central tenets of the Faith. Cornelia Connelly, who followed her husband in becoming a Catholic, in later years told the nuns of the Society of the Holy Child Jesus which she founded 'that her actual conversion dated from a retreat

---

[12] Although it was said by one member of its first Birmingham audience of 1900 to 'stink of incense', its devotional quality earned it acclaim from Protestants and Catholics alike during the period 1901–14. As *Grove's Dictionary of Music* has put it, the ostensible criticism was in fact 'a tribute, though a superficial one, to the sympathy existing between poet and composer' (*Grove's Dictionary of Music and Musicians*, ed. H. C. Colles (5 vols.; 4th edn., London, 1940), ii. 152). See also *The Concise Oxford Dictionary of Music*, ed. M. Kennedy, 3rd edn., based on the original publication by P. Scholes (Oxford, 1980), 203, and H. Belloc, *The Path to Rome* (1902; London, 1952), pp. 416–18.

[13] Embarrassed by the earnestness which characterized works like his *Orthodoxy* of 1909, Chesterton later dismissed it as having been composed 'with all the solemnity of youth' (G. K. Chesterton, *Autobiography* (London, 1937), 177).

she made . . . in December, 1839. She had been a Catholic for four years
but this was the first time that the fact held any reality for her."[14]

Nor was it only literal converts to Catholicism who desired and set
store by such intense and emotional reappropriations of the doctrines of
faith as those entailed in a conversion experience. Although born a Catholic,
William Ullathorne, whose youth was spent at sea, felt little compunction
to go to church, and recalled that 'when abroad I had never tried to go
to Mass, and probably I should not have been permitted to go alone. Yet
I always stuck to the confession of my Catholicity and was proud of
it.'[15] One Sunday, however, while his ship was docked at Memel, 'Mr
Craythorne, the mate, said to me: "William, let us go to Mass." I fished
up *The Garden of the Soul* from the bottom of my sea chest, and we set
off'.[16] It is difficult to judge from Ullathorne's account why this particular occasion should have affected him so powerfully, but:

The moment I entered I was struck by the simple fervour of the scene: it threw
me into a cold shiver; my heart was turned inward upon myself; I saw the claims
of God upon me, and felt a deep reproach within my soul . . . A life filled with the
sense of God and devoted to God was what I had never realized [17]

As his biographer Butler reports, 'in after-life he used to speak of the
experience in the chapel at Memel as a "conversion" '.[18] He adds, not
altogether approvingly, that

it does seem to have been of the nature of the conversions so frequent a phenomenon in all forms of evangelical religion, but infrequent in Catholicism. We see
the sudden awakening of conscience, the conviction of sin, the stimulating of the
religious sense, the changed life. That Ullathorne went through such a conversion
may be attributed to his boyhood having been without the Sacraments and care-
less in regard to religion, which hitherto had no vital grip on him.[19]

Although Butler was reluctant to admit that 'conversions' like Ullathorne's
ever formed an important part of Catholic experience, missions, such as
those given in England from about 1840 by Redemptorists, Passionists,
Marists, Dominicans, and Jesuits, were designed to stimulate just such
vivid apprehensions of the Faith as Butler describes. These periodic
renewals, initiated by Italian orders under the auspices of the English
hierarchy but soon adopted by Jesuits and Dominicans as well, had clear
parallels in the Protestant revivalist tradition. Featuring sobs and wailings

---

[14] J. Wadham, *The Case of Cornelia Connelly* (London, 1956), 56.
[15] As cited in C. Butler, *The Life and Times of Bishop Ullathorne* (2 vols.; London, 1926),
i. 10.   [16] Ibid. 13.
[17] Ibid. 14.   [18] Ibid.   [19] Butler, *Life and Times of Ullathorne*, i. 14 n.

as the appropriate response to evocations of hell-fire and accusations of sinfulness and ingratitude, Catholic mission sermons were usually followed by public acknowledgements of particular sins, and ended with testimonies of personal salvation through the renewal of baptismal vows.[20] It was in the context of analogous Protestant developments that the Passionist Dominic Barberi first realized that he had a ready audience in the promotion of such methods. After the first (and generally disappointing) mission which he gave outside his own parish, at Lane End, Staffordshire, from 24 to 31 March 1844, and which he left 'on the verge of tears',

a big strapping Irishman came bounding in, flung himself at his feet, and, to the accompaniment of sobs and sighs, begged him to hear his confession. Barberi, curious to know what in his sermon had so moved the man, was told that '. . . the whole sermon struck me all of a heap; I did not understand more than a few words of it, and don't know from Adam what foreign language you were talking. But I saw you stretch out your arms, and your voice had something so kind in it, that I said to myself, though I am the biggest blackguard in the whole Church— more shame on me!—that holy man won't scold me, and I'll make my confession to him.'[21]

It was the adoption of an excitable approach to sin and grace, not the introduction of Italian or continental forms of devotion *per se*, which marked a departure in Victorian Catholic piety from the more gentlemanly tone of the eighteenth century. Ullathorne, himself a convert to the new style, remained gentle in his appraisal of what had come to seem an old-fashioned approach, that still current at Prior Park in 1845. As Ullathorne wrote that year of Dr Brindle of Prior Park, he was 'a gentleman in the true sense of the word'. 'I do not think it a school of perfection,' Ullathorne considered, 'but of sensible, as well as earnest (for I do think) so religion.' In the bishop's house, he mused,

the whole set-out is gentlemanlike, yet accompanied with the deep impression of religion as an objective fact. I think I should get on well with Dr Brindle and the bursar, Mr Shaddock, who is very like a fellow of Magdalen or St John's, in externals. I was amused at the set-out.[22]

---

[20] John Kent has found much overlap between the techniques of revivalists Moody and Sankey and those used by Anglo-Catholics at the Twelve Days Mission to London of 1869 and the longer session of 1875. As he points out, High-Church clerics made their revivals explicitly 'Catholic' by calling them 'missions'. Although Kent assumes that the term must have been taken from 'French Roman Catholic usage', it is just as likely to have been contemporary English Catholic practice which was being imitated. See J. Kent, *Holding the Fort: Studies in Victorian Revivalism* (London, 1978), 236.

[21] A. Wilson, *Blessed Dominic Barberi: Supernaturalized Briton* (London, 1967), 262.

[22] As cited in Butler, *Life and Times of Ullathorne*, i. 141.

Both Protestant and Catholic revivalist forms, as John Sharp has pointed out, stressed 'the need for individual salvation and . . . saving grace' and 'were based on a thoroughly evangelical view of redemption as the bringing by Christ of the message and the dynamic of the Father's love for all men'.[23] Not only were English Protestant and Catholic approaches analogous; they could even overlap. It was a point of pride with missioners like Barberi that Protestants should also be attracted and thereby perhaps be led to the true path to salvation. A fair proportion of outsiders, like Annie Foley of Southwark, who 'went to Catholic missions, [though she] wasn't a Catholic',[24] evidently found that the idiom and substance of a mission, for all its peculiarly Catholic devotions and doctrines, effectively conveyed a Christian view which was both recognizable and palatable to an English working-class sensibility.

But just as Protestant revivals aimed to renew fervour among nominal members, it was primarily to the consciences of lapsed or sinful Catholics that missions were designed to appeal; and it was with these, unsurprisingly, that they were most successful. Two hours after an early Redemptorist mission in London, an observer found a working man still sobbing from the effects of a sermon designed to return sinners to righteousness. This observer 'did not wonder at the women sobbing and crying this afternoon', but was suitably impressed that

at the sermon this evening, when there was not even one woman present in the chapel, and it was crowded to suffocation, the whole of the men, young and old, borne along, as it were, on a resistless tide, burst forth into one long continual wail and lament during, but particularly towards the end of the Fathers' farewell address.[25]

This heightened revivalist spirit continued to colour Catholic approaches long after the second-spring optimism of the 1840s had given way to deepening worries about 'leakage' from the Faith. The parish priest of St Peter's, Lytham, could still note with satisfaction in his visitation return of 1865 that 'having had a mission lately nearly all are in the Church. I think there are not more than ten or twelve of the regular Catholics out of the Church.'[26] At Our Lady's, Birkenhead, 'the number of Communions in 1874 was 7,580 no doubt boosted by the mission. There was no

---

[23] J. Sharp, *Reapers of the Harvest: The Redemptorists in Great Britain and Ireland 1843–1898* (Dublin, 1989), 159.
[24] P. Schweitzer and C. Wegner (eds.), *On the River: Memories of a Working River* (1989), 40.   [25] As cited in Sharp, *Reapers of the Harvest*, 159.
[26] Lancashire Record Office, The Bishop of Lancaster, St Peter's Lytham, RCLy 5/3, Answers to Visitation Questions, 26 Oct. 1865, fo. 8.

mission in 1875 and the number of Communions came to 6,956. In 1877 they went up to 8,258 and until 1881 were always 7,000 annually.'[27] As late as 1901 the priest of the Sacred Heart and English Martyrs at Thornley, in the diocese of Hexham and Newcastle, found that the scandal caused by drunkenness in his parish had noticeably 'lessened since the mission'.[28]

Mission sermons were of their nature an occasional, if recurrent, feature of English Catholic experience. But they gave in concentrated form what was to become, over the course of the century, a message as widespread among Catholics as among Protestants. Sermons designed to provoke a vivid recognition of one's sinfulness or inadequacy, and a corresponding desire to renew fervour and earnestness, came to be the characteristic fare of retreats and mass sermons as well as of missions. During her fifth retreat, taken in 1862, Lady Georgiana Fullerton 'Prayed as we were desired to do, that we may all see more than we have yet done, the evil, the badness of sin, and feel shame and confusion at having offended infinite goodness.'[29] Later, after a sermon 'On the vileness and hideousness of sin, even if it was not forbidden. The soul a running ulcer', she 'Saw the Father immediately afterwards—told him how depressed I was in body and mind. He helped and strengthened me.'[30] Herbert, later Cardinal, Vaughan was similarly affected with a combination of self-reproach and spiritual refreshment when, returning from a retreat in Holy Week 1869, he wrote that 'to enter such a haven after tossing about for so long in such an angry sea is not only the most grateful calm but a necessary precaution to prevent "going to pieces"'. On the Friday, he recalled how he had

walked up and down my room as one going to execution or rather to Judgment and then made a General Confession again of my whole life. How salutary! how little it makes one! how fitting it is that we should again and again bear the shame which we cast upon Him in the Garden, the sins which at last broke His Heart on the Cross! And yet, alas! how far, far one falls short of everything one ought to think of oneself.[31]

There is a broad similarity between such fervent expressions of sinfulness among Catholics and Protestants alike. Walter Houghton has

[27] E. M. Abbott, 'History of Our Lady's—Birkenhead', unpublished manuscript, 1991, fo. 14.
[28] Hexham and Newcastle Diocesan Archives, The Sacred Heart and English Martyrs, Thornley Archives, 'Visitation Papers', 8 June 1902.
[29] Anon., *The Inner Life of Lady Georgiana Fullerton* (London, 1899), 293.
[30] Ibid. 294.
[31] *Letters of Herbert, Cardinal Vaughan, to Lady Herbert of Lea 1867 to 1903*, ed. S. Leslie (London, 1942), 146.

usefully pointed out that the Victorian 'Puritan' conscience was 'hardly less common among Anglo-Catholics than Evangelicals and Dissenters'.[32] He might have added that it was equally characteristic of Roman Catholics in the period. Herbert Vaughan was the first to acknowledge such a sense of personal failure: 'Like you, I often find myself staring into the fire or pacing my room almost for hours wondering what I can do during this my brief span of life in the midst of all this evil,' he wrote to Lady Herbert of Lea; 'looking at the Apostles and the Saints and then broken-hearted at myself: contrasting this love and my tepidity and misery . . .'.[33] On another occasion he lamented that: 'My naked crucifix standing here before me seems to say all day long, "Poor Herbert, what have you done, how little do you, what would you ever do for me?" This it is which makes life sad and, I must almost say, bitter . . .'.[34]

English Catholicism certainly did not require converts like Newman to bring that sense of doubt and devotional inadequacy which, in a climate which put a high premium on enthusiastic apprehensions of grace, was, as Houghton points out, the *mal du siècle*.[35] Vaughan, who came from a prominent Catholic family, echoed Newman's regret, both as an Anglican and as a Catholic, that he was 'tethered in his moral circle'. '*Quis infirmatur et ego non infirmor?*', he once wrote:

I do indeed feel these words—they go through me, they set me on fire. But when the moment, the unsought-for moment, comes for throwing myself into the weaknesses of others, for sympathising with them—in a word, for assimilating myself to them—I do not, I cannot, do it. I am closed up in myself—I am simply Herbert Vaughan.[36]

Lady Georgiana Fullerton, on the eve of a retreat in 1868, was similarly alarmed to find that she felt 'No joy on entering the Retreat—different from anything I ever felt before—dull, indifferent—hard irritable feeling.' Nevertheless, she was able to reassure herself somewhat by being able to note that 'when in the opening discourse the Father said, that Father Segneri had gone into retreat an ordinary man, and had come out a Saint, I felt an ardent desire that such a change might come over me, this time'. As she reasoned to herself, 'My soul does find joy in magnifying the Lord, and my spirit generally rejoices in God my Saviour,' though she added anxiously: 'I wonder how I shall get on to-morrow.'[37]

---

[32] W. Houghton, *The Victorian Frame of Mind, 1830–1870* (1957; New Haven, Conn., 1984), 62.　　　　[33] 13 Jan. 1867, *Vaughan Letters*, 1.

[34] 22 Dec. 1867, ibid. 47.　　　[35] Houghton, *Victorian Frame of Mind*, 65.

[36] J. Brodrick, in *Vaughan Letters*, p. xvi.　　　[37] *The Inner Life*, 291.

Again, the Methodist J. A. Symonds, who had developed such an acute
sense of his own evil by the age of 7 that he 'screamed at night about
imaginary acts of disobedience',[38] had much in common with lower-
middle-class English Catholic Teresa Higginson, who, by the time she
had grown up to be a schoolteacher in Bootle and Neston, had developed
such a morbid sense of sin that she considered her first trespass to have
been committed at age 4, or in about 1849, when she 'wilfully pretended
not to hear' her mother calling her.[39] What might be called a 'Puritan'
conscience or 'evangelical' tendency towards scrupulosity underpinned
both the desire for vivid apprehensions of grace and a corresponding self-
doubt which was a mark of Victorian piety.

Penance, Reparations, and Sanctity

Protestant denominations offered explanations and methods of their own
for coping with such a widespread sense of sin, doubt, dryness, and
religious anxiety as we have seen. For Catholics, the primary means of
comfort and renewal was to be sought through the sacrament of penance,
which was increasingly both urged from above and desired from below.
As John Kent reminds us, this distinctively Catholic institution, which
objectified forgiveness in a way which an 'uncritical Evangelical demand
for "repentance"' left to the mercy of private conscience, was the envy of
some of the younger Anglo-Catholics of the 1840s. As W. J. Butler wrote
to John Keble in 1845, 'Many of . . . my own personal friends, are now
repenting bitterly; their sins are lying like a heavy load upon them, and
torturing them indescribably. They long to go through some form of
prescribed penance.'[40] Some sensitive souls, like Lady Georgiana Fullerton,
went so far as to change their religion[41] for the sake of finding solace in
the confessional. As her biographer has put it, 'she may be said to have
had a "devotion" to the Sacrament of Penance, approaching it when she
could, twice in the week'.[42] At her retreat in 1868, although one day was

---

[38] As cited in Houghton, *Victorian Frame of Mind*, 63.

[39] A. M. O'Sullivan, *Teresa Higginson the Servant of God School Teacher 1845–1905*
(London, 1924), 29–30.   [40] As cited in Kent, *Holding the Fort*, 264–5.

[41] As a child, Fullerton had imagined herself worthy of death for cursing her governess.
She later explained that: 'A Catholic child would have been told by a confessor what had
been the amount of sin, and would have received absolution. But I tormented myself some
time about this, and then forgot to be sorry for it, till I made my general confession as a
Catholic' (*The Inner Life*, 3).

[42] Ibid. 30–1. She also points out that Lady Georgiana Fullerton's three favourite
poems—Longfellow's 'Evangeline', Mrs Norton's 'The Lady of La Garaye', and Tennyson's
'Guinevere'—were all concerned with forgiveness and absolution (ibid. 29).

'somewhat spoilt by anxiety about going to confession', Fullerton 'at last . . . got in, so that I am at peace'.[43] She soon 'got a new light—about making frequent confession a still greater means of grace'.[44]

Such fervent desires for the formal transmission of divine forgiveness, which had come to be shared by many Anglicans, were hardly confined to one class of Catholic. Wiseman meant to touch a nerve when he observed publicly in 1848 that, while the Tractarian 'sees the poor in flocks gather round the confessional of the Catholic priest, in fullness of faith, crying out for forgiveness', he found his 'own ministry powerless and flat among the masses . . .'.[45] Anglo-Catholics took up the suggestion at their Twelve Days Mission of 1869 and London Mission of 1874, making the practice of auricular confession a feature. While this provoked accusations of 'Romanism' from the Evangelical press, it was remarkably effective in drawing crowds of penitents.[46] Particularly after the effects of a good mission, Roman Catholics filled the confessional in gratifyingly large numbers. When Fr Slaughter, priest of Our Lady's, Birkenhead, brought four Jesuits over to conduct his first mission in March 1873, 'the missioners heard over 2,000 confessions' in three weeks, while Fr Slaughter and his curate heard 135.[47] This was no isolated phenomenon: as can be seen from the architectural plans of nineteenth-century English Catholic churches throughout the country, confessionals, which were built as separate rooms into the structure of the churches themselves, aimed to cater for enormous numbers of penitents at a given time.[48]

Just as the sacrament of penance offered a distinctively Catholic solution to a common Christian difficulty, so did a range of Catholic devotions, many of which could effectively soothe that sense of sin which had been highlighted and sharpened by evangelical approaches. The desire to make amends, as well as to acknowledge blame for sins, could be accommodated through reparations to the Sacred Heart, a devotion which had

[43] Ibid. 300.

[44] When she showed her spiritual director the 'rules' which she had set herself as resolutions to follow the retreat, 'he made some changes—diminutions about Penance. Approved of the rest' (ibid. 304).

[45] N. Wiseman, *Conversion: A Letter to Mr Alexander Chiriol and his Family on their Happy Admission to the Communion of the Holy Catholic Church* (London, 1848), 33, as cited in S. W. Gilley, 'Heretic London, Holy Poverty, and the Irish Poor, 1830–1870', *Downside Review*, 89 (1971), 80.

[46] G. Parsons, 'Emotion and Piety: Revivalism and Ritualism in Victorian Christianity', in G. Parsons (ed.), *Religion in Victorian Britain* (4 vols.; Manchester, 1988), i. 227–8.

[47] Abbott, 'History of Our Lady's', fo. 14.

[48] R. McDonnell, 'Church Architecture as a Primary Document for Nineteenth Century Catholic History', paper read to the Catholic Record Society Conference, Plater College, Oxford, 1 Aug. 1989.

been known in the recusant tradition but which began to make a much stronger appeal to English Catholics after the trans-denominational revival of the 1840s. At Our Lady's, Birkenhead, it was noted in 1863 that 'women wish to raise an altar in honour of the Sacred Heart',[49] and in 1872 the local priest and 'John Barnack, a dock labourer and Y[oung] M[en's] S[ociety] president went on pilgrimage to Paray-le-Monial' together, while the next year a memorial was presented to James Brown, bishop of the diocese, 'with 2,000 signatures begging that the parish might be consecrated to the Sacred Heart'. This request was not only granted but celebrated with a certain amount of festivity. Before the High Mass, at a ceremony at which '713 received Communion' and which boasted a procession of the Blessed Sacrament in the evening, 'the Bishop blessed the new statue of the Sacred Heart [which] . . . cost £22.7.11, to which the Y[oung] M[en's] S[ociety] contributed £2, dock labourers 10/- and Mr E. Singleton 10/-'.[50]

Again, it was in a climate in which the US evangelicals Dwight Moody and Ira Sankey were conducting their most successful national tour of 1873–5, and infusing Protestants with a revivalist fervour which was well documented in the press,[51] that a still greater proportion of Catholic churches began to advertise extra-liturgical devotions.[52] As we have already seen, 364 Catholics, of English as well as of Irish origin,[53] voluntarily joined the Confraternity of the Sacred Heart which had just been established by their parish priest at St Peter's, Lytham. Such devotions were equally appealing to many converts from the Church of England, most notably Henry Manning, who, like cradle-Catholic James Guiron before him, published a devotional work to acknowledge his sense of debt to, and to further spread the message of, this path to spiritual consolation.[54] It was hardly in obedience to Rome but rather in order to assuage an acute sense of personal guilt as well as the heavy sense of living in particularly sinful times that Catholics increasingly turned to those

----

[49] Abbott, 'History of Our Lady's', fo. 9. See also his less detailed, but published, account in 'Our Lady's, Birkenhead: Growth, Destruction, Resurgence and Renewal', *North West Catholic History*, 19 (1992), 47–50.   [50] Abbott, 'History of Our Lady's', fo. 15.
[51] Parsons, *Religion in Victorian Britain*, i. 219.   [52] See Appendices I and II.
[53] So one presumes from the mixture of Irish and English names given in the membership lists. These included such names as Arrowsmith, Rourke, Newsham, Parker, Ainscough, Pendlebury, Maloney, Thistleton, Walmsley, Johnson, Cross, Morris, Ethrington, and Whiteside. Lancashire Record Office, The Bishop of Lancaster, Archives of St Peter's, Lytham, RCLy 7/14, 'Roll of Members of the Confraternity of the Sacred Heart of Jesus, 6 June 1875'.
[54] See J. Guiron, *The Sacred Heart* (London, 1873), and H. E. Manning, *The Glories of the Sacred Heart* (London, 1876).

denominationally specific practices, like confession or devotions to the Sacred Heart, which addressed themselves to such feelings.

David Bebbington has identified one of the main strands of nineteenth-century evangelicalism as characterized by an intense concentration on the crucifixion. Set devotional forms, such as meditating on the five wounds of Christ or symbolically taking part in the Passion through the enactment of the Stations of the Cross, focused a more broadly 'crucicentric'[55] Victorian apprehension of the faith in specifically Catholic ways. For Catholics, there existed a range of forms of self-denial or self-torture whose end was to 'mortify' the self, in other words to contradict one's natural inclinations. All ordinary sufferings were similarly to be 'offered' to God as the necessary and, at least theoretically, welcome means of striving to imitate Christ's own perfect self-sacrifice.

Thus Herbert Vaughan attempted to steer Lady Herbert, who gave up eating foods she particularly liked, from physical to spiritual forms of self-denial, chiding her teasingly:

If your Ladyship will insist on their serving you up a warm unbuttered cinder and a glass of water for breakfast, you will find yourself without strength for the trials Our Lord will send you and your life will be a failure, through imprudence. Mortification of the will, mind and heart, as you know, avail more. But I think you promised me to behave yourself properly on this score of health?[56]

Instead of fasting, he recommended that she take her crucifix as her master and 'Study those wounds. I cannot tell you how much I owe to the study of them, which I began some years ago.'[57] He also attempted to console her, even to congratulate her, on having 'one child away ill . . . another delicate, one sent off to the South, and one at home laid up and that poor desolate heart of yours suffering in so many ways'. Such misfortunes, properly handled, could only lead to sanctity and were the best of divine gifts. 'I can only find interpretation in that Sacred Heart which was sad and sorrowful and bled in the Garden and on the Cross,' he wrote:

Somehow or other after having made you and after you had left Him, He has fallen in love with your soul. And in His love He is refining and purifying it in the crucible, a burning painful process, but how wonderfully blessed when accepted and received with the eyes of faith! Accept all your trials calmly and lovingly, with an interior spirit, thinking of His love and sufferings rather than of yourself.[58]

---

[55] D. W. Bebbington, *Evangelicalism in Modern Britain: A History from the 1730s to the 1980s* (London, 1989), 3.   [56] *Vaughan Letters*, 33.
[57] 17 Oct. 1867, ibid.   [58] 30 Jan. 1868, ibid. 60.

Like other Christians, Catholics believed that it was through the conscious imitation of Christ and a striving for sanctity that the perfect
Christian life should be sought. Again, Protestant and Catholic interpretations of this Victorian commonplace overlapped, but were not precisely
the same. Alexander M'Laren, thinking of Low-Church Frank Crossley,
once claimed that a truly Christian life was 'recognised by all who knew
it even slightly and unsympathetically as beautiful in its unworldliness, its
faithfulness to conscience, its unstinted liberality, and its self-oblivion'.[59]
Such a broad conception of Christianity did indeed have a powerful pull
for many Victorians of all denominations and classes, and was often
recognized across denominational boundaries. The prevalence among even
lapsed proletarians of what might be termed a latent Christian sensibility,
however maddeningly vague to many clergyman, and hardly orthodox,
certainly appears to have been widespread. So one gathers from Henry
Mayhew's famous interviews with London labourers, and from common
working-class maxims of the middle of the nineteenth century, like: 'All
religious sects were right in some respects, but all had fallen short of the
truth . . . What was wanted was love.'[60] It seems to have been Fr Dominic
Barberi's voluntary poverty, for example, together with his powerful
imitation of recognizably Christ-like gestures, as when he kissed stones
which some local youths had hurled at him in 1842, which gave pause to
Protestants and Catholics alike.[61]

Even the generally hostile English gutter press, when it drew breath
from condemning the alleged captivity of nuns, the sinister manœuvres of

[59] A. M'Laren, Preface to J. Rendel Harris (ed.), *The Life of Francis William Crossley*
(London, 1899), p. iii.

[60] D. G. Paz, 'Anti-Catholicism, Anti-Irish Stereotyping, and Anti-Celtic Racism in
Mid-Victorian Working-Class Periodicals', *Albion*, 18 (1986), 604. Paz draws his examples
from the following: *Family Herald*, 14 Dec. 1850, 524–5; 21 Dec. 1850, 540–1; 4 Jan. 1851,
572–3; 1 Feb. 1851, 636–7; *Lloyd's Entertaining Journal* 5, 7 Mar. 1846, 48. See also H.
McLeod, 'New Perspectives on Victorian Working-Class Religion: The Oral Evidence',
Oral History Journal, 14 (1986), 31–49, on the continued importance of Christian tenets
among even non-practising working-class men and women in the period, and in particular
the high regard in which the 'real Christian' continued to be held (ibid. 35).

[61] He soon developed a reputation for miraculous powers in Aston and Stone. There,
'as he passed through the streets, bystanders lowered their voices in conversation as they
do when they are speaking of death or hell . . . A Protestant woman angrily rebuked her
own husband when he dared to ridicule Dominic. . . . "He was esteemed a saint by all the
Catholics," Mrs Mary Hearney testified, "and when he walked through the streets, we
children used to go down on our knees to receive his blessing . . . mothers, who had babies
in their arms, held them up for his blessing as he passed by" ' (Wilson, *Blessed Dominic
Barberi*, 258). Charles Booth observed in 1902 that it was the self-imposed poverty of
Anglo-Catholic priests living in the poorest areas which particularly impressed parishioners
(cited in Parsons, *Religion in Victorian Britain*, i. 233).

the Jesuits, and the persecuting tendencies of the Roman church, was prepared to recognize in at least some contemporary English Catholics a 'truly' Christian spirit. As D. G. Paz found in his minute study of working-class periodicals of the mid-nineteenth century, 'the only real clergyman of any sort whom the [Protestant] gutter press praised was a Roman Catholic priest—Father Matthew [*sic*], the famous temperance evangelist' who, although he was 'a popish priest', the writers judged to be '"great apostle" with a "God-like mission" and a "holy task", whose name should be placed on the calendar [of saints] not far below the apostles'.[62]

Although M'Laren claimed that St Francis of Assisi would have recognized in Frank Crossley 'a brother in faith and spirit',[63] Protestant approaches to sanctity were not exactly like Catholic ones. Protestant devotion to St Francis, for example, tended rather to concentrate on his poverty than on his literal imitation of Christ crucified and shied away from accounts of his supernatural feats or stigmata, which were regarded as superstitious medieval accretions.[64] On the other hand, Catholic approaches to perfection stressed the sanctification of suffering in ways which were partially alien to Protestant conceptions. When Vaughan urged Lady Herbert of Lea (whom he affectionately called 'St Paula') to strive for sainthood, he drew on a tradition which stressed martyrdom as much as Christian goodness and morality. Having already urged her, in January 1868, 'to become an interior soul',[65] he suggested to her in the following year not to 'grieve because you are misunderstood and calumniated', since, 'if you were simply human . . . if there were no other interpretation to your life than that which the world must put on it, you might grieve indeed',[66] but

you, my dearest child, have invoked suffering . . . Why? because you believed in the School of suffering: because of a closer conformity with your Spouse Our Lord: because you believed it to be in every way good for you to be scourged and crowned with contempt and fastened on your Cross . . . He has added to the sufferings chosen by your generous will, sufferings chosen by His deepest love for you. Is this not true? And is this not the explanation and key to your life?[67]

[62] Paz, 'Anti-Catholicism', 607–8.
[63] M'Laren, Preface to Harris (ed.), *Life of Crossley*, p. iii.
[64] For a discussion of the contrast between the Oratorian approach to St Francis and that of Mrs Oliphant, for example, see R. Townsend, 'Hagiography in England in the Nineteenth Century: a Study in Literary, Historiographical and Theological Developments' (D.Phil. thesis, Oxford University, 1981), 37.   [65] 30 Jan. 1868, *Vaughan Letters*, 60.
[66] 6 July 1869, ibid. 152.   [67] Ibid. 153.

Lady Georgiana Fullerton, who also regarded her life as a training for the hereafter, and tortured herself with doubt as to whether she might ever achieve her ambition of sainthood,[68] pondered in a similar vein in 1868:

September 16th. St Francis of Assisi's Stigmata. *If any man will come after me let him deny himself, and take up his Cross, and follow me. (St Matt. xvi. 24).* Abnegation of self—carrying the Cross—following Christ. We might be what the Saints are, if we would do what the Saints did. (*St Chrysostom*).[69]

Although a concentration on the 'school of suffering' was broadly shared by Protestants, Catholic approaches seem to have given an added stress to the value of physical suffering as a path to holiness. A marked concentration on the wounds of Christ, emulation of the crucifixion, and the horror as well as the consolation of the Sacred Heart could lead some Catholics, like Teresa Higginson of Bootle, to saintly extremes. As she recalled for her spiritual director in 1880, as a child she had felt that she had been 'the cause of all that Our Blessed Lord suffered, and I tried each day to hurt myself in some way'.[70] Although Teresa's approach was clearly considered excessive by the nuns at her school, one of whom caught her trying to burn herself in self-chastisement and forbade such behaviour,[71] it arose from a deeply rooted desire for atonement and sanctification which was focused through a distinctively Catholic hagiographical tradition. By the 1870s Teresa, who clearly meant to emulate the saints and in particular her namesake St Teresa, had already claimed the mystical experiences of visions, bilocation, and wrangles with the devil, and was to go on to develop stigmata. While such a case was clearly extraordinary, and was viewed with mingled reactions even by her Catholic neighbours,[72] her case was an exaggerated case of feelings which were, in a less extreme form, not uncommon, and which appear to have been shared by Catholics of very different social backgrounds.

Holy Simplicity

English Catholic devotion had a great deal in common with contemporary Protestant spirituality. In its anxious and scrupulous attention to sin, its

---

[68] 'My God make me a saint' is said by her biographer to be a constant prayer in her diary (*The Inner Life*, 147). [69] Ibid. 338.

[70] O'Sullivan, *Teresa Higginson*, 29–30. [71] Ibid. 57.

[72] Moves for Teresa Higginson's beatification, which have been recently rekindled in Neston and Bootle, were not taken up with much zeal until the 1930s. Mrs F. Julien, born in 1920, remembered, as a child in Lancashire, coming into 'contact with older people who had heard quite a lot about her holiness from relatives of theirs who were Teresa's contemporaries' (letter from Mrs F. Julien to the present writer, 12 Mar. 1990).

hunger for vivid apprehensions of grace such as those entailed in a 'conversion' experience, and its striving for spiritual perfection, a Victorian religious sensibility is readily identifiable. Catholic attitudes to reparations, suffering, and sanctification were more distinctive, but arose out of a broadly shared religious climate in which earnest Protestants and Catholics endeavoured to follow the cross and to imitate the perfect Christian model of Christ's self-sacrifice. If we were to single out one aspect of a Victorian and Edwardian Christian sensibility which united Catholics where it divided Protestants, we might suggest a particularly English Catholic stress on the value and holiness of simplicity.

At various points in this work a tendency has been observed among nineteenth-century English Catholics to allow, and even to champion, those devotional elements open to the simplest of approaches. We have seen how the significance of the traditional service of Benediction was left open to a variety of interpretations which enabled it to respond to the spiritual needs of a highly disparate collection of Catholics living in England. We have also seen how, in spite of some embarrassment, the unintellectual devotion of the rosary came to be said by ever-increasing numbers of the faithful, educated and uneducated alike. It also seems to have been the devotional elasticity of the *Memorare* which led to its becoming, alone of modern prayers, nearly as familiar among English Catholics as the Hail Mary or Our Father. Those aspects of devotion which were new or newly emphasized in the latter half of the nineteenth century tended to be just those which were as accessible to the poor and illiterate as to the learned.

There were good reasons why the English hierarchy should have felt it necessary to concentrate in earnest on integrating the Catholic community from the 1840s and certainly by about 1850. The arrival of large numbers of Irish Catholics, churched and unchurched, presented a particularly acute problem of denominational accommodation. This historical accident had some important repercussions, one of which was to force rich and poor Catholics into greater contact with one another through the sheer scarcity of churches and of diocesan and parish funds. 'In west and central London,' as Sheridan Gilley has found, 'the Irish settlements, or rookeries, stood within a stone's throw of the houses of the Catholic rich.' This meant that 'in the late 1840s in Kensington and Kentish Town, Fulham and Holborn, Brook Green, Hammersmith and the Strand, the poor and prosperous worshipped in the same churches'.[73] By the late

---

[73] S. W. Gilley, 'The Roman Catholic Mission to the Irish in London', *Recusant History*, 10 (1969), 126.

1850s the same pattern had been reproduced in urban and rural centres throughout the country.

While unsought external circumstances imposed a certain amount of social mixing on the English Catholic community, integration was undoubtedly helped by the spread of an idealized view of the holiness of the poor. This view was promoted not only by the ecclesiastical hierarchy but also by the Vincentians and Franciscans, who urged Catholics to accept one another in a spirit of holy charity as brothers and sisters in the true church of Christ. Gilley is undoubtedly right to caution us that 'the pious commonplaces of devotional literature tell the great mass of men what they ought to be, and only the saints what they are'.[74] But a range of evidence suggests that the deliberate building of bridges between rich and poor, Irish and English, members of the Catholic community gradually came to be accepted by a majority of Catholics living in England as both a holy ideal and a religious duty.

The ideal of mutual acceptance among Catholics in England has been recognized by some historians through its perceptible influence on approaches to social problems in the Victorian and Edwardian periods. Robert Donovan and Sheridan Gilley have both stressed the difference in philosophical outlook between the Catholic charitable effort and that of contemporary Protestants. As Gilley has put it, the often 'striking' resemblance between evangelical and Catholic methods of evangelism can nevertheless be distinguished by their different approaches to the poor and outcast, as manifested in 'notably dissimilar notions of almsgiving, and a notably dissimilar charitable idea'.[75] That official Catholic attitudes to the very poorest members of society were influenced by a notion of the holiness of poverty and a spiritual ideal of charity far removed from the thinking behind the English Poor Laws undoubtedly accounts in part for the legendary high popularity in which the parish priest—and by association his church—was often held among the destitute. However unevenly practised, the notion of holy poverty certainly became a commonly held pious maxim, and marked the behaviour of at least some Catholics in the period.

Ideals such as those expressed by the particularly widespread Society of St Vincent de Paul and the Third Order of Franciscans, as Gilley has remarked, 'have their influence' and should not be dismissed too

---

[74] Gilley, 'Heretic London, Holy Poverty and the Irish Poor', 64.

[75] S. W. Gilley, 'Papists, Protestants and the Irish in London, 1835–70', in G. J. Cuming and D. Baker (eds.), *Popular Belief and Practice* (Studies in Church History 8, Cambridge, 1972), 261.

readily;[76] we have already seen how many earnest laypeople attempted to 'practise' poverty themselves while simultaneously providing charitable assistance to others. Barberi himself attributed his own success to 'first, example which the ministers cannot match; secondly, almsgiving. "They cannot understand how people who are so poor themselves can give so much alms. If an accurate account were made, it would probably be found that we have spent more on the poor than on ourselves."'[77] Manning, whose later championship of the poor during the London dockers' strike of 1889 made him something of a folk hero, may have touched on a kernel of truth, but certainly voiced a quintessentially English Catholic ideal, when he declared with satisfaction in 1873 that:

> The poor in England have no animosities against the Faith of their fathers. Our people are mingled with them: they labour together and live together. They are accustomed to see with no wonder, and with good will, our Clergy and our Sisters visiting the sick and the dying in the same neighbourhood, in the same hospital, and even in the same house where they dwell. They have learned that the Catholic religion is the religion of charity, and that the Catholic Church is the Church of the poor.[78]

The ideal of closeness between all Catholics, rich and poor, which came to be widely advocated in the latter half of the nineteenth century was neither meant to be, nor was it in practice, characteristically expressed as a material and this-worldly one. Rather, Catholics of all classes, intellectual abilities, and ethnic origins were encouraged to join together in a distinctively Catholic experience which became increasingly accessible in order that it should become more widespread. Signs of such a *rapprochement* have been seen throughout the course of this work. Through increased attention to Benediction and the rosary, the spread of catechizing, greater Mass attendance, and more frequent confessions; in the following of the Stations of the Cross, meditations on the Sacred Heart, the recitation of common prayers, and through membership in exclusively denominational societies, Catholics were drawn together into what was becoming an increasingly exclusive Catholic world. The holy language of simplicity which invited the humblest to participate was not the preserve of Irish proletarians or of 'Romans' like Ward or Faber, but was just as

---

[76] Gilley, 'Heretic London, Holy Poverty and the Irish Poor', 81.

[77] Wilson, *Blessed Dominic Barberi*, 259.

[78] H. Manning, Synodal Letter to the Fourth Synod of Westminster, 12 Aug. 1873, in *The Synods in English: Being the Text of the Four Synods of Westminster, translated into English . . .* , ed. R. E. Guy (Stratford, 1886), p. 298.

earnestly appropriated by intellects as sophisticated, and sometimes troubled, as Newman's or Tyrrell's.

Just as approaches to established devotions became more elastic, so the
realm of the miraculous broadened to provide another meeting-point for
Catholics of different social classes and backgrounds. Gerard Connolly
has found that in Manchester in 1837, where slum priest Fr Hearne 'was
almost worshipped'[79] by the poor of his parish, he, along with other local
clergy, had been 'continually at pains to disclaim reputations as wonder
workers attributed to them by Irish congregations'.[80] But, while before
the revival of the 1840s Catholics expressed the kind of disdain for Irish
'superstition' which continued to be characteristic of Protestant middle-
class commentators like Booth, a substantial number of Catholic priests,
bishops, and educated laypeople came to tolerate, single out for praise,
and even to seek to emulate many aspects of the 'simple' faith of Catholic
slum-dwellers.

However patronizing approval of simplicity may sound to the modern
ear, praise for the piety of the poor was no disparagement, but was meant
approvingly, even reverently. In the full flush of the Catholic revival even
attributions of signs and wonders to priests began to be tacitly tolerated
or lauded as commendable signs of affection for the church, and as
betraying a pious predisposition, however partially misguided in specifics.
Barberi, who was called 'a saint on earth'[81] by the time of his second
mission, in Swynnerton from 11 to 19 May 1844, was hardly being critical when he reported to his superior, of the next mission, at Tixall from
21 to 29 July 1844, that he had been 'occupied from morning to night
in preaching, hearing confessions, instructing Protestants, etc'. Not even
in Italy, he commented with astonishment,

have I come across a more fervent people. All came to hear me in the early
morning, in the afternoon, and in the evening! . . . What fine people! . . . You
could not believe the impression our habit makes when we go to preach any-
where. Heavens above, people take me for a saint! They kneel down in crowds
just to receive my blessing. We do more preaching here with bare feet and
religious restraint and modesty than with the tongue. When they can understand
me, they are overjoyed.[82]

Ullathorne, writing to Manning after a return visit, in 1865, to the Coventry he had known in the middle 1840s, similarly found grounds only

---

[79] B. T. Swindells, *Manchester Streets and Manchester Men* (Manchester, 1908), 176–7, as
cited in G. P. Connolly, 'Little Brother be at Peace: The Priest as Holy Man in the
Nineteenth-Century Ghetto', in S. Mews (ed.), *Religion and National Identity* (Studies in
Church History 18; Oxford, 1982), 198 n.   [80] Ibid. 193.
[81] As cited in Wilson, *Blessed Dominic Barberi*, 264.   [82] As cited in ibid. 263.

for praise when he declared that the Catholics of the town were 'a simple and a pious people'. The poor had 'flocked in upon me in the sacristy whenever I was not officiating, from morning till night for three days, with their simple faith, weeping, kissing feet as well as hands, and all wanting some little word to take home and live upon'. Musing on the quality of their devotion, Ullathorne concluded that the Catholics of Coventry were 'an English people of converts, and yet they have the deep Irish faith, together with the English quality of good works. It has been a feast to be among them.'[83]

Such acceptance of working–class spirituality appears to have won a corresponding enthusiasm from a substantial proportion of the poor. Fr Dominic Barberi was initially ridiculed rather than revered by the Midlands Catholics he had fondly imagined would welcome his attempts to convert the Protestant majority to the true faith: at Prior Park in 1841 he was called 'Paddy-Whack' because of his 'far from elegant' appearance, and 'even the pious' at Aston could 'not Suppress their amusement' when, in broken English, he first 'stood up boldly and preached Christ crucified' in 1842.[84] Soon, however, he was treated as a saint possessed of miraculous powers. Not long after his reception as a laughing-stock, a story began to circulate concerning a shoemaker who, having met with him,

afterwards went home and entertained the family-circle by mimicking and ridiculing him. Finally, spurred on by applause, he drew a cross on the wall, and began to strike it, and spit at it, and fling at it everything that came to hand, including one of his tools. The blasphemous mockery stopped suddenly. Before the eyes of a horrified family, his arm withered and was completely paralysed. Though he later became a Catholic, the arm remained withered, a visible warning to any would-be insultors of the Christian religion . . .[85]

It is worth stressing that apprehensions of the miraculous, like other devotional tastes, were not confined to Irish proletarians of the 1840s, but tended rather to join Catholics of different ethnic origins. Susan Ryland and Teresa Higginson of Bootle, both lower-middle-class English Catholics, still believed in 1880 that their priest had powers over the devil.[86] They also providentially found a bar of soap when they had run short[87] and, asking St Joseph for some kindling, found that 'nice pieces not like the wood we bought'[88] were miraculously provided. Those who were successful in finding supernatural cures through the agency of St Winefride's well at Holywell included pilgrims of both Irish and English

[83] Butler, *Life and Times of Ullathorne*, i. 133–4.
[84] Wilson, *Blessed Dominic Barberi*, 235, 242.   [85] Ibid. 252.
[86] Kerr, *Teresa Helena Higginson*, 51.   [87] Ibid. 53.   [88] Ibid. 53–4.

descent such as Lancaster Catholic Mary Standen, who went in 1896,[89] Bootle Catholic John Murphy, and Millicent Bradley from Preston, who was cured in 1910.[90] It was Fr Quigley of Cwmbran who had the idea of sending one of his parishioners, Kitty O'Brien, to Holywell, where she was cured in 1914,[91] but the shrine's spontaneous popularity seems evident from the fact that even the occasional non-Catholic was drawn, like baker-turned-coal-miner Daniel Maddock of Audley, who went there to be healed in 1908.[92]

Nor was such simple-minded faith meant only for the humble, Irish or English. Wiseman urged Catholics of all stations in life to

hold fast the doctrine of your holy Mother, the Church, in all simplicity of heart, without cavil, and without anxiety. Accept the truths of faith in the plain meaning in which they were taught you in your infancy, nor fear that the progress of human learning, or the discoveries of modern science, can shake the foundations of your everlasting belief. Keep ever 'the form of sound words', which you have learnt, without innovation, without attempts to adapt it to any particular theory. Be content to remain docile children of the Church.[93]

For at least some educated and genteel Catholics it was not a very large step from that longing for sanctity which Gerard Connolly has called a 'swoon for life everlasting' to a sense of the immediacy and accessibility of the miraculous in everyday life.

Increased emphasis on the reality of the intercession of the saints led logically to an acknowledgement of their possible intervention in natural affairs. As Ralph Townsend points out, Newman in his essay *On Ecclesiastical Miracles* of 1842–3 'defended ecclesiastical miracles, despite their legendary air, on the grounds that it was only distance in time from their genuine point of origin which injured the record of saints having performed them'.[94] This insistence upon simple acceptance of the marvellous also served to sharpen a sense of difference between the holy and Catholic and the surrounding and sceptical world. As a particularly uncompromising article in the *Rambler* put it in 1850:

We see that the English mind has no true faith in the supernatural; that its imaginary belief in the reality of the scripture miracles is a deception; that it

[89] Thurston, 'Holywell in Recent Years', 46.
[90] She afterwards suffered a relapse. Ibid. 44–5.   [91] Ibid. 39–40.
[92] Ibid. 43.
[93] Wiseman, Synodal Letter to the Third Synod of Westminster, 16 July 1859, in *The Synods in English*, ed. Guy, 289.   [94] Townsend, 'Hagiography in England', 37.

knows but one reality—this visible universe; and that it worships a false god, namely *itself*.[95]

The acceptance of contemporary miracles and pious legends was not quite as straightforward as the Oratorians or former Tractarians would have liked to believe. Educated Catholics were not unaffected by those currents of thought which demanded that the same 'scientific' approach as that which was coming to be expected of ordinary biographies also be applied to the lives of saints.[96] But, while Acton made himself unpopular in some Catholic circles of the 1860s, as Thurston was to do in the early years of the twentieth century, by the deliberate pointing to errors of fact in the legends of the saints, others—Newman, Manning, and Faber among them—put their abilities to the task of reviving such tales of saintly edification. By the end of the century the more credulous approach appears to have been the one which was most commonly expressed in devotional literature and official Catholic publications, in self-conscious defiance of an unbelieving world. Catholic newspapers like the *Month*, or the Jesuit magazine the *Messenger of the Sacred Heart* (which began publishing in about 1885), heightened accounts of the miraculous. Stories for children, such as those edited by Lady Georgiana Fullerton or published by the Catholic Truth Society, brimmed with such tales. As can be seen from the similar devotional content of a range of differently priced editions of such works, tales of saintly wonders and contemporary miracles were not addressed exclusively to the poorest, or even the youngest, members of the community but were meant to edify Catholics of all stations, and stages, of life.[97]

Like Protestant devotional literature, Catholic lives of saints were meant primarily as spurs to imitate the life of Christ. To further this end,

---

[95] Anon., 'The Miracle at Rimini', *Rambler*, 6 (1850), 177, as reproduced in ibid. 122.

[96] See Ralph Townsend's admirable discussion of this complex subject in ibid. 151.

[97] Lady Georgiana Fullerton published translations of *The Life, Virtues and Miracles of John Berchmans* by François Deynoodt and Jean Philippe Verdenal's *The Miracle at Metz* in 1866; and brought out *The Miraculous Medal. Life and Visions of Catherine Labouré* in 1880. Publication lists of the Catholic Truth Society at the turn of the century include, among the 'shilling publications': *The Catholic's Library of Tales, Legends of St Francis, St Brigid, Ven. Oliver Plunket, Ven. Edmund Arrowsmith, The Curé d'Ars* by Lady Herbert, *The Holy Coat of Trèves* by Canon Moyes, *St Teresa* by David Lewis, *St Philip Neri*, and *Blessed John Fisher*. 'Sixpenny publications' include: *A Few Flowers from St Francis' Garden, Life of the Curé d'Ars, The Catholic's Library of Tales, Ireland's Spiritual Shamrock: Being Lives of St Patrick, St Brigid, and St Columba*, and *St Francis and You*. 'Penny publications' include more merely informative works like *What is the Mass?* and *A Simple Prayer Book*, but also *Good Words from the Curé d'Ars, St Brigid* by Mrs Atkinson, *St Francis of Assisi* by J. Prendergast, *Ven. Oliver Plunket, St Philip Neri*, and *St Teresa*. Clearly, the same pious tales were meant to edify Catholics of all income-levels.

Catholics were encouraged to follow those deemed to have been especially close to Christ, figures like St Francis of Assisi or St Teresa. Increasingly, however, the acceptance by Catholics of miracles associated with the saints was taken as a sign of genuine faith, to be praised in the simple and aspired to by the more sophisticated. The reluctance to disturb pious beliefs undoubtedly rested in part on fears that questions surrounding the lives of the saints would in turn shed doubt on biblical and doctrinal miracles, thus unravelling the whole fabric, not only of Catholic, but of Christian belief. But official acceptance of a working-class readiness to believe in wonders and contemporary miracles was not a purely pragmatic expedient; nor was it meant as a condescension on the part of the hierarchy.

Reluctant to denounce reports of current miracles to the disedification of the simple, and themselves eager to have such immediate signs of the truth of revelation, educated Catholic responses could range from the hopeful or diffident to the frankly sanguine. Thus in 1846 Cornelia Connelly longed to see significance in the fact that at Pius IX's election 'there was a dove flying around the Chamber of the Conclave of Cardinals during the whole time of the election, which they endeavoured in vain to drive out'.[98] Herbert Vaughan seemed unsure quite what to think when he agreed, in a letter of 14 September 1883 to Lady Herbert of Lea, that a knocking at the door which came as a friend lay dying 'was a very curious circumstance'. As he added thoughtfully, 'Such things certainly do happen with Souls in Purgatory.'[99] More positively, an enthusiast for Holywell remembered, in 1916, how her friend Lady Mary Plowden had once sent some moss and water from the well to add to an ill daughter's medicine. It was to this action that she attributed the child's subsequent recovery.[100]

It will be remembered how even those Catholics who disbelieved in the supernatural sanction sometimes attributed to the rosary were annoyed to have 'pious legends' disturbed. The vague sense that pious credulity might contain truth in a realm in which scientific method had no business to meddle led to a predisposition to accept supernatural explanations if possible; and at all times to take care not to disturb the simple, and therefore commendable, faith of others. An example of the extent to which such apprehensions had become a widely shared feature of Catholic piety may be seen from Herbert Thurston's observation of 1916 that

[98] Wadham, *Case of Cornelia Connelly*, 93.   [99] *Vaughan Letters*, 358.
[100] Thurston, 'Holywell in Recent Years', 51.

there are many intelligent people, quite sane, and normally free from superstition, who taught, as they believe, by long personal experience, maintain that the intervention of St Anthony in finding lost objects produces results far beyond anything which it is in the power of coincidence to explain.[101]

As Thurston, despite his own uncomfortable reputation for challenging superstitious elements within the Catholic tradition, cheerfully acknowledged, he 'personally share[d] the conviction'.[102]

The Ultramontane Question

The experience of Catholicism in the nineteenth and early twentieth centuries was not the same in all countries. Despite the prevalence of the view that an ultramontane conception of Catholicism was imposed on the entire Catholic world in the latter half of the nineteenth century, this does not seem to have happened in England. Although English, French, Irish, and other national variants of Catholicism are argued to have been abandoned from about 1850 in favour of a newly universal and Roman conception of devotion, in England at least it was an idiosyncratic tradition which was deliberately, and for the most part successfully, preserved. Furthermore, where the native English Catholic tradition was modified, it seems to have been for reasons which owed little to Roman pronouncements but had more to do with local problems, the need to compete effectively with rival denominations, and the desire to recast traditional piety into the idiom of the day. As a final response to the ultramontane question, it seems worth underlining the fact that English Catholicism not only remained distinct from continental Catholicism, but such devotional change as did occur did not come about for the reasons which historians' accounts of continental ultramontanism have suggested. Let us briefly compare the case of England with that of France, whose devotional practice, which included a marked concentration on the rosary and the Blessed Sacrament, and attention to devotions like the Sacred Heart and the Stations of the Cross, most nearly resembled the English situation.

Gérard Cholvy, Yves-Marie Hilaire, and Ralph Gibson have argued that, in contemporary France, a new 'ultramontane' spirituality was successfully imposed on Catholics, partly by means of the clergy's skilful redirection of older, unorthodox forms of religiosity and, above all, through the presentation of God as a God of love rather than of fear. This

---

[101] Ibid. 49.   [102] Ibid.

account, however compelling in itself, does not present a convincing model for contemporary England.

We have already seen how, as with curative powers attributed to Benediction, miraculous sanctions attached to the rosary, and special powers associated with the *Memorare*, English Catholic bishops in the period alternatively tolerated, incorporated, or tried to rechannel elements of Irish and English piety which bordered on the superstitious. But there is little evidence to suggest that in England it was the deliberate redirection of unorthodox 'holy places' or reverence for dubious saints which fuelled devotion to what have in any case misleadingly been called 'ultramontane' ends. As with attempts to tinker with Benediction, or to supplant *The Garden of the Soul* with the *Manual of Prayers for Congregational Use*, popular devotions were in practice notoriously difficult to impose from above. Nor is it clear that most members of the English episcopate would have wished to impose an overtly Roman spirituality on their flocks: we have already seen the English bishops' reluctance to abandon their own penny catechism and have noted even Wiseman's and Manning's reverence for the devotional legacy of Richard Challoner.

The bishops in synod did occasionally feel the need to discourage what seemed unseemly behaviour, as when in 1885 they suggested that 'any abuse of the practice of using flowers at Funerals should be prudently discouraged'[103] or when, in 1889, they felt that 'steps should be taken to prevent Catholics celebrating the Feast of a Saint in Lent by a meat tea and dancing; but no special resolution was come to'.[104] But while the occasional parish notice, like that of Fr Daly, priest of Our Lady's, Birkenhead, in 1866, does reveal some activity to redirect Irish 'superstition' which seems closer to Gibson's model of accommodation, such isolated examples can hardly be seen as providing the main impetus for devotional change in the period. This particular announcement read:

All notices of Funerals must be brought in to us at least the day before the Funeral is to take place in order to ensure the attendance of a priest at the Cemetery. . . . In all cases when wakes are held it is the express order of the Bishop that no priest attend the Funeral. It appears that a most disgraceful wake was held last night in Price Street. No priest will therefore attend the funeral.[105]

Devotional 'abuses' were not, in England, an exclusively Irish-working-class phenomenon; nor were they generally linked to non-

<hr>

[103] Westminster Archdiocesan Archives, 'Bishops' Meetings 1858–1909', Acta, Meeting of the Bishops in Low Week, 1885, xviii. 190.   [104] Ibid. 1889, xv. 222.
[105] Abbott, 'History of Our Lady's', fo. 12.

Christian folk traditions or superstitions, as has too often been assumed.[106]
In the same year that wakes were being discouraged at Birkenhead, Bishop
Goss of Liverpool felt obliged to remind a nun in Preston that, since 'Our
Lord says that the first commandment of all is "the Lord thy God is *one*
God"', she must choose between 'the statue of the Holy Child & Jesus
Christ, whose body, blood, soul & divinity are truly present in the Blessed
Eucharist. You cannot set up both for adoration, nor can you divide with
a graven image the worship due to the God of heaven.'[107] English bishops
seem to have been roused to restrain excesses of the kind of devotion
which Gibson and others have called 'ultramontane' at least as often as
they felt it necessary to forbid dubious popular practices.

As we have seen in their approaches to *The Garden of the Soul* and the
penny catechism, for all that bishops hoped to 'improve' the faith of their
flocks through a call to greater 'earnestness' and 'devotion', they were just
as adamant that their distinctively English Catholic tradition should be
preserved. Thus it was not inconsistent for the episcopate to decline, in
1902, to support 'a petition promoted in France and elsewhere, to add
to the Litany of Loreto an invocation such as *"Regina Purgatorii"'*[108]
and again in 1908 to decide that they 'were opposed to the extension to
England of the Feast of the Miraculous Medal'.[109] The bishops sometimes felt it necessary to curb the devotional fervour of their own clergy,
as when in 1908 'a recent practice of having public devotions before the
Altar of Repose on Maundy Thursday'[110] was condemned, and it was
insisted that 'With regard to funerals, the Clergy are bound to recite the
whole of the Latin prayers in the *Ordo Exequiarum*. After that is finished,
any English prayers may be said.'[111] As with its attitude to the rosary or
to Benediction, it seems that the English hierarchy sought a devotional
middle ground, a compromise between popular feeling on the one hand
and some clerical over-enthusiasm on the other.[112] The bishops' prime

---

[106] Largely, one suspects, owing to the enormous influence of Keith Thomas's brilliant
but (in this writer's opinion) misleading *Religion and the Decline of Magic* (Harmondsworth,
Middlesex, 1978). As we have seen, superstitious 'abuses' like those connected with St
Bridget in approaches to the rosary, or evident in the 'Red Cross Chain', were hardly
'pagan' but had clearly Catholic roots, however confused.

[107] Lancashire Record Office, The Archbishop of Liverpool, 'Bishop Goss Letter Book
1855–1872', RCLv 14 5/2, Alexander Goss to Sr Lucy, St Wilfrid's Convent, Preston, 13
May 1866, fo. 112.

[108] Westminster Archdiocesan Archives, 'Bishops' Meetings 1858–1909', Meeting of the
Bishops in Low Week, Acta, 1902, xii. 324.   [109] Ibid. 1908, vi. 387.

[110] Ibid. 1908, viii. 387.   [111] Ibid. 1908, xxiii. 389.

[112] So it would also seem from the majority of bishops' moderate stance on papal infallibility, and their approaches to revisions to *The Garden of the Soul* which have already been
discussed.

concern was to attract the greatest possible following among the Catholic population and to maintain an English spiritual tradition while continuing to make room for what appeared to be genuine devotional improvement from whatever source it might appear.

Gibson's account of a shift from a religion of fear in roughly the first half of the nineteenth century to one of love in the second does not seem any more helpful in understanding the character of devotional change in England. Since England did not share the Jansenist background of pre-revolutionary France, it is hardly surprising that this particular contrast should not fit the English case. While nineteenth- and early twentieth-century English Catholic devotion was characteristically sentimental in expression, eminently accessible, and did have its consoling aspects, the recusant tradition was in many ways the gentler of the two.

As Geoffrey Rowell has observed, *The Garden of the Soul* is 'unusually restrained in its descriptions of hell, and forbears from anatomizing the details of physical torment compared, for example, with the contemporary work of St Alphonsus Liguori'.[113] Challoner, following Francis de Sales rather than more rigorist continental devotional writers, made clear that his own notion of the horror of hell was one of the absence of God rather than fire and brimstone when, 'coming in the midst of a sober catalogue of the losses endured in hell', he wrote, '"Ah! unhappy wretches that cannot love!"'[114] When Challoner wrote of divine flames in his *Meditations*, it was in quite another sense than this. 'We have this loving and most lovely God always with us and always in us,' he mused;

> why do we not run to His embraces? He is a fire that ever burns; this fire is in the very centre of our souls; how is it that we feel so little of its flames? It is because we will not stand by it. It is because we will not keep our souls at home, attentive to that great guest who resides within us, but let them continually wander abroad upon vain created amusements.[115]

One could argue that, if anything, it was popular mission sermons from the 1840s, preached to match Protestant revivals, which introduced the horrors of a material hell to English Catholics; but evidence as to the increase or decrease in severity of the Catholic message is contradictory and points to no clear conclusion. Since there is no evidence to suggest that a clear shift of emphasis from fear to love took place in England, the point need not be laboured further.

[113] G. Rowell, *Hell and the Victorians* (Oxford, 1974), 154.
[114] As cited in M. Trappes-Lomax, *Bishop Challoner: A Biographical Study Derived from Dr. Edwin Burton's 'The Life and Times of Bishop Challoner'* (1936; London, 1947), 135.
[115] As cited in ibid. 22.

The Jansenist pre-conditions for an ultramontane revolution did not exist in eighteenth-century England; neither has this examination of English Catholic devotion found evidence to suggest that a change of the kind which historians describe as ultramontane actually occurred in Victorian or Edwardian times. As we have seen, most genuinely Roman devotions were neglected in the post-1850 period, while virtually every aspect of recusant devotion was highlighted and further popularized. Not only did England fail to import Roman spirituality wholesale, but in many respects English Catholic devotion was more closely influenced by parallel developments within other English churches. Most prayers which English Catholics said were common to all Christians; anxieties about the state of one's soul, the longing for perfection, and a marked desire for vivid apprehensions of grace were loosely Victorian; and the tactics of missioners were decidedly evangelical.

Where Catholic approaches differed most sharply from Protestant ones—in the desire to attend Benediction, to say the rosary, or to recite the *Memorare*—it seems generally to have been at the point where the importance of keeping the Catholic community together overrode other considerations. Whereas class, social, and devotional differences among Protestants tended to separate along a range of high, low, and dissenting churches, the Catholic community's highest endeavour was to keep its own small community whole. It seems to have been in order to keep Catholics together that an increasingly simple devotional language was advocated for all and that apprehensions of the miraculous were not only allowed but positively encouraged.

While the specifically Catholic content of the English Catholic message intensified in order to give members a clear denominational loyalty, broader English church trends continued to influence developments within the English Catholic community. It was no accident that mission sermons, whose excitement matched that of contemporary Protestant revivals, were introduced in the 1840s. This was, after all, the period when the need to bring lapsed proletarians back to the fold, and particularly refugees from Ireland, were at their most acute. Even that enthusiast for Roman forms F. W. Faber found at about this time that 'One of the most striking things is that the more Roman I get, the more I seem to recover, only in a safe way and with make-weights, of old boyish evangelical feelings instead of the cold gentilising ethics of Williams and others which never came natural to me.'[116]

---

[116] F. W. Faber to J. B. Morris, 5 Aug. 1846, as cited in R. Chapman, *Father Faber* (London, 1961), 148–9.

By the 1870s, in the midst of renewed Protestant revivals, it would seem that it was rather through a dramatic increase in extra-liturgical devotions like Benediction and Public Rosary, and in the catering for a heavy sense of sin, that Catholic tastes were best accommodated. These developments arose from a widespread Victorian *malaise* which sought reassurance as to prospects for salvation and desired constancy in belief. It was during this period that Bishop Goss showed impatience with a priest of his diocese who imagined that there existed any 'power or authority in the Church' which could 'compel the people to attend' his services. 'If your services are rightly carried out,' he wrote testily, 'if you are punctual . . . for the services on week days as well as on Sundays, & if you dont [*sic*] scold, & if you preach and don't talk, you will find that your Church will fill.'[117] Not surprisingly, given the widespread sense of sin and inadequacy which we have already seen, the bishop added: 'Ordinarily it is thro[ugh] the Confessional that the Church is filled.'[118]

To Catholics as well as to Christians of other denominations, secularizing influences appeared inexorable from about 1880. Such perceptions were partly the inevitable reaction of disappointment to hopes which had been inflated by the trans-denominational revival of the 1840s but whose promise could never have been fulfilled. Jeffrey Cox has usefully pointed out that this perception of failure has been reiterated far too uncritically by religious historians, who have tended both to accept Victorian self-assessments at face value and to see lower church growth as part of an ineluctable process of secularization. As he writes, 'They judge a Victorian religious movement by the standard of the movement itself, even though its goal was the conversion of an entire city or an entire social class or an entire nation, a goal which could only be achieved by force of arms.'[119] Late Victorian pessimism also reflected a belief that the masses were in danger of dechristianization, a view which was widely held in the wake of sensationalist publicity given to the extent of working-class 'indifference' in the great industrial cities.[120]

Such widespread perceptions of 'leakage' led many Catholic priests to imitate Protestant endeavours to make the parish an attractive place to the less religiously minded, so that it might effectively compete with rival

[117] Lancashire Record Office, The Archbishop of Liverpool, 'Bishop Goss's Letter Book 1855–1872', RCLv 14 5/2, Bp Goss to Fr Tobin, 6 May 1866, fo. 105.   [118] Ibid.

[119] J. Cox, *The English Churches in a Secular Society: Lambeth, 1870–1930* (Oxford, 1982), 265.

[120] e.g. A. Mearns, *The Bitter Cry of Outcast London: An Inquiry into the Condition of the Abject Poor* (London, 1883), and W. Booth, *In Darkest England and the Way Out* (London, 1890).

secular attractions. Thus in 1896 the curate of All Souls, Peterborough, Dudley Cary-Elwes, spent an inordinate amount of time organizing outings, treats, and plays for the amusement of Catholic schoolchildren and their families. After staging *Santa Claus* within a few days of his arrival at the parish in 1896,[121] a performance which had so much success that it was repeated the following week,[122] a concert for the grown-ups followed.[123] Fun was not only for the Christmas season: in February the curate records:

Children's tea at 5.30. Canon Moser presided over girls' table, Fr C-Elwes over boys'. Magic lantern afterwards . . . boys then gave spontaneous entertainment of a sanguine kind, i.e. Charade in wh[ich] murders-executions were the chief features. Ended with ghost story by Fr C-Elwes.[124]

By about the turn of the century, the tone had become more desperate. James Britten, writing about Catholic boys' clubs in 1901, stressed the 'absolute necessity of immensely increased effort, if we are to succeed in stemming the leakage which confronts us on every side'.[125] He believed that 'the religious side must be worked in with much tact, and with every consideration for the weaker brethren'[126] if the boys were not to flee, taking the club's dominoes set or boxing gloves with them.[127] The sense that devotional fervour had slackened was as commonly expressed among Catholics as among Protestants. As one Irish Redemptorist father complained in 1894, in a climate in which missions, by now a parish institution, catered for an ever smaller number of the devout, revivals had become 'only a huge station . . . a hullabaloo mission', rather than a spur to mass reappropriation of an earnest religion. G. E. Anstruther wrote to the editor of the *Ransomer* in a similar vein in 1893, arguing that 'I am much afraid that the excelsior of ambition with some of us' to bring Catholic boys back to the Faith is to urge them to 'join a "Club", where the principal attractions are a few illustrated papers, some draughts, and a box or two of dominoes. Surely we can aim higher than this.'[128]

However far Catholic practice in the late Victorian and Edwardian periods fell short of the ideals of its hierarchy and more earnest members,

[121] Archives of the Church of St Peter and All Souls, Peterborough, Box 3, 'All Souls Mission Log Book', i, 16 Dec. 1896.   [122] Ibid., 22 Dec. 1896.

[123] Ibid., 21 Jan. 1897.

[124] Ibid., 15 Feb. 1897. It was only a week before a 'Nigger Minstrel Entertainment' continued the social calendar (ibid., 22 Feb. 1897).

[125] J. Britten, 'Boys' Clubs', *Month*, 97 (1901), 57.   [126] Ibid. 62.   [127] Ibid.

[128] G. E. Anstruther, letter to the editor, 'What Shall We Do with Our Boys in their Teens', *Ransomer*, 1 (1893), 150.

the piety of the Victorian period had left its stamp on Catholic practice and continued to mark the religious feelings of those who remained within the fold. At Grimsby in 1890, as John Sharp reports, although half of the town's 2,000 Catholics were 'left totally unimpressed' by a mission held there and 'were deemed to have lapsed altogether', the remaining 1,000 were earnest enough to wish to attend.[129] Similarly, in Manchester in 1892, 'scarcely any of those lost to the Faith could be got up; but nearly all the rest came'.[130] Congregations may have grown smaller, but those who remained bore the unmistakable stamp of the Catholic revival of the 1840s, a recognizable blend of earnestness with simplicity, notable for its open-mindedness in the face of the marvellous and supernatural. Not only the Catholic sacraments, but Benediction, the rosary, the Stations of the Cross, devotions to the Sacred Heart, and prayers and devotions drawn from *The Garden of the Soul* marked religious apprehensions and experience and distinguished Catholic from Protestant practice.

This distinctively Catholic piety continued to join together those who had much else to divide them. Bruce Marshall's proudly affectionate portrait of the social mix characteristic of Scottish Catholics in the 1930s, for all its sentimentality, is none the less recognizably British. 'About twenty minutes to eleven on Sunday the faithful of the quarter began to enter the church for the eleven o'clock High Mass', he wrote:

These faithful included Irish labourers and their families, Italian ice-cream merchants and their families, French mistresses from some of the more exclusive girls' schools, a flock of Belgian nuns, a few University lecturers who had been converted to Catholicism by reading history or theology, a handful or so of Real Ladies and Gentlemen who saw no inconsistency in accepting both haggis *and* papal infallibility and a horde of publicans whose piety would have shamed a Carthusian monk.[131]

Members of the Catholic community in England remained as English as the Scots remained Scottish. But they had also become more distinctively Catholic. While class and ethnicity undoubtedly remained in many respects an obvious point of division within the community, the revivalist spirit of devotional change which aimed to sustain a sense of the otherworldly among Catholics of all backgrounds effectively provided a point of affinity to which Catholics as Catholics were able to respond. Meeting together more frequently for Mass, Catholics of all classes, ethnic backgrounds, and political persuasions were also joined together in a range of

[129] Sharp, *Reapers of the Harvest*, 224.   [130] As cited in ibid.
[131] B. Marshall, *Father Malachy's Miracle* (1931; London, 1947), 17.

extra-liturgical activities which catered for their individual spiritual and psychological make-up rather than their social place. In their holy aspiration to accept one another as Catholics first, despite class, ethnic, and political differences, they had also become more catholic in the other sense. It was perhaps in this surprising degree of class and ethnic tolerance that English Catholics had grown most unlike the majority of their fellow countrymen. One home may have been little England, but another stretched beyond and above, and was shared by all members of the Catholic body. This Catholic world within England was not an outpost of Rome but remained both an English and a Catholic community.

Appendix I

Devotional Statistics of the Churches, Chapels, and Stations in England and Wales

TABLE I gives the number of churches, chapels, and stations in all the dioceses of England and Wales, as well as the number of distinct confraternities, guilds, and sodalities attached to them for the sample years between 1850 and 1914. Figures are also given by year and diocese of the number of churches offering catechizing, confession, Benediction of the Blessed Sacrament, Public Rosary, *Quarant'ore* or Forty Hours' Devotion, the Stations or Way of the Cross, and Exposition of the Blessed Sacrament.

The figures in Table I have been taken from church advertisements listed in the *Catholic Directory* for the relevant years; according to the *Directory*, some details of confraternities and services were omitted from 1890, and so information for the years 1890–1914 must be treated as approximate and as under-representing the real number of devotional services and societies offered by the churches of England and Wales.

Since several dioceses changed their boundaries and/or their names over the course of the period under scrutiny, it seemed useful to list the information both by diocese proper and by 'diocesan group', an invented category which remains constant over time. Thus the diocese of Beverley, which split into the dioceses of Leeds and Middlesbrough in 1878, but continued to minister to the same geographical area of Yorkshire, has been treated as the diocese of 'Beverley' until 1878, and the combined figures given for the dioceses of Leeds and Middlesbrough have been treated as those of the 'diocesan group of Beverley' thereafter in order to allow for comparisons of the devotional activity of Yorkshire churches to be made both before and after 1878. Similarly, Southwark diocese was divided into the dioceses of Southwark and Portsmouth in 1882; after that date Southwark and Portsmouth dioceses are treated together in all calculations as the 'diocesan group of Southwark'.

Name changes have been preserved in this table of raw data but regularized for the purpose of calculations. Thus Hexham diocese, which changed its name to the diocese of Hexham and Newcastle in 1861, has been assigned the 'diocesan-group' name of Hexham and Newcastle throughout. Similarly, the diocese of Newport and Menevia, which became Newport diocese in 1896, is treated for computational purposes as the 'diocesan group' of Newport. The diocese of

Shrewsbury, which ceased to include northern Wales under its jurisdiction from 1896, has been adjusted for the earlier period by omitting the figures given for the churches of northern Wales even before 1896, so that comparisons can be made of the number of devotions offered in the English portion of Shrewsbury diocese over time.

In two cases, it has not been possible to accommodate minor diocesan changes so easily; but these hardly affect the overall picture. Jurisdiction over the area of Leyland shifted from Salford to Liverpool diocese in 1852, but this change has not been taken into account in the figures given, since no county breakdown in the figures for the diocese is given for 1851 in the *Directory*; neither have the figures for the Scilly Isles, which were added to the diocese of Plymouth in 1853, been traced for 1851.

The information given in Table 1 represents the raw statistical information which has been used to calculate the proportion of churches within each diocese which offered various devotions, figures which (in order to allow for comparisons easily to be made across dioceses and over time) are more vividly represented by the figures which follow. This table is therefore given primarily for reference purposes, and may be used for a more detailed examination of the devotional information gleaned from the *Catholic Directory* which the figures illustrate.

TABLE 1. *Devotional Statistics of the churches, chapels, and stations in England and Wales, 1850–1914*

Year	Diocese name	Catechizing	Public Rosary	Benediction	Confraternities, sodalities, and guilds	Confession	Exposition	Stations	Quarant'ore	Number of churches	Diocesan-group name
1851	Beverley	1	0	3	1	0	0	0	0	61	Beverley
1851	Birmingham	3	1	4	5	0	0	0	0	82	Birmingham
1851	Clifton	1	0	2	0	0	0	0	0	30	Clifton
1851	Hexham	0	0	0	0	0	0	0	0	56	Hexham & Newcastle
1851	Liverpool	5	2	6	4	0	0	0	0	–	Liverpool
1851	Newport & Menevia	0	1	0	0	0	0	0	0	13	Newport
1851	Northampton	0	0	0	1	0	0	0	0	26	Northampton
1851	Nottingham	1	1	2	1	0	0	0	0	42	Nottingham
1851	Plymouth	0	0	1	0	0	0	0	0	29	Plymouth
1851	Salford	3	1	4	3	0	0	0	0	–	Salford
1851	Shrewsbury	1	1	2	1	1	0	0	0	29	Shrewsbury
1851	Southwark	3	5	9	10	0	1	1	0	56	Southwark
1851	Westminster	9	3	15	9	3	1	0	0	47	Westminster
1855	Beverley	2	0	3	4	2	0	0	0	76	Beverley
1855	Birmingham	9	2	9	6	0	0	0	0	90	Birmingham
1855	Clifton	3	2	3	0	1	0	0	0	36	Clifton
1855	Hexham	3	0	4	9	1	0	0	0	59	Hexham & Newcastle
1855	Liverpool	8	7	11	6	3	0	2	0	88	Liverpool
1855	Newport & Menevia	2	1	1	0	0	0	0	0	35	Newport
1855	Northampton	2	0	2	2	0	0	0	0	28	Northampton
1855	Nottingham	1	0	3	1	0	0	0	0	40	Nottingham
1855	Plymouth	1	0	3	0	0	0	0	0	27	Plymouth
1855	Salford	8	3	9	3	1	0	0	0	44	Salford
1855	Shrewsbury	3	3	6	1	5	0	1	0	50	Shrewsbury
1855	Southwark	10	11	11	8	1	0	2	0	72	Southwark
1855	Westminster	17	11	22	23	15	0	2	0	54	Westminster

Year	Diocese									Diocese	Total
1860	Beverley	3	2	8	3	2	0	1	0	Beverley	79
1860	Birmingham	7	3	13	0	2	0	1	0	Birmingham	94
1860	Clifton	6	5	9	3	2	0	3	0	Clifton	35
1860	Hexham	9	3	9	17	4	0	4	0	Hexham & Newcastle	66
1860	Liverpool	12	7	14	0	2	0	4	0	Liverpool	94
1860	Newport & Menevia	6	5	8	0	0	0	2	0	Newport	35
1860	Northampton	4	1	5	4	1	0	1	0	Northampton	30
1860	Nottingham	8	3	5	0	0	0	1	0	Nottingham	47
1860	Plymouth	3	2	6	0	0	0	0	0	Plymouth	33
1860	Salford	8	5	11	7	3	0	2	0	Salford	54
1860	Shrewsbury	7	7	9	0	2	0	0	0	Shrewsbury	52
1860	Southwark	16	24	29	17	4	2	10	0	Southwark	89
1860	Westminster	25	17	39	33	22	2	10	1	Westminster	59
1865	Beverley	7	1	12	6	4	0	2	0	Beverley	90
1865	Birmingham	12	7	21	1	5	0	4	0	Birmingham	100
1865	Clifton	9	5	21	12	10	0	6	0	Clifton	49
1865	Hexham & Newcastle	7	4	12	25	6	1	3	0	Hexham & Newcastle	81
1865	Liverpool	20	19	29	7	13	1	8	0	Liverpool	110
1865	Menevia & Newport	9	5	14	0	1	0	4	0	Newport	42
1865	Northampton	10	1	11	6	3	0	1	0	Northampton	36
1865	Nottingham	11	3	12	0	3	0	2	0	Nottingham	52
1865	Plymouth	6	4	16	2	2	0	1	0	Plymouth	35
1865	Salford	16	9	21	10	6	0	3	0	Salford	70
1865	Shrewsbury	10	9	18	0	2	0	16	6	Shrewsbury	59
1865	Southwark	32	32	55	40	19	14	25	1	Southwark	100
1865	Westminster	32	29	64	108	41	8	1	0	Westminster	117
1870	Beverley	9	1	8	3	5	0	10	0	Beverley	107
1870	Birmingham	20	9	34	0	0	0	8	0	Birmingham	114
1870	Clifton	14	7	19	17	13	0	3	0	Clifton	53
1870	Hexham & Newcastle	12	7	15	28	4	0	13	0	Hexham & Newcastle	94
1870	Liverpool	34	29	46	19	19	0	4	0	Liverpool	130
1870	Menevia & Newport	16	14	24	5	4	1		0	Newport	46

TABLE I. (Cont'd)

Year	Diocese name	Catechizing	Public Rosary	Benediction	Confraternities, sodalities, and guilds	Confession	Exposition	Stations	Quarant'ore	Number of churches	Diocesan-group name
1870	Northampton	12	2	14	9	3	0	2	0	49	Northampton
1870	Nottingham	11	5	14	2	5	0	2	0	64	Nottingham
1870	Plymouth	11	8	17	6	2	0	5	0	41	Plymouth
1870	Salford	15	11	26	37	8	0	6	0	95	Salford
1870	Shrewsbury	15	11	21	17	11	0	5	0	73	Shrewsbury
1870	Southwark	27	34	50	54	22	15	22	6	159	Southwark
1870	Westminster	46	29	64	143	47	10	28	0	126	Westminster
1875	Beverley	5	1	10	3	8	0	1	0	109	Beverley
1875	Birmingham	19	17	44	0	0	0	10	0	103	Birmingham
1875	Clifton	11	8	20	15	7	0	7	0	38	Clifton
1875	Hexham & Newcastle	7	4	19	26	2	1	3	0	91	Hexham & Newcastle
1875	Liverpool	25	31	51	27	22	0	14	0	122	Liverpool
1875	Newport & Menevia	4	13	24	6	4	1	7	0	56	Newport
1875	Northampton	8	4	14	11	0	1	1	0	40	Northampton
1875	Nottingham	10	9	19	14	6	0	3	0	58	Nottingham
1875	Plymouth	8	9	22	3	2	0	4	0	36	Plymouth
1875	Salford	16	22	53	49	9	1	4	0	83	Salford
1875	Shrewsbury	6	8	28	12	10	0	2	0	70	Shrewsbury
1875	Southwark	24	31	66	70	23	1	24	6	134	Southwark
1875	Westminster	28	28	69	169	29	13	25	0	101	Westminster
1880	Birmingham	25	18	53	14	1	0	10	0	108	Birmingham
1880	Clifton	7	10	25	31	28	0	6	0	41	Clifton
1880	Hexham & Newcastle	6	6	23	41	3	0	3	0	104	Hexham & Newcastle
1880	Leeds	4	3	5	2	5	0	1	0	74	Beverley
1880	Liverpool	31	32	54	52	31	0	15	0	141	Liverpool
1880	Middlesbrough	1	1	7	3	3	0	1	0	47	Beverley

Year	Diocese										Diocese
1880	Newport & Menevia	13	9	24	4	3	0	4	0	58	Newport
1880	Northampton	7	4	19	13	0	0	0	0	47	Northampton
1880	Nottingham	28	16	34	30	15	0	7	0	76	Nottingham
1880	Plymouth	9	11	24	8	3	0	7	0	37	Plymouth
1880	Salford	15	24	68	54	8	1	1	0	104	Salford
1880	Shrewsbury	3	7	23	21	10	0	1	6	71	Shrewsbury
1880	Southwark	14	34	73	90	31	3	18	0	145	Southwark
1880	Westminster	33	27	70	193	55	17	24	0	105	Westminster
1885	Birmingham	30	30	68	24	2	1	3	0	118	Birmingham
1885	Clifton	11	11	37	7	32	0	5	0	44	Clifton
1885	Hexham & Newcastle	7	13	40	22	3	0	5	0	108	Hexham & Newcastle
1885	Leeds	8	5	11	5	7	0	0	0	83	Beverley
1885	Liverpool	86	115	125	26	34	0	8	0	145	Liverpool
1885	Middlesbrough	0	2	8	3	4	0	0	0	52	Beverley
1885	Newport & Menevia	17	13	28	4	4	0	2	0	67	Newport
1885	Northampton	7	6	25	2	4	0	0	0	51	Northampton
1885	Nottingham	23	22	49	9	21	0	1	0	91	Nottingham
1885	Plymouth	10	20	30	5	5	0	5	0	45	Plymouth
1885	Portsmouth	6	15	32	6	12	0	3	0	62	Southwark
1885	Salford	22	33	90	6	21	3	1	0	108	Salford
1885	Shrewsbury	6	20	45	5	20	0	3	0	74	Shrewsbury
1885	Southwark	21	35	73	43	52	1	7	0	100	Southwark
1885	Westminster	36	25	84	102	48	14	18	0	115	Westminster
1890	Birmingham	28	35	73	15	2	0	1	0	121	Birmingham
1890	Clifton	11	11	34	7	28	0	5	0	45	Clifton
1890	Hexham & Newcastle	5	13	38	21	5	0	4	0	111	Hexham & Newcastle
1890	Leeds	8	6	15	6	8	0	0	0	86	Beverley
1890	Liverpool	109	134	142	31	38	0	8	0	152	Liverpool
1890	Middlesbrough	2	6	14	6	6	0	0	0	57	Beverley
1890	Newport & Menevia	14	26	47	7	7	1	3	0	68	Newport
1890	Northampton	10	9	32	3	9	1	0	0	54	Northampton
1890	Nottingham	31	27	55	11	23	1	0	0	89	Nottingham

TABLE I. (Cont'd)

Year	Diocese name	Catechizing	Public Rosary	Benediction	Confraternities, sodalities, and guilds	Confession	Exposition	Stations	Quarant'ore	Number of churches	Diocesan-group name
1890	Plymouth	19	28	43	3	10	1	7	0	52	Plymouth
1890	Portsmouth	14	20	46	12	19	1	3	0	67	Southwark
1890	Salford	22	35	90	13	24	1	1	0	111	Salford
1890	Shrewsbury	14	25	45	4	19	0	2	0	74	Shrewsbury
1890	Southwark	30	48	84	47	54	4	8	0	111	Southwark
1890	Westminster	33	26	73	103	51	15	21	0	124	Westminster
1895	Birmingham	28	36	76	29	4	1	1	0	131	Birmingham
1895	Clifton	13	16	39	15	32	1	7	0	46	Clifton
1895	Hexham & Newcastle	7	21	48	34	8	0	4	0	115	Hexham & Newcastle
1895	Leeds	9	7	20	8	9	0	0	0	89	Beverley
1895	Liverpool	121	140	151	37	45	0	7	0	162	Liverpool
1895	Middlesbrough	2	8	16	7	9	0	0	0	61	Beverley
1895	Newport & Menevia	22	24	41	10	10	0	4	0	67	Newport
1895	Northampton	13	13	33	3	8	0	0	0	61	Northampton
1895	Nottingham	41	28	57	7	34	2	0	0	91	Nottingham
1895	Plymouth	20	26	39	4	13	3	5	0	52	Plymouth
1895	Portsmouth	16	30	54	17	24	2	2	0	77	Southwark
1895	Salford	26	45	104	26	28	2	1	0	117	Salford
1895	Shrewsbury	15	25	45	4	22	0	3	0	78	Shrewsbury
1895	Southwark	44	60	105	62	71	7	7	0	141	Southwark
1895	Westminster	53	41	99	137	67	17	22	0	135	Westminster
1900	Birmingham	36	44	82	27	9	1	3	0	134	Birmingham
1900	Clifton	15	13	36	17	27	3	7	0	50	Clifton
1900	Hexham & Newcastle	10	24	63	43	7	0	4	0	123	Hexham & Newcastle
1900	Leeds	9	13	23	9	9	0	0	0	91	Beverley
1900	Liverpool	113	135	144	36	46	0	11	0	171	Liverpool

1900	Middlesbrough	3	10	19	8	10	0	0	0	Beverley	63
1900	Newport	22	20	31	11	8	0	4	0	Newport	56
1900	Northampton	17	17	38	2	14	0	1	0	Northampton	63
1900	Nottingham	48	27	63	7	33	1	0	0	Nottingham	121
1900	Plymouth	25	26	39	5	21	2	4	0	Plymouth	52
1900	Portsmouth	20	34	57	16	36	2	3	0	Southwark	77
1900	Salford	26	43	105	40	31	2	1	0	Salford	126
1900	Shrewsbury	11	25	41	3	17	0	1	0	Shrewsbury	58
1900	Southwark	45	62	113	54	78	5	3	0	Southwark	152
1900	Westminster	65	41	100	128	79	17	19	0	Westminster	153
1905	Birmingham	42	48	99	27	17	1	4	0	Birmingham	135
1905	Clifton	20	18	48	22	35	3	8	0	Clifton	56
1905	Hexham & Newcastle	11	28	89	38	11	0	4	0	Hexham & Newcastle	128
1905	Leeds	15	14	32	12	14	0	1	0	Beverley	102
1905	Liverpool	120	150	161	43	50	1	10	0	Liverpool	185
1905	Middlesbrough	5	10	19	8	14	0	0	0	Beverley	67
1905	Newport	24	24	39	13	8	0	5	0	Newport	69
1905	Northampton	19	19	44	3	17	0	1	0	Northampton	65
1905	Nottingham	48	30	71	8	44	0	1	0	Nottingham	97
1905	Plymouth	24	29	51	3	25	2	3	0	Plymouth	62
1905	Portsmouth	22	36	61	13	41	2	3	0	Southwark	83
1905	Salford	25	46	116	49	36	1	1	0	Salford	138
1905	Shrewsbury	16	30	39	3	19	0	1	0	Shrewsbury	60
1905	Southwark	57	78	156	59	99	13	1	0	Southwark	180
1905	Westminster	66	44	112	125	82	18	20	0	Westminster	168
1910	Birmingham	45	62	113	29	25	2	5	0	Birmingham	144
1910	Clifton	25	19	46	20	37	2	7	0	Clifton	63
1910	Hexham & Newcastle	17	26	104	42	15	0	4	0	Hexham & Newcastle	139
1910	Leeds	25	34	63	14	32	1	3	0	Beverley	109
1910	Liverpool	127	154	168	49	57	1	11	0	Liverpool	183
1910	Middlesbrough	10	15	30	12	25	0	0	0	Beverley	67
1910	Newport	22	28	44	13	10	0	4	0	Newport	77

TABLE I. (Cont'd)

Year	Diocese name	Catechizing	Public Rosary	Benediction	Confraternities, sodalities, and guilds	Confession	Exposition	Stations	Quarant'ore	Number of churches	Diocesan-group name
1910	Northampton	20	18	60	3	30	0	2	0	73	Northampton
1910	Nottingham	49	30	75	14	55	0	2	0	106	Nottingham
1910	Plymouth	27	38	57	3	29	3	2	0	62	Plymouth
1910	Portsmouth	29	38	66	15	45	2	2	0	99	Southwark
1910	Salford	29	47	112	53	40	1	0	0	139	Salford
1910	Shrewsbury	18	36	48	4	26	0	1	0	63	Shrewsbury
1910	Southwark	82	89	175	68	136	8	3	0	217	Southwark
1910	Westminster	80	55	142	161	107	24	16	0	176	Westminster
1914	Birmingham	44	70	119	36	70	2	4	0	153	Birmingham
1914	Clifton	22	23	49	19	51	4	4	0	71	Clifton
1914	Hexham & Newcastle	19	29	112	61	101	0	3	0	148	Hexham & Newcastle
1914	Leeds	30	32	72	22	62	1	2	0	116	Beverley
1914	Liverpool	125	156	175	63	80	1	12	0	185	Liverpool
1914	Middlesbrough	10	18	33	10	30	1	0	0	68	Beverley
1914	Newport	26	28	48	17	21	0	3	0	76	Newport
1914	Northampton	24	17	59	5	48	0	2	0	77	Northampton
1914	Nottingham	52	34	75	15	66	0	2	0	98	Nottingham
1914	Plymouth	28	42	61	3	48	4	2	0	77	Plymouth
1914	Portsmouth	32	38	75	15	65	2	3	0	101	Southwark
1914	Salford	33	56	124	61	75	1	0	0	145	Salford
1914	Shrewsbury	19	36	48	6	34	0	1	0	60	Shrewsbury
1914	Southwark	95	91	184	83	165	11	3	0	222	Southwark
1914	Westminster	94	54	159	167	147	30	13	0	192	Westminster

Note: A dash indicates no information in the *Directory*.

Appendix II

Proportion of Church-Based Devotions by Year and Diocese

FIGURES 1–14 illustrate graphically the proportions of churches offering different devotional services for the same sample of years from 1850 to 1914. The vertical axis of each figure gives percentages of the total number of churches in each diocese, while the horizontal axis gives the 'diocesan-group' name; each figure represents a particular year. Thus each bar represents a single diocese in a single year, and has been subdivided by the percentage of churches in that diocese which offered devotional extras such as Public Rosary, Exposition of the Blessed Sacrament, Benediction of the Blessed Sacrament, the Stations or Way of the Cross, and *Quarant'ore* or the Forty Hours' Devotion.

The proportions represented have been calculated by dividing the number of churches in a given diocese offering a particular devotion by the total number of churches in that diocese, multiplied by one hundred. Thus if diocese X contained ten churches in 1850, five of which offered Public Rosary, the relevant shading in the bar chart given for diocese X would equal 50 per cent. Since eight churches, or 80 per cent of the total number of churches, might also offer Benediction, the shaded areas in these charts should be considered separately, and do not add up to the total number of churches or 100 per cent. The reason for expressing the absolute devotional statistics given in Table 1 as a percentage in these figures, and for keeping the scale constant for all years, has been to facilitate comparisons of particular devotions between dioceses of differing size over time in order to reveal the importance of individual devotions. These charts omit information about confessions, catechizing, and confraternities, sodalities, and guilds, which may be consulted in Table 1, in order to show the purely devotional figures more clearly. Statistics of *Quarant'ore* have been include in all calculations, but the numbers involved are too insignificant to be visible in the figures.

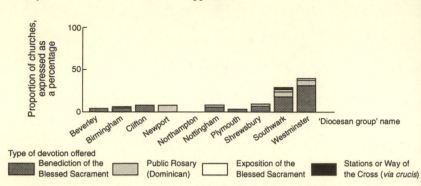

FIG. 1. Church–based devotions by year and diocese, 1851

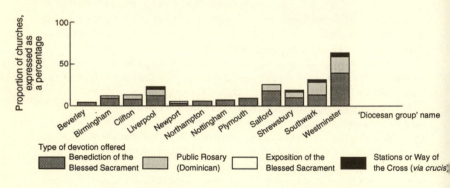

FIG. 2. Church–based devotions by year and diocese, 1855

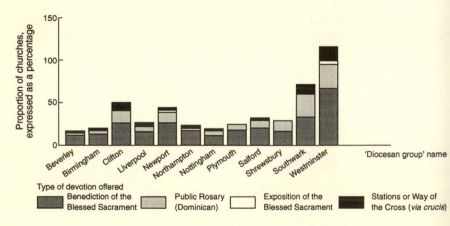

FIG. 3. Church–based devotions by year and diocese, 1860

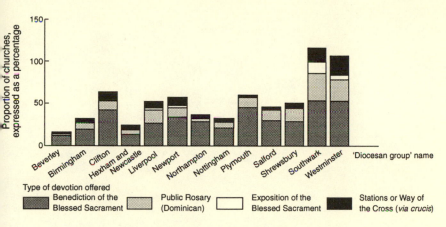

FIG. 4. Church-based devotions by year and diocese, 1865

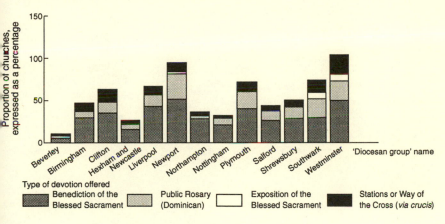

FIG. 5. Church-based devotions by year and diocese, 1870

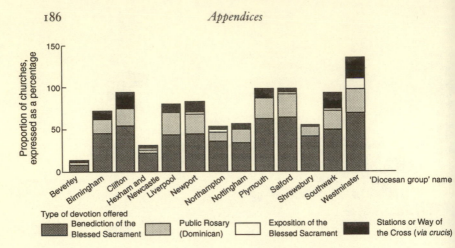

FIG. 6. Church-based devotions by year and diocese, 1875

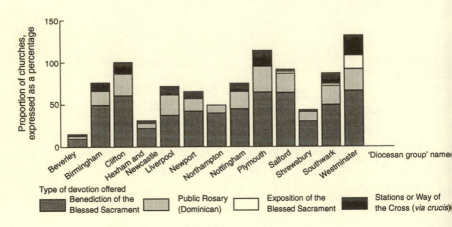

FIG. 7. Church-based devotions by year and diocese, 1880

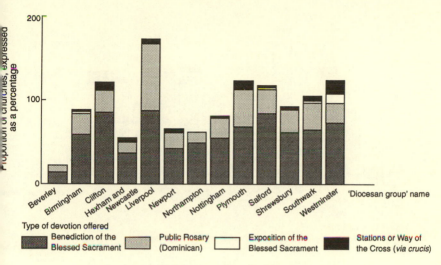

FIG. 8. Church-based devotions by year and diocese, 1885

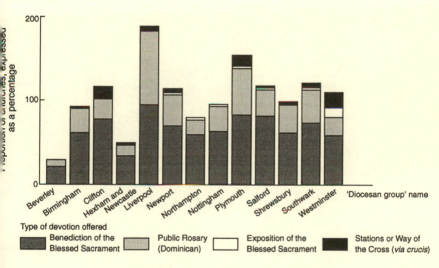

FIG. 9. Church-based devotions by year and diocese, 1890

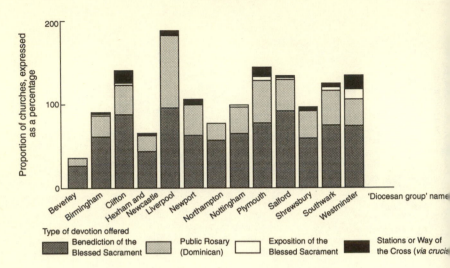

FIG. 10. Church-based devotions by year and diocese, 1895

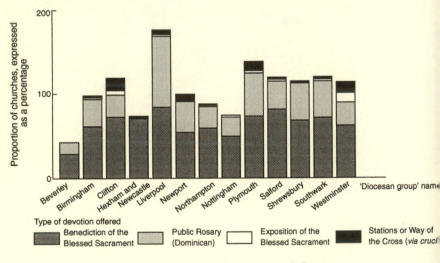

FIG. 11. Church-based devotions by year and diocese, 1900

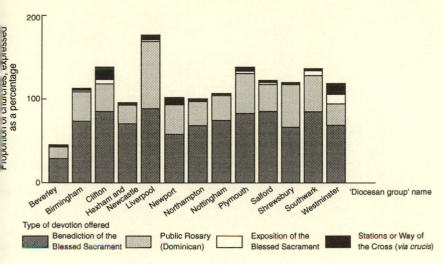

FIG. 12. Church-based devotions by year and diocese, 1905

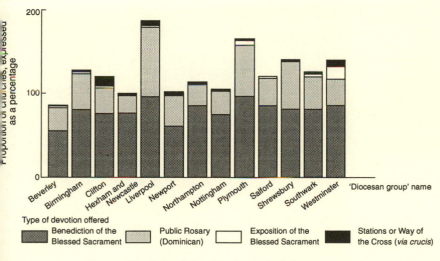

FIG. 13. Church-based devotions by year and diocese, 1910

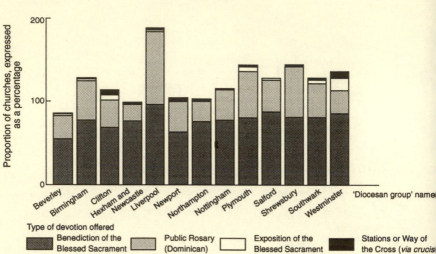

FIG. 14. Church-based devotions by year and diocese, 1914

Note: Statistics of churches offering *Quarant'ore* have been included in all calculations, but are too insignificant to show up in the figures.

Appendix III

The Revelations of St Bridget

THE following Revelation was made by the mouth of Our Blessed Saviour to St Bridget, who desired to know somewhat of the Passion he endured, to whom after much prayer, he spoke as follows:—

    1st.—When I was apprehended in the garden I received 30 cuffs and 820 blows.

    2nd.—Going to the house of Annas I got 7 falls.

    3rd.—They gave me 540 blows on my breast.

    4th.—They gave me 5 cruel blows on my shoulders.

    5th.—They raised me by the hair of my head 630 times.

    6th.—They gave me 30 blows on my mouth.

    7th.—With anguish I sighed 888 times.

    8th.—They drew me by the beard 308 times.

    9th.—They gave me 6666 stripes with whips.

    10th.—I was bound to a pillar and they spat upon my face 68 times.

    11th.—They put a crown of thorns upon my head.

    12th.—The soldiers gave me 558 stripes with whips.

    13th.—Falling upon my cross I received mortal wounds.

    14th.—They gave me gall and vinegar to drink.

    15th.—When I was hanging on the cross I received 5 large wounds.

To all persons who say devoutly Seven Paters and Seven Aves with the Creed every day for 15 Years, in honour of my Passion, shall enjoy the blessings herein mentioned. They shall receive a plenary indulgence from all their sins. They shall not suffer the pains of Purgatory. If they die before the 15 years are ended, they shall enjoy the same happiness as if they had suffered martyrdom. I will come myself to receive their souls and bring them to everlasting bliss. Whosoever will carry this Revelation about them shall be preserved from crimes, neither shall they die suddenly. If a woman with child will carry this Revelation and perform this devotion, she shall have a safe delivery. In whatever part of the house this Revelation is kept that place shall not be infected with any contagious distemper. Whosoever will carry this Revelation, and perform the devotion, the most glorious and Blessed Virgin will appear to them three days before their death.—Amen.

(H. Thurston, 'Uses that are Really Superstitious', *Month*, 133 (1919), 57–8)

Appendix IV

Letter from Herbert Vaughan, Bishop of Salford, to Edmund Knight, Bishop of Shrewsbury, 23 December 1884

'Gloria Patri'

Bishop's House,

Salford

Dec. 23, 1884

My dear Lord,

The reasons for a new version having been submitted to your Lordship, I now beg to submit the reasons which may be alleged for retaining the present translation.

1. It was urged that the present translation is not Catholic, but Protestant.

No proof of this has ever been established. On the contrary, the Catholic origin would seem to be clear. Thus in a Primer belonging to the Bishop of Clifton, printed about 1528 in black letter, we have the following:—'Glory be to the Father &c. as it *is* now & ever *shall be*. So be it. It will be noted that the words *et in saecula saeculorum* are not rendered in this translation: they are however rendered in this same book, at the end, of all the Collects by the translations at present in use, viz:—'worlde without ende.' The date of this Primer shews that the translation, interpolation of the verbs and the phrase 'world without end', said to have been of Protestant, are in reality of Catholic origin.

In another Catholic Book, called *Church Prayer Book* of date 1563, at S. Edward's College, Liverpool, we find, though the rendering 'even as it was in the beginning, and now & ever', is more correct than the earlier & than our actual translation—the expression 'world without end' given, this time as part of the 'Glory be to the Father'.

Johnson (but voce 'world') says that 'world without end' is a survival of the Saxon use of 'world' for 'time'.

It must be remembered that the actual translation has now been in possession for 300 years; that it is used wherever the English Language is the language of prayer; that it is common to Catholic & Protestant alike.

It must be admitted that as a translation it is faulty, and that were the Bishops undertaking to revise and perfect all our translations, & not merely to secure a *uniform* version of English prayers for popular use, they might feel called upon to amend the present translation of the Gloria Patri, but if they attempted this, they would have to proceed to a new translation of the Our Father & the Creed—for 'trespasses' & 'hell', not to speak of other expressions, are equally well called into question by purists.

Is it desirable to draw a fresh & additional distinction between Catholics & the English people, by declaring, after 300 years, that we can no longer use the same version of the Doxology?

Were the English Bishops to publish a new translation of the Doxology, would they succeed in getting it adopted—even by their own flocks? Is there not a very strong feeling among Catholics to hold to their traditions & customs? Would not a large number of the clergy feel an equal repugnance with the laity to make this change?

Would the reasons for the change be so cogent & manifest as to induce the hierarchies in other English-speaking countries to adopt it? If the English Bishops are not unanimous for a change, is it likely that there would be an inclination to follow their example in Ireland & the United States &c. Is there so general a feeling of dissatisfaction among English Catholics with the present version? Is not the discontent confined to a few purists, who have considered the question simply as one of grammar and translation?

The proposal to give a new translation has been (unofficially) brought under the notice of one of the chief theologians of the Holy Office, who understands English. His opinion is that the present translation, though faulty, should be retained—

1) because it gives a good sense
2) because it is in possession, no matter even if it sh[oul]d have been borrowed from the Protestants

The same kind of criticisms as are made in England upon the translation of the Gloria, are frequently made by purists in Italy & France on translations that are in vogue in these countries: but no change is considered expedient.

These appear to be the chief reasons for leaving the translation as it has been for 300 years.

Will your Lordship please vote '—

1. As to whether there shall be any change in the translation.'
2. And if so, which of the suggested changes, given in the previous paper shall be adopted.

Yours,
Herbert Bp Salford

P.S. Is it proposed to translate in the Te Deum, the words '*Deus Sabaoth*' by 'God of Hosts' instead of 'God of Sabaoth' which the people are apt to confound with the word Sabbath.

One person has suggested that Dr. Lingard's rendering of 'Te *Deum*' by the accusative instead of by the vocative, should be adopted, 'We praise Thee, God' instead of 'We praise Thee, O God' which is the translation generally used by Catholics & Protestants.

(Copy of this letter kindly sent by John Marmion, Archivist of Shrewsbury Diocese.)

Appendix V

Chronological List of Confraternities, Sodalities, and Guilds, 1850–1914

THE names of the following Catholic societies are taken from the *Catholic Directory* for the years 1850–60 inclusive, 1865, 1870, 1875, 1880, 1890, and 1900. The date given in parentheses after the title of the society indicates the earliest reference found in the *Catholic Directory* for the sample years examined.

1. Holy Ghost, *see* Servants of . . .
2. Blessed Virgin, Confraternity (1851)
3. Bona Mors, Confraternity (1851)
4. Blessed Sacrament, Confraternity (1851); *see also* Most Holy, Holy . . .
5. Dead, Confraternity for the = Holy Guild of St George & Blessed Virgin (1851)
6. Immaculate Heart of Mary, Confraternity (1851)
7. Most Holy Rosary, Confraternity (1851)
8. Passion, Confraternity (1851); *see* Red Scapular
9. Sacred Heart, Confraternity = ?Sacred Heart of Jesus (1851)
10. St George and Blessed Virgin = Confraternity for the Dead
11. Christian Doctrine, Confraternity (1852); *see also* St Charles . . .
12. Passion of Our Lord, Confraternity (1852)
13. Rosary of the Holy & Immaculate Heart of Mary for the Conversion of Sinners (1852)
14. Way of the Cross, Confraternity (1852)
15. Conversion of England, Confraternity (1853)
16. Heart of Mary, Confraternity (1853); *see also* Immaculate Heart
17. Our Lady of Mount Carmel, Confraternity (1853)
18. Sacred Heart of Jesus, Confraternity = ?Sacred Heart (1853)
19. Rosary, Confraternity = ?Rosary of Holy and Immaculate Conception (1853)
20. Blessed Virgin Mary and St Joseph, Most Holy Guild of (1854)
21. Most Precious Blood, Confraternity (1854)
22. Holy and Immaculate Heart of the BVM for the Conversion of Sinners (1855)
23. Holy Rosary, Confraternity; *see* Rosary, Most Holy Rosary . . . (1855)
24. Living Rosary, Sodality of; *see* Confraternity of (1855)

25. Most Holy Sacrament, Confraternity (1855); *see also* Most Blessed . . .
26. Scapular of Mount Carmel, Confraternity (1855)
27. Seven Dolours, Confraternity (1855)
28. Holy Family, Confraternity (1856)
29. Our Lady of Victories, Confraternity (1856)
30. Stigmata of St Francis for Religious Care of the Dead, Confraternity (1856)
31. Precious Blood, Confraternity (1857) = ?Most Precious Blood; *see also* Seven Mysteries of the Precious Blood
32. St George, Holy Guild of = ?Confraternity of the Blessed Sacrament (1857)
33. Sacred Heart, Association (1858)
34. St Patrick, Confraternity (1858)
35. St Philip Neri, Companions (for Young Men) (1858)
36. St Vincent of Paul, Brotherhood of (1858); *see* Confraternity of, Society of
37. B[lessed] S[acrament] of Christ[ian] Doctrine (1859)
38. Blessed Virgin Mary and St Elizabeth for Visiting the Sick (1859)
39. Carmelite Confraternity (1859)
40. Congregation of Our Blessed Lady for Scholars of the Institute [of St Philip Neri] (1859)
41. Consolation; *see* Our Lady of, Association
42. Christian Doctrine of the Confrat[ernity] of the B[lessed] S[acrament] (1859) = B[lessed] S[acrament] of Christ[ian] Doctr[ine]
43. Immaculate Heart of Mary for the Conversion of Sinners (1859)
44. Most Sacred and Most Holy Heart of Mary (1859)
45. Purgatory Society (1859)
46. Young Men's Society (1859)
47. Altar Society, Guild (1860)
48. Penance and Conversion of Sinners (1860)
49. Sacred Hearts of Jesus and Mary, Confraternity (1860)
50. St Joseph's Guild (for Girls) under care of Sisters of Mercy (1860)
51. Sanctuary Guild of St Aloysius (1860)
52. Temperance Guild of Our Lady and St John the Baptist (1860)
53. Angelic Warfare, Confraternity (1865)
54. Benevolent Society for Relief of Aged and Infirm Poor (1865)
55. Blessed Sacrament, Guild (1865)
56. Blessed Sacrament of Our Lady of Sorrows (1865)
57. Blessed Virgin Mary, Guild (1865)
58. Brown Scapular, Confraternity (1865)
59. Cincture of S[aints] Augustine and Monica (1865)
60. Constant Homage to St Joseph, Association (1865)
61. Cord of St Francis (1865)
62. Cord of St Thomas (1865)
63. Faithful Departed, Confraternity (1865)
64. Holy Angels [for Children], Confraternity (1865)

65. Men's Society (1865)
66. Most Blessed Sacrament, Confraternity (1865); *see also* Most Holy . . .
67. Night Refuge for Homeless Women of Good Character (1865)
68. Provident Society (1865)
69. Sacred Heart of Mary, Confraternity = ?Sacred Heart of Mary in Union with Notre-Dame des Victoires, Paris (1865)
70. Sacred Heart of Mary in Union with Notre-Dame des Victoires, Paris (1865)
71. St Charles Confraternity of Christian Doctrine (1865)
72. St Joseph, Confraternity (1865)
73. St Vincent of Paul, Confraternity (1865)
74. Scapular of Seven Dolours (1865)
75. Temperance Association (1865)
76. Temperance Guild (1865)
77. Total Abstinence Society (1865)
78. Third Order of St Francis (1865) = Tertiaries
79. Apostleship of Prayer, Association (1870)
80. Boys' Guild (1870)
81. Burial Guild (1870)
82. Catholic Married Women, a Guild of, under Sisters of Mercy (1870)
83. Children, Guild for (1870)
84. Children of Mary (1870)
85. Christian Mothers (1870)
86. Guard of Honour of the Sacred Heart (1870) = ?Guard of Honour of the Sacred Heart of Jesus (1870)
87. Guardian Angels, Association (1870)
88. Holy Family Provident Society (1870)
89. Holy Family Total Abstinence Society (1870)
90. Holy Hours, Confraternity (1870)
91. Immaculate Conception, Archconfraternity (1870)
92. Immaculate Conception for the Suppression of Drunkenness (1870)
93. Immaculate Heart, Confraternity (1870)
94. Immaculate Heart of the Blessed Virgin Mary (1870)
95. Men, Guild for (1870)
96. Mount Carmel, Confraternity (1870); *see also* Our Lady of . . .
97. Night Refuge for Homeless Men, Women & Children of Good Character (1870)
98. Our Lady, Confraternity (1870)
99. Our Lady Guard of Honour, Association = Perpetual Rosary (1870)
100. Our Lady of Sorrows (1870)
101. Perpetual Rosary; *see also* Our Lady Guard of Honour
102. Peter's Pence (1870)
103. Purgatorial Society (1870)

104. Sacred Heart, Confraternity for Children (1870)
105. St Aloysius, Confraternity (1870); *see* Sanctuary Guild of
106. St Anthony, Confraternity (1870)
107. S[aints] Augustine and Monica (1870); *see also* Cincture
108. St Charles, Confraternity (1870)
109. St Joseph, Association of (1870)
110. St Joseph for the Young, Confraternity (1870)
111. St Peter, Confraternity (1870)
112. St Vincent of Paul, Society (1870)
113. Savings Bank (1870)
114. Scapular of Our Lady of Mount Carmel, Confraternity (1870)
115. Thanksgiving, Confraternity (1870)
116. Unmarried Women, Guild for (1870)
117. Temperance Guild of St Patrick (1870); *see also* St Patrick
118. Working Men's Club (1870)
119. Young Men, A Sodality of (1870)
120. Young Men's Catholic Brotherhood (1870)
121. Ladies' Soc[iety] of St Anne (1875)
122. Little Oratory (Men only), Confraternity (1875)
123. Perpetual Daily Adoration of the Blessed Sacrament, Confraternity (1875)
124. Sacred Heart for Education of Poor Children, Society (1875)
125. Sacred Thirst, Confraternity (1875)
126. St Aloysius, Guild of (1875)
127. St Joseph for the Suppression of Drunkenness (1875)
128. St Joseph's Guild for Boys (1875)
129. St Joseph's, for Men (1875)
130. St Norbert, Confraternity (1875)
131. St Patrick's Temperance Association (1875); *see also* St Patrick, Temperance, St Patrick's Total Abstinence . . .
132. St Patrick's Total Abstinence Association (1875)
133. St Thomas, Confraternity (1875)
134. St Wilfrid, Confraternity (1875)
135. Temperance (1875)
136. Young Men, Confraternity (1875)
137. Young Women, Confraternity (1875)
138. Children, Confraternity (1875)
139. Dolours, Confraternity (1875)
140. Girls' Guild (1875)
141. Holy Name, Guild (1875)
142. Holy Warfare (1880)
143. Kensington Young Men's Catholic Association (1880)
144. Ladies' District Visiting Society (1880)
145. League of the Cross (1880)

146. S[ervants] of Holy Ghost, [Arch-]Confraternity (1880) = Servants of Holy Ghost, Archconfraternity
147. Young Men's Guild (1880)
148. Holy Name, Confraternity (1885)
149. Marie Reparatrice, Society of (1885)
150. Catholic Truth Society (1890)
151. Expiation, Confraternity (?1890)
152. Perpetual Succour, Our Lady of, Confraternity (1890)
153. Reparation, Confraternity (?1890)
154. Tertiaries (1890); *see also* Third Order of St Francis
155. Divine Expiation, Confraternity
156. Corpus Christi, Guild (1900)
157. Men's Confraternity (1900)
158. Our Lady of Consolation, Association (1900)
159. Pious Union of St Anthony (1900)
160. St Anthony, Guild (1900)
161. St Joseph Guild (1900)
162. Soldiers' Confraternity (1900)
163. CBB (1910)
164. CYM (1910)
165. CYMS (1910)
166. S (1910)
167. St Michael, Confraternity (1910)
168. Our Lady of Light, Confraternity (1914)
169. S St E (1914)

BIBLIOGRAPHY

I. PRIMARY SOURCES

A. Manuscript

Archives of the Church of St Peter and All Souls, Geneva Street, Peterborough
Boxes 1–33; 3: 'All Souls Mission Log Book', i (11 Dec. 1896–31 Dec. 1910),
incl. photograph of First Communion group, 2 Apr. 1899; 13: 'Canon Moser's
Intentions' book; 17: 'Conference of St Wilfrid. Minute Book', 1908; 19: 'Copy
Letter Book' 1891–1914; inserts: 'Holy Family', 'Chapel', Letters 1880–91; 24:
photographs of high altar Christmas decorations 1910, 'Red Mount' procession
to King's Lynn, 17 May 1913, high altar pre-1914; 26: letters 1900–12; 31:
letters 1891, 'Decorations for All Souls Church'; 'All Souls Stations of the
Cross [correspondence and draft drawings] 1912'; 'Miscellaneous'.

Birkenhead Central Library, Metropolitan Borough of Wirral
Papers of Sir William Jackson (Archive class YJA), Jackson to G. Clive;
H. Segar to Jackson (concerning 'Garibaldi Riots' of 1862).

Birmingham Archdiocesan Archives, Cathedral House, St Chad's, Birmingham
'St Chad's Cathedral Records', nos. 13 (29 Sept. 1850–31 Dec. 1880), 14 (12
Jan. 1874–29 May 1895); 'Notice Books' of St Peter's, Broad St, 29 Sept.
1889–8 May 1898; 3 Mar. 1889–30 Oct. 1892; 12 Jan. 1908–2 Apr. 1911; 10
Mar. 1901–29 Dec. 1907; 'St Chad's Confraternity of the Blessed Sacrament',
Altar Society Minute Book, 14 Nov. 1867–11 Nov. 1895.

Centre for North-West Regional Studies, University of Lancaster
Oral History Archives, transcripts of interviews with Mr S. 4. P (Sept. 1979),
RSC/79/290/291/312 and Miss T. 2. B. (Apr. and June 1975), RSC/75/147;
RSC/75/153.

Clifton Diocesan Archives, St Ambrose, Bristol
Clifford papers: Letters to Clifford 1854–74: from Errington, 13 Dec. 1855, 9
Jan. 1856; Newman, 4 Mar. 1858; Turner, 15 Aug. 1862; Neve, 13 Feb. 1864.
Letter Book no. 3 (4 Nov. 1892–16 July 1866).

Dorset County Record Office, Dorchester
Weld of Chideock MSS, C15: Clifford to Weld; C40: Manning to Weld; C44:
Lady Petre to Weld; D16: F26: 'Authentication of relics belonging to the Weld
family of Chideock, 1836–1881', 'Affiliation of Charles Weld to Carmelite
Order, 1848', 'Petitions for Plenary Indulgences', 1858 and ?1868, 'Indulgence,
Chideock, 1869'; F34: 'Commander E. F. Weld, R.N. papers', incl. devotional
c.1864; L15: 'Description of Chideock Church 1880'. Weld of Lulworth Castle
MSS, D/10: C259: 'E. J. Weld to Fr Thomas Seed, 1864'; C290: 'J. B. Rowe
to Joseph Weld II, 1857'.

Downside Abbey Archives, Stratton-on-the-Fosse, near Bath
R. Simpson MSS, Notebooks: 8: 'Shakespeare'; 15–23: 'Spiritualia'. Box II, vii: 'Notes for article on the Invocation of the Saints', n.d.; xv: 'A paper on Ecclesiastical Architecture'; xvi: 'A Paper (possibly review) on a work of Faber'.

Durham County Record Office, County Hall, Durham
D/Sa/F 421: 'Diary of Winefred Salvin, Croxdale', 1 Jan.–31 May 1851; 422: 'Diary for 1852'; 423: 'Diary of Winefred Salvin of Croxdale', 1 Jan.–28 Feb., 22 May–13 Sept. 1853; 424: 'Diary of Winefred Salvin, Tours', 13 Feb.–20 July 1866.

Hexham and Newcastle Diocesan Archives, Bishop's House, Newcastle upon Tyne
Pastoral letters 1851–2; 'Notice Books 1854–1856'; 'Notice Books 1867–1871'; 'Notice Books 1877–1883'; 'Notice Book 1886'; 'Correspondence Files 75–78'; 'Visitation Papers', 1855, 1868, 1875, 1879, 1880, 1885, 1900, 1901, 1902, 1907, 1911, 1912, 1914.

Lancashire Record Office, Preston
Roman Catholic Records: RCFe 1/1: 'Money Donors, 1727'; RCFe 2/1: 'Our Lady's Well . . . at Fernyhalgh', 1714–23; RCLv 13 and 18: 'Correspondence 1850s–1890s'; RCLv 14 5/2: 'Bishop Goss's Letter Book 1855–1872; RCLv 15: 'Bishop O'Reilley's Letter Books from 1877'; RCLy 15 5/3: 'Copy Replies to the Visitations Questions, 1865', St Peter's, Lytham; RCLy 15 5/4: 'Proceedings and Statutes of Liverpool Diocesan Synods, nos. 2–7 (3 vols.), 1856–68; RCLy 7/13: 'Circle Lists of the Confraternity of the Living Rosary, 6 June 1875'; RCLy 7/14: 'Roll of Members of the Confraternity of the Sacred Heart of Jesus, 6 June 1875'; RCLy 7/18: 'Register of Members of the Living Rosary, 1896'; RCPa 13: 'Notice Book 8 Jan. 1855–11 July 1858, St Augustine, Preston'; RCPa 1/16–22: 'St Augustine's Parochial Notice Books, 1870–1900', 3 vols.

Northampton Diocesan Archives, Bishop's House, Marriot Street, Northampton
Original transcripts of interviews by Fr Dudley Cary-Elwes with Peterborough Catholics, 'Miss Copeland's Narrative' and 'Mr. John Copeland's Narrative', c.1896.

Oratory of St Philip Neri Archives, Edgbaston, Birmingham
Newman papers: book of newspaper cuttings; 'Letter to Duke of Norfolk' (Oct.–Dec. 1874): Emly to JHN, 1875–1892. Oct. 1874, 11 Oct. 1874, 28 Oct. 1874, 27 Oct. 1874, 6 Nov. 1874; A. P. de Lisle to JHN, 2 Nov. 1874, 8 Nov. 1874; JHN to de Lisle, 6 Nov. 1874; T. Galton to JHN, 9 Nov. 1874; Lady G. Fullerton to JHN, 9 Nov. 1874.

St Dominic's Convent Archives, Stone, Staffs.
Ullathorne MSS G/ULL/I 20–1; G/ULL/II; Letters by Ullathorne, G/ULL/III; Letters to Ullathorne, G/ULL/IV; Ecclesiastical and Diocesan Documents G/ULL/V; Official Documents concerning the Stone Congregation G/ULL/VI.

Shrewsbury Diocesan Archives, Curial Offices, 2 Park Road South, Birkenhead
'Gloria Patri', Vaughan to Knight, 23 Dec. 1884.
Society of Jesus (British Province) Archives, 114 Mount Street, London
Thurston papers: 'Rosary', 'Holy Water', 'Red Cross Chain', 'Nine Fridays correspondence', 'Stations of the Cross', 'Knock', 'Notes on Stigmatics', 'Notes on Eucharistic Fast, Benediction, etc.', 'Altars and Bells', 'Blood Prodigies. Naples, Liquefaction of the Blood of Januarius'; Letters 1894–1915.
Southwark Archdiocesan Archives, Archbishop's House, 150 St George's Rd, Southwark, London
'Societies pre-1900', J89: 'Catholic Union 1871', 'St Cuthbert 1855'; 'St Edward Confraternity 1858', 'Catholic Servants 1850', 'Association of Ladies 1871', 'Sufferers in Indian Mutiny', 'Newman House 1892', 'Catholic Aid 1859', 'St Anselm's 1866', 'Altar Society 1867', 'Crusaders 1879', 'League of St Sebastian 1870', St Elizabeth of Hungary 1880', 'Immaculate Conception Charity' (n.d.), 'Catholic Order of Oddfellows 1871', 'Catholic Association 1891–1892', 'Ladies' Association for Catholic Soldiers 1892', 'Workhouse Association' (n.d.), 'Catholic Union' (n.d.), 'Catholic Club' (n.d.), 'Catholic Registration Society' (n.d.), pamphlet entitled 'Constitution of the Temperance Society of the Cross' (n.d.). Visitation reports, 1863: 'Bermondsey', 'Clapham', 'Greenwich-St Mary's', 'Woolwich', 'St Elizabeth's, Richmond', 'Canterbury', 'Ashford', 'St Mary's, Chislehurst, Kent', 'Mortlake', 'Gravesend'.
Staffordshire County Record Office, Stafford
Stafford Family Collection (Fitzherberts), D641: Henry V. S. Jerningham, 9th Baron Stafford: 3/P/3/23/73–160: Letters from J. C. Buckler re: improvements to Costessey Hall, Building of Catholic Poor School and Chapel at Shifnal, etc., 1846, 1857–64; 3/P/3/23/218–45: appeals for charity, subscriptions, etc. 1857–63; 5/P(C)/3/2/12: appeals for funds from religious causes 1850, 1860; 5/P(C)/4/7: more appeals 1851–61; 5/P(C)/7/4: William Singleton to Pius IX, 10 May 1868; (Gifford family) D590/346: 'Regina v. Grosvenor', case and depositions, 1853; 347/10: will of Thomas William Gifford of Chillington, 1861.
Westminster Archdiocesan Archives, 16a Abingdon Rd, Kensington, London
'Bishops' Meetings 1858–1909'; 'Bishops' Meetings 1867–1974', 'Manning 1867–1891' folder.

B. Printed Sources

(The place of publication is London unless otherwise stated. Additional details of publication are given where numerous editions of the same catechism or prayer-book might otherwise lead to confusion.)

An Abridgment of Christian Doctrine or First Catechism Published for the Use of the London District (Keating, Brown, & Co., 1816).

An Abridgment of Christian Doctrine: or, the First Catechism. Published for the Use of the London District (Keating, Brown, & Co., *c.*1820).

An Abridgment of Christian Doctrine, Revised, Improved, and Recommended by Authority for the Use of the Faithful in All the Districts of England (Dolman, 1836).

Acta et Decreta Primi Concilii Provincialis Westmonasteriensis (Paris, 1853).

ACTON, J., 'Medieval Fables of the Popes', *Home and Foreign Review*, 3 (1863), 610–37.

—— 'Conflicts with Rome', *Home and Foreign Review*, 4 (1864), 667–90.

—— *Selections from the Correspondence of the First Lord Acton*, ed. J. N. Figgis and R. V. Laurence (1917).

—— *The Correspondence of Lord Acton and Richard Simpson*, ed. J. L. Altholz, D. McElrath, and J. C. Holland (3 vols.; 1971–5).

ADDINGTON, R., *Faber, Poet and Priest: Selected Letters 1833–1863* (1974).

ANON., 'The Ancient Saints of God', *Month*, 1 (1864), 202–8.

ANON., 'Catechesis', *New Catholic Encyclopedia* (17 vols.; London, New York, etc., 1967–79), iii. 214–29.

ANON., 'Catholic Controversies', *Dublin Review*, NS 12 (1869), 361–84.

ANON., 'Catholicism in Bavaria', *Contemporary Review*, 14 (1870), 495–510.

ANON., 'The Convent Case', *Dublin Review*, 12 (1869), 385–98.

ANON., 'A Council on the Council', *Month*, 11 (1869), 474–88.

ANON., 'Current Events', *Home and Foreign Review*, 1 (1862), 567–9.

ANON., 'Doctrine, Christian', *The Catholic Encyclopedia*, (17 vols.; 1909), v. 87–8.

ANON., 'English Catholics at Oxford', *Chronicle*, 1 (1867), 874–6.

ANON., *The English Pilgrimage to Lourdes May 1883: By One of the Pilgrims* (1883).

ANON., *A History of St Chad's Cathedral Birmingham 1841–1904: Compiled by the Cathedral Clergy* (Birmingham, 1904).

ANON., *The Inner Life of Lady Georgiana Fullerton* (1899).

ANON., 'An Irish Churchman's View of Irish Politics', *Contemporary Review*, 10 (1869), 53–73.

ANON., 'John Henry Newman as Preacher', *Contemporary Review*, 10 (1869), 37–52.

ANON., *Legends of Our Lady and the Saints; or, Our Children's Book of Stories, In Verse, Written for the Recitations of the Pupils of the Schools of the Holy Child Jesus, St Leonards-on-Sea* (1870).

ANON., *Letters of Teresa Higginson . . . by a Monk of Ramsgate* (London and Glasgow, 1937).

ANON., 'The Life of F. Faber', *Dublin Review*, NS 13 (1869), 109–43.

ANON., 'The Malines Exhibition of Religious Objects of Art', *Month*, 1 (1864), 383–94.

ANON., 'The Massacre of St Bartholomew', *Chronicle*, 2 (1867), 158–60.

ANON., 'Medieval Fables of the Popes', *Home and Foreign Review*, 3 (1863), 610–37.

ANON., 'Milner and his Times', *Home and Foreign Review*, 2 (1863), 531–57.

ANON., 'Mr Ffoulkes's Letter to Archbishop Manning', *Dublin Review*, NS 12 (1869), 269–308.

ANON., 'The Munich Congress', *Home and Foreign Review*, 4 (1864), 209–44.

ANON., 'Nationality', *Home and Foreign Review*, 1 (1862), 1–25.

ANON., 'Note to the 100th Number of the North British Review', *North British Review*, 50 (1869), 602–5.

ANON., 'The Oecumenical Council', *Edinburgh Review, or Critical Journal*, 130 (1869), 297–336.

ANON., 'Papal Infallibility', *Quarterly Review*, 128 (1870), 162–95.

ANON., 'The Pope and the Council', *Month*, 11 (1869), 529–44.

ANON., 'Priest-Ridden Ireland', *Blackwood's Edinburgh Magazine*, 154 (1893), 264–71.

ANON., 'Recent Irish Legislation', *Home and Foreign Review*, 1 (1862), 52–78.

ANON., 'Roman Catholicism in France on the Eve of the Oecumenical Council of 1869', *British Quarterly Review*, 49 (1869), 391–435.

ANON., 'Roman Catholicism: Present and Future', *Westminster Review*, NS 38 (1870), 116–60.

ANON., 'Roman Documents', *Dublin Review*, NS 13 (1869), 185–97.

ANON., *The Second National Congress, Newcastle Upon Tyne, 4th–8th August, 1911. Handbook and Souvenir* (Newcastle, 1911).

ANON., 'Some Myths of the Middle Ages', *Month*, 1 (1864), 362–8.

ANON., 'Ultramontanism', *Home and Foreign Review*, 3 (1863), 162–206.

ANON., 'University Education in Ireland', *Home and Foreign Review*, 2 (1863), 32–58.

ANON., 'The Vatican Council', *Edinburgh Review or Critical Journal*, 134 (1871), 131–61.

ANON., 'The Vatican Council', *North British Review*, NS 14 (1870–1), 183–229.

ANON., 'What is Going on at the Vatican?', *Contemporary Review*, 33 (1878), 665–82.

ANON., 'What is Papal Infallibility?', *Weekly Register and Catholic Standard*, 50 (1874), 19–20.

ANSTRUTHER, G. E., 'What Shall We Do with Our Boys in their Teens', *Ransomer*, 1 (1893), 150.

BAGSHAWE, J. B., *The Catechism Illustrated by Passages from the Holy Scriptures. With an Appendix and Notes* (R. Washbourne, 1870).

BAMBER, G. A. H., *Popular Sermons on the Catechism* (1914).

BELLOC, H., *The Path to Rome* (1902; 1952).

BELLORD, J., *A New Catechism of Christian Doctrine and Practice for School and Home Use* (Catholic Truth Society, 1901).

BENSON, R. H., *Come Rack! Come Rope!* (1912).

—— *Lourdes* (1914).

—— *Spiritual Letters* (1915).

BLAKISTON, N. (ed.), *The Roman Question: Extracts from the Despatches of Odo Russell from Rome, 1858–1870* (1962).

BOOTH, C. (ed.), *Life and Labour* (2 vols.; 1889).

BOOTH, W., *In Darkest England and the Way Out* (1890).

BOWDEN, T. W., *The Life and Letters of Frederick William Faber* (1869).

BRITTEN, J., 'Boys' Clubs', *Month*, 97 (1901), 57–66.

BUTLER, J., *Catechism. Revised, Enlarged, Approved, and Recommended by the Four R.C. Archbishops of Ireland, as a General Catechism for the Kingdom* (Dublin: Gerald P. Warren, n.d.).

CAMPION, E. (ed.), *Lord Acton and the First Vatican Council: A Journal* (Sydney, 1975).

CAPES, A., and CAPES, J. M., *The Old and New Churches of London* (1880).

CAPES, J. M., *Reasons for Returning to the Church of England* (1871).

—— *To Rome and Back* (1873).

CARY-ELWES, D., 'Catholic Peterborough, Past and Present', *St Francis' Magazine*, NS 27 (1910), 11–15; 28 (1915), 121–5; 30 (1916), 39–43, 78–83; 32 (1916), 99–103; 33 (1917), 11–15; 34 (1917), 33–7, 54–9; 36 (1917), 81–5; 37 (1918), 102–8; 38 (1918), 130–6; 39 (1918), 149–54; 40 (1918), 176–83; 41 (1919), 10–16; 43 (1919), 98–103; 45 (1920), 37–42; 46 (1920), 61–5; 47 (1920), 82–6; 48 (1921), 107–13; 49 (1921), 135–42.

CASWALL, E., *Confraternity Manual of the Most Precious Blood* (1861).

A Catechism of Christian Doctrine, no. II. Approved by the Cardinal Archbishop and Bishops of England and Wales, and Directed to be Used in all their Dioceses (London and Leamington, c.1860).

Catechism of Christian Doctrine, with the Questions Numbered. Approved for the Use of the Faithful, in all the Dioceses of England and Wales (Liverpool: Rockliff Brothers, 1876).

Catechism of Christian Doctrine, with the Questions Numbered. Approved for the Use of the Faithful, in all the Dioceses of England and Wales (Liverpool: Rockliff Brothers, c.1876).

A Catechism of Christian Doctrine, (no. 2), Approved by the Cardinal Archbishop and Bishops of England and Wales, and Directed to be Used in all their Dioceses (Manchester: Thomas Walker, c.1880).

A Catechism of Christian Doctrine, (no. 2), Approved by the Cardinal Archbishop and Bishops of England and Wales, and Directed to be Used in all their Dioceses (London and Derby: Thomas Richardson, c.1880).

A Catechism of Christian Doctrine, no. II. Approved by the Cardinal Archbishop and the Bishops of England and Wales, and Directed to be Used in all their Dioceses (London and Derby: Thomas Richardson & Son, 1883).

A Catechism of Christian Doctrine, no. II. Approved by the Cardinal Archbishop and the Bishops of England and Wales, and Directed to be Used in all their Dioceses (London: Burns & Oates, 1883).

A Catechism of Christian Doctrine, no. II. Approved by the Cardinal Archbishop and the Bishops of England and Wales, and Directed to be Used in all their Dioceses (Manchester, 1887).

A Catechism of Christian Doctrine (W. Knott, [1895]).

A Catechism of Christian Doctrine, Approved by the Cardinal Archbishop and Bishops of England and Wales, and Directed to be Used in all their Dioceses, with a Compendium of Bible History and Prayer Book (R. & T. Washbourne, 1903).

A Catechism of the Sacraments of the Catholic Church (*c*.1872).

The Catholic Directory and Annual Register (1850–5; 1860, 1865, 1870, 1875, 1880, 1885, 1890, 1895, 1890, 1895, 1900, 1905, 1910, 1914).

Catholic Hours, or, The Family Prayer-Book (1868).

Catholic Manual for Children Compiled and Translated from Approved Sources (London, Dublin, and Derby, 1869).

A Catholic's Manual of Instructions and Devotions (Liverpool, 1867).

The Catholic Penny Prayer Book: Designed for the Use of Schools (1873).

The Catholic Prayer Book. A Short Manual of Private Devotions (1888).

Catholic Religious Instruction: Suitable for Standard 1 (London and Derby, 1879).

Catholic Religious Instruction: Suitable for Standard 2 (London and Derby, 1879).

Catholic Religious Instruction: Suitable for Standard 3. Revised Edition of 1883 (London and Derby, 1883).

CATHOLIC TRUTH SOCIETY, *Prayers on the Anima Christi* (1900).

—— *A Catechism of Christian Doctrine* (1985).

—— *The Teaching of the Catholic Church. A New Catechism of Christian Doctrine* (1985).

Catholics [sic] Vade Mecum· A Select Manual of Prayers for Daily Use (1851).

CAVENDISH, F., *The Diary of Lady Frederick Cavendish*, ed. J. Bailey (2 vols.; 1927).

CHALLONER, R., *The Unerring Authority of the Catholick Church, in Matters of Faith . . . In Which the Infallibility of the Church of Christ is Demonstrated . . .* (1732).

—— *The Garden of the Soul. A Manual of Spiritual Exercises and Instructions for Christians, Who, Living in the World, Aspire to Devotion* (*c*.1740).

—— *Memoirs of the Missionary Priests, as Well Secular as Regular and of other Catholics of both Sexes, that have Suffered Death in England, on Religious Accounts . . . 1577 to 1684* (2 vols.; 1741–2).

—— *Britannia Sancta: or the Lives of the Most Celebrated British, English, Scottish and Irish Saints: Who Have Flourished in these Islands, from the Earliest Times of Christianity, Down to the Change of Religion in the Sixteenth Century* (1745).

[CHALLONER, R.], *The Garden of the Soul: A Manual of Spiritual Exercises and Instructions for Christians, Who, Living in the World, Aspire to Devotion* (1755).

—— *The Garden of the Soul: A Manual of Spiritual Exercises and Instructions for Christians, Who, Living in the World, Aspire to Devotion* (1798).

—— *The Garden of the Soul; or, A Manual of Spiritual Exercises and Instructions for Christians, Who, Living in the World, Aspire to Devotion* (London and Wolverhampton, 1801).

—— *Bishop Challoner's Meditations for Every Day in the Year. A New Edition*, ed. F. C. Husenbeth (1839).

—— *The Garden of the Soul: A Manual of Spiritual Exercises and Instructions for Christians, Who, Living in the World, Aspire to Devotion* (Birmingham, 1844).

—— *The Garden of the Soul: A Manual of Spiritual Exercises and Instructions for Christians . . . Enlarged edition* (Dublin, 1854).

—— *The Garden of the Soul: A Manual of Spiritual Exercises and Instructions for Christians Who, Living in the World, Aspire to Devotion. New Edition. Miniature Golden Manual* (London: Burns & Lambert, 1856).

—— *The Garden of the Soul: A Manual of Spiritual Exercises, in which Are Included Many Devotions of Recent Practice and Approved of by the Church* (1872).

—— *The Garden of the Soul. A Manual of Devotion. A New Edition, Containing Devotions to the Sacred Heart, Visits to the Blessed Sacraments* [*sic*], *Way of the Cross, Bona Mors, Indulgenced Prayers, Administration of the Sacraments . . .* (Edinburgh: John Chisholm, 1874).

—— *The Garden of the Soul or, Manual of Spiritual Exercises and Devotions, for Christians, Who, Living in the World, Aspire to Devotion. A New Edition, Containing: Devotions to the Blessed Sacrament, to the Sacred Heart, to St Joseph, and a Collection of Indulgenced Prayers. By Lawful Authority* (London and Derby: Thomas Richardson & Sons, 1877).

—— *The Garden of the Soul: A Manual of Spiritual Exercises, in Which Are Included Many Devotions of Recent Practice, and Approved of by the Church* (R. Washbourne, 1877).

—— *Instructions and Devotions for Hearing Mass . . . (from The Garden of the Soul)* (1877).

—— *Parochial Garden of the Soul* (1877).

—— *Little Garden of the Soul* (R. Washbourne, 1878).

—— *The Catholic Christian Instructed in the Doctrines and Ceremonies of the Church, by way of Question and Answer . . . A new edition* (London: Burns & Oates, 1881).

—— *The Garden of the Soul: A Manual of Spiritual Exercises and Instructions for Christians Who, Living in the World, Aspire to Devotion . . . A New Edition. Approved by the Cardinal Archbishop of Westminster* (London: Burns & Oates, 1883).

—— *The Garden of the Soul. A Manual of Spiritual Exercises and Instructions. Approved by the Cardinal Archbishop of Westminster* (London: Burns & Oates, 1884).

—— *The Garden of the Soul; Combined with the 'Manual of Prayers'. Version prescribed by the Cardinal Archbishop of Westminster and the Bishops of England. Edited by Monsignor McKenna, V.G.* (Dublin: James Duffy & Co., Ltd., 1892).

—— *The Garden of the Soul. A Manual of Devotion Containing Devotions to the Sacred Heart, Way of the Cross, Ordinary of the Mass . . .* (R. & T. Washbourne, 1899).

—— *Sunday Evening Devotions* [*Extracted from The Garden of the Soul*] (1900).

CHEETHAM, S., 'The Roman Curia', *Contemporary Review*, 13 (1870), 1–15.

CHESTERTON, G. K., *Autobiography* (1937).

—— *Orthodoxy* (1909).

Child's Key of Heaven. A Prayer Book for Catholic Children, Compiled from Approved Sources (1900).

The Child of Mary's Little Handbook: A Manual of the Rule, Ritual and Devotion for the Use of Sodalities of Children of Mary affiliated to the Primaria, or Arch-Sodality, of the Immaculate Virgin and of St Agnes (1901).

CLARKE, C. C., *Handbook of the Divine Liturgy: A Brief Study of the Historical Development of the Mass* (1910).

A Companion to the First Catechism or Abridgement of Christian Doctrine (1853).

The Crown of Jesus: A Complete Catholic Manual of Devotion, Doctrine, and Instruction (London and Derby, 1862).

DE SALES, F., *An Introduction to the Devout Life* (1609; ed. P. Toon, 1988).

Devotions and Prayers: A Book for the Use of the Boys of Ampleforth College at the Benedictine Abbey of Saint Lawrence the Martyr (Ampleforth, 1933).

DÖLLINGER, J. J. I. von, *Döllinger, Johann Joseph Ignaz von. Briefwechsel 1820–1890: mit Lord Acton: I 1850–1869, II 1869–70*, ed. V. Conzemius (Munich, 1963–5).

ERRINGTON, G., *Four Lectures on the Hierarchy* (1850).

The Explanatory Catechism of Christian Doctrine . . . (1877).

FABER, F. W., *The Blessed Sacrament* (1845).

—— *All for Jesus* (1854).

—— *Growth in Holiness; or the Progress of the Spiritual Life* (1854).

—— *Devotion to the Pope* (1860).

—— *The Precious Blood* (1860).

First[–Fourth] Standard Catechism, Extracted from the Catechism of Christian Doctrine, approved by the Bishop for the Diocese of Nottingham, and Directed to be Used in all the Schools of the Diocese (Nottingham, 1891).

FLETCHER, P., *Recollections of a Ransomer by the . . . Co-Founder, and Master, of the Guild of Our Lady of Ransom*, ed. G. E. Anstruther and W. A. Spence (1928).

A Form of Prayers following the Church Office, for the Use of Catholics Unable to Hear Mass upon Sundays and Holidays (1896; 2nd edn., 1900).

Franciscan Tertiary Manual: Containing Rule and Ceremonial of the Third Order. Encyclical of Pope Leo XIII, and An Explanation of the New Rule (Pantasaph, 1904).

FROHSCHAMMER, J., 'The Papacy and National Life', *Contemporary Review*, 15 (1870), 327–47.

FULLER, M. J., '*Our Lady*' of Walsingham (1886).

FULLERTON, G., *The Miraculous Medal* (1880).

—— *Faithful and True: The Life of Elizabeth Twiddy* ([1860]; 1900).

GEMMINGER, L., *All Souls' 'Forget-Me-Not': A Prayer and Meditation Book for the Solace of the Poor Souls in Purgatory. By Louis Gemminger, Priest of the Archdiocese of Munich*, trans. W. Moser (1890).

A General Catechism of the Christian Doctrine (R. Washbourne, 1872).

GIBSON, H., *Catechism Made Easy, being a Familiar Explanation of the Catechism of Christian Doctrine* . . . (3 vols.; Liverpool: Rockliff Brothers, 1865–77).

GLADSTONE, W. E., 'Ritualism and Ritual', *Contemporary Review*, 24 (1874), 663–81.

GODDARD, G. F., 'Gregory the Great and Pius IX', *Contemporary Review*, 13 (1870), 422–38.

The Golden Manual: A Guide to Catholic Devotion (1850).

The Golden Manual: A Guide to Catholic Devotion Public and Private Compiled from Approved Sources (*c*.1885).

GORMAN, W. G., *Converts to Rome* (1910).

GREENE, G. P. (ed.), *Letters from Baron Friedrich von Hügel to a Niece* (1928; 1965).

GUIRON, J., *The Sacred Heart* (1873).

HARRIS, J. R. (ed.), *The Life of Francis William Crossley* (1899).

HESELTINE, G. C., *The English Cardinals* (1931).

HOWE, G. E., *The Catechist: or, Headings and Suggestions for the Explanation of the Catechism of Christian Doctrine (No. 2). With Numerous Quotations and Examples from Scripture* (2 vols.; Newcastle-on-Tyne, 1895).

HUGHES, H. G., 'On Pilgrimage', *Month*, 104 (1904), 584–8.

HUNT, J., 'Three Broad Church Catholics: Döllinger, "Janus", Froschammer', *Contemporary Review*, 14 (1870), 311–28.

HUSENBETH, F. C., *Life of the Rt. Rev. Monsignor Weedall, D.D.* . . . *President of St Mary's, Oscott; Including Incidentally the Early History of Oscott College* (1860).

—— *Life of the Rt. Rev. John Milner, D.D.* (Dublin, etc., 1862).

—— *Our Blessed Lady of Lourdes* (1870).

The Jesus Psalter (1894).

KEENAN, S., *Controversial Catechism: or, Protestantism Refuted, and Catholicism Established, by an Appeal to the Holy Scriptures, the Testimony of the Holy Fathers, and the Dictates of Reason; in which Such Portions of Scheffmacher's Catechism as Suit Modern Controversy are Embodied* (London, Manchester, and Edinburgh, 1854).

KEENAN, S., and CORMACK, G., *Controversial Catechism: or, Protestantism Refuted, and Catholicism Established, by an Appeal to the Holy Scriptures, the Testimony of the Holy Fathers, and the Dictates of Reason; in which Such Portions of Scheffmacher's Catechism as Suit Modern Controversy are Embodied* (London, New York, etc., 1896).

KELLY, B. W., *The Little Catechism explained* (1905).

The Key of Heaven: A Manual of Catholic Devotion (33rd edn., Dublin, 1839).

The Key of Heaven, or a Posy of Prayer . . . (Dublin, 1820).

The Key to Heaven: A Manual of Prayers. With Epistles and Gospels (1884).

The Laity's Directory for the Year 1823 (1823).

Large Type Edition. Catechism of Christian Doctrine, Approved for the Use of the Faithful, in all the Dioceses of England and Wales (London and Derby: Thomas Richardson & Sons, 1876).

LINGARD, J., *Catechetical Instructions on the Doctrines and Worship of the Catholic Church* (London, Liverpool, and Dublin, 1841).

MACAULAY, G., 'Ranke's History of the Popes', *Lord Macaulay's Essays and Lays of Ancient Rome* (1909), 547–69.

MAHER, M., 'Holywell in 1894', *Month*, 83 (1895), 153–82.

MANNING, H. E., *The Blessed Sacrament the Centre of Immutable Truth: A Sermon* (1864).

—— *The Vatican Council: A Pastoral Letter* (1870).

—— *Petri Privilegium: Three Pastoral Letters* (1871).

—— *The Vatican Decrees in their Bearing on Civil Allegiance* (1875).

—— *The Glories of the Sacred Heart* (1876).

—— *The True Story of the Vatican Council* (1877).

—— *The Eternal Priesthood* (1883; 10th edn., n.d.).

—— *The Temporal Mission of the Holy Ghost: or Reason and Revelation* (1892).

MANNOCK, J., *The Poor Man's Catechism: or, the Christian Doctrine Explained. With Short Admonitions* (Dublin, 1825).

Manual of Prayers for Congregational Use (London and Derby, 1886).

MARTIN, A., 'What Hinders the Ritualists from Becoming Roman Catholics?', *Contemporary Review*, 33 (1878), 113–36.

MAYHEW, H., *London Labour and the London Poor* (2 vols., 1851; 4 vols., 1861–2).

MAYO, H., 'Letters on the Truths Contained in Popular Superstitions', *Blackwood's Magazine*, 61 (1847), 368–74.

MEARNS, A., *The Bitter Cry of Outcast London: An Inquiry into the Condition of the Abject Poor* (1883).

The Missal for the Laity, according to the Use of the Holy Roman Church (Derby, etc., 1846).

The Missal for the Use of the Laity, arranged by Provost Husenbeth (1897).

MONAHAN, M., *Life and Letters of Janet Erskine Stuart: Superior General of the Society of the Sacred Heart 1857–1914* (1922; 1943).

NEWMAN, J. H., *Loss and Gain* (1848), ed. A. G. Hill (Oxford, 1986).

—— *Lectures on the Present Position of Catholics in England: Addressed to the Brothers of the Oratory* (1851; 1951).

—— *Sermons Preached on Various Occasions* (1857).

—— *On Consulting the Faithful in Matters of Doctrine* (1859), ed. J. Coulson (1961).

—— *Apologia Pro Vita Sua* (1864; 1945).

—— *Parochial and Plain Sermons* (8 vols.; 1872–9).

—— *The Letters and Diaries of John Henry Newman*, ed. C. S. Dessain *et al.* (31 vols.; 1964–).

O., A., 'The Confraternity of Our Lady of Compassion', *Month*, 97 (1901), 39–46.

O'DOHERTY, T., 'A Scandalous Imposture', *Irish Ecclesiastical Record*, 5th ser., 12 (1918), 421–2.

190th Thousand. The Explanatory Catechism of Christian Doctrine, Chiefly Intended for the Use of Children in Catholic Schools. With an Appendix (Burns & Oates, 1884).

The Path of Holiness, a First Book of Prayers . . ., ed. T. T. Carter (1871).

POLLEN, J. H., *The Life and Labours of Father John Morris, S.J.* (1896).

The Poor Man's Manual; or, Devout Christian's Daily Companion (n.d.).

The Poor Man's Posey of Prayers: or, The Key of Heaven (1769).

A Popular Missal for the Use of the Laity (1893; 2nd edn., 1898).

Practical Meditations for Every Day in the Year on the Life of. . . Jesus Christ, by a Father of the Society of Jesus (1868).

PRICE, B., 'Catholicity', *Contemporary Review*, 12 (1869), 161–85.

—— 'Mr. Ffoulkes' Letter', *Contemporary Review*, 10 (1869), 481–502.

Private Devotions for Every Day in the Week (1868).

Raccolta di Orazioni e pie Opere per le quali sono state concedute dai Sommi Pontefici le S. Indulgenze (Rome, 1807; 12th edn., 1849).

The Raccolta: or Collection of Indulgenced Prayers, ed. T. Galli; trans. A. St John (1857).

The Raccolta: or Collection of Indulgenced Prayers, ed. A. St John (5th edn., 1880).

The Raccolta: or Collection of Indulgenced Prayers, ed. R. G. Bellasis (6th edn., 1909).

RAMSAY, G. [K. O'MEARA], *Thomas Grant: First Bishop of Southwark* (1874).

RANKEN, T. E., 'Sir Walter Scott and Mediaeval Catholicism', *Month*, 101 (1903), 146–52.

RICHARDS, W. J. B., *Catechism on Virtues and Vices: Compiled Chiefly from Bellarmine* (1879).

The Roman Missal Adapted to the Use of the Laity (London, 1887).

The Roman Missal for the Use of the Laity. New Edition (1852).

The Roman Missal for the Use of the Laity. New Edition (1890).

The Second Catechism, being an Abstract of the Douay Catechism (Keating, Brown, & Co., *c.*1820).

A Short Abridgment of Christian Doctrine for the Instruction of Beginners (1745).

A Short Catechism, extracted from the Douuay [sic] Catechism and from the Historical Catechism of M. l'Abbé Fleury (Malta, 1829).

SIMPSON, R., 'The Conservative Reaction', *Home and Foreign Review*, 1 (1862), 26–51.

—— 'Milner and his Times', *Home and Foreign Review*, 2 (1863), 531–57.

SMITH, S. F., 'Anti-Miraculous Pre-Suppositions', *Month*, 126 (1915), 1, 17.

—— 'Contemporary Miracles', *Month*, 124 (1914), 561–76; 125 (1915), 113–26.

—— 'Ecclesiastical Miracles', *Month*, 125 (1915), 249–65, 371–84.

SWINDELLS, B. T., *Manchester Streets and Manchester Men* (Manchester, 1908).

The Synods in English: Being the Text of the Four Synods of Westminster, translated into English . . ., ed. R. E. Guy (Stratford, 1886).

Tenth Thousand. The Explanatory Catechism of Christian Doctrine, Chiefly intended for the Use of Children in Catholic Schools. With an Appendix (Burns & Oates, 1877).

THURSTON, H. (ed.), *First Communion* (1897).

—— 'The Rosary', *Month*, 96 (1900), 403–18, 513–27, 620–37; 97 (1901), 67–79, 172–88, 286–304, 382–404.

—— 'The Stations of the Cross', *Month*, 96 (1900), 1–12, 153–66, 282–93.

—— 'The Angelus. I. The Hail Mary', *Month*, 98 (1901), 483–99.

—— 'The Angelus. II. The Curfew Bell', *Month*, 98 (1901), 607–16.

—— 'Benediction of the Blessed Sacrament', *Month*, 97 (1901), 587–97; 98 (1901), 58–69, 186–93, 264–76.

—— 'The Dedication of the Month of May to Our Lady', *Month*, 97 (1901), 470–83.

—— 'Walsingham, the English Loreto', *Month*, 98 (1901), 236–44.

—— 'The Angelus. III. Compline or Curfew Bell—Which?', *Month*, 99 (1902), 61–73.

—— 'The Angelus. IV. The Mid-Day Angelus', *Month*, 99 (1902), 518–32.

—— 'The So-Called Bridgettine Rosary', *Month*, 100 (1902), 189–203.

—— 'Easter Sepulchre, or Altar of Repose?', *Month*, 101 (1903), 404–14.

—— 'The Holy Shroud as a Scientific Problem', *Month*, 101 (1903), 162–78.

—— 'The Holy Shroud and the Verdict of History', *Month*, 101 (1903), 17–29.

—— 'The Nine Fridays', *Month*, 101 (1903), 635–49.

—— 'Abbot Anselm of Bury and the Immaculate Conception', *Month*, 103 (1904), 561–73.

—— 'The Antiquity of the Angelus', *Month*, 103 (1904), 57–66.

—— 'England and the Immaculate Conception', *Month*, 104 (1904), 561–76.

—— 'The Irish Origins of our Lady's Conception Feast', *Month*, 103 (1904), 449–65.

—— 'Our English Benediction Service', *Month*, 106 (1905), 394–404.

—— *The Stations of the Cross* (1906).

—— (ed.), *Report of the Nineteenth Eucharistic Congress, Held at Westminster from 9th to 13th September 1908* (1909).

—— 'The First Edition of the Penny Catechism', *Tablet*, NS 16 (1910), 1052–5.

—— 'The "Douay Abstract" and the "Short Abridgement" ', *Tablet*, 117 (1911), 8–10.

—— 'The Confiteor', *Month*, 124 (1914), 50–63.

—— 'The Early Ritual of Holy Communion', *Month*, 124 (1914), 159–68.

—— '"Omens, Dreams and Such-like Fooleries"', *Month*, 124 (1914), 630–3.

—— 'The Sanctus Bell', *Month*, 124 (1914), 189–91.

—— 'The Anima Christi', *Month*, 125 (1915), 493–505.

—— 'English Ritualia, Old and New', *Month*, 126 (1915), 60–73.

—— 'The Holy Eucharist and the "Rituale Romanum"', *Month*, 126 (1915), 291–300.

—— 'Genuflexions and Aves: A Study in Rosary Origins', *Month*, 127 (1916), 441–52, 546–59.

—— 'Holywell in Recent Years', *Month*, 128 (1916), 38–51.

—— 'The Salve Regina', *Month*, 128 (1916), 248–60; 300–14.

—— 'The Feast of the Assumption', *Month*, 130 (1917), 121–34.

—— 'Prayer Beads', *Month*, 129 (1917), 352–7.

—— 'Reservation in its Historical Aspects', *Month*, 130 (1917), 233–43.

—— 'The Reserved Sacrament', *Month*, 129 (1917), 472–3.

—— 'Benediction *with* the Blessed Sacrament', *Month*, 132 (1918), 219–21.

—— 'The Benediction Service amongst Anglicans', *Month*, 132 (1918), 141–4.

—— 'The "De Profundis"', *Month*, 132 (1918), 358–68.

—— 'The Gloria Patri', *Month*, 131 (1918), 406–17.

—— 'The Memorare', *Month*, 132 (1918), 269–78.

—— 'Some Physical Phenomena of Mysticism', *Month*, 133 (1919), 266–77, 321–35, 401–13; 134 (1919), 39–50, 144–57, 243–55, 531–41.

—— 'Uses that are Really Superstitious', *Month*, 133 (1919), 56–8.

—— *Familiar Prayers* ([publ. posthumously] 1953).

TODD, W. G., 'The Roman Catholic Marriage Laws: From a Roman Catholic Point of View', *Contemporary Review*, 26 (1875), 412–29.

TURBERVILLE, H., *Abridgment of Christian Doctrine* (*c*.1649).

TYRRELL, G., 'The Relation of Theology to Devotion', *Month*, NS 94 (1899), 461–73.

—— *Hard Sayings: A Selection of Meditations and Studies* (1910).

—— *George Tyrrell's Letters*, ed. M. Petre (1920).

ULLATHORNE, W. B., *The Holy Mountain of La Salette: A Pilgrimage of the Year 1854* (1854).

—— *The Immaculate Conception of the Mother of God* (1855).

—— *The Accord of the Infallible Church with the Infallible Pontiff: A Discourse* (*c*.1890).

—— *Autobiography and Letters* (2 vols.; 1891–2).

—— *From Cabin-Boy to Archbishop: The Autobiography of Archbishop Ullathorne*, ed. S. Leslie (1941).

The Ursuline Manual, or a Collection of Prayers, Spiritual Exercises . . . Arranged for the Young Ladies at the Ursuline Convent, Cork (Dublin, 1875).

V., A. E., 'Joseph Mazzini', *Contemporary Review*, 15 (1870), 383–407.

VAUGHAN, H., *Letters of Herbert, Cardinal Vaughan, to Lady Herbert of Lea 1867 to 1903*, ed. S. Leslie (1942).

—— Preface (1893) to *Franciscan Tertiary Manual . . .* (Pantasaph, 1904), pp. ix–xvii.

VAUX, L., *Catechism, or Christian Doctrine necessary for Children and Ignorant People* (1562).

VERDENAL, J. P., *The Miracle at Metz Wrought by the Blessed Sacrament, June 14, 1865*, trans. G. Fullerton from *Relation de la guérison d'une malade* (1866).

VON HÜGEL, F., *Baron von Hügel: Selected Letters, 1896–1924*, ed. B. Holland (1927).

—— *Spiritual Counsels and Letters of Friedrich von Hügel*, ed. D. V. Steere (1964).

W., T. A., *A Companion to the First Catechism or Abridgment of Christian Doctrine: Intended Principally to Assist the Pastor in Examining Children before their Admission to Communion* (Preston, 1853).

WENHAM, J. G., *A Manual of Instructions in Christian Doctrine* (1861).

WHALE, W. S., *The Life of a Priest: My Own Experience 1867–1912*, trans. A. Houtin (1927).

WISEMAN, N., 'Prayer and Prayer-books', *Dublin Review*, 13 (1842), 448–85.

—— *Conversion: A Letter to Mr. Alexander Chiriol and his Family on their Happy Admission to the Communion of the Holy Catholic Church* (1848).

II. SECONDARY WORKS

ABBOTT, E. M., *History of the Diocese of Shrewsbury* (Bolton, 1987).

—— 'The Foundation of Our Lady's, Birkenhead', *North West Catholic History*, 18 (1991), 11–15.

—— 'Our Lady's, Birkenhead: Growth, Destruction, Resurgence and Renewal', *North West Catholic History*, 19 (1992), 47–50.

—— 'History of Our Lady's—Birkenhead' (unpublished manuscript, kindly lent by the author, 1991).

ABERCROMBIE, N. J., 'Edmund Bishop and the Roman Breviary', *Clergy Review*, NS 38 (1953), 75–86, 129–39.

—— 'The English Catholic Enlightenment: A Review', *North West Catholic History*, 9 (1982), 26–9.

ADAMS, P. A., 'Converts to the Roman Catholic Church in England *circa* 1830–70' (B.Litt. thesis, Oxford University, 1977).

ADDINGTON, R., *The Idea of the Oratory* (1966).

ADDIS, W. E., and ARNOLD, T. (eds.), *A Catholic Dictionary* (9th edn., 1917).

ALLIES, M. H., *Thomas William Allies* (1907).

ALMOND, C., *The History of Ampleforth Abbey* (1903).

ALTHOLZ, J. L., *The Liberal Catholic Movement in England: The 'Rambler' and its Contributors 1848–1864* (1962).

—— 'The Vatican Decrees Controversy, 1874–1875', *Catholic Historical Review*, 57 (1972), 593–605.

ANON., *Infallibility in the Church: An Anglican-Catholic Dialogue* (1968).

ANON., *The Inner Life of Lady Georgiana Fullerton* (1899).

ANON., *Life of Teresa Higginson the Teacher Mystic 1845–1905* (Rochdale, 1937).

ANON., *The Life of the Very Reverend Mother Mary Philomena Juliana Morel: By a Servite Nun* (1942).

ANON., *Life and Work of Mother Mary St Ignatius (Claudine Thévenet) 1774–1837: Foundress of the Congregation of Jesus and Mary. By a Religious of Jesus and Mary* (London and Dublin, 1953), ch. xxxii.

ANON., *Message of Our Lord to Teresa Higginson* (1984).

ANSON, P. F., *The Religious Orders and Congregations of Great Britain and Ireland* (Worcester, 1949).

ANSTRUTHER, G. E., and HALLETT, P. E., *Catholic Truth Society: The First Fifty Years* (1934).

ARNSTEIN, W. L., *Protestant versus Catholic in Mid-Victorian England: Mr Newdegate and the Nuns* (Columbia, 1982).

ASPINWALL, B., 'The Second Spring in Scotland', *Clergy Review*, 66 (1981), 281–90, 312–19.

—— 'The Formation of the Catholic Community in the West of Scotland: Some Preliminary Outlines', *Innes Review*, 33 (1982), 44–57.

—— [review article], *Heythrop Journal*, 31 (1990), 362–3.

—— 'The Welfare State within the State: The Saint Vincent de Paul Society in Glasgow, 1848–1920', in W. J. Sheils and D. Wood (eds.), *Voluntary Religion* (Studies in Church History 23; 1986), 445–59.

ATTWATER, D., *The Catholic Church in Modern Wales* (1935).

—— (ed.), *The Penguin Dictionary of Saints* (Harmondsworth, 1983).

AUBERT, R., *Histoire de l'église depuis les origines jusqu'à nos jours*, xxi. *Le Pontificat de Pie IX (1846–1878)* (Paris, 1952).

—— 'Ultramontanisme', in ibid. 262–310.

AVELING, J. C. H., *The Handle and the Axe: The Catholic Recusants in England, from Reformation to Emancipation* (1976).

BAKER, D. (ed.), *Church, Society and Politics* (Oxford, 1975).

BARROW, L., *Independent Spirits: Spiritualism and English Plebeians 1850–1910* (1986).

BASTABLE, J. D. (ed.), *Newman and Gladstone: Centennial Essays* (Dublin, 1978).

BEBBINGTON, D. W., *Evangelicalism in Modern Britain: A History from the 1730s to the 1980s* (1989).

BECK, G. A. (ed.), *The English Catholics 1850–1950: Essays to Commemorate the Centenary of the Restoration of the Hierarchy of England and Wales* (1950).

BELLENGER, D., 'The French Exiled Clergy in England and National Identity, 1790–1815', in S. Mews (ed.), *Religion and National Identity* (Studies in Church History 18; Oxford, 1982), 397–407.

—— 'The Emigré Clergy and the English Church, 1789–1815', *Journal of Ecclesiastical History*, 34 (1983), 392–410.

—— (ed.), *Opening the Scrolls: Essays in Catholic History in Honour of G. Anstruther* (Bath, 1987).

BENTLEY, J., *Ritualism and Politics in Victorian Britain: The Attempt to Legislate for Belief* (Oxford, 1978).

BETJEMAN, J., Preface to *Guide to the Architecture and Interior, the History and the Pastoral Functions of the Metropolitan Cathedral of Westminster* (1968).

BODLEY, J. E. C., *Cardinal Manning: The Decay of Idealism in France: The Institute of France. Three Essays* . . . (1912).

BOGAN, B. J., *The Great Link: A History of St George's Cathedral, Southwark, 1786–1948* (1948; 1958).

BOLTON, C. A., *Salford Diocese and its Catholic Past* (Manchester, 1950).

BOND, A., *The Walsingham Story through Nine Hundred Years* (1960).

BOSSY, J., *The English Catholic Community 1570–1850* (1975).

—— *Christianity in the West 1400–1700* (Oxford, 1985).

—— 'Christian Life in the Later Middle Ages: Prayers', *Transactions of the Royal Historical Society*, 6th ser., 1 (1991), 137–50.

—— 'English Catholics after 1688', in O. P. Grell, J. I. Israel, and N. Tyacke (eds.), *From Persecution to Toleration: The Glorious Revolution and Religion in England* (Oxford, 1991), 369–87.

BOUYER, L., *Newman: His Life and Spirituality*, trans. J. L. May (1958).

BOWDEN, J. E., *The Life and Letters of Frederick William Faber, D.D.: Priest of the Oratory of St Philip Neri* (1869).

BOWEN, D., *Paul Cardinal Cullen and the Shaping of Modern Irish Catholicism* (Dublin, 1983).

BRADLEY, G. T. (ed.), *Yorkshire Catholics: Essays Presented to the Rt. Rev. William Gordon Wheeler* (Leeds Diocesan Archives Occasional Publications No. 1; Leeds, 1985).

BRITTEN, J., 'The Armagh Hymnal', *Month*, 126 (1915), 503–11.

BROOKS, P. (ed.), *Christian Spirituality: Essays in Honour of Gordon Rupp* (1975).

BURKE, T., *Catholic History of Liverpool* (Liverpool, 1910).

BURTON, E., *The Life and Times of Bishop Challoner* (2 vols.; 1909).

BUSCHKÜHL, M., *Great Britain and the Holy See 1746–1870* (Dublin, 1982).

BUTLER, A. S. G., *John Francis Bentley the Architect of Westminster Cathedral: An Essay* (1961).

BUTLER, B. C., 'Vatican I a Hundred Years Later', *Tablet*, 224 (1970), 3.

BUTLER, C., *The Life and Times of Bishop Ullathorne* (2 vols.; 1926).

—— *The Vatican Council* (2 vols.; 1930).

BUTLER, P., *Gladstone: Church, State, and Tractarianism: A Study of his Religious Ideas and Attitudes, 1809–1859* (Oxford, 1982).

BUTTERFIELD, H., *Lord Acton* (1948).

CAHILL, M., 'More about the Catechism', *Month*, 132 (1918), 350–7.

CAPES, H. M., *The Life and Labours of Father Bertrand Wilberforce, O.P.* (1906).

CARWARDINE, R., *Trans-Atlantic Revivalism: Popular Evangelicalism in Britain and America, 1790–1865* (Westport and London, 1978).

CARY-ELWES, C., *Experiences with God: A Dictionary of Spirituality and Prayer* (1986).

CASHDOLLAR, C. D., *The Transformation of Theology, 1830–1890: Positivism and Protestant Thought in Britain and America* (Princeton, 1989).

CASHMAN, J., 'The 1906 Education Bill: Catholic Peers and Irish Nationalists', *Recusant History*, 18 (1987), 422–39.

—— 'Bishop Baines and the Tensions in the Western District, 1823–1843' (M.Litt. thesis, Bristol University, 1989).

CHADWICK, O., *From Bossuet to Newman* (1957).

—— *The Victorian Church* (2 vols.; 1966–70; 1987).

—— 'Lord Acton at the First Vatican Council', *Journal of Theological Studies*, NS 28 (1977), 465–97.

—— *The Popes and European Revolution* (Oxford, 1981).

—— *Newman* (Oxford, 1983).

CHAMP, J. F., 'Bishop Milner, Holywell, and the Cure Tradition', in S. Mews (ed.), *Religion and National Identity* (Studies in Church History 18; Oxford, 1982), 153–64.

CHAPMAN, R., 'English Spiritual Writers 8: Father Faber', *Clergy Review*, NS 44 (1959), 385–94.

—— *Father Faber* (1961).

CHARLES, C., 'The Origins of the Parish Mission in England and the Early Passionist Apostolate, 1840–1850', *Journal of Ecclesiastical History*, 15 (1964), 60–75.

CHINNICI, J. P., 'English Catholic Tradition and the Vatican II *Declaration on Religious Freedom*', *Clergy Review*, 60 (1975), 487–98.

—— 'Liberal Catholicism and Newman's *Letter to the Duke of Norfolk*', *Clergy Review*, NS 60 (1975), 498–511.

—— 'Organization of the Spiritual Life: American Catholic Devotional Works, 1791–1866', *Theological Studies*, 40 (1979), 229–55.

—— *The English Catholic Enlightenment: John Lingard and the Cisalpine Movement 1780–1850* (Shepherdstown, W. Va., 1980).

—— *Devotion to the Holy Spirit in American Catholicism* (Mahwah, NJ, 1985).

CHOLVY, G., and HILAIRE, Y.-M., *Histoire religieuse de la France contemporaine 1800–1930* (2 vols.; Toulouse, 1986).

CLIFTON, M., *The Quiet Negotiator* (Liverpool, 1990).

COLLINGWOOD, C., 'The Catholic Truth Society', *Clergy Review*, 37 (1952), 641–58.

—— *The Catholic Truth Society* (1965).

The Concise Oxford Dictionary of Music, ed. M. Kennedy (3rd edn., based on the original publication by P. Scholes; Oxford, 1980).

CONNOLLY, G. P., 'Catholicism in Manchester and Salford, 1770–1850: The Quest for "le chrétien quelconque"' (Ph.D. thesis, 3 vols.; Manchester University, 1980).

—— 'Little Brother be at Peace: The Priest as Holy Man in the Nineteenth-Century Ghetto', in S. Mews (ed.), *Religion and National Identity* (Studies in Church History 18; Oxford, 1982), 191–205.

—— '"With more than Ordinary Devotion to God": The Secular Missioner of the North in the Evangelical Age of the English Mission', *North West Catholic History*, 10 (1983), 8–31.

—— 'The Transubstantiation of Myth: Towards a New Popular History of Nineteenth-Century Catholicism in England', *Journal of Ecclesiastical History*, 35 (1984), 78–104.

—— 'Irish and Catholic: Myth or Reality? Another Sort of Irish and the Renewal of the Clerical Profession among Catholics in England, 1791–1918', in R. Swift and S. Gilley (eds.), *The Irish in the Victorian City* (Beckenham, Kent, 1985), 225–54.

CONNOLLY, S. J., *Priests and People in Pre-Famine Ireland 1780–1850* (Dublin, 1982).

CONZEMIUS, J. V., 'Lord Acton and the First Vatican Council', *Journal of Ecclesiastical History*, 20 (1969), 267–94.

CONZEMIUS, V., 'Acton, Döllinger and Gladstone: A Strange Variety of Anti-Infallibilists', in J. Bastable (ed.), *Newman and Gladstone: Centennial Essays* (Dublin, 1978), 39–55.

COOTER, R. J., 'Lady Londonderry and the Irish Catholics of Seaham Harbour: "No Popery" Out of Context', *Recusant History*, 13 (1976), 288–98.

COPE, N., *Stone in Staffordshire: The History of a Market Town* (Hanley, 1972).

CORISH, P. J., 'Cardinal Cullen and Archbishop McHale', *Irish Ecclesiastical Record*, 5th ser. 91 (1959), 393–408.

—— *The Irish Catholic Experience: A Historical Survey* (Wilmington, Del., 1985).

COX, J., *The English Churches in a Secular Society: Lambeth, 1870–1930* (Oxford, 1982).

CRANSTON, R., *The Miracle of Lourdes* (New York, 1955; 1988).

CRAVEN, P. M., *The Life of Lady Georgiana Fullerton*, trans. H. J. Coleridge (1888).

CREHAN, J. H., *Father Thurston: A Memoir with a Bibliography of his Writings* (1952).

CRICHTON, J. D., *English Catholic Worship* (1979).

—— 'Richard Challoner: Catechist and Spiritual Writer', *Clergy Review*, 66 (1981), 269–75.

CROSS, F. L., and LIVINGSTONE, E. A. (eds.), *The Oxford Dictionary of the Christian Church* (Oxford, 1957; repr. 1988).

CUMING, G. J., and BAKER, D. (eds.), *Popular Belief and Practice* (Studies in Church History 8; Cambridge, 1972).

CURRIE, R., *Methodism Divided: A Study in the Sociology of Ecumenicalism* (1968).

—— GILBERT, A., and HORSLEY, L., *Churches and Churchgoers: Patterns of Church Growth in the British Isles since 1700* (Oxford, 1977).

CWIEKOWSKI, F. J., *The English Bishops and the First Vatican Council* (Louvain, 1971).

DAVIES, H., 'Is Newman's Theory of Development Catholic?', *Blackfriars Magazine*, 39 (1958), 310–21.

—— *Worship and Theology in England: From Newman to Martineau, 1850–1900* (4 vols.; 1962), iv.

DAVIES, J., 'Parish Charity: The Work of the Society of St Vincent de Paul, St Mary's, Highfield St, Liverpool, 1867–1868', *North West Catholic History*, 17 (1990; 1991), 37–46.

DAVIES, J. G. (ed.), *A New Dictionary of Liturgy and Worship* (1986; 1991).

DE L'HÔPITAL, W., *Westminster Cathedral and its Architect* (2 vols.; 1919).

DERRETT, J. D. M., ' "Thou Art the Stone, and Upon this Stone . . ." ', *Downside Review*, 106 (1988), 276–85.

DESSAIN, C. S., ' "Heart Speaks to Heart": Margaret Mary Hallahan and John Henry Newman', *Month*, NS 34 (1965), 360–7.

Dictionnaire de théologie catholique, ed. A. Vacant and E. Mangenot (17 vols.; Paris, 1899–1950).

DOLAN, J. P., *Catholic Revivalism: The American Experience, 1830–1900* (Notre Dame, Ind., 1978).

—— (ed.), *The American Catholic Parish: A History from 1850 to the Present* (2 vols.; Mahwah, NJ, 1987).

DONOVAN, R. K., 'The Denominational Character of English Catholic Charitable Effort, 1800–1865', *Catholic Historical Review*, 62 (1976), 200–23.

DOYLE, P. H., 'The Episcopate of Alexander Goss of Liverpool, 1856–1872: Diocesan Organisation and Control after the Restoration of the Roman Catholic Hierarchy' (Ph.D. thesis, London University, 1981).

—— 'Bishop Goss of Liverpool (1856–1872) and the Importance of Being English', in S. Mews (ed.), *Religion and National Identity* (Studies in Church History 18; Oxford, 1982), 433–47.

—— 'The Education and Training of Catholic Priests in Nineteenth-Century England', *Journal of Ecclesiastical History*, 35 (1984), 208–19.

—— 'An Episcopal Historian: Alexander Goss of Liverpool (1865–1872)', *North West Catholic History*, 15 (1988), 6–15.

DOYLE, P. J., 'Catholics and the Social Question', *London Recusant*, 3 (1973), 68–73.

DRANE, A. T., *Life of Mother Margaret Mary Hallahan* (1929).

DREW, M., *Acton, Gladstone and Others* (1924).

DUFFY, E. (ed.), *Challoner and his Church: A Catholic Bishop in Georgian England* (1981).

—— 'The English Secular Clergy and the Counter-Reformation', *Journal of Ecclesiastical History*, 34 (1983), 214–30.

—— 'Them Dry Bones', *New Blackfriars*, 66 (1985), 365–72.

DUGGAN, T., 'College Rectors: V. Robert Cornthwaite (1851–1857)', *Venerabile*, 4 (1930), 352–72.

DUNSTAN, P., 'William Cornwallis Cartwright: A Foreign Correspondent in Rome in the 1860s' (Ph.D. thesis, Cambridge University, 1985).

DUTHIE, J. L., 'The Fishermen's Religious Revival', *History Today*, 33 (1983), 22–7.

DYOS, H. J., and WOOLF, M. (eds.), *The Victorian City* (2 vols.; 1973).

EDWARDS, F., 'An English Bishop and the Other Council', *Month*, 28 (1962), 319–35.

ELLIOTT-BINNS, L. E., *The Development of English Theology in the Later Nineteenth Century* (1952).

ELWES, W., *The Fielding Album* (1950).

EMERY, C. J., *The Rosminians* (1960).

EVINSON, D., 'William Wardell and the Gothic Revival' (paper read to the Catholic Record Society Conference, Plater College, Oxford, 26 July 1989).

—— *The Lord's House: A History of Sheffield's Roman Catholic Buildings 1570–1990* (Sheffield, 1991).

FEHENEY, F., 'Catholic Orphanages in the Nineteenth Century', *Clergy Review*, 67 (1982), 355–61.

FITZSIMONS, J. (ed.), *Manning: Anglican and Catholic* (1951).

FLETCHER, J. R., 'Early Catholic Periodicals in England', *Dublin Review*, 198 (1936), 284–310.

FORD, J. T., 'Infallibility: A Review of Recent Studies', *Theological Studies*, 40 (1979), 273–305.

GASQUET, F. A. (ed.), *Lord Acton and his Circle* (1906).

GASQUET, J. R., *Cardinal Manning* (1896).

GIBSON, R., *A Social History of French Catholicism 1789–1914* (1989).

—— untitled paper on French Catholicism read to History of Religion Seminar (University of Birmingham, 5 Feb. 1992).

GILLEY, S. W., 'The Roman Catholic Mission to the Irish in London, 1840–1860', *Recusant History*, 10 (1969), 123–45.

—— 'Evangelical and Roman Catholic Missions to the Irish in London, 1830–70' (Ph.D. thesis, Cambridge University, 1970).

—— 'Protestant London, No-Popery and the Irish Poor 1830–60', *Recusant History*, 10 (1970), 210–30; 11 (1971), 21–46.

—— 'Heretic London, Holy Poverty, and the Irish Poor, 1830–70', *Downside Review*, 89 (1971), 64–89.

—— 'Papists, Protestants and the Irish in London, 1835–70', in G. J. Cuming and D. Baker (eds.), *Popular Belief and Practice* (Studies in Church History 8; Cambridge, 1972), 259–66.

—— 'Supernaturalised Culture: Catholic Attitudes and Latin Lands 1840–60', in D. Baker (ed.), *The Materials, Sources and Methods of Ecclesiastical History* (Studies in Church History 11; Oxford, 1975), 309–23.

—— 'Challoner as Controversialist', in E. Duffy (ed.), *Challoner and his Church: A Catholic Bishop in Georgian England* (1981), 90–111.

—— 'Vulgar Piety and the Brompton Oratory, 1850–1860', *Durham University Journal*, 43 (1981), 15–21.

—— 'Newman and Prophecy, Evangelical and Catholic', *Journal of the United Reformed Church History Society*, 3 (1985), 160–88.

GOODALL, D., 'How I Pray: 6. Habit of a Lifetime', *Tablet*, 246 (1992), 466–7.

GORMAN, W. G. (ed.), *Converts to Rome: A Biographical List of the More Notable Converts to the Catholic Church in the United Kingdom during the Last Sixty Years* (1910).

GRATTAN FLOOD, W. H., 'Ireland's Contribution to English Hymnody', *Month*, 127 (1916), 36–41.

GREELEY, A. M., *The Persistence of Religion* (1973).

GREEN, B., 'Adieu Mass', *Ampleforth Hospitalité de Lourdes Newsletter*, 16 (1992), 6–7.

Grove's Dictionary of Music and Musicians, ed. H. C. Colles (5 vols.; 4th edn., London, 1940).

GWYNN, D. R., *Cardinal Wiseman* (1929).

—— *A Hundred Years of Catholic Emancipation 1829–1929* (1929).

—— *The Second Spring, 1818–1852: A Study of the Catholic Revival in England* (1942).

—— 'England and the Foreign Missions', *Clergy Review*, NS 26 (1946), 57–65.

—— *Lord Shrewsbury, Pugin and the Catholic Revival* (1946).

—— 'Father Gentili', *Irish Ecclesiastical Record*, 70 (1948), 769–84.

—— 'Father Paul Pakenham, Passionist', *Clergy Review*, NS 42 (1957), 400–19.

—— 'Heralds of the Second Spring—Baines—Philipps—Gentili—Pugin—Walsh—Barberi—Cardinal Acton—Lucas—Ullathorne', *Clergy Review*, NS 29 (1948), 94–109, 251–65, 395–412; 30 (1948) 39–53, 100–18, 176–96, 248–65, 310–27, 389–406.

HALES, E. E. Y., *Pio Nono: A Study in European Politics and Religion in the Nineteenth Century* (New York, 1954).

HARDING, J. A., 'The Rebirth of the Roman Catholic Community in Frome' (Ph.D. thesis, Bristol University, 1986).

HASLER, A. B., *How the Pope became Infallible: Pius IX and the Politics of Persuasion*, trans. P. Heinegg, intro. Hans Küng (New York, 1981).

HASTINGS, A., 'Some Reflexions on the English Catholicism of the Late 1930's', in A. Hastings (ed.), *Bishops and Writers: Aspects of the Evolution of Modern English Catholicism* (Cambridge, 1977), 107–25.

HEILER, F., *Prayer: A Study in the History and Psychology of Religion*, trans. and ed. S. McComb (New York, 1932).

HELMREICH, E. C. (ed.), *Problems in European Civilization: A Free Church in a Free State? The Catholic Church, Italy, Germany, France, 1864–1914* (Boston, 1964).

HENNESSEY, J., *The First Council of the Vatican: The American Experience* (New York, 1963).

HERBERMANN, C. G., *et al.* (eds.), *The Catholic Encyclopedia*, (17 vols.; 1907–).

HEYDT, O. VAN DER, 'Monsignor Talbot de Malahide', *Wiseman Review*, 502 (winter 1964), 290–308.

HICKEY, J., *Urban Catholics: Urban Catholicism in England and Wales from 1829 to the Present Day* (1967).

HILTON, B., *The Age of Atonement: The Influence of Evangelicalism on Social and Economic Thought 1795–1865* (Oxford, 1988).

HILTON, J. A., '"The Science of the Saints": The Spirituality of Butler's Lives of the Saints', *Recusant History*, 15 (1980), 189–93.

—— 'Lingard's Hornby', in J. A. Hilton (ed.), *Catholic Englishmen: Essays Presented to Rt. Rev. Brian Charles Foley, Bishop of Lancaster* (Wigan, 1984), 37–44.

HIRST, J., 'On the Origin of Exposition of the Blessed Sacrament', *Month*, 68 (1890), 86–96.

HOLLIS, C., 'The Syllabus of Errors: Its Genesis and Implications', in L. Sheppard (ed.), *Twentieth Century Catholicism* (New York, 1915), 12–46.

HOLMES, D. J., 'Liberal Catholicism and Newman's Letter to the Duke of Norfolk', *Clergy Review*, 60 (1975), 498–511.

—— 'A Note on Newman's Reaction to the Definition of Papal Infallibility', *Spode House Review Occasional Papers*, 3 (1976), 39–58.

—— 'Newman's Attitude to Ultramontanism and Liberal Catholicism on the Eve of the First Vatican Council', in A. Hastings (ed.), *Bishops and Writers: Aspects of the Evolution of Modern English Catholicism* (Cambridge, 1977), 15–33.

—— *More Roman than Rome: English Catholicism in the Nineteenth Century* (1978).

—— *The Triumph of the Holy See: A Short History of the Papacy in the Nineteenth Century* (Shepherdstown, W. Va., 1978).

HOPPEN, K. T., 'W. G. Ward and Liberal Catholicism', *Journal of Ecclesiastical History*, 23 (1972), 323–44.

HORNSBY-SMITH, M. P., and TURCAN, K. A., 'Are Northern Catholics Different?', *Clergy Review*, 66 (1981), 231–41.

HOUGHTON, W. E., *The Victorian Frame of Mind, 1830–1870* (1957; New Haven, Conn., 1985).

—— (ed.), *The Wellesley Index to Victorian Periodicals 1824–1900* (5 vols.; London, etc., 1966–89).

INGLIS, K. S., 'Patterns of Religious Worship in 1851', *Journal of Ecclesiastical History*, 11 (1960), 74–86.

—— *Churches and the Working Classes in Victorian England* (1963).

IPPOLITO, R., 'Archbishop Manning's Championship of Papal Infallibility, 1867–72', *Ampleforth Journal*, 77 (1972), 31–9.

ISAACSON, C. S., *The Story of the Later Popes* (1906).

JAMES, W., *The Varieties of Religious Experience* (1902; 1960).

JAY, E., *Faith and Doubt in Victorian Britain* (1986).

JONES, C., WAINWRIGHT, G., and YARNOLD, E. (eds.), *The Study of Spirituality* (1986).

KEENAN, D. J., 'The Catholic Church in Ireland 1800–1860: Social and Sociological Study' (Ph.D. thesis, Queen's University, Belfast, 1979).

KENT, J., *Holding the Fort: Studies in Victorian Revivalism* (1978).

KER, I., *John Henry Newman: A Biography* (Oxford, 1988).

KERR, C., *Teresa Helena Higginson: Servant of God 'The Spouse of the Crucified' 1844–1905* (1927).

—— *Teresa Helena Higginson: School Teacher and Mystic 1844–1905* (Edinburgh, 1928).

KERR, D., 'The Early Nineteenth Century: Patterns of Change', in M. Maher (ed.), *Irish Spirituality* (Dublin, 1981).

KERR, D. A., 'Under the Union Flag: The Catholic Church in Ireland, 1800–1870', in *Ireland after the Union: Proceedings of the Second Joint Meeting of the Royal Irish Academy and the British Academy, London, 1986* (Oxford, 1989), 23–44.

KNOX, R., *The Creed in Slow Motion* (1949).

—— *Enthusiasm: A Chapter in the History of Religion* (Oxford, 1950).

KOLLAR, R., *Westminster Cathedral: From Dream to Reality* (Edinburgh, 1987).

KÜNG, H., *Infallible: An Enquiry* (1970).

LARKIN, E., 'The Roman Catholic Hierarchy and the Fall of Parnell', *Victorian Studies*, 4 (1961), 315–36.

—— 'The Devotional Revolution in Ireland, 1850–75', *American Historical Review*, 77 (1972), 625–52.

—— 'Church, State and Nation in Modern Ireland', *American Historical Review*, 80 (1975), 1244–76.

—— *The Roman Catholic Church in Ireland and the Fall of Parnell 1888–1891* (Liverpool, 1979).

—— *The Making of the Roman Catholic Church in Ireland, 1850–1860* (Chapel Hill, NC, 1980).

LEES, L., *Exiles of Erin: Irish Migrants in Victorian London* (Ithaca, NY, 1979).

LEETHAM, C., *Rosmini: Priest, Philosopher and Patriot* (1957).

—— 'Gentili's Reports to Rome', *Wiseman Review*, 498 (1963–4), 395–414.

—— *Luigi Gentili: A Sower for the Second Spring* (1965).

LESLIE, S., *Henry Edward Manning: His Life and Labours* (1921).

—— *Cardinal Gasquet: A Memoir* (1953).

L'ESTRANGE, P. J., 'The Nineteenth-Century British Jesuits, with Special Reference to their Relations with the Vicars Apostolic and the Bishops' (D.Phil. thesis, Oxford University, 1990).

LEWIS, C. S., *Letters to Malcolm Chiefly on Prayer* (1964).

LEYS, M. D. R., *Catholics in England 1559–1829: A Social History* (1961).

LITTLE, B., *Catholic Churches since 1623* (1966).

LOWE, W. J., 'The Lancashire Irish and the Catholic Church, 1846–1871: The Social Dimension', *Irish Historical Studies*, 20 (1976), 129–55.

LUCAS, M., *Two Englishwomen in Rome, 1871–1900* (1938).

LUCKETT, R., 'Bishop Challoner: The Devotionary Writer', in E. Duffy (ed.), *Challoner and his Church: A Catholic Bishop in Georgian England* (1981), 71–89.

LUKER, D., 'Revivalism in Theory and Practice: The Case of Cornish Methodism', *Journal of Ecclesiastical History*, 37 (1986), 603–19.

McCABE, H., introduction to *The Teaching of the Catholic Church: A New Catechism of Christian Doctrine* (1985).

McCAFFREY, J., 'Roman Catholics in Scotland in the Nineteenth and Twentieth Centuries', *Records of the Scottish Church History Society*, 21 (1983), 275–300.

McCLELLAND, V., *Cardinal Manning: His Public Life and Influence, 1865–1892* (1962).

—— 'The Irish Clergy and Archbishop Manning's Apostolic Visitation of the Western District of Scotland, 1867', *Catholic Historical Review*, 53 (1967), 1–27, 229–50.

McCORMACK, A., *Cardinal Vaughan: The Life of the Third Archbishop of Westminster, Founder of St Joseph's Missionary Society, Mill Hill* (1966).

McDONALD, W. J., *et al.* (eds.), *New Catholic Encyclopedia* (17 vols.; New York, 1967–79).

McDONNELL, R., 'Church Architecture as a Primary Document for Nineteenth Century Catholic History' (paper read to the Catholic Record Society Conference, Plater College, Oxford, 1 Aug. 1990).

MacDOUGALL, H. A., *The Acton–Newman Relations: The Dilemma of Christian Liberalism* (New York, 1962).

McELRATH, D., *The Syllabus of Pius IX: Some Reactions in England* (Louvain, 1964).

—— 'Richard Simpson and Count de Montalembert, the *Rambler* and the *Correspondant*', *Downside Review*, 84 (1966), 150–70.

—— 'Richard Simpson and John Henry Newman: *The Rambler*, Laymen and Theology', *Catholic Historical Review*, 52 (1967), 509–33.

—— (ed.), *Lord Acton, the Decisive Decade* (1970).

—— *Richard Simpson, 1820–1876, a Study in XIXth Century English Liberal Catholicism* (Louvain, 1972).

MacGREGOR, G., *The Vatican Revolution* (1958).

MACHIN, G. I. T., *Politics and the Church in Great Britain 1832–1868* (1977).

McINTIRE, C. T., *England against the Papacy 1858–1861: Tories, Liberals, and the Overthrow of Papal Temporal Power during the Italian Risorgimento* (Cambridge, 1983).

McLEOD, H., *Class and Religion in the Late Victorian City* (1974).

—— *Religion and the People of Western Europe 1789–1970* (Oxford, 1981).

—— *Religion and the Working Class in Nineteenth-Century Britain* (1984).

—— 'Building the "Catholic Ghetto": Catholic Organisations 1870–1914', in W. J. Sheils and D. Wood (eds.), *Voluntary Religion* (Studies in Church History 23; 1986), 411–44.

—— 'New Perspectives on Victorian Working Class Religion: The Oral Evidence', *Oral History Journal*, 14 (1986), 31–49.

—— 'Female Piety and Male Irreligion', originally published as 'Weibliche Frömmigkeit—männlicher Unglaube?: Religion und Kirchen im bürgerlichen 19. Jahrhundert', in Ute Frevert (ed.), *Bürgerinnen und Bürger: Geschlechterverhältnisse im 19. Jahrhundert* (Göttingen, 1988), 134–56.

MacManus, F. R., *The Congregation of Sacred Rites* (1954).

Macready, S., and Thompson, F. H., *Influences in Victorian Art and Architecture: Occasional Paper (New Series) VII* (1985).

MacSuibhne, P., *Paul Cullen and his Contemporaries* (5 vols.; Naas, 1961–77).

McSweeney, B., *Roman Catholicism: The Search for Relevance* (Oxford, 1980).

Maher, M. (ed.), *Irish Spirituality* (Dublin, 1981).

Mallin, D., ' "Rome on the Rates" in Wigan; the Founding of Sacred Heart School, 1904–6', *North West Catholic History*, 5 (1978), 34–41.

Mangenot, E., 'Catéchisme', in *Dictionnaire de théologie catholique*, ed. A. Vacant and E. Mangenot (17 vols.; Paris, 1899–1950), ii (1903), cols. 1896–1968.

Manion, M. M., 'What Happened to Devotion?', *The Way*, 27 (1987), 192–200.

Marron, S., 'Bishop Challoner and our Catechism', *Douai Magazine*, NS 9 (1936), 111–20.

Marshall, B., *Father Malachy's Miracle* (1931; 1947).

—— *All Glorious Within* (1944).

Martin, D., *A General Theory of Secularization* (Oxford, 1978).

Martindale, C. C., 'Stigmata and Sanctity', *Clergy Review*, 37 (1952), 659–66.

Mathew, D., *Catholicism in England* (1936; 1948).

—— *Acton* (1946).

—— 'English Spiritual Writers 6: Provost Husenbeth', *Clergy Review*, NS 44 (1959), 257–64.

—— *Lord Acton and his Times* (1968).

Maunder, C., 'Authenticity Criteria for Marian Apparitions' (early draft chapter for inclusion in forthcoming Leeds University Ph.D. thesis).

Mayor, S. M., 'The "Nonconformist" and the Roman Catholic Church', *Recusant History*, 9 (1988), 183–97.

Mews, S. (ed.), *Religion and National Identity* (Studies in Church History 18; Oxford, 1982).

Milburn, D., 'Impressions of an English Bishop at the First Vatican Council', *Wiseman Review*, 493 (1962), 217–35.

Miller, D. W., 'Irish Catholicism and the Great Famine', *Journal of Social History*, 9 (1975), 81–98.

Monahan, M., *Life and Letters of Janet Erskine Stuart: Superior General of the Society of the Sacred Heart 1857 to 1914* (1922).

Mooney, D., 'Popular Religion and Clerical Influence in Pre-Famine Meath', in R. V. Comerford, M. Cullen, J. R. Hill, and C. Lennon (eds.), *Religion, Conflict and Coexistence in Ireland: Essays Presented to Monsignor Patrick Corish* (Dublin, 1990), 188–218.

Moorhouse, G., *Against all Reason* (1969).

Murphy, T. A., 'Newman and Devotion to Our Lady', *Irish Ecclesiastical Record*, 5th ser. 72 (Dublin, 1949), 385–96.

Murray, R. H., *Church of England Handbooks: No. 8. Is the Pope Infallible?* (London, n.d.).

NEAL, F., 'The Birkenhead Garibaldi Riots of 1862', *Transactions of the Historic Society of Lancashire and Cheshire*, 131 (1981), 87–111.

NEMER, L., 'Anglican and Roman Catholic Attitudes on Missions. A Comparison of the Church Missionary Society with the Society of St Joseph of the Sacred Heart for Foreign Missions in their Home Structures and Life between 1865 and 1885' (Ph.D. thesis, Cambridge University, 1979).

The New Oxford Book of Victorian Verse, ed. C. Ricks (Oxford, 1987).

NEWSOME, D., *The Parting of Friends: The Wilberforces and Henry Manning* (1966).

—— 'Newman and Manning: Spirituality and Personal Conflict', in P. Brooks (ed.), *Christian Spirituality: Essays in Honour of Gordon Rupp* (1975).

—— *The Convert Cardinals: John Henry Newman and Henry Edward Manning* (1993).

NORMAN, E., *Anti-Catholicism in Victorian England* (1968).

—— *The Catholic Church and Ireland . . . 1859–1873* (1968).

—— *The English Catholic Church in the Nineteenth Century* (Oxford, 1984).

—— *Roman Catholicism in England: From the Elizabethan Settlement to the Second Vatican Council* (Oxford, 1986).

OBELKEVICH, J., ROPER, L., and SAMUEL, R. (eds.), *Disciplines of Faith* (1987).

O'BRIEN, S., 'Terra Incognita: The Nun in Nineteenth Century England', *Past and Present*, 121 (1988), 183–97.

—— 'Roman Catholic Nuns in England 1829–1920' (paper read to Social History seminar, University of Birmingham, 17 May 1989).

OLDMEADOW, E., *Francis, Cardinal Bourne* (2 vols.; 1940–4).

O'SULLIVAN, A. M., *Teresa Higginson the Servant of God: School Teacher 1845–1905* (1924).

ÖTUATHAIGH, M., 'The Irish in Nineteenth-Century Britain: Problems of Integration', *Transactions of the Royal Historical Society*, 5th ser. 31 (1981), 149–74.

PALLEN, C., and WYNNE, J. (eds.), *The New Catholic Dictionary* (1929).

PARSONS, G. (ed.), *Religion in Victorian Britain* (4 vols.; Manchester, 1988).

PAWLEY, B., and PAWLEY, M., *Rome and Canterbury through Four Centuries: A Study of the Relations between the Church of Rome and the Anglican Churches 1530–1981* (Oxford, 1981).

PAZ, D. G., 'Anti-Catholicism, Anti-Irish Stereotyping and Anti-Celtic Racism in Mid-Victorian Working-Class Periodicals', *Albion*, 18 (1986), 601–16.

PERRY, N., and ECHEVERRIA, L., *Under the Heel of Mary* (1988).

PLUMB, B., 'Some Religious Orders in the North West: A Select Bibliography', *North West Catholic History*, 16 (1989), 28–37.

PRITCHARD, G., 'College Rectors: II. Nicholas Wiseman (1828–1840)', *Venerabile*, 4 (1928), 39–62.

PURCELL, E. S., *Life of Cardinal Manning, Archbishop of Westminster* (2 vols.; 1896).

—— and DE LISLE, E., *Life and Letters of Ambrose Phillipps de Lisle* (2 vols.; New York, 1900).

QUINN, D. A., 'English Roman Catholics and Politics in the Second Half of the Nineteenth Century' (D.Phil. thesis, Oxford University, 1985).

RAMSAY, G. [K. O'MEARA], *Thomas Grant: First Bishop of Southwark* (1874; 2nd edn., 1886).

RAVITCH, N., *The Catholic Church and the French Nation* (1990).

REARDON, B., 'Roman Catholic Modernism', in N. Smart, J. Clayton, S. Katz, and P. Sherry (eds.), *Nineteenth Century Religious Thought in the West* (3 vols.; Cambridge, 1985), ii. 141–77.

RHODES, J., 'The Rosary in Sixteenth-Century England', *Mount Carmel*, 31 (1983), 180–91; 32 (1984), 4–17.

RICKABY, J., 'The Church and Liberal Catholicism', *Month*, 97 (1901), 337–46.

ROBBINS, K., 'Religion and Identity in Modern British History' (Presidential Address), in S. Mews (ed.), *Religion and National Identity* (Studies in Church History 18; Oxford, 1982), 465–87.

ROBERTS, R., *The Classic Slum: Salford Life in the First Quarter of the Century* (1971).

ROE, W. G., *Lamennais and England: The Reception of Lamennais's Religious Ideas in England in the Nineteenth Century* (Oxford, 1966).

ROOT, J. D., 'Catholicism and Science in Victorian England', *Clergy Review*, 66 (1981), 138–47, 162–70.

ROSKELL, M. F., and VAUGHAN, H. F. J., *Memoirs of Francis Kerril Amherst D.D., Lord Bishop of Northampton* (1903).

ROSS, A., 'The Development of the Scottish Catholic Community 1878–1978', *Innes Review*, 29 (1978), 30–55.

ROWELL, G., *Hell and the Victorians* (Oxford, 1974).

SACKVILLE-WEST, V., *The Eagle and the Dove: A Study in Contrasts. St Teresa of Avila. St Thérèse of Lisieux* (1943).

SAGOVSKY, N., *'On God's Side': A Life of George Tyrrell* (Oxford, 1990).

SCHIEFEN, R. J., 'The Organisation and Administration of Roman Catholic Dioceses in England and Wales in the Mid-Nineteenth Century' (Ph.D. thesis, London University, 1970).

—— 'Some Aspects of the Controversy between Cardinal Wiseman and the Westminster Chapter', *Journal of Ecclesiastical History*, 21 (1970), 128–48.

—— ' "Anglo-Gallicanism" in Nineteenth-Century England', *Catholic Historical Review*, 60 (1977), 14–44.

—— *Nicholas Wiseman and the Transformation of English Catholicism* (Shepherdstown, W. Va., 1984).

SCHWEITZER, P., and WEGNER, C. (eds.), *On the River: Memories of a Working River* (1989).

SEWELL, B., 'Frederick William Rolfe and the Scots College', *Innes Review*, 26 (1976), 20–6.

SHARP, J., 'The Influence of St Alphonsus Liguori in Nineteenth-Century Britain', *Downside Review*, 101 (1983), 60–76.

—— 'Juvenile Holiness: Catholic Revivalism among Children in Victorian Britain', *Journal of Ecclesiastical History*, 35 (1984), 220–38.

—— *Reapers of the Harvest: The Redemptorists in Great Britain and Ireland 1843–1898* (Dublin, 1989).

SHEILS, W. J., and WOOD, D. (eds.), *The Churches, Ireland and the Irish* (Studies in Church History 25; Oxford, 1986).

—— *Voluntary Religion* (Studies in Church History 23; Oxford, 1986).

SINGLETON, J., 'The Virgin Mary and Religious Conflict in Victorian Britain', *Journal of Ecclesiastical History*, 43 (1992), 16–34.

SMART, N., CLAYTON, J., KATZ, S., and SHERRY, P. (eds.), *Nineteenth Century Religious Thought in the West* (3 vols.; Cambridge, 1985).

SNEAD-COX, J. G., *The Life of Cardinal Vaughan* (2 vols.; 1910).

SPERBER, J., *Popular Catholicism in Nineteenth-Century Germany* (Princeton, 1984).

STANTON, P., *Life of Pugin* (1971).

STEELE, E. D., 'Cardinal Cullen and Irish Nationality', *Irish Historical Studies*, 19 (1975), 239–60.

STRACHEY, L., *Eminent Victorians* (1918).

STUART, E. B., 'Bishop Baines and his 1840 Lenten Pastoral: The Last Full-Scale Manifesto of Traditional English Catholicism?', *Downside Review*, 358 (1987), 40–59.

—— 'Roman Catholic Reactions to the Oxford Movement and Anglican Schemes for Reunion, from 1833 to the Condemnation of Anglican Orders in 1896' (D.Phil. thesis, Oxford University, 1987).

SUPPLE, J. F., 'Catholicism in Yorkshire, 1850–1900' (Ph.D. thesis, Leeds University, 1982).

—— 'The Catholic Clergy of Yorkshire, 1850–1900: A Profile', *Northern History*, 21 (1985), 212–35.

—— 'Robert Cornthwaite: A Neglected Nineteenth Century Bishop', *Recusant History*, 17 (1985), 399–413.

—— 'Ultramontanism in Yorkshire', *Recusant History*, 17 (1985), 274–86.

—— 'The Political Attitudes and Activities of Yorkshire Catholics, 1850–1900', *Northern History*, 22 (1986), 231–49.

SUPPLE-GREEN, J. F., *The Catholic Revival in Yorkshire 1850–1900* (Leeds, 1990).

SWEENEY, G., 'The Forgotten Council', in A. Hastings (ed.), *Bishops and Writers: Aspects of the Evolution of Modern English Catholicism* (Cambridge, 1977), 161–78.

SWIFT, R., 'Anti-Catholicism and Irish Disturbances: Public Order in Mid-Victorian Wolverhampton', *Midland History*, 9 (1984), 87–108.

SWIFT, R. and GILLEY, S. (eds.), *The Irish in the Victorian City* (Beckenham, Kent, 1985).

SYMONS, A. J. A., *The Quest for Corvo* (1955).

TAVES, A., *The Household of Faith: Roman Catholic Devotions in Mid-Nineteenth-Century America* (Notre Dame, Ind., 1986).

THACKRAY, D., and THACKRAY, L., *A Brief History of St Marie's Church 1844 to 1986* (Rugby, 1987).

THILS, G., *L'Infallibilité pontificale* (Gembloux, 1969).

THOMAS, K., *Religion and the Decline of Magic* (Harmondsworth, 1978).

THUREAU-DANGIN, P., *The English Catholic Revival in the Nineteenth Century* (2 vols.; New York, 1899).

TIERNY, B., *The Origins of Papal Infallibility 1150–1350* (Leiden, 1972).

TOPLISS, J., 'A London Precursor of the Catholic Truth Society', *London Recusant*, 4 (1974), 100–7.

TOWNSEND, R., 'Hagiography in England in the Nineteenth Century: A Study in Literary, Historiographical and Theological Developments' (D.Phil. thesis, Oxford University, 1981).

TRAPPES-LOMAX, M., *Pugin* (1932).

—— *Bishop Challoner: A Biographical Study Derived from Dr. Edwin Burton's 'The Life and Times of Bishop Challoner'* (1936; 1947).

TREVOR, M., 'Post-Conciliar Problems: 1870 and 1967', *Ampleforth Journal*, 72 (1967), 8–15.

TULLOCH, H., *Acton* (1988).

VIDLER, A. R., *The Modernist Movement in the Roman Church. Norrisian Prize Essay, 1933* (Cambridge, 1934).

—— *A Variety of Catholic Modernists* (Cambridge, 1970).

WADHAM, J., *The Case of Cornelia Connelly* (1956).

WAKE, E. H., 'College Rectors. IV: Thomas Grant', *Venerabile*, 4 (1929), 245–63.

WALSH, W., 'The Alleged Gallicanism of Maynooth and of the Irish Clergy', *Dublin Review*, 3rd ser., 5 (1880), 210–53.

WARD, B., *The Sequel to Catholic Emancipation 1830–1850* (2 vols.; 1913–15).

WARD, M., *The Wilfrid Wards and the Transition* (2 vols.; 1934–7).

—— 'W. G. Ward and Wilfrid Ward', *Dublin Review*, 198 (1936), 235–52.

WARD, W. P., *William George Ward and the Catholic Revival* (1893).

—— *The Life of John Henry Cardinal Newman* (2 vols.; 1912).

WASZAK, P., *Roman Catholic Schools in Peterborough: A History* (Peterborough, 1984).

—— 'The Revival of the Roman Catholic Church in Peterborough *c.*1793–1910', *Peterborough Past: The Journal of the Peterborough Museum Society*, 3 (1988), 27–39.

—— 'The Parish Archives of All Souls Church, Peterborough', *Catholic Archives*, 11 (1991), 31–4.

WATKIN, E. I., *Roman Catholicism in England from the Reformation to 1950* (1957).

WAUGH, E., *Brideshead Revisited* (1945).

WERFEL, F., *The Song of Bernadette* (1942).

WHELAN, J. P., *The Spirituality of Friedrich von Hügel* (1971).

WHYTE, J. H., *Catholics in Western Democracies: A Study in Political Behaviour* (Dublin, 1981).

WILLIAMS, S., 'Religious Belief and Popular Culture: 1865–1939' (paper read to the British History since 1830 seminar held at Merton College, Oxford, 16 Oct. 1990).

WILSON, A., *Blessed Dominic Barberi: Supernaturalized Briton* (London, 1967).

WILSON, B. R. (ed.), *Patterns of Sectarianism: Organisation and Ideology in Social and Religious Movements* (1967).

WILSON, I., *The Bleeding Mind: An Investigation into the Mysterious Phenomenon of Stigmata* (1988).

WILSON, J. A., *The Life of Bishop Hedley* (1930).

WILSON, S. (ed.), *Saints and their Cults* (Cambridge, 1983).

YATES, N., 'Pugin and the Medieval Dream', *History Today*, 37 (1987), 33–40.

YEO, S., *Religion and Voluntary Organisations in Crisis* (1976).

YOUNG, U., *Life and Letters of Ven. Dominic Barberi, C.P.* (1926).

—— *Life of Father Ignatius Spencer, C.P.* (1933).

—— (ed.), *Dominic Barberi in England* (1935).

ZIMDARS-SWARTZ, S. L., *Encountering Mary from La Salette to Medjugorje* (Princeton, 1991).

INDEX

Abridgement of Christian Doctrine, An, *see* catechisms
Acton, John E. E. D., first Baron 69
  and Döllinger 21
  faith of 112 n.
  and German Catholicism 21, 23
  and the liberal Catholic 'party' 3, 18, 20, 105
  and papal infallibility 112
  and pious legends 163
Adams, Pauline 13 n.
Adoremus 51
Adrian VI, Pope 68
Alacoque, Margaret Mary St, *see* St Margaret Mary Alacoque
alcoholism 148
  see also temperance
All Souls, Peterborough, *see* Peterborough
altar societies, *see* Catholic societies
Altholz, Josef 6 n., 18–22
America, *see* United States of America
Ampleforth Abbey 98
Ampleforth College 98–9
angels 115
Angelus, the 80, 91
Anglicanism 20, 21, 29, 49, 80, 88, 116, 119, 120, 142, 143, 151
  see also Anglo-Catholicism; converts; Oxford Movement; Tractarians
Anglo-Catholicism 146 n., 149, 150, 151
Anglo-Gallicanism, *see* Gallicanism
Anima Christi, the 90, 91, 92–3
Anstruther, G. E. 171
Antonelli, Giacomo, Cardinal 19 & n.
Apostles' Creed, *see* Creed
Apostleship of Prayer, *see* Catholic societies
apparitions of the Blessed Virgin Mary 25, 68, 137
  see also Lourdes; La Salette; Mary
archbishops, *see* bishops
archconfraternities, *see* Catholic societies
archdioceses, *see under individual names*
architecture, ecclesiastical vi, 26, 151
aristocracy, *see* class

Ark of Salvation 115
Ash Wednesday 46
Aspinwall, Bernard 3
Aston 161
Athanasian Creed, *see* Creed
atheism, *see* 'leakage'
Audley 162
Augustine of Canterbury, St, *see* St Augustine
Austria 112, 125
Ave Maria, see Hail Mary
Ave Maria Stella 79
Aveling, John 77

Bagshawe, Edward, bishop of Nottingham 74–5, 121
Bagshawe, John B. 108
Balliol College, *see* Oxford University
baptism 38, 41, 122–3, 144, 146
Barberi, Fr Dominic 146, 147, 154, 159, 160, 161
Barnabò, Cardinal 19, 119
Barnack, John 152
Bathurst, Catherine 29
Bebbington, David 153
Belgium 67, 125
Bellarmine, Robert, St 102, 103 n.
  catechism of 100–5, 107, 118, 138
Bellasis, R. G. 73
Belloc, Hilaire 143
Benedict XIV, Pope 65
Benedictines, *see* St Benedict, Order of
Benediction of the Blessed Sacrament 7, 36, 40
  in Bridgewater 48
  for the Conversion of England 56 & n.
  in Coventry 48, 61
  description of 46, 49, 50
  and devotional unity 50–3, 58, 99, 100, 135, 157, 159, 169, 172
  and the ecclesiastical hierarchy 54–9
  at Embassy chapels 11–12
  English tradition of 47–51, 83, 140
  and The Eucharistic Congress (1908) 52 & n.

Benediction of the Blessed Sacrament
  (*cont.*):
  and Evensong 49
  and Exposition of the Bl. Sacr. 50,
    55–6
  Faber on 50
  in *Garden of the Soul* 47–8, 50, 54, 61,
    68, 79, 80, 82, 138
  and Hallahan 61
  and Lady Herbert of Lea 51–2
  and Litany of Loreto 46, 50, 51
  in Liverpool 42
  in London 42, 48, 52 n.
  and Manning 25, 50
  and *Manual of Prayers for
    Congregational Use* 54–6
  and the Mass 45, 49, 52, 53, 58
  and *Memorare* 91, 94–8
  and miracles 53–4, 97–9
  neglect by historians of 45, 50 n.
  novelty of 46–7
  and old Catholics 12, 47–51, 61
  origins of 47–8, 53
  in Peterborough 52
  popularity of 45–66, 68–9, 176–90
  resilience to change of 54–8, 80, 82
  and the rosary 45, 58–60, 61, 68, 69
  and *Salve Regina* 91
  and social unity 50–1, 69, 99, 100, 135,
    157, 159, 169, 172
  statistical importance of 42, 44, 176–90
  and superstitions 53–4, 166
  H. Thurston and 51, 69
  H. Thurston on 45–51
  and W. Ullathorne 61 & n.
  in the United States 89
  and the Vatican 46–7, 49, 56, 58, 68
  and H. Vaughan 51–2
  and W. G. Ward 50
  in Whitby 48
  and N. Wiseman 52, 55, 69
  see also eucharist; Exposition of the
    Blessed Sacrament; *Quarant' ore*;
    Visitation of the Blessed Sacrament
Beverley:
  bishop of, *see* Cornthwaite, Robert
  diocese of 36–7, 42, 44, 45, 60, 109,
    125 n., 127
Bidding Prayers 91
bilocation 156
Birkenhead:
  Our Lady's, Birkenhead 130 n., 133,
    147–8, 151, 152, 166, 167

Birmingham:
  bishop of 109; *see also* Ullathorne
  diocese of 41, 42, 45, 60, 115 n., 125,
    127 n.
  St Chad's, Birmingham 128, 130 n.,
    134
  see also Oratory of St Philip Neri
bishops, the English Catholic, *see*
  hierarchy; *see also under individual
  names of bishops and of dioceses*
Blessed Sacrament 36, 51, 134, 167
  as 'Captive victim' 50
  in the catechism 116–17
  English attitudes towards the 56–8, 140
  in France 126
  and Manning 25
  and von Hügel 26
  see also Benediction of the; communion;
    Corpus Christi; eucharist; Exposition
    of the Blessed Sacrament; Mass;
    Quarant' ore; transubstantiation;
    Visitation of the Blessed Sacrament
Blessed Virgin Mary, *see* Mary
Bodleian Library 71, 73, 75, 106, 110
Bodley, John 25 n.
bona mors 71, 80, 84, 87, 126–7
books:
  'bad' 22, 114, 143
  'good' 123, 131 & n.
Booth, Charles 13, 160
Bootle 43, 150, 156, 161, 162
Borromeo, Charles, St, *see* St Charles
  Borromeo
Bossy, John:
  on Benediction of the Bl. Sacr. 53
  on Challoner's *Garden of the Soul*
    9–10, 77–8, 79
  on the importance of devotion 2
  on old Catholics 9–10
  on the 'second spring' 6
  on the Toleration Act 11–12
Bowdlerization 86, 87
Bowness, Mary 140 n.
Bradley, Millicent 162
Bremond, Henri 25
Brice, Adele 129 n.
Bridgewater 48 & n.
Brigittines 65
Brindle, Dr Robert 146
British Library 71, 73, 75, 106, 110
Britten, James 171
Brompton Oratory, *see* Oratory of St
  Philip Neri

Brook Green 157
Brown, Father 143
Brown, James, bishop of Shrewsbury:
  on the catechism 102–3, 109–10, 119,
    120
  on Challoner's *Garden of the Soul*
    73–4, 119
  and ecclesiastical authority 119
  and the Errington case 118–19
  on the *Manual of Prayers for*
    Congregational Use 73–4, 119
  moderation of 119–20
  on prayer-book revisions 73–5, 119–20
  and the Sacred Heart 152
Brown, Thomas Joseph, bishop of
  Newport and Menevia 119
Burnet, Bishop Gilbert 11
Burns, Paul 71 n.
Burton, Canon Edwin 76
Butler, Alban 83
Butler, Dom Cuthbert:
  on Benediction of the Bl. Sacr. 61 n.
  on the catechism 101–2
  on 'conversion' experiences 145
  on education 124
  on the First Vatican Council 101–2
  on Manning 18 n.
  on papal infallibility 101–2
  on Pugin 26
  on the rosary 44, 61 n.
  and the 'second spring' 6
  on Ullathorne 61 n., 145
  and von Hügel 25–6
  on W. G. Ward 26
Butler, William John, Dean of Lincoln
  150

Cambridge Camden Society 142
Cambridge University Library 71, 75,
  106, 110
Camdenians, *see* Cambridge Camden
  Society
Canisius, Peter, St 103 & n., 106,
  see also catechisms
Canonization of the Japanese Martyrs
  102–3
caritas 103, 134, 154, 157–61
  see also poverty; tolerance; unity
Carmelites 132
Cary-Elwes, Dudley 52, 171
catechisms:
  debate at the First Vatican Council on
    100–5

  and the English bishops 100–5,
    109–10, 117–24, 166, 167
  in France 105, 111
  in Germany 100–5
  history and use of catechisms in
    England 105–10
  importance of 100
  and the pope 100–5, 111–12
  in Rome 100–5
  'the' catechism 108, 109
  see also Clifford; penny catechism
  INDIVIDUAL CATECHISMS:
  An Abridgment of Christian Doctrine: or,
    the First Catechism. Published for the
    Use of the London District (London:
    Keating, Brown, & Co., Printers to
    R. R. the Vicars Apostolic, *c.*1820),
    see proto-penny catechism
  Bagshawe's, *see The Catechism*
    Illustrated . . .
  Bellarmine's 100–5, 107, 118, 138
  Canisius's 100–5
  The Catechism Illustrated . . . 108
  Catechism Made Easy (Liverpool,
    1865–77) 108
  Catholic Truth Society's, *see The*
    Teaching of the Catholic Church . . .
  Challoner's, *see* penny catechism
  Controversial Catechism . . . 111
  Douay Abstract 107
  Douai Catechism 107
  Gibson's, *see Catechism Made Easy*
  Gother's 107
  Keenan's, *see Controversial*
    Catechism . . .
  Large Type Edition . . . (1876; 1859
    version), *see* penny catechism
  Luther's 106
  of Montpellier diocese 111
  190th Thousand . . . (London, 1884;
    *c.*1880 version), *see* penny catechism
  A Short Abridgment of Christian Doctrine
    for the Instruction of Beginners (1745)
    107
  The Teaching of the Catholic Truth: A
    New Catechism of Christian Doctrine
    (London, 1889) 106
  'the' catechism, *see* penny catechism
  Turberville's 107
  Vaux's 106–7
  see also Confraternity of Christian
    Doctrine; penny catechism
Catholic Dictionary 45, 46, 58–9

Catholic Directory 40–1, 44, 56, 60, 89,
    109, 125, 127
Catholic Emancipation:
    Relief Acts 11–12
    and the 'second spring' 10–12
    significance accorded to 4–7
    Toleration Act, enforcement of 11
Catholic Encyclopedia 62
    see also *New Catholic Encyclopedia*
'Catholic ghetto' 83–4, 143
Catholic societies 32, 34, 35, 41, 126, 127,
    134
    altar societies 131, 134
    boys' 126, 129–30, 135
    burial guilds 135
    choir guilds 131
    common spirit of 129, 132–6
    complete list of 195–9
    and devotional unity 132–6
    embroidery guilds 131
    in England 35, 125–36, 174–82,
        183–90, 195–9
    in France 126, 132
    girls' 126, 129–30
    lack of work on 125
    and the Mass 129, 133
    men's 126, 129–30
    night refuges 130
    and penance 129, 133
    purpose of 124, 125–36
    and the rosary 126–7, 134 n.
    and the Sacred Heart 94, 97, 126, 127,
        152
    and social class 132–6
    statistics of 174–82
    temperance societies 130, 133–4
    in the United States 34
    women's 126, 127, 129–30
    INDIVIDUAL SOCIETIES:
    Altar Society, St Chad's, Birmingham
        134
    Apostleship of Prayer 126, 132, 136
    Association of the Cross 133–4
    Boys' Guilds 129
    Catholic Boys' Brigade 52 n., 130 n.
    Catholic Clothing Club, Newcastle 131
    Catholic Total Abstinence League
        134 n.
    Catholic Women's League, Newcastle
        130 n.
    Catholic Young Men's Society,
        Newcastle 130 n.
    Children of Mary 128–9

Confraternity of Christian Doctrine
    109, 125 n.
Confraternity of Christian Mothers 129
Confraternity of the Living Rosary 126
Confraternity of the Sacred Heart 126,
    152
Converts' Aid Society 130
Girls' Guilds 129
Guild of Our Lady of Ransom, see
    Ransomer
Immaculate Conception Charity 130
League of English Martyrs 130
Men's Sodality, St Chad's, Birmingham
    130 n.
St Vincent de Paul Society 127–8, 130,
    134, 158
Temperence Guild of Our Lady and St
    John the Baptist 130
Temperence Guild of St Patrick 130
Young Men's Society 130 n., 133, 152
*for comprehensive list of Catholic societies
    in England see* 195–9
    see also Catholic Truth Society, St
    Dominic (Third Order of) St Francis
    (Third Order of), Society of the
    Holy Child Jesus
Catholic Truth Society 68, 93, 106, 163
Chadwick, Bishop 24
Chadwick, Owen 142–3
Challoner, Richard 166
    and Benediction of the Bl. Sacr. 47–8
    as controversialist 77, 83–4
    criticisms of 86
    as devotional enthusiast 84, 140
    esteem for 72–7, 79, 80–5
    on hell 168
    influence of 72–8, 81–9
    and the penny catechism 80–1, 84,
        105–9, 138
    and the rosary 61–2
    and the Sign of the Cross 84
    Think Well On It 16
    unoriginality of 84–5, 86
    and 'the world' 9–10, 78, 79, 82–3, 84
    see also catechisms; *Garden of the Soul*
charity, see *caritas*; poverty
Chelsea 157
Cheshire 128 n.,
    see also Bootle, Neston
Chesterton, Gilbert Keith 143, 144 & n.
childbirth 66
Children of Mary, *see* Catholic Societies
Cholvy, Gérard 33–4, 165–6

Christ, imitation of 153–7
Christian's Rule of Life 123
Christian Doctrine, Confraternity of, *see* catechisms; Catholic societies
Christianity, broad conception of 148–57, 169
Christmas 171
Chronicle 24
Church of England, *see* Anglicanism
churches:
  architecture of, *see* architecture
  devotions offered in, *see* devotions
  statistics of English and Welsh 174–90
  see also under individual names
Cisalpinism 8, 21
class, social:
  and Benediction of the Bl. Sacr. 51–3, 69, 99, 100, 135, 157, 159, 169, 172
  and the catechism 109, 117
  and Catholic societies 132–6
  and devotional stereotypes 13–14, 31, 39
  and devotions 151–3, 157–65, 169–73
  see also tolerance; unity
Clement XI, Pope 65
Clifford, William, bishop of Clifton 101, 119
  and catechisms 101–5
  and papal infallibility 101–2
  and 'party' 105, 117–19
Clifton:
  bishop of, *see* Clifford, William
  diocese of 42, 45, 60, 125, 127 & n.
Commandments, the Ten 82, 114, 122, 167
Commandments of the Church 116
communion 7, 8, 34, 35, 69
  in Challoner's *Garden of the Soul* 86
  First Communion 126, 129
  and missions 147–8, 152
  see also Benediction of the Bl. Sacr.; Blessed Sacrament, Corpus Christi; eucharist; Exposition of the Blessed Sacrament; Mass; *Quarant' ore*; transubstantiation; Visitation of the Blessed Sacrament
Compline 48, 79, 91
Confession, *see* penance
Confiteor 79, 90, 91
Connelly, Cornelia 144–5, 164
Connolly, Gerard:
  on Catholics in Manchester and Salford 13, 36, 160

on Challoner's *Garden of the Soul* 77–8, 79
on the Irish in England 13 n., 12–14
on miracles 160
on old Catholic spirituality 9–10
on sanctity 162
on the 'second spring' 6, 12–14
confraternities, *see* Catholic societies
Continent, the European 3–5, 19–21, 140
  see also under individual countries
Controversial Catechism, see catechisms
convents, *see under individual names of orders*
conversion:
  to Catholicism 3–5, 7, 8, 12, 124, 130, 161
  to earnestness in practice 13, 144–50
Conversion of England 12, 55–6, 78, 80, 82
  see also 'second spring'; Oxford Movement; Tractarians
converts:
  devotional caricatures of 3–5, 8
  and 'ultramontane-triumph' thesis 17–25
  see also marriages; Oxford Movement; Tractarians
copyright libraries, *see* Bodleian; British; Cambridge University
Corish, Patrick 15
Cornthwaite, Robert, bishop of Beverley 36
Corpus Christi 36, 47
  see also Benediction of the Bl. Sacr.; Blessed Sacrament; communion; eucharist; Exposition of the Blessed Sacrament; Mass; processions; *Quarant' ore*; transubstantiation; Visitation of the Blessed Sacrament
Counter-Reformation 91
Coventry 48, 160–1
Cox, Jeffrey 170
Craythorne 145
Creed, The Apostles' 79, 111
Creed, The Athanasian 79
Crichton, James 10, 108
Cross, *see* crucifix; crucifixion; Stations of the Cross
Cross, Association of the, *see* Catholic societies
Cross, Sign of the 46 & n., 84, 90, 91, 131
Cross, F. L., see *Oxford Dictionary of the Christian Church*

Crossley, Frank 154, 155
Crown of Jesus 71, 73, 75
crucifix 25 n., 27, 67, 115, 133, 133–4,
    153
    see also Cross; crucifixion; Passion
crucifixion 27, 42, 67, 148, 153–6, 157
Cullen, Paul, Cardinal, Archbishop of
    Dublin 14–17, 33, 34
cures, miraculous, *see* miracles
Cwiekowski, Frederick 8, 17–18, 60–1,
    101, 103–4
Cwmbran 162

Daly, Fr 166
Danell, James, bishop of Southwark
    74 & n., 75
Dante Alighieri 98
Darwin, Charles, *see Origin of Species*
Davies, Horton 9
Dead, Office of the 91
Death, Exercises for a Happy, *see bona mors*
Dechamps, Archbishop of Malines 18 n.
dechristianization, *see* 'leakage'
de Lisle, Ambrose Phillips 138
De Profundis 47, 90, 91–2
Derby 74 & n., 75, 87 n., 108
de Sales, Francis, *see* St Francis de Sales
Deus, qui nobis 46
devil, the 68, 156, 161
devotion, devotions:
    DEVOTION:
        absence of work on 1–3
        caricatures of, *see* 'second spring';
            'uitramontane-triumph' thesis; *under*
            individual names of devotions
        centrality of 2, 39, 70
        in Cheshire 128 n.
        consensus on 26–30
        definition of 26, 38
        devotional pictures 1, 40, 115
        'devotional revolution' 14–17, 34, 42
        English-Irish 15–17, 141, 161
        excesses in 167
        and feeling 24–30, 38–9, 84
        and gender 127
        intimate nature of 3
        in Lancashire 128 n.
        latitude in 26–30, 38–9, 100, 137
        modern revulsion to 1–2
        as prayer 70
        and social class 151–3, 157–65, 169–73
        and social divisiveness 5, 26
        and 'ultramontanism' 32–4, 165–6, 168

'vulgar piety' 28, 31
    see also devotions; prayers; tolerance;
        unity; *and under individual names of*
        devotions
DEVOTIONS:
    church-based 40–5, 174–90
    definition of 27, 38
    and the ecclesiastical hierarchy 40,
        54–8, 87–9
    'Italianate' 3–4, 9, 17, 24–6, 38–9,
        42–5, 47, 61, 138–9
    latitude in 26–30, 100, 137
    Manual of Prayers for Congregational
        Use on 57–8
    May devotions, *see* Mary
    to the pope 139
    'popular' 39–40
    significance of 26–30, 38–42
    and social class 151–3, 157–65, 169–73
    statistics of church-based 40–5, 174–90
    voluntary nature of 38
    see also under names of individual
        countries, devotions, and persons
Dictionnaire de théologie Catholique 105
Digby, Mother 67
dioceses 174–82, 183–90
    see also under individual names
dissent 142, 149, 169
    see also under individual names of
        denominations
distemper, contagious 66
dockers' strike (1889), 159
Doctrine, Christian, *see* catechisms;
    Catholic societies
Dolan, Jay 34
Döllinger, Dr J. J. I. von 18, 21
Dominicans, *see* St Dominic
Donovan, Robert 132, 158
Douai 47, 48, 51, 61–2, 84, 107, 109
    see also catechisms; old Catholics
Douay, *see* Douai
Downside Abbey 62
Doxology, Little 58, 74–5, 90, 91 & n.,
    192–3
Drane, Augusta 69
Dream of Gerontius, see Elgar; Newman
Dublin, Archbishop of, *see* Cullen, Paul
Dublin Review 18, 20, 77
Duffy, Eamon 77, 79
Durantus, Gonsalvo 67

Easter 38, 91
education 114, 116, 123–4, 143

Edwardian 141, 143
Elevation of the Host, *see* Mass
Elgar, Sir Edward 143
Emancipation Acts, *see* Catholic Emancipation
Embassy chapels (London) 11–12, 44–5, 45 n.
England:
  attitudes to the Bl. Sacr. in 56–8, 140
  and Benediction of the Bl. Sacr. 45–58, 83, 140
  caricatures of Catholics in 3–5, 24–30, 82–9
  and catechisms 100–5, 105–10, 117–24, 166, 167
  Catholic societies in 35, 174–82, 183–90, 195–9
  church-based devotions in 40–5, 174–90
  devotional statistics of 42–5, 174–90
  English–Irish spirituality in 15–17, 141
  Exposition of the Bl. Sacr. in 44, 55–8, 174–90
  and Jansenism 168, 169
  number of Catholic churches in 174–82
  Quarant' ore in 42, 44, 61
  and the rosary 42, 58–69 & n., 80–1, 174–90
  Sacred Heart devotions in 43–4, 126–7, 151–3
  Stations of the Cross in 42–4, 139 n., 174–90
  Visitation of the Bl. Sacr. in 44
  see also ethnicity; 'second spring'; simplicity; tolerance; ultramontane-triumph' thesis; unity
English Catholics, *see* old Catholics
English-Irish 15–17, 141, 161
Errington, George, bishop of Plymouth, titular Archbishop of Trebizond 118–19
Ethelbert 5
ethnicity 3–5, 13–17, 34, 39, 51–3, 100, 135–6, 151–3, 157–65, 169–73
eucharist 25, 40, 52 & n., 167
  'captive victim' 50
  and the ecclesiastical hierarchy 55–8, 116–17
  Elevation of the Host 53
  in France 33
  Manning and the 25
  plaster made from the 53
  and superstition 53–4, 97–8, 167

in the United States 34
and von Hügel 25–6
see also Benediction of the Bl. Sacr.; Blessed Sacrament; communion; Corpus Christi; Exposition of the Blessed Sacrament; Mass; *Quarant' ore*, transubstantiation, Visitation of the Blessed Sacrament
Eucharistic Congress, The (1908) 52 & n.
Evangelicals 29, 70, 149, 151, 158, 169
'evangelicalism' among Catholics 34–5, 144–56, 169
Evensong 49, 79
Exposition of the Blessed Sacrament 36, 40
  and Benediction of the Bl. Sacr. 50, 55–6
  and devotional stereotypes 42
  and the ecclesiastical hierarchy 55–8
  in England 44, 55–8, 174–90
  and prayer 70
  see also Benediction of the Bl. Sacr.; Blessed Sacrament; communion; Corpus Christi; eucharist, Mass; *Quarant' ore*, transubstantiation; Visitation of the Blessed Sacrament

Faber, Frederick William 159, 163
  on Benediction of the Bl. Sacr. 50
  on devotional tolerance 26–8, 99, 100
  enthusiam of 29, 38–9, 99, 169
  on evangelical feelings 169
  and Lady G. Fullerton 135
  'God Bless our Pope' 139
  The Growth in Holiness 26–7, 28–9
  and Italianate devotions 9, 26, 38–9, 139
  and legends of the saints 162
  on Mary 27, 99
  Newman to 29–30
Farm Street 66
Fenians 121
First Communion, *see* communion
First Vatican Council 3, 7–8, 18–24, 76
  and the catechism 100–5, 110–12, 118–19
  and 'party' divisions 18–24, 100–5, 118–21
  and 'ultramontane-triumph' thesis 18, 23–4, 100–5, 118–24
First World War vi, 5, 53, 67, 76, 141
Five Wounds 27, 133–4, 135, 153, 156
flowers 67, 79, 80, 166

Foley, Annie 147
Forty Hours' devotion, see *Quarant' ore*
France 138
    catechisms in 105, 111
    Catholic societies in 126, 132
    clergy in 33
    and the eucharist 25, 40, 52 & n., 53,
      126
    Jansenist background of 168, 169
    and Marian devotion 33
    and the *Memorare* 94
    revivalism in 30, 32–4
    revolutions in 4, 123, 138, 141, 168
    Robert, king of 91
    and the Sacred Heart 43 & n., 126
    and Stations of the Cross 42
    and 'superstitions' 33, 53, 165–7
    and 'ultramontane piety' 23, 165–6,
      167, 168
    see also Gallicanism; Gibson, Ralph;
      'ultramontane-triumph' thesis
Franciscans, *see* St Francis of Assisi,
    Order of, Third Order of
Freemasons 120
Froude, Mrs William 27
Fulham 157
Fullerton, Lady Georgiana 130, 132,
    163 & n.
    and Faber 135
    and miracles 53 n.,
    and penance 148, 149, 150–1, 150 n.
    pious books by 53 n., 163 & n.
    and St Vincent de Paul Society 130
    and sanctity 156
    and Stations of the Cross 43
    and Third Order of St Francis 132
funerals 14, 67, 133, 166, 167
    see also Catholic societies

Gallicanism 19, 20, 118, 119, 120, 139
Gallipoli 53
Gallwey, Fr Peter 63 n.
Garden of the Soul, The 172
    alternative title of 78, 87 & n.
    and Benediction of the Bl. Sacr. 47–9,
      50, 54, 61, 68, 79, 80, 82, 138, 168
    on communion 86
    on Compline 79
    'deformations' of 77–89
    Derby edition of 74 & n.
    and devotional unity 72–8, 85–9, 100
    and the ecclesiastical hierarchy 73–6,
      77, 85–9, 119–20, 137–8, 167

    editions in England of the 72–3, 78–89
    on hell 168
    historians on the 9–10, 47, 61, 76,
      77–8, 83–7, 168
    increased inclusiveness of 78–89, 100
    in Ireland 16–17
    litanies in 8, 79, 82, 137–8
    and *Manual of Prayers for
      Congregational Use* 73–4, 80, 87,
      119–20, 166
    Mary in 61, 79
    and the Mass 71, 80–2, 138
    and *Memorare* 80, 91, 94–6
    Newman on 80
    and old Catholics 8–9, 25, 61, 72,
      74–5, 82–9, 172
    popularity of 71, 72–6
    prayers in 8, 73–5, 78–9, 80–2, 137
    and *Quarant' ore* 80, 84
    resilience to change of 55, 81–2, 166
    and the rosary 61, 65–6, 68, 79, 80–1
    and the Sacred Heart 80, 82, 87
    and St Bernard's hymn 79
    and Stations of the Cross 80, 84, 87
    stereotype version of 78–80, 78 n.,
      81–3, 137, 167
    tolerance of 9–10, 77–9
    and Ullathorne 145
    unoriginality of 84–5
    in the United States 61
    and Visitation of the Blessed Sacrament
      80
    EDITIONS OF:
    first Derby edn. 74 & n.
    pre-1850 72
    post-1850 72–3, 81–2
    *c.*1740 (first edn.) 9, 47, 61, 72, 73, 76,
      78 & n., 119, 168
    1755 (London, stereotype edn.) 78 & n.,
      80–2
    1844 edition (Birmingham) 54 n., 94
    1854 edition (Dublin) 65, 80
    1856 edition (miniature golden)
      (London: Burns & Lambert) 65, 72,
      80, 81, 87
    1872 (London: R. Washbourne) 87 n.
    1873 (little) 72
    1874 edition (Edinburgh: John
      Chisholm) 65, 72, 82, 87 n.
    1877 edition (London and Derby: T.
      Richardson and Sons) 72, 74 n.
    1877 edition (London: T. Richardson
      and Sons; Parochial) 72, 87 n.

1877 edition (London: R. Washbourne) 80, 81–2, 87, 127–8
1883 edition (London: Burns & Oates) 65, 72, 81–2, 87 n.
1884 (London: Burns & Oates) 72, 87 n.
1892 (Dublin: James Duffy & Co., Ltd.; combined with *Manual of Prayers for Congregational Use*) 72, 80, 81–2, 87
1899 (London: R. & T. Washbourne) 81–2
see also bibliography 203–15
'Garden-of-the-Soul Catholics' 8, 25, 51, 61, 72, 76, 85
see also R. Challoner; old Catholics
Gasquet, Francis Neil (Dom Aidan), Cardinal 62, 63, 64
gender 127
Gentili, Fr Luigi 4
Germany 21, 23, 30, 100–1, 102, 112, 125, 139
ghost stories 171
Gibson, Henry 108
Gibson, Ralph 32–4, 126, 132, 163 8
Gilley, Sheridan 158–9
    on Catholic societies 125
    on Challoner 83, 84
    on devotion 2
    on holy poverty 157–8
    on London 44–5, 45 n., 157
    on the rosary 67
    on 'vulgar' piety 31
Gloria Patri, *see* Doxology
'God Bless Our Pope' 139
Golden Manual 71
Golden Sequence, the, *see* Veni Sancte Spiritus
Gordon, John 30
Gosling, Fr 9
Goss, Alexander, bishop of Liverpool 56, 167, 170
Gother, Fr John 85, 107
Gothic architecture 26
Grant, Thomas, bishop of Southwark 106, 118
Great Famine, the 12, 15–16
Grimsby 172
The Growth in Holiness 26–7, 28–9
guilds, *see* Catholic societies
Guiron, James 152
gutter press, the 154–5
Gwynn, Denis 6

Hail Mary 56, 58, 79, 90, 91, 113, 115, 133, 157
    see also Mary; rosary
Hales, E. E. Y. 21 n.
Hallahan, Margaret Mary 60–1, 69 n.
Hammersmith 157
Hampstead Heath 25
Harrow School 22
Hearne, Fr Daniel 160
Hearney, Mary 154 n.
Helbert, Mrs 27
hell 33, 146, 168
Hennessey, James 104–5
Herbert, Lady Elizabeth of Lea 51–2, 130, 149, 153, 155, 164
Hexham diocese 109
    see also Hexham and Newcastle
Hexham and Newcastle:
    diocese of 41, 42, 43, 44, 45, 60, 109, 125, 127 & n., 132, 148
    Sacred Heart and English Martyrs, Thornley 132 & n., 148
    St Mary's, Newcastle 43, 130 n., 131 n.
hierarchy, the ecclesiastical 138, 157–65, 166–73
    and Benediction of the Bl. Sacr. 54–9
    and catechisms 100–5; *see also* penny catechism
    and Catholic societies 125–36
    and Challoner's *Garden of the Soul* 73–6, 77, 85–9, 119–20, 137–8, 167
    and charity 103, 157–61
    and devotions 40, 54–8, 87–9
    and the eucharist 55–8, 116–17
    lack of guile of 102–3
    and *Manual of Prayers for Congregational Use* 54–8, 73–5, 87–9, 119–20, 166
    and the *Memorare* 95–7
    and the penny catechism 100–5, 109–10, 117–24, 166, 167
    and prayer-books 72–83, 85–9, 100, 120
    and 'party' feeling 118–21
    restoration of the 5, 7, 9, 118, 123; *see also* Catholic Emancipation; synods; *and under names of individual bishops and dioceses*
    and the rosary 60–1, 65–6
    and sectarianism 113–17, 120–4
    and the 'world' 123–4, 135, 143
Higginson, Teresa Helena:
    local reputation of 156 n.

Higginson, Teresa Helena (*cont.*):
  morbid sense of sin of 150, 156
  and Stations of the Cross 43
  and the supernatural 156, 161
  and Third Order of St Francis 129 n.
Hilaire, Yves-Marie 33–4, 165–6
Hilton, John 78
Holborn 157
holiness, *see* devotion; sanctity; simplicity
Holly Place 26
Holmes, Derek 17–20, 22
Holy Child Jesus, *see* Society of the Holy
  Child Jesus
Holy Family 36, 40, 92
  see also Jesus; Mary; St Joseph
Holy Ghost (Holy Spirit) 25, 27
holy poverty, *see* poverty
Holy Week, *see* Easter, Lent
Holywell, shrine at 140 & n., 161–2, 164
Home and Foreign Review 19, 23
  see also *Rambler*
Hopkins, Gerard Manley 140 n.
Host, the, *see* eucharist; Mass
Houghton, Walter 148–9
Husenbeth, Frederick Charles 71
Huvelin, Abbé Henri 69
hymnody vi
  see also under individual titles of hymns

Immaculate Conception, *see* Mary
Index of prohibited books 22
indulgences 8, 31–2, 49, 65–6, 72–3, 79,
  89–90, 93–4, 135
  and Catholic societies 135–6
  and penny catechism 115, 116
  Sacred Congregation of 73
infallibility, *see* papal infallibility
Innocent III, Pope 91
'inopportunism', *see* papal infallibility
Introduction to a Devout Life 61, 79, 82,
  85
  see also St Francis de Sales
Ireland, the Irish:
  IRELAND:
    Catholic revival in 12–17, 30
    and Challoner's *Garden of the Soul* 16
    and the *De Profundis* 91–2
    and devotion to the pope 139
    'devotional revolution' in 14–17, 34, 42
    and *Key of Heaven* 16, 75
    most popular devotional manuals in 16
    and old Catholicism 3, 16–17, 141, 161
    and 'Red Cross Chain' 67

  and the rosary 67–8
  St Bridget, patron saint of 64
  and 'second spring' mythology 12–17,
    34, 42
  and 'ultramontane-triumph' thesis
    17–24, 139
  see also Cullen, Paul
  THE IRISH:
    3–5, 12–17, 34, 60, 67
    see also ethnicity; tolerance; unity
Irish Rosary 68
Italy 19, 42, 61, 137
  see also Rome; Vatican
Ivison, Alice 128
Ixelles 67

Jansenism 168, 169
Japanese, *see* Canonization of the Japanese
  Martyrs
Jesus, the only thought of thee, see St
  Bernard, hymn of
Jesus Prayer 64
Jesus Psalter 8, 71, 79
Jesuits, *see* Society of Jesus
Jews 11, 65
Julian of Norwich 43
Julien, Mrs Florence 128 n., 156 n.

Keble, John 150
Keenan, see *Controversial Catechism*
Keenan, Desmond 139
Kensington 157
Kent, John 146 n., 150
Kentish Strand 5
Kentish Town 157
Kerr, Donal 2, 3, 16
Key of Heaven 16, 71, 75, 80
Knight, Edmund 74 & n., 75, 192–4
  see also Shrewsbury, bishop of

labourers 152, 154
  see also class
Laity's Directory 48 n.
Lancashire 45 n., 57, 128 & n., 162
Langton, Stephen 91
Larkin, Emmett 14, 34
La Salette 25
  see also apparitions of the Blessed
    Virgin Mary
Laudi 47
Lauds 91
Lausanne and Geneva, bishop of, *see*
  Marilley, Etienne

'leakage' 16, 32, 123, 141, 142–3, 147, 170–2
Leary, Paddy 16
Leeds, diocese of 127 n.
Lees, Lynn 13 n.
Lent 166, 167
Leo X, Pope 65, 68
Leo XIII, Pope 32, 65
Lescher, Fr Wilfrid 62
Leslie, Shane 18 n., 21 n.
Liberal Catholicism 3–5, 17–30, 105
  see also 'ultramontane-triumph' thesis
Liguori, *see* St Alphonsus Liguori
Lilley, A. L. 25
litanies:
  from *Garden of the Soul* 8, 79, 82, 137–8
  for the intercession of England 56
  of Loreto 46, 48, 49, 50, 51, 167
liturgical movement 71–2
Liverpool:
  bishop of, *see* Goss, Alexander
  city of 42
  diocese of 41, 42, 45, 60, 109, 125,
    127 & n., 128, 133, 152, 167, 170
  see also Birkenhead; Salford
Liverpool Daily Post 36
Livingstone, E. A., *see Oxford Dictionary
  of the Christian Church*
Lof 47
London: 42, 48, 52 n.
  Catholic societies in 174–82, 195–9
  churches in 174–90
  church-based devotions in 174–90
  Embassy chapels in 11–12, 44–5, 45 n.
  missions to 146 n., 147, 151, 169
  old diocese of 19, 118, 157
  social mixing in 157
  statistical eccentricity of 44–5, 45 n.
  see also Southwark; Westminster
Lord's Prayer, the 79, 90–1, 133, 157
Loreto, *see* Litany of
Lourdes 1, 32, 53, 92, 140
Lucas, Frederick 134
Luckett, Richard 76
Luther, Martin 70, 106
Lytham, St Peter's, Lytham:
  Confraternity of the Sacred Heart at
    126, 127, 152
  Living Rosary at 60 & n., 126, 127
  mission at 147

McCabe, Herbert 106
McDonnell, Rory 26

M'Laren, Alexander 154, 155
McLeod, Hugh 125, 126, 143
MacSuibhne, Fr 15
McSweeney, Bill 1
Maddock, Daniel 162
Magdalen College, *see* Oxford University
Maher, Michael 14
Malines, Archbishop of, *see* Dechamps
Manchester 13, 36, 56, 160, 172
  St Gertrude's convent in 56
Mangenot, E., see *Dictionnaire de théologie
  Catholique*
Manning, Henry Edward, Cardinal
  Archbishop of Westminster:
  asceticism of 25 n.
  and Benediction of the Bl. Sacr. 25, 50
  on Challoner 85, 166
  'chief whip' of the ultramontane party
    18 & n.
  and dogmatism 20, 120, 138
  devotional life of 25 & n.
  and the English bishops 102–3, 118–20
  at First Vatican Council 18, 20, 21,
    22–4, 102
  on First Vatican Council 104
  and legends of the saints 163
  and London dockers's strike 159
  and *Manual of Prayers for
    Congregational Use* 74 & n., 75
  on Newman 21–2
  on poverty 159
  on the priesthood 50, 51
  reputation of 21–2, 21 n.
  and the Sacred Heart 152
  Ullathorne to 160
  and ultramontanism 18 & n., 19–24
  and Wiseman 22, 23 n., 118
Manual of Devout Prayers 9, 85
*Manual of Prayers for Congregational
  Use* 119–20, 166
  and Benediction of the Bl. Sacr. 54–6
  combined with the *Garden of the Soul*
    80, 87
  on devotions 57–8
  function of the 88–9
  influenced by the *Garden of the Soul*
    73–4, 119–20, 166
  and the *Memorare* 93
  origins of the 73–5
Marian, *see* Mary
Marilley, Etienne, bishop of Lausanne and
  Geneva 101, 104
Marists 145

marriages, 'mixed' 114, 116, 123–4, 143
Marron, Stephen 106, 108, 110
Marshall, Bruce 54, 172
Mary, Blessed Virgin:
  called 'mamma' 99
  in the catechism 112–14, 115, 117, 122
  in Challoner's *Garden of Soul* 61, 79
  Children of Mary 128–9
  Faber on 27, 99
  Immaculate Conception of 36, 112–14, 120
  May devotions 7, 61
  in the *Memorare* 93–9
  Memorare to Our Lady of the Sacred Heart 95, 96
  Newman on devotion to 27
  and old catholics 8
  in 'Revelations of St Bridget' 66
  and the rosary 58, 62–3, 68
  in the rosary 58–9
  statues of 1, 40
  J. E. Stuart on 97
  Ullathorne and 25
  and von Hügel 25
  Wiseman and 55
  see also apparitions of the Blessed Virgin; Catholic societies; Hail Mary; litanies; Lourdes; *Memorare*; *Regina Caeli*; rosary; *Salve Regina*
Mary Catherine, Sister 63 & n., 64
Mass, the:
  attendance at 35, 38, 172
  and Benediction of the Bl. Sacr. 45, 49, 52, 53, 58
  and Catholic societies 129, 133
  Elevation of the Host at 53
  at Embassy chapels 11–12
  and *Garden of the Soul* 71, 138
  in *Garden of the Soul* 80–2
  and Office of the Sacred Heart 43
  in the penny catechism 80–1, 116
  prayers said at 91–2, 138
  sermons at 148
  see also communion; eucharist; *Garden of the Soul*; missals
Mathew, David 112 n., 143
Mathew, Fr Theobald 155
May devotions, *see* Mary
Mayes, Lawrence 83
Mayhew, Henry 13, 154
medals 7, 67
  see also Miraculous Medal
Memel 145

Memorare or Prayer of St Bernard 169
  in Dante's *Paradiso* 98
  devotional elasticity of 135, 157
  and devotional unity 92, 97–9, 169
  and the ecclesiastical hierarchy 95–7
  in France 94
  in *Garden of the Soul* 80, 91, 94–6
  immediacy of 94–9, 166
  in Latin 96 n.
  in *Manual of Prayers for Congregational Use* 93
  naïve views of 97–9
  to Our Lady of the Sacred Heart 96
  in the penny catechism 93, 94, 96–7
  popularity of 90–1, 93–4, 97
  reassurance of 94–9
  relation to Benediction of the Bl. Sacr. 91, 97–9
  relation to the rosary 97–9
  to the Sacred Heart 95–6
  and J. E. Stuart 97
  Thurston on 93–4
  translation by A. St John of 93, 96
  variations in the 93–9
  see also Mary
Messenger of the Sacred Heart 163
Methodism 116
Metz, the miracle at 53 n.
Middle Ages 1, 92, 134
middle class, *see* class
Middlesbrough, diocese of 127 n.
Midland district 43, 140
Miller, David 15
Milner, John, vicar-apostolic Midland district 43, 140
miracles:
  acceptance of 160–5
  and devotional unity 162–5
  and the eucharist 53–4, 97–8, 167
  at Holywell 140, 161–2, 164
  at La Salette 25
  at Lourdes 53, 140
  and the *Memorare* 97–9
  and the rosary 58, 62–3
  and St Joseph 161
  see also apparitions; Miraculous Medal
Miraculous Medal, Feast of the 167
missals 71
  see also prayer-books
missionary priests 14, 77, 83, 139
missions 36, 138, 139, 171–2
  Anglo-Catholic 146 n., 151
  at Birkenhead 147–8, 151

and communion 147–8, 152
and devotional stereotypes 4, 7
dwindling appeal of 34, 171–2
at Grimsby 172
and hell-fire sermons 33, 145–6, 168
'hullabaloo' 171
at Lytham 147
at Manchester 172
and penance 146–53, 160, 171–2
and Protestant revivals 145–53, 169
in Southwark 147
in Staffordshire 146
at Swynnerton 160
at Thornley 148
at Tixall 160
in the United States 34
see also evangelicalism; retreats
modernism 25, 28
monasteries, *see under individual names of
orders*
Monsell, William 23 n.
Month 7–8, 18, 63, 90, 163
Montpellier, diocese of 111
Moody, Dwight 146 n., 152
see also Sankey
Morris, John Brande 99
Moser, Canon William 52, 139 & n., 171
Murphy, John 162
mysticism, *see* sanctity

Neston 150
Netherlands 125
New Catholic Encyclopedia 105
*New Manual of Catholic Devotion, see
Ursuline Manual*
Newcastle, *see* Hexham and Newcastle
Newman, John Henry, Cardinal:
as an Anglican 29, 30
to C. Bathurst 29
and devotional inadequacy 29–30, 149,
160
devotional life of 25
on devotional tolerance 27–30, 38–9,
99, 100
and devotions at Birmingham Oratory
25
and difficulties with Rome 23, 25
Dream of Gerontius 143–4
On Ecclesiastical Miracles 162
on evangelicalism 29–30
and F. W. Faber 29–30
to Mrs Wm. Froude 27
on *Garden of the Soul* 80

to Gordon 30
to Mrs Helbert 27
and 'inopportunist' party at the First
Vatican Council 18, 21, 25, 105, 120
on the *Key of Heaven* 80
and legends of the saints 162, 163
Letter to Pusey 80
Manning on 21–2
on Mary 27
and papal infallibility 18, 21, 25, 120
Parochial and Plain Sermons 29 n.
'second spring' sermon 5–6, 9
to Simpson 21
on Ullathorne 21
and 'ultramontane-triumph' thesis
17–25, 105
works on 1
Newport and Menevia:
bishop of, *see* Brown, Thomas Joseph
diocese of 42, 45, 60, 125, 127
Newsome, David 21 n.
Nine Fridays, the 62
nonconformity, *see* dissent
Norman, Edward 2, 3–4, 23, 102, 118
Northampton:
diocese of 41, 42, 45, 52, 60, 125,
127 & n., 171
Nottingham:
bishop of, *see* Bagshawe, Edward
diocese of 42, 45, 60, 125, 127 & n.
novenas 7, 36, 58
see also devotions; prayers

O Salutaris Hostia, see Benediction of the
Bl. Sacr.
Oblates of St Charles, *see* St Charles
O'Brien, Kitty 162
Odd Fellows 121
Old Catholic Churches, the 112
old Catholics:
and Benediction of the Bl. Sacr. 12,
47–51, 61
devotional caricatures of 3–5, 7–8,
8–10, 10 n., 19, 24–30, 82–9
devotional rehabilitations of 9–10, 36–7
and Embassy chapels 11–12
and First Vatican Council 7–8
and *Garden of the Soul* 8–9, 25, 61, 72,
74–5, 82–9, 172
and Irish Catholicism 3, 15–17, 141,
161
and the penny catechism 106–8, 121–4
and the rosary 61–2, 138

old Catholics (*cont.*):
  and the Sacred Heart 43–4, 151–2
  and the Sign of the Cross 84
  and the Stations of the Cross 42–3
  and Stockholm syndrome 7
  see also Catholic Emancipation;
    Challoner; *Garden of the Soul*
Oliphant, Mrs 155
O'Meara, Kathleen 106
Oratio sine intermissione 48
Oratory of St Philip Neri 155 n., 163
  in Birmingham (Edgbaston) 25, 29
  in London (Brompton) 26, 29, 31, 39,
    44, 51
Orders, religious vi, 12
  see also under names of individual
    communities
Origin of Species 142
Orthodox Church, the 64
Oscott, provincial synod at, *see* synods
Our Father, *see* Lord's Prayer
Our Lady's, Birkenhead, *see* Birkenhead
*Oxford Dictionary of the Christian
  Church* 105
Oxford Movement, the 3, 4, 7, 12, 21,
  142
  see also Anglicanism; converts;
    Tractarians
Oxford University 21, 22, 146

papacy, temporal power of the, *see* pope
papal indulgences, *see* indulgences
papal infallibility 7–8, 17–25, 101–5,
  111–12, 120, 122
  see also First Vatican Council;
    'ultramontane-triumph' thesis
Paray-le-Monial 43 n., 152
parents, the duties of 114
Parliament 1–12, 142
Parochial and Plain Sermons, *see* Newman
Parsons, Gerald 34–5
Passion, the 27, 42, 43, 47, 65–6, 153
  see also Cross; crucifix; crucifixion; Five
    Wounds; Stations of the Cross
Passionists 145, 146
  see also Barberi
Path of Heaven 73, 75
Path of Holiness 71
pattern 14
Pawley, Bernard 10
Pawley, Margaret 10
Paz, D. G. 155
Penance, sacrament of 7, 35, 170

and Catholic societies 129, 133
and evangelicalism 146–53
in France 33
and *Garden of the Soul* 79
and missions 146–53, 160, 171–2
obligation of 49
and the Sacred Heart 151–3
and the Stations of the Cross 42–3, 153
in the United States 34
see also sin
penny catechism:
  and baptism 122–3
  *Catechism of Christian Doctrine, with the
    Questions Numbered. Approved for the
    Use of the Faithful, in all the Dioceses
    of England and Wales* (*c.*1876) 108
  and Challoner 80–84, 105–9, 138
  and the Christian's Rule of Life 123
  committee to revise the 109–10,
    117–24
  and devotional unity 119–21
  and the ecclesiastical hierarchy 100–5,
    109–10, 117–24, 166, 167
  and education 114, 116, 123–4
  and the eucharist 115–17
  history of the 105–9
  *Large Type Edition. Catechism of
    Christian Doctrine, Approved for the
    Use of the Faithful, in all the Dioceses
    of England and Wales* (1876; 1859
    version) 108–9, 111 n., 111–17,
    122–4
  on the Mass 80–1, 116
  and 'mixed marriages' 114, 116, 123–4
  on Mary 112–17, 122
  Memorare in the 93, 94, 96–7
  *190th Thousand. The Explanatory
    Catechism of Christian Doctrine,
    Chiefly Intended for the Use of
    Children in Catholic Schools . . .*
    (London, 1884; *c.*1880 version)
    109–10, 111 n., 112 n., 111–18,
    120–3
  origins of the 105–9
  on the pope 111–12, 120, 122
  proto-penny catechism 107, 121–3
  revisions to the 107–17, 123
  rosary in the 61, 91
  and the sacraments 80–1, 115–16
  on St Peter 111–12, 120, 122
  on secret societies 120–1
  sectarian emphasis of 110–24
  and social class 109, 117

Ten Thousand. The Explanatory Catechism of Christian Doctrine (London, 1877) 110 n.
'the' catechism (1859 version) 108–9
Thurston on the 107–8
for proto-penny catechism, *see* penny catechism; *for versions of the* penny catechism *see Large Type Edition . . .* (1859 version), *190th Thousand . . .* (*c.*1880 version)
see also catechisms
Peter's Pence 139
Peterborough 52, 128, 139 & n., 171
Philadelphia 16
pictures, holy, *see* devotion
piety, *see* devotion
Pilate 65
pilgrimages 7, 24, 32, 36, 42, 68, 140, 152, 161–2
see also Holywell; La Salette; Lourdes; Paray-le-Monial
Pio Nono, *see* Pius IX, Pope
Pius IX, Pope: 114
and the *Anima Christi* 93
and catechisms 100–5, 111–12
election of 164
and Gallicanism 19
and indulgences 32, *see also separate entry under indulgences*
and the *Memorare* 94
papal chamberlain to, *see* Talbot
and the Sacred Heart 43–4
Syllabus of Errors 18–20, 23, 120
and the temporal power 21, 22, 23, 32, 138
see also papal infallibility; pope; Rome; Vatican
Plowden, Lady Mary 164
Plymouth:
bishop of 101, *see also* Errington, George; Vaughan, William
diocese of 42, 45, 60, 125, 127 & n.
Polish, prayers in 88
Poor Laws 134, 158
pope:
and catechisms 100–5, 111–12
devotion to the 139
infallibility of the, *see* papal infallibility
in the penny catechism 111–12, 120, 122
temporal power of the 21, 22, 23, 32, 138
see also Adrian; Benedict; Clement; First Vatican Council; Innocent; Leo; Pius, St Peter

poverty 157–65
and English bishops 103, 157–8, 159, 160–1
holiness of 134, 154, 158–9
Protestant attitudes towards 132, 134, 155, 158
voluntary 128, 130, 131, 134–5, 154, 158–9
see also class
prayers and prayer-books:
PRAYERS:
bidding prayers 91
familiar prayers 90–9
importance of prayer 70
novenas 7, 36, 58
see also Angelus; *Anima Christi*; Apostleship of Prayer; Catholic Societies; *De Profundis*; devotion; devotions; Hail Mary; Mass; *Memorare*; *Regina Caeli*; *Salve Regina*; Soul of my Saviour; *Te Deum*; *Veni Sancte Spiritus*
PRAYER-BOOKS:
and the ecclesiastical hierarchy 72–5, 81–2, 85–7, 88–9, 100, 120
most popular in England 70–3
Tavesian analysis of 89–90
see also Crown of Jesus; *Garden of the Soul*; *Key of Heaven*; *Manual of Prayers for Congregational Use*; missals; *Raccolta*
Precious Blood 27
Preston 51, 167
Priest, 'eternal', 46 n., 50
Primrose League 121
Prior Park 146, 161
processions 7, 36, 52, 56, 61, 128, 152
prône, *see* Bidding Prayers
Propaganda, Prefect of, *see* Barnabò
Protestantism, *see under individual denominations*
Public Rosary, *see* rosary
Pugin, Augustus Welby 26, 138
Purcell, Edmund Sheridan 21 n., 23, 24, 119
see also Westminster Review
purgatory 66, 139 n., 164, 167
Puritanism 149–50
Pusey, Edward Bouverie, *Letter to* 80

Quakers, *see* Society of Friends
Quarant' ore 35, 40
in England 42, 44, 61

Quarant' ore (*cont.*):
  in *Garden of the Soul* 80, 84
  'Italianate' devotion 42, 45
  and prayer 70
Quigley, Fr 162
Quinn, Dermot 6, 23, 103

Raccolta . . . 71, 72–3, 73 n., 88, 93–6, 138
railway 140
Rambler 18–24, 27–8, 162
Ransomer 171
recusancy, *see* Catholic Emancipation;
    Challoner; old Catholics
'Red Cross Chain' 66–7, 106 n.
Redemptorists 145, 147, 171
Reformation, the 2, 19, 60
Regina Caeli, the 90, 91
Regina Purgatorii 167
relics 115
relief acts, *see* Catholic Emancipation
religious orders, *see under individual names
    of orders*
restoration of ecclesiastical hierarchy in
    England, *see* hierarchy, the
    ecclesiastical
retreats 36, 129, 139, 144, 148–51
'Revelations of St Bridget' 66–7, 191,
    see St Bridget of Sweden
revolutions:
  in devotion, *see* devotion
  in France, *see* France
Riley, Michael 133
Rites, Sacred Congregation of 47
Robert, king of France 91
Rome:
  bishop of, *see* pope
  in the 1860s 20, 22, 139
  English bishops at 19, 20–4, 100–5,
    119
  'more Roman than Rome' 18, 23 n., 35,
    36, 138
  see also First Vatican Council; Italy;
    'ultramontane-triumph'; Vatican
rosary 36, 40, 70, 164, 166, 167, 169, 170,
    172
  beads for telling the 7, 24, 58–9
  and Benediction of the Bl. Sacr. 45,
    58–60, 61, 68, 69
  and Catholic societies 126–7, 134 n.
  and Challoner 61–2
  considered childish 69 & n.
  considered effeminate 69 n.
  description of 58–9

and devotional unity 60–2, 69, 99
the Dominican 58–9, 64
and Drane 69
and embarrassment 62–9, 69 n., 157
in England 42, 58, 59–62, 69 & n.,
    80–1, 174–90
in *Garden of the Soul* 61, 65–6, 68, 79,
    80–1
and the Irish 59–60, 67, 68
in Italy 61
and Jesus Prayer 64
'Living' 59, 126, 127, 135
and old Catholics 61–2, 138
in the penny catechism 61, 91
and pious legends 58, 62–4, 67–8
Public Rosary 7, 44, 59–60, 61, 174–90
and 'Revelations of St Bridget' 64–7
'ring' for telling the 59
of St Bridget 64–7
sanctioned by Mary 58, 62–4, 68
and 'second spring' 59–60
and social unity 58–60, 69, 157, 159,
    169
and J. E. Stuart 67
and superstition 62–9, 164
Thurston and the 63, 69
Thurston on the 62–3
and Ullathorne 25, 60–1, 61 n., 69
and 'ultramontane-triumph' thesis
    59–60
unintellectual quality of 63–4, 68–9,
    69 n.
variations on the 58–9, 59 n.
and the Vatican 65, 68
and H. Vaughan 69 n.
and von Hügel 69
and Wilberforce 63, 64
and Wiseman 61
Rosary 62
Rowell, Geoffrey 4, 168
Ryland, Susan 161

sacraments 14, 34, 80–1, 115–16, 122,
    145, 172
  see also under individual sacraments
Sacred Heart 1, 40
  and Catholic societies 94, 97, 126, 127,
    152
  and devotional stereotypes 7, 35–6, 45,
    92
  in England 43–4, 126–7, 151–3
  and Faber 27
  in France 43 & n., 126

in *Garden of the Soul* 80, 82, 87
history of devotions to the 43 & n.
and Manning 152
Mass and Office of the 43
and the *Memorare* 95–6
Messenger of the 163
and old Catholics 43–4, 151–2
and penance 151–3
and prayer 70
and the Vatican 43–4, 43 n.
and H. Vaughan 153
see also Memorare to the; Nine Fridays;
   Paray-le-Monial; St Margaret Mary
   Alacoque
Sacred Heart and English Martyrs,
   Thornley, *see* Hexham and Newcastle
St Alphonsus Liguori 33, 168
St Anthony 165
St Augustine 5, 91
St Benedict, Order of:
   at Ampleforth 98–9
   at Downside 62
St Bernard, Hymn of 73, 79
St Bernard, Prayer of, see *Memorare*
St Bridget, patron saint of Ireland 64
St Bridget of Sweden 64–7
St Buonaventura, Psalter of 27
St Chad's, Birmingham, *see* Birmingham
St Charles, Oblates of 118–19
St Charles Borromeo 48
St Dominic 58, 62–3
   Order of 59, 60, 64, 103, 145
   Third Order of 61, 132
   see also rosary
St Dominic's, Stone 103
St Edmund's College 118
St Francis de Sales 61, 79, 82, 85, 168
St Francis of Assisi: 135, 155 & n., 156,
   164
   Order of 42, 158
   Third Order (Tertiaries) of 129, 131–2,
     134, 136
St Gertrude, Manchester, *see* Manchester
St Ignatius, Preston, *see* Preston
St John the Baptist, *see* Catholic Societies
St John, Ambrose 73, 93, 96
St John's College, *see* Oxford University
St Joseph 36, 40, 80, 89, 92, 161
   see also Holy Family
St Leonards-on-Sea 68
St Margaret Mary Alacoque 43
   see also Paray-le-Monial; Sacred Heart
St Mary's, Newcastle 43, 131 n.

St Maurus 62
St Michael's 56
St Omer 47, 48
St Patrick, *see* Catholic Societies
St Paul 25
St Paula 155
St Peter 111–12, 120, 122
   see also pope; Rome; Vatican
St Peter Canisius, *see* Canisius
St Peter and All Souls, Peterborough, *see*
   Peterborough
St Peter's, Lytham, *see* Lytham
St Philip Neri 30
   see also Oratory of
St Placid 62
St Robert Bellarmine, *see* Bellarmine
St Teresa 156, 164
St Vincent de Paul 128
   see also Catholic societies
St Winefride, *see* Holywell
Sagovsky, Nicholas 28
Salford:
   bishop of 109; *see also* H. Vaughan
   diocese of 42, 45, 56, 60, 109, 125,
     127 & n.
   township of 13, 36, 160
Salut 47
Salve 47
Salve Regina 47, 90, 91, 93
sanctity 153–6, 160–5, 169
Sankey, Ira 146 n., 152
   see also Moody
Santa Claus 171
Satan, *see* devil
scapular 7, 126, 132
Schleiermacher, Friedrich Daniel
   Ernst 70
science 23, 142, 162, 163, 164
Scotland 54 n., 82, 172
Scott, Sir Walter 142
Searle, Mgr. Francis 19
'second spring' 5–10, 72, 86
   and Catholic emancipation 10–12
   and Challoner's *Garden of the Soul*
     76–7, 77–8
   and devotional caricatures 7, 39, 77–8,
     137, 140–1, 147
   and Irish Catholics 12–17, 34, 42
   Newman's sermon on the 5–6, 9
Second Vatican Council vi, 86
Second World War 54 n.
secret societies 120–1
secularization, *see* 'leakage'

Segneri, Fr 149
Sequence:
  definition of 92 & n.
  the Golden Sequence, see *Veni Sancte*
    Spiritus
Shaddock, Mr 146
Shakespeare, William 86, 87
Sharp, John 147, 172
Shrewsbury:
  bishop of 109, see also J. Brown;
    Knight
  diocese of 44, 45, 60, 109, 125,
    127 & n.
Sign of the Cross, see Cross
simplicity, holiness of 157–65, 169, 171–2
Simpson, Richard 18, 21, 27–8, 105,
  123–4
  and devotional tolerance 27–8, 123–4
  and liberal Catholic 'party' 18, 105
  on 'mixed' marriages 123–4
  on university education 123–4
sin:
  and indulgences 115, 135
  and missions 145–53
  in the penny catechism 115, 116, 123–4
  and the Sacred Heart 151–3
  the sense of 135, 145–53, 156–7, 170
  and the Stations of the Cross 42–3, 153
  see also penance
Singleton, E. 152
Slaughter, Fr 151
Smith, Fr 54
social class, see class
Society of Friends 11, 134
Society of the Holy Child Jesus 68, 144–5
Society of Jesus 145, 151, 155
societies, see Catholic societies
sodalities, see Catholic societies
Soul of my Saviour 93
  see also Anima Christi
Southwark 128, 147
  bishop of, see Danell; Grant
  diocese of 19, 41, 42, 44, 45, 60, 109,
    118, 125, 127 & n.
Spain 100–1, 102
Spencer, Fr Ignatius 56
Spirit of Prayer, The, see *Ursuline Manual*
spirituality, see devotion
Staffordshire 146
Standen, Mary 162
Stations of the Cross 40, 44
  and devotional stereotypes 7, 35, 42, 45
  in England 42–4, 139 n., 174–90

and France 42
in *Garden of the Soul* 80, 84, 87
and prayer 70
and sin 42–3, 153
statistical irregularity of the 42–3
statistics of 174–90
in the United States 89–90
statues 1, 40, 167
  bleeding, see Italy
Steele, Edward 15
stereotypes, devotional 3–5, 25–30
stigmata 129, 155, 156
Stockholm syndrome 7
Stone, Staffordshire 103, 154 n.
Strachey, Lytton 21 n.
Strand, the 5, 157
Stuart, Janet Erskine 67, 97
suffering, school of, see penance
superstitions 14, 16, 165
  and the eucharist 53–4, 166–7
  in France 33, 53, 165–7
  and funerals 14, 166, 167
  and the Nine Fridays 62–3
  and the 'Red Cross Chain' 66–7
  and the 'Revelations of St Bridget'
    64–6
  and the rosary 62–9, 164
  and St Maurus 62–3
  and St Placid 62–3
  see also miracles; simplicity
Supple, Jennifer 36–7, 59, 139
Sweden, see St Bridget of
Switzerland 112, 125
Swynnerton 160
Syllabus of Errors 18, 19–20, 23, 120
  see also Pius IX
Symonds, J. A. 150
synods, provincial 5–6, 7, 85, 109, 118,
  162 n., 166

Tablet, The 18, 134
Talbot, Mgr George 19, 120
Tantum Ergo, see Benediction of the
  Bl. Sacr.
Taves, Ann 2–3, 31–2, 50 n., 61, 89–90
Te Deum 46, 52, 56, 73, 74, 93, 193–4
teetotalism, see Catholic societies
temperance, see Catholic societies
temporal power, see pope
Ten Commandments, see Commandments
tertiaries, see Third Order
Tertullian 91
The Times 102

Think Well On It, see Challoner
Third Order:
of St Dominic, *see* St Dominic
of St Francis, *see* St Francis of Assisi
Thomas, Keith 167 n.
Thornley, *see* Hexham and Newcastle
Thureau-Dangin, Paul 6
Thurston, Herbert 163, 165
on the *Anima Christi* 90, 92–3
apocryphal story about 63 & n.
and Benediction of the Bl. Sacr. 51, 69
on Benediction of the Bl. Sacr. 45–51
on the *De Profundis* 47, 90, 91–2
on familiar prayers 90–6
on the *Memorare* 93–4
on the penny catechism 107–8
on the *Raccolta* 73 n., 93
on the 'Red Cross Chain' 66–7
reputation for scepticism of 63 & n.,
165
and 'Revelations of St Bridget' 66–7
and the rosary 63, 69
on the rosary 62–3
on St Anthony 165
on the *Salve Regina* 47, 90, 91, 93
on superstitions 53, 66–7, 164–5
on the *Te Deum* 46, 93
on the *Veni Sancte Spiritus* 90, 92
Tixall 160
tolerance, devotional 25–30, 38–9,
97–100, 119–24, 132–7, 141,
158–65
Toleration Acts, *see* Catholic
Emancipation
Total Abstinence, *see* Catholic societies
Townsend, Ralph 155 n., 162, 163 n.
Tractarians 13, 130, 151, 163
see also Oxford Movement
transubstantiation 50, 54, 116
see also Benediction of the Bl. Sacr.;
Blessed Sacrament; communion;
Corpus Christi; eucharist; Exposition
of the Blessed Sacrament; Mass;
Quarant' ore; Visitation of the Bl.
Sacr.
Trappes-Lomax, Michael 72, 83–4, 84–5,
86, 86–7
Traynor, Jack 53
Trebizond, titular Archbishop of, *see*
Errington, George
Trent, Council of 14, 30, 33
Turberville, Henry 107
Tyrrell, George 28, 99, 100, 160

Ullathorne, William Bernard, bishop of
Birmingham:
and Benediction of the Bl. Sacr. 61
'conversion' of 145, 146
devotional life of 25, 61, 160–1
and *Garden of the Soul* 145
and papal infallibility 21, 24, 120
and 'party' spirit 21, 24, 119
on Prior Park 146
at Rome 24, 103
and rosary 25, 61 & n., 69
and the See of Westminster 24
on simple piety 160–1
and Society of St Vincent de Paul 128
H. Vaughan on 119
'ultramontane-triumph' thesis:
applied to England 17–25, 31, 100–5
applied to France 32–4, 165–9
applied to Ireland 12–17, 34, 42
applied to the United States 31–2
and devotional caricature 3–5, 39, 45,
46, 59–60
irrelevance to the English case 17–24,
25–30, 31, 36, 37, 46, 76–7, 85, 92,
105, 118–24, 137–41, 165–73
see also devotions; ethnicity; *Garden of
the Soul*; tolerance; unity
Uniformity, Act of, *see* Catholic
Emancipation
Unitarians 11
United States of America:
Catholic revival in 30, 34–5
Catholic societies in 125
devotions in 2–3, 31–2, 89–90
missions in 34
prayer-books in 31–2, 89–90
and 'ultramontane-triumph' thesis
31–2
unity, devotional:
and Benediction of the Bl. Sacr. 50–3,
58, 99, 100, 135, 157, 159, 169, 172
and Catholic societies 132–6
and Challoner's *Garden of the Soul*
72–8, 85–9, 100
English and Irish 15–17, 141, 161
and the *Memorare* 92, 97–9, 169
and miracles 162–5
and the penny catechism 119–21
as a principle of devotion 25–30, 38–9,
100, 141, 158–62
and the rosary 60–2, 69, 99
university education, *see* education
upper class, *see* class

Urban IV, Pope 68
Ursuline Manual, The 73, 75

Vade Mecum, see *Path of Holiness*
Vatican 1, 4, 18–24, 35
  and Bellarmine's catechism 100–5
  and Benediction of the Bl. Sacr. 46–7,
    49, 56, 58, 68
  and devotion in England 137–40,
    152–3, 173
  devotional 'strategy' of 1
  and indulgences 32
  and the *Memorare* 93–4, 96
  Newman's difficulties with the 23, 25
  and the rosary 65, 68
  and the Sacred Heart 43–4, 43 n.
  see also Rome; 'ultramontane-triumph'
    thesis
Vatican Councils, see First Vatican
  Council; Second Vatican Council
Vatican decrees, see papal infallibility
Vaughan, Herbert, Cardinal:
  and Benediction of the Bl. Sacr. 51–2
  on the crucifix 153
  and devotional inadequacy 148, 149
  and the Errington case 118
  to Knight, Bp. of Shrewsbury 192–4
  on miracles 164
  and the penny catechism 119, 120
  and prayer-books 74 & n., 75, 120,
    192–4
  and the rosary 69 n.
  on the Sacred Heart 153
  on sanctity 153, 155
  sense of sin in 148, 149, 153
  on the Sign of the Cross 131
  and Third Order of St Francis 131
  on Ullathorne 119
Vaughan, William, bishop of Plymouth
  101–5
Vaux, Laurence 106
Veni Creator 73
Veni Sancte Spiritus (the Golden Sequence)
  90, 91, 92
Vespers 48 n., 79, 131 n.
Veuillot, Louis 33
via crucis, see *Stations of the Cross*
Vidler, Alec 25
Virgin Mary, see Mary
Visitation of the Blessed Sacrament 36, 40
  and Benediction of the Bl. Sacr. 49–50
  and devotional stereotypes 44
  in England 44

in *Garden of the Soul* 80
and von Hügel 25–6
see also Benediction of the Bl. Sacr.;
  Blessed Sacrament; communion;
  Corpus Christi; eucharist; Exposition
  of the Blessed Sacrament; Mass;
  Quarant' ore; transubstantiation
von Hügel, Baron Friedrich 25–6, 28, 69,
  100
'vulgar piety' 28, 31

wakes 14, 166, 167
Wales 140
  Catholic societies in England and
    174–82, 195–9
  churches in England and 174–82
  devotions in England and 174–90
  see also Cwmbran; Holywell
Ward, William George 18, 26, 50, 51,
  138, 159
Way of the Cross, see Stations of the Cross
Weekly Register 24
Westminster:
  archbishopric of 24, see also Manning;
    H. Vaughan; Wiseman
  archdiocese of 42, 44, 45, 60, 109, 118,
    125, 127 & n.
  provincial synods of, see synods
Westminster Review 24
Whitby 48
White, Winefrid 140 n.
Whitty, M. J. 36
Whyte, John 15
Wigan 57
Wilberforce, Fr Bertrand 63, 64
Williams, Isaac 169
Wiseman, Nicholas, Cardinal 24, 138
  appointment to Westminster of 4
  and Benediction of the Bl. Sacr. 52, 55,
    69
  and the catechism 108
  on Challoner 77, 85, 86, 166
  and the English bishops 118, 119
  and 'Italianate' devotions 4, 9, 17, 25,
    61, 138
  on Mary 55
  on penance 151
  prayers by 55
  and *Quarant' ore* 61
  in Rome 19 & n., 61
  and the rosary 61, 69
  and the 'second spring' 6, 9
  on simplicity 162

working class, *see* class
'world', the 39, 159, 172–3
  Challoner and 9–10, 78, 79, 82–3, 84
  the ecclesiastical hierarchy and 123–4,
    135, 143
  the laity and 123–4, 135

Manning and 22, 23 n., 118
wounds of Christ, *see* crucifixion; Five
    Wounds; Passion

Yorkshire 36, 45 n., 139
  see also Beverley, diocese of

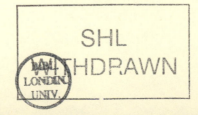